PRACTICAL MVS JCL EXAMPLES

An Introduction to MVS/ESA

Related Wiley Books

System 370/390 JCL by Gary DeWard Brown is the third edition of this classic reference book of JCL.

Advanced MVS/ESA JCL Examples by Jim Janossy demonstrates how to use JCL features provided only by MVS/ESA Release 4 and beyond, to support programming in COBOL, PL/I, C, PASCAL, and FORTRAN on IBM System 3090 and ES/9000 mainframes.

VS COBOL II: Highlights and Techniques by Jim Janossy gives you crucial information about using VS COBOL II and also shows you how to use MicroFocus, RM/COBOL-85, and CA-Realia PC-based COBOL compilers.

Advanced ANSI COBOL With Structured Programming (second edition) by Gary DeWard Brown provides ready reference to VS COBOL and VS COBOL II syntax.

Structured COBOL Programming (sixth edition) by Robert and Nancy Stern is an excellent standard textbook for learning COBOL.

Practical VSAM For Today's Programmer by Jim Janossy

Practical TSO/ISPF For Programmers and the Information Center by Jim Janossy

CICS Command Level Programming (second edition) by Alida M. Jatich

PRACTICAL MVS JCL EXAMPLES
An Introduction to MVS/ESA

JAMES G. JANOSSY

DePaul University, Chicago

John Wiley & Sons, Inc.
New York • Chichester • Brisbane • Toronto • Singapore

In recognition of the importance of preserving what has been written, it is a policy of John Wiley & Sons, Inc. to have books of enduring value published in the United States printed on acid-free paper, and we exert our best efforts to that end.

This publication is designed to provide accurate and authoritative information in regard to the subject matter covered. It is sold with the understanding that the publisher is not engaged in rendering legal, accounting, or other professional service. If legal advice or other expert assistance is required, the services of a competent professional person should be sought. FROM A DECLARATION OF PRINCIPLES JOINTLY ADOPTED BY A COMMITTEE OF THE AMERICAN BAR ASSOCIATION AND A COMMITTEE OF PUBLISHERS.

Library of Congress Cataloging-in-Publication Data
Janossy, James G. (James Gustav)
    Practical MVS JCL Examples / James G. Janossy.
        p.   cm.
    Includes bibliographical references and index.
    ISBN 0-471-57316-7 (pbk.)
    1. IBM 370 (Computer)–Programming. 2. IBM System/390 (Computer)–Programming.
3. IBM MVS. 4. Job Control Language (Computer program language) I. Title.
QA76.8.I123J35   1993
005.4'3—dc20   92-28504
                                                                         CIP

Printed in the United States of America
10   9   8   7

C'est passionant parce
que c'est une grande entreprise!

Offering new levels of mainframe price/performance, IBM's ES/9000 processors are among the newest models of the System/390. These innovative machines require less than 30% of the space of older mainframes by using four-megabit chips, surface-mounting techniques, and RAID (redundant array of inexpensive disk) model 9345 hard disks. The ES/9000 moves mainframe power out of the traditional data center environment and competes directly with minicomputers and microcomputer workstations. DePaul University (Chicago) installed its 128-megabyte ES/9000 in 1992 and uses it to support MVS/ESA Release 4, VS COBOL II, CICS 3.3, and DB2. (*Photo courtesy of International Business Machines Corporation*)

PREFACE

MVS JCL is simple (and fun) to use! This is true for me. In this book, I show you how to make this true for you as well.

You may have heard that MVS JCL is a bit unfriendly. MVS is among the oldest commercial software. It was invented in 1962–1964, when nothing like PCs, fourth generation languages, Windows, Apples, UNIX, interactivity, or concepts of user-friendly interaction were known. And in its three decades of life, MVS JCL hasn't changed much more than a glacier!

But learning MVS JCL doesn't have to be difficult. I show you here how to tame it and harness it to your purposes. The satisfaction you will develop from using MVS JCL easily and well will be pleasing in its own right. And knowing JCL will pay you immense dividends. Despite hype to the contrary, IBM mainframes will remain in use for at least another 20 years. Many high-volume data processing requirements can only be met using mainframe computers. People will need to know JCL even when many mainframes become "information server" nodes on PC networks!

I designed the chapters in this book to be your learning materials; Chapters 1 through 10 even include glossaries and review materials. I also included an index and a thorough appendix on error messages that you will encounter using MVS JCL, so this book will serve you well on the job. But this is not a reference book in the classic sense. You will find it valuable in your professional work to have Gary Brown's legendary *System/390 JCL* at hand. I shaped this book specifically with the intention of complementing Gary's JCL "bible."

Enough talk. Let me help you become productive with MVS JCL!

With thanks . . .

Thanks to Dr. Helmut Epp, Steve Samuels, Rich Orth, Cindy Llewellyn, Joel Bernstein, Rich Guzik, Norm Noerper, Morris Broker, Bill Cronin, Forest Key, and the late Jerry Wasserman. The work of these people has had a significant impact on me over the last 20 years. It's impossible to itemize the JCL knowledge and techniques that I've picked up from these people. But I'd like you to know their names and the fact that the skills of each played a role in shaping this book.

Thanks also to Dawne Tortorella, Bob Dameron, and Larry Wheeler of DePaul's Academic Computing Services for their superb work in installing and supporting our new ES/9000 mainframe, which I used to run most of the examples in this book. Thanks to Norm Noerper of Caliber Data Training for his many suggestions on content and coverage and his perceptions of the audience for this book. Thanks to David Mullen, president of Certified Collateral Corporation, and Louis Navarro of GIS Information Systems, Oakbrook, Illinois for their help in running some of these examples on the large MVS/ESA systems supporting their firms. And a special thanks to Nancy Friedland and Sam Fatigato of IBM, who helped immensely in configuring, acquiring, and installing our ES/9000 and in securing the photo illustration for this book!

Jim Janossy

About the Author

James G. Janossy is a fulltime faculty member of the Department of Computer Science and Information Systems at DePaul University, Chicago. He teaches COBOL, MVS JCL. systems analysis and design, software testing, project management, relational database, and on-line programming on IBM and VAX systems. Prior to joining DePaul he worked in the industry 17 years as manager of systems and programming and data processing project leader and programmer. Jim earned his B.A. at Northwestern University, his M.S. at California State University, Los Angeles, and is completing a Ph.D. in computer science.

Jim has written several books including *Practical MVS, JCL, Practical VSAM* (with Richard Guzik), *Practical TSO/ISPF For Programmers and the Information Center, VS COBOL II: Highlights and Techniques,* and *VAX COBOL On-Line,* published by John Wiley & Sons. He also wrote *COBOL: A Software Engineering Introduction* for Dryden Press, Inc. He has authored columns and numerous articles for *Data Training magazine,* and given presentations on course development at the annual Data Training conference.

CONTENTS IN BRIEF

CONTENTS

Chapter One

THE MAINFRAME ENVIRONMENT

In this chapter I'll give you the perspective you need to be comfortable with the IBM mainframe environment. I will explain what the MVS operating system is, what it does, and how job control language is your interface to it. I'll also show you how TSO/ISPF, IBM's Time-Sharing Option, enables you to create programs and job control language.

1.1 Three Worlds to Conquer

If you are a newcomer to computer programming in the IBM mainframe environment, you face the hurdle of learning about *three* different things all at once:

- *A programming language*—such as COBOL, PL/I, FORTRAN, C, or Assembler—to express processing logic and algorithms
- *Job Control Language (JCL)*—to tell the computer system what programs you want it to run and what files these programs will read or create
- *Time-Sharing Option (TSO/ISPF),* which is the mainframe "programmer's word processor" you'll use to create programs and job control language and to access the computer system

When you are learning about programming, the added tasks of becoming comfortable with JCL and TSO/ISPF may seem like a heavy extra burden. I'll show you by example that neither JCL nor TSO/ISPF is hard to learn or use.

Your programming language statements and your job control language statements are two different things, but both have to be "typed up" in machine readable form to enter the computer. In the early days of computers, you would have used a keypunch machine to translate program statements and JCL into machine readable form. Nowadays, you use your mainframe word processor, TSO/ISPF, to do this.

1

1.2 IBM and Punch Card History

IBM has been in business since 1911. In case your knowledge of the history of automation is a bit rusty, that's nearly 40 years before the commercialization of business data processing computers began! What did IBM sell during those 40 years? Among other things, IBM sold punch cards and related processing equipment.

Punch cards were invented by Herman Hollerith in the 1880s. They were the first way that information expressed with letters and numbers could be represented in machine readable form. These cards were roughly 3 by 7 inches in size and could be physically punched with holes in 80 columns. The combination of holes punched in each column of a punch card represented a letter or number. Machinery could sense the holes and print out the information, mechanically add up numbers, or rearrange (sort) the cards into piles.

Punch cards are now almost entirely obsolete, but they have left their mark on the world. IBM dominated the punch card equipment business; it sold card stock itself but also leased the equipment required to punch information onto cards and process them. Its customers included the largest businesses in the world and the governments of many countries.

When the era of electronic information processing began in the 1950s, IBM recognized the computer as a better and faster manipulator of information. But IBM continued to see information entering and leaving the machine on 80-column punch cards. This is why mainframe computing languages (and job control language) take the form of statements 80 characters long. And this is why computer terminal screens, even today, are 80 columns wide.

1.3 TSO/ISPF: The Time-Sharing Option

By the 1970s, it had become possible to manufacture computer terminals at a cost low enough to justify their common use. But just having this hardware did not make it possible to eliminate the keypunch. Software was needed to interact with the terminal and provide the interface between programmers and the mainframe. IBM developed *TSO*, or *Time-Sharing Option*, to meet this need. You can think of TSO as a word processor for punch cards.

But TSO is more than just a word processor. It's the mainframe programmer's workbench. You not only create and mold your program statements and job control language with TSO. You also use TSO to submit your work to the computer system for processing, and you use it to see the results of your computer runs, as shown in Figure 1.1.

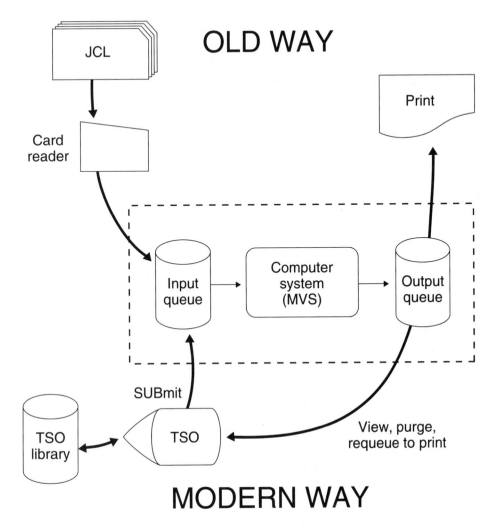

Figure 1.1   TSO Replaces Punch Cards on IBM Mainframes

When IBM mainframes were invented, you prepared programs and job control language on punch cards. You submitted your work by physically dropping punch cards into a "reader." Now you use TSO, the Time-Sharing Option, to prepare your programs and JCL, and you use the **SUB** command to send your JCL into the system. Instead of waiting for printout, you use TSO to view your output and decide if it should be printed or deleted.

1.4 What Is the MVS Operating System?

MVS stands for *Multiple Virtual Storages.* This name describes how the MVS operating system manages and allows programs to use the memory of the computer.

What is the computer's operating system? The easiest way to visualize what an operating system does is to picture a large, busy airport such as O'Hare International in Chicago. The airport consists of huge, paved runways, each of which can be used by one airplane at a time. Many airplanes have to use the runways. To keep them from colliding or interfering with one another, air traffic controllers manage the airport and dictate where each airplane is to go, and when. If the airport had no air traffic controllers to do this, there would be no practical way for large numbers of airplanes to land or take off.

The operating system of a computer serves the same function as the air traffic controllers at a major airport. The "runways" of the computer are its electronic memory and its input and output devices, such as terminals, printers, and magnetic disk and tape information storage devices. The "airplanes" using this facility are *programs.* Just as with airplanes and airports, more programs exist to be run than can be accommodated at one time. The operating system manages computer resources so that as many programs as possible can be active at one time, just as several airplanes can take off at the same time from parallel runways. Figure 1.2 shows you some of the software that MVS manages.

Where does job control language fit into this analogy? Pilots of commercial aircraft have to file flight plans before they take off, mapping out where they will be going, how they plan to get there, and when they will do it. As a programmer running programs on a mainframe computer, you're very much like an airplane pilot. You have to express your flight plan in job control language, which is the only language that MVS understands.

The grammar of JCL is similar to the terse but very precise language that pilots and air traffic controllers speak when they are exchanging information. Neither pilot/controller conversation nor JCL is elegant or even understandable to the uninitiated. But both express essential information in a standardized way.

Even small personal computers have an operating system. On smaller machines, the operating system is simpler to use because there is less to manage. That makes sense. Smaller airports have less elaborate air traffic control arrangements than major airports.

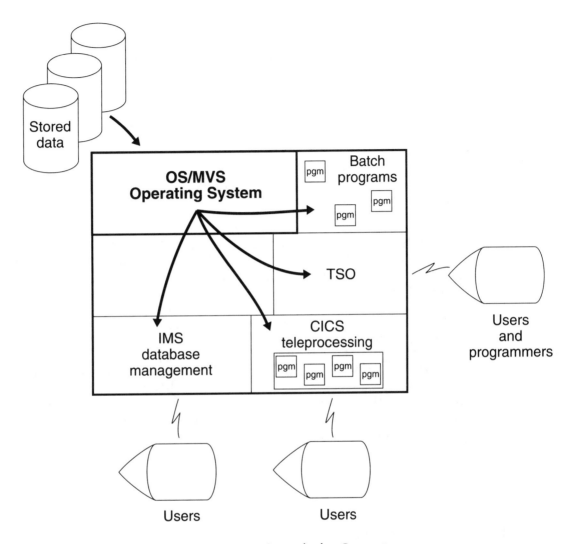

Figure 1.2   The MVS Operating System Controls the Computer

MVS manages the memory and data storage devices of the mainframe. It controls what programs run, where in memory they run, and how much of the computer's processing time each program gets. TSO is a program managed by MVS, just as are your own programs. CICS (Customer Information Control System), a product that supports interactive programs, and IMS (Information Management System), a database, are other system software products managed by MVS.

1.5 What Is JCL?

JCL stands for *Job Control Language.* It is the command language of the MVS operating system. Even though MVS has been upgraded from earlier versions to MVS/XA and MVS/ESA, job control language remains essentially unchanged.

JCL is the way you "talk" to MVS and tell it what you want it to do for you. You use JCL to

1. Tell MVS what programs you want to run
2. Tell MVS what files these programs will use
3. Tell MVS what you want done with the files after the programs have used them

Although JCL may look strange to you, this is all that JCL ever does. Some sets of JCL are short and some are long. Why? Some sets of JCL run one or a few programs (one after another), whereas other sets of JCL run many programs (one after another).

JCL starts with two slashes in the very first column on punch cards. But on TSO screens, you'll view JCL with line numbers in front. The line numbers are not a part of the actual JCL. They are on the screen only because TSO provides them as a place for you to put editing commands. Notice the COLUMNS 001 072 at the far upper right corner of the TSO editing screen in Figure 1.3. This tells you that the editable area of the screen (where the slashes start in this example) begins with column 1. The format of actual JCL remains the same as it was on punch cards, even though we now use terminals and TSO rather than punch cards to prepare it.

1.6 Running a Program by Submitting JCL

The seven lines of JCL you see on the TSO screen in Figure 1.3 represent the shortest set of JCL you can prepare and run. This JCL executes just one program, named IEFBR14. This program doesn't do anything; it simply starts and stops. But if you run a job like this, you'll see the basic amount of reporting you get from MVS when you interact with it.

I submitted this job for execution by putting SUB on the command line of the TSO/ISPF function 2 editing screen. In response, MVS issued a job number to me. Because the job finished almost immediately, I also got the job completion message you see at the bottom of the screen. The *** indicates that TSO is waiting for me to read the message and press the *<Enter>* key.

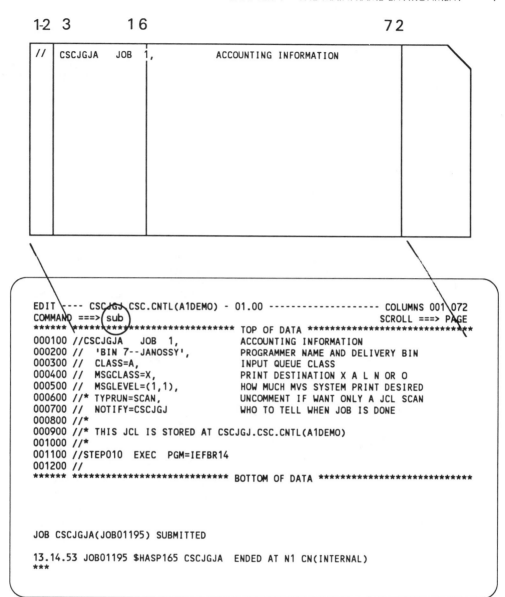

Figure 1.3 The Format of Job Control Language Statements

Each JCL statement starts with two slashes. Most JCL statements carry a statement label immediately following the two slashes (such as CSCJGJA and STEP010 here). In this example, JOB and EXEC are two JCL statement types. You continue a JCL statement with a comma and start the continuation indented as you see at line 000200, but don't indent beyond column 16 or the line will be ignored! JCL lines starting with //* are comment lines but you can also put comments (like "accounting information") on the same line as a JCL statement.

```
SDSF OUTPUT DISPLAY CSCJGJA  JOB01195 DSID    2 LINE 0      COLUMNS 02- 81
COMMAND INPUT ===>                                          SCROLL ===> PAGE
******************************** TOP OF DATA ********************************
                      J E S 2   J O B   L O G  --  S Y S T E M   I B M 1  --  N

13.10.52 JOB01195  IRR010I  USERID CSCJGJ    IS ASSIGNED TO THIS JOB.
13.10.53 JOB01195  ICH70001I CSCJGJ   LAST ACCESS AT 13:04:48 ON THURSDAY, SEPTE
13.10.53 JOB01195  $HASP373 CSCJGJA  STARTED - INIT  1 - CLASS A - SYS IBM1
13.10.53 JOB01195  $HASP395 CSCJGJA  ENDED
------ JES2 JOB STATISTICS ------
      10 SEP 92 JOB EXECUTION DATE
          11 CARDS READ
          30 SYSOUT PRINT RECORDS
           0 SYSOUT PUNCH RECORDS
           2 SYSOUT SPOOL KBYTES
        0.00 MINUTES EXECUTION TIME
        1 //CSCJGJA   JOB  1,            ACCOUNTING INFORMATION
          //  'BIN 7--JANOSSY',          PROGRAMMER NAME AND DELIVERY BIN
          //  CLASS=A,                   INPUT QUEUE CLASS
          //  MSGCLASS=X,                PRINT DESTINATION X A L N OR O
          //  MSGLEVEL=(1,1),            HOW MUCH MVS SYSTEM PRINT DESIRED
          //* TYPRUN=SCAN,               UNCOMMENT IF WANT ONLY A JCL SCAN
          //  NOTIFY=CSCJGJ              WHO TO TELL WHEN JOB IS DONE
          //*
```

1.7 Seeing Job Output Using TSO

I submitted JCL using TSO in Figure 1.3, using the SUB command in TSO edit mode (selection 2 from the TSO/ISPF main menu). When the job finished, MVS sent a message telling me so, as you also saw on the previous page. To actually see the result of the job, I then went to TSO function S to view its print output (this is function 3.8 on some systems).

The figure above shows you what the output of my first job looks like on the screen. If this strikes you as confusing, don't be alarmed. What you are looking at is reporting from the MVS operating system indicating how it processed the job. The appearance of this output is not particularly friendly, but it is easy to learn how to read it.

Realize that this screen is showing you lines that are intended to be printed! By using TSO's "view the output" function, you are looking at part of a large file that houses many lines of print. This file is called the **output queue** or **spool**. Before TSO was invented, you couldn't see this output before it printed. Waiting for it to print could take hours, as it waited its turn to get to the printer.

You will almost always view the results of your jobs using TSO in this way. But the printed form of MVS output is easier to read and explain. I have listed the printed form of this job output in Figure 1.4. Look at that illustration and compare it to the TSO screen version!

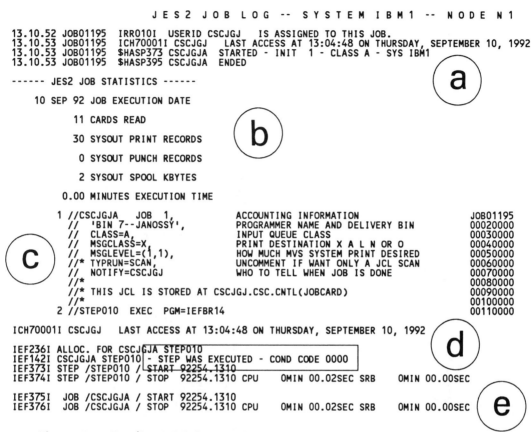

```
                    J E S 2   J O B   L O G  --  S Y S T E M   I B M 1  --  N O D E   N 1

13.10.52 JOB01195  IRR010I  USERID CSCJGJ   IS ASSIGNED TO THIS JOB.
13.10.53 JOB01195  ICH70001I CSCJGJ   LAST ACCESS AT 13:04:48 ON THURSDAY, SEPTEMBER 10, 1992
13.10.53 JOB01195  $HASP373 CSCJGJA  STARTED - INIT 1 - CLASS A - SYS IBM1
13.10.53 JOB01195  $HASP395 CSCJGJA  ENDED

------ JES2 JOB STATISTICS ------

     10 SEP 92 JOB EXECUTION DATE

        11 CARDS READ

        30 SYSOUT PRINT RECORDS

         0 SYSOUT PUNCH RECORDS

         2 SYSOUT SPOOL KBYTES

       0.00 MINUTES EXECUTION TIME

      1 //CSCJGJA   JOB  1,            ACCOUNTING INFORMATION           JOB01195
        //   'BIN 7--JANOSSY',         PROGRAMMER NAME AND DELIVERY BIN 00020000
        //   CLASS=A,                  INPUT QUEUE CLASS                00030000
        //   MSGCLASS=X,               PRINT DESTINATION X A L N OR O   00040000
        //   MSGLEVEL=(1,1),           HOW MUCH MVS SYSTEM PRINT DESIRED 00050000
        //*  TYPRUN=SCAN,              UNCOMMENT IF WANT ONLY A JCL SCAN 00060000
        //   NOTIFY=CSCJGJ             WHO TO TELL WHEN JOB IS DONE     00070000
        //*                                                            00080000
        //*  THIS JCL IS STORED AT CSCJGJ.CSC.CNTL(JOBCARD)            00090000
        //*                                                            00100000
      2 //STEP010  EXEC PGM=IEFBR14                                    00110000

ICH70001I CSCJGJ   LAST ACCESS AT 13:04:48 ON THURSDAY, SEPTEMBER 10, 1992

IEF236I ALLOC. FOR CSCJGJA STEP010
IEF142I CSCJGJA STEP010 - STEP WAS EXECUTED - COND CODE 0000
IEF373I STEP /STEP010 / START 92254.1310
IEF374I STEP /STEP010 / STOP  92254.1310 CPU    0MIN 00.02SEC SRB    0MIN 00.00SEC

IEF375I  JOB /CSCJGJA / START 92254.1310
IEF376I  JOB /CSCJGJA / STOP  92254.1310 CPU    0MIN 00.02SEC SRB    0MIN 00.00SEC
```

Figure 1.4   Reading MVS System Output

You submit JCL to run programs. Your submission is called a *job.* MVS always gives you several lines of print output telling you what it did to run your job. Here is what this print output means:

a.   The ''job log'' tells you when the job started and stopped.

b.   JOB STATISTICS tells you the date, number of JCL statements (**cards**), and amount of print output produced.

c.   The JCL you submitted is listed, with statements numbered by MVS. (There were only two actual JCL statements in this job.)

d.   ALLOC. tells you which devices and how much memory were allocated for the job step, as well as the central processing unit (CPU) time required to process the job step. (One ''step'' is the running of one program.) Each program leaves behind a **COND CODE** in the range of 0000 to 4095 as a crude form of communication.

e.   The final messages tell you the amount of time the whole job took. The codes such as IEF375I are message identifiers that you could use to look up documentation about each line in IBM manuals.

TSO/ISPF

```
-------------------- ISPF/PDF PRIMARY OPTION MENU --------------------
OPTION  ===>                                              USERID   - CSCJGJ
                                                          TIME     - 17:36
   0  ISPF PARMS   - Specify terminal and user parameters TERMINAL - 3278
   1  BROWSE       - Display source data or output listings PF KEYS - 24
   2  EDIT         - Create or change source data
   3  UTILITIES    - Perform utility functions
   4  FOREGROUND   - Invoke language processors in foreground
   6  COMMAND      - Enter TSO Command, CLIST, or REXX exec
   C  CHANGES      - Display summary of changes for this release
   S  SDSF         - Spool Display and Search Facility
   T  TUTORIAL     - Display information about ISPF/PDF
   X  EXIT         - Terminate ISPF using log and list defaults

Enter END command to terminate ISPF.
```

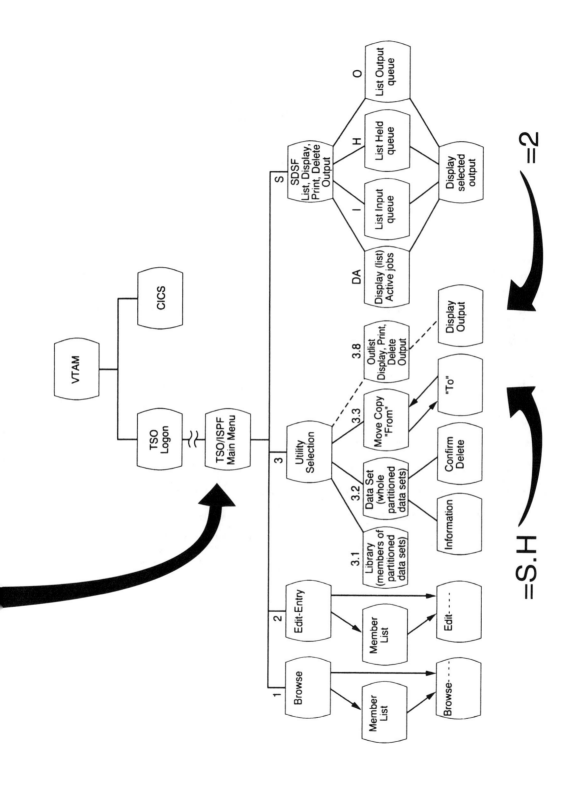

Figure 1.5 Road Map to TSO/ISPF and the Main Menu

1.8 A Road Map to TSO/ISPF

TSO/ISPF has no direct connection to job control language. It is simply your means of building JCL (and program) statements, submitting JCL for job execution, and seeing the results. TSO serves as your mainframe programmer's workbench.

Figure 1.5 is a diagram of the most useful screens in TSO/ISPF. The screen at the top, labeled "VTAM," is where your computer terminal is positioned before you log on to TSO. When you log on, you reach the TSO/ISPF main menu. From the main menu you select function 2 to edit and submit JCL and function S to view your output. You can select function 3 to copy or move files. You select X to leave TSO/ISPF.

TSO/ISPF makes it easy to jump from screen to screen without going through the main menu screen. You can enter =S.H on the command line of the edit screen to go immediately to the SDSF "table of contents" screen for your print output as I did below. You can either enter =2 to get back to the edit screen from SDSF or enter =X on any command line to leave TSO/ISPF.

This book is not about TSO/ISPF; that is a subject unto itself. If you are new to the IBM mainframe environment and are learning TSO/ISPF at the same time you are learning JCL, you will find a "learning materials" book on TSO/ISPF very handy. I wrote a companion to *Practical MVS JCL Examples*. It's called *Practical TSO/ISPF* (John Wiley & Sons, Inc., 1988). Figure 1.5 is from that book.

```
EDIT ---- CSCJGJ.CSC.CNTL(A1DEMO) - 01.00 ------------------- COLUMNS 001 072
COMMAND ===> =s.h                                         SCROLL ===> PAGE
****** ********************************* TOP OF DATA *******************************
000100 //CSCJGJA    JOB  1,            ACCOUNTING INFORMATION
000200 //  'BIN 7--JANOSSY',           PROGRAMMER NAME AND DELIVERY BIN
000300 //  CLA        ,                INPUT QUEUE CLASS
000400 //  M        X,                 PRINT DESTINATION X A L N OR O
000500 //  MSG      L=(1,1),           HOW MUCH MVS SYSTEM PRINT DESIRED
000600 //* TYP      SCAN               UNCOMMENT IF WANT ONLY A JCL SCAN
000700 //  NOT      CSCJGJ             WHO TO TELL WHEN JOB IS DONE
000800 //*
000900 //* THIS JCL IS STORED AT CSCJGJ.CSC.CNTL(A1DEMO)
001000 //*
001100 //STEP010  EXEC  PGM=IEFBR14
001200 //
****** *************************** BOTTOM OF DATA ******************************
```

1.9 Using TSO/ISPF: Function Keys

TSO/ISPF provides you with a consistent way to manipulate programs, JCL, and output that you view. Your access to all of these items is aided by these program function keys:

Key	Emitted Word	Actual Meaning
PF1	HELP	Access help text files
PF2	SPLIT	Split screen into two sessions
PF3	END	Move up the menu hierarchy
PF4	RETURN	Go directly to the main menu
PF5	RFIND	Repeat your last FIND command
PF6	RCHANGE	Repeat your last CHANGE command
PF7	UP	Move screen up in the viewed item
PF8	DOWN	Move screen down in the viewed item
PF9	SWAP	Switch to other split-screen session
PF10	LEFT	Move screen left in the viewed item
PF11	RIGHT	Move screen right in the viewed item
PF12	RETRIEVE	Bring back your previous command

Pressing one of these PF keys "emits" the word shown as if you had entered it on the command line, and then sends the same signal as does the <*Enter*> key. You can make these meanings display at the bottom of your screen by putting PFSHOW ON on the command line. You can shut off the screen display of these key meanings by putting PFSHOW OFF on the command line.

If you are working on a microcomputer emulating an IBM terminal, you may not have special keys labeled as PF keys, or your PF keys may not actually send the same electronic signals as those of a real IBM terminal. On a non-IBM terminal try pressing the <*Escape*> key then a number key, such as <*Escape*>3 for "end." If all else fails, you can always type the actual word shown on the second column on the command line, and press the <*Enter*> key. For example, to move downward while editing a program, JCL, or viewing output, you can put the word DOWN on the command line and press <*Enter*>. DOWN moves you down in the item the amount of lines specified in the SCROLL field at the top of the screen. UP moves you up this amount; LEFT and RIGHT move you this amount of columns left and right (useful for viewing print output).

Chapter 1 Review

Mini-Glossary

Mainframe   A large-scale computer system that can support thousands of terminals and data storage devices. Many manufacturers make large computers, but "mainframe" has traditionally referred to IBM's larger systems.

TSO   Time-Sharing Option

ISPF   Integrated System Productivity Facility (the component of TSO that provides full-screen editing)

JCL   Job Control Language

MVS   Multiple Virtual Storages computer operating system

SDSF   Spool Display and Search Facility, a software product you can access from TSO to preview output on your screen

Review Questions

1. Explain how IBM's roots in punch card information processing affect programming, job control language, and the screen size of modern computer terminals.
2. Describe the role of TSO in the IBM mainframe environment.
3. Compare the old and modern ways of submitting job control language to the computer system for processing.
4. Describe why an operating system such as MVS is like the air traffic controllers at a large airport.
5. Explain the three things that JCL does.

Exercises

A. Find out what the format of the JOB statement is in your installation and use it to compose JCL similar to that in Figure 1.3. Submit the JCL. When the job executes, view your output and compare it to Figure 1.4.
B. After completing Exercise A, modify your JCL to misspell EXEC as EXXX. Submit the job and view your output to see how MVS complains about this error!

Chapter Two

MAINFRAME INFORMATION REPRESENTATION AND STORAGE

IBM mainframes are unique in some of the terms they use to describe the electronic storage of information. In this chapter I'll describe how bits, bytes, and fields build records and how records "live" in files. I'll also explain how the IBM mainframe supports several different types of files and show you how hard disks and MVS keep track of where data is being stored.

2.1 Components of the Mainframe Computer System

The major components of any digital computer system are its electronic memory and its central processing unit (CPU). The memory stores information in electronically coded form. The CPU manipulates this information and makes simple decisions based on it. Programs are logical sequences of instructions that reside in memory and tell the CPU what actions to take. How is electronically coded information stored when it's not required to be in memory? It's out of memory. The IBM mainframe was designed to support hundreds of information storage devices such as disk and tape drives. These devices connect to memory through small auxiliary computers called ***channel processors.*** Each channel deals with a group of information storage devices and relieves some of the input/output processing burden from the CPU. Modern mainframes have 32 or more channels.

2.2 How the Mainframe Represents Data

Millions of tiny transistors form the memory of a computer. Each transistor can be carrying or not carrying an electric charge. Each transistor stores one ***bit,*** or binary digit.

A single bit can represent only two different things. But we have over 100 symbols to represent to be able to store information. We have 26 letters (actually, 52 because we want to distinguish between lowercase letters like "a" and uppercase letters like "A"); ten number symbols (0, 1, 2, 3, 4, 5, 6, 7, 8, and 9); symbols such as +, -, *, and /; and more than a dozen punctuation symbols. To represent these electronically we group several bits together for each character.

2.3 Eight Bits Form a Character (Byte)

Characters formed with eight bits are called **bytes.** When you press a key on a video terminal keyboard, imagine that eight bits squirt out of the cable attached to it, one after another, as shown in Figure 2.1. Each key creates a unique combination of eight on- or off-bits.

Because we use eight bits to store each character of data, a total of 2^8 (or 256) possible bit patterns exists. Which bit patterns represent each letter or number symbol? IBM's mainframe designers "mapped" bit patterns to our language symbols in a scheme named Extended Binary Coded Decimal Interchange Code, EBCDIC. This is different from the American Standard Code for Information Interchange, ASCII.

2.4 Fields, Records, Files, and Data Sets

If you group characters together to store a customer name, address, and other items of information, each group of characters is called a **field.** A field can be as short as one byte or as long as a systems analyst or programmer feels is required, subject to the programming language you use.

If you group fields together to collect all the information about a given occurrence of something (such as a customer), you form a **record.** A record can contain any number of fields. Records of 80-byte length are common on mainframes because punch cards were 80 bytes in length, but MVS can handle records up to 32,760 bytes long.

You can place records together physically in the computer's memory. The common name for such a grouping is a **table.** If you copy such a group of records out of memory and house them on disk or tape, the result is called a **file.** IBM mainframe designers coined the word **data set** as a synonym for file.

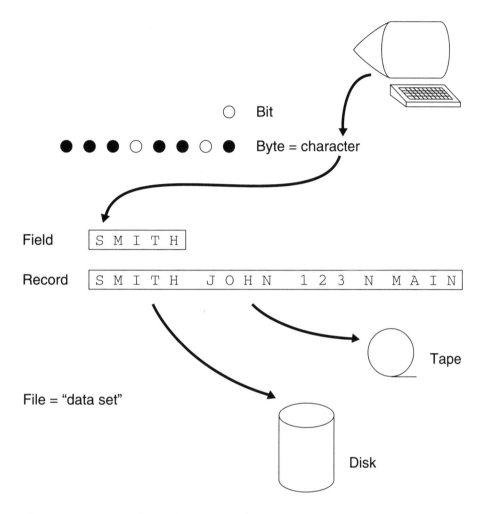

Figure 2.1   How Information Is Stored

This is the electronic information storage hierarchy. IBM mainframes use the term *data set* instead of *file.*

2.5 Bytes as Binary or Decimal Numbers

Eight bits make up one byte, or character, of information. Each bit can be either "on" or "off." We represent the status of the bits in a byte with the numerals 0 and 1. The lowest possible bit pattern is 00000000 (all bits off), and the highest is 11111111 (all bits on).

A byte may store a character, a numeric value, or a machine language instruction. But regardless of how its contents will be interpreted, the contents of any byte can be depicted as a number in base-2 (binary) arithmetic. The lowest bit pattern, 00000000, carries a decimal value of 0, whereas the highest bit pattern, 11111111, is equivalent to 255 in our familiar decimal (base-10) form.

2.6 Hexadecimal Representation of Byte Contents

You will occasionally have to deal with **hexadecimal** representation of data when you work on a mainframe. Hexadecimal, or hex, is a base-16 numbering system. Hex uses 16 different numerals rather than the 10 used in the decimal system. Hex is commonly used by IBM system software because it provides a more compact shorthand for representing the contents of bytes than either binary or decimal:

Binary	Decimal	Hex
0000	0	0
0001	1	1
0010	2	2
0011	3	3
0100	4	4
0101	5	5
0110	6	6
0111	7	7
1000	8	8
1001	9	9
1010	10	A
1011	11	B
1100	12	C
1101	13	D
1110	14	E
1111	15	F

Hex is used to abbreviate the eight bits of a byte in two groups of four. For example, suppose you examined a byte of memory containing the bits 11000001. You could abbreviate the first four bits (1100) as decimal 12 or hex "C." You could abbreviate the last four bits (0001) as hex "1." Decimal 12,1 or hex C1 is the abbreviation for 1100 0001. Figure 2.2 shows you the EBCDIC bit representations of some letters and numbers in hex. Appendix C shows you all 256 bit patterns, their hex representations, and what (if anything) each prints.

```
EDIT ---- CSCJGJ.CSC.CNTL(RHYME) - 01.01 -------------------- COLUMNS 001 072
COMMAND ===>                                               SCROLL ===> PAGE
****** **************************** TOP OF DATA ******************************
000001 0123456789 Aa Bb Cc Dd Ee Ff Gg Hh Jj Kk Ll Mm Nn Oo Pp Qq Rr Ss
000002 THE TIME HAS COME,
000003 THE WALRUS SAID,
000004 TO TALK OF MANY THINGS.
```

```
EDIT ---- CSCJGJ.CSC.CNTL(RHYME) - 01.01 -------------------- COLUMNS 001 072
COMMAND ===> hex on                                        SCROLL ===> PAGE
****** **************************** TOP OF DATA ******************************


--------------------------------------------------------------------------
000001 0123456789 Aa Bb Cc Dd Ee Ff Gg Hh Jj Kk Ll Mm Nn Oo Pp Qq Rr Ss
       FFFFFFFFFF4C84C84C84C84C84C84C84C84D94D94D94D94D94D94D94D94D94EA44444444
       012345678901102203304405506607708801102203304405506607708809902200000000
--------------------------------------------------------------------------
000002 THE TIME HAS COME,
       ECC4ECDC4CCE4CDDC644444444
       38503945081203645B00000000
-------------------------------------
000003 THE WALRUS SAID,
       ECC4ECDDEE4ECCC64444444444
       385061394202194B0000000000
-------------------------------------
000004 TO TALK OF MANY THINGS.
       ED4ECDD4DC4DCDE4ECCDCE444444444444444444444444444444444444444444444444444444
       360313206604158038957 2B0000000000000000000000000000000000000000000000000000
--------------------------------------------------------------------------
```

If you change the hex representation the character data will change. This is how you can enter values for which no keys exist on your keyboard.

Figure 2.2 Seeing Data in Hex Using TSO

You can see the contents of data sets in hexadecimal using TSO/ISPF. Just put the words "hex on" on the command line when you are editing or browsing an item. You'll see the hexadecimal value listed vertically under each character. You can see the actual bit pattern contents of any byte, even if the bit pattern has no corresponding representation as a printed symbol. Return to normal viewing by putting "hex off" on the command line. (Hex 40 is 0100 0000, the code for a space.)

2.7 Forming Data Set Names

A data set is a collection of records. A typical mainframe computer system will have to manage thousands of data sets. It makes sense that we have to name each data set uniquely.

MVS supports very large data set names. A data set name (abbreviated in JCL as DSN) can be 44 characters long in this format:

XXXXXXXX.XXXXXXXX.XXXXXXXX.XXXXXXXX.XXXXXXXX

You can compose a data set name using groups of up to eight characters. Each of the groups must start with a capital letter; you can use either letters or numbers for the last seven characters of each group. You can also use the symbols @, #, and $ in data set names, although many people consider them highly unusual.

2.8 Data Set Names and TSO

MVS keeps track of groups of data sets by referring to the front part of the names, which are sometimes called **qualifiers.** When you use TSO/ISPF, a special requirement applies to most data sets that you work with. The first part of the name must be your TSO user-id, such as CSCJGJ. For example, the data set I store my JCL in is named

```
CSCJGJ.CSC.CNTL
```

while my data set for COBOL source code is named

```
CSCJGJ.CSC.COBOL
```

You can see that it's not necessary to use the full 44 characters to name a data set, nor do you have to use all eight characters in any of the groups between periods.

You represent data set names differently on TSO/ISPF screens and in JCL. Figure 2.3 illustrates how you code data set names in JCL all in a row, with periods separating the parts of the name. When you use TSO/ISPF to access a data set such as your JCL or program library, you code the parts of the name vertically, with no periods.

2.9 Data Set Names and Security

Mainframe security software controls access to data sets by referring to the first part of the data set name. Using either TSO or JCL, you will be able to access only data sets starting with certain names, as permitted by your installation's security mechanism.

2.10 Sequential Data Sets

Sequential data sets are the simplest form or organization of data set. A sequential data set just contains records placed one after another as shown

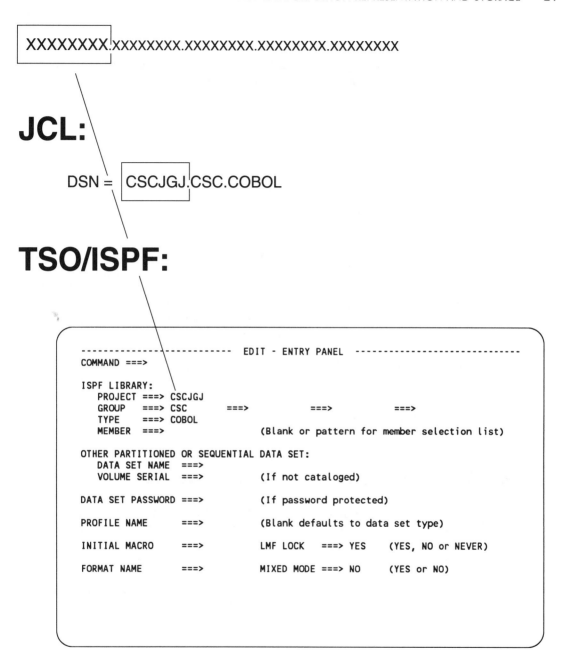

Figure 2.3   Data Set Name in JCL and on TSO Screens

You enter the same data set name differently in JCL and on TSO/ISPF screens. Neither place ordinarily uses surrounding apostrophes.

in Figure 2.4. A sequential data set can contain zero records (that is, it can be empty), several records, or millions of records. Its size (how many records it can hold) depends only on how much space you provide for it on disk or how many magnetic tapes you allow it to use.

2.11 Creating a Sequential Data Set: What Happens

The creation process for a sequential data set is different, from the *system's* point of view, depending on whether you write it to tape or disk. But from your *program's* point of view, there is no difference. MVS isolates your program from the electronic details of how the records are written.

When you direct a program to write records to tape, your program is executed (via JCL) and the system provides "scratch" tapes to receive the records. You output records one by one. As the tape is pulled past the read/ write mechanism of the tape drive, the bit patterns representing the bytes of each record are copied to tape. You can continue outputting records even beyond one reel or cartridge of tape, and MVS will supply additional tapes automatically. I'll explain more about tapes in Chapter 15.

When you write a sequential data set to disk, disk space has to be allocated for it. You may have previously done the allocation yourself, or MVS may do it automatically for you. Your program outputs records one by one. If you fill up your allocated disk space, your job will fail. I'll explain a lot more about disk space in Chapter 14.

2.12 Reading a Sequential Data Set: What Happens

When you read records from a sequential data set on either tape or disk, you obtain the records one by one, beginning with the first record recorded in the data set. This is fine for some purposes such as printing a report, where you will read and perhaps print all of the records in the data set.

For interactive (on-line) information retrieval or information update you'll typically need to obtain specific records from a data set immediately. Sequential data sets don't support this type of access. To obtain the 50,000th record in a sequential data set containing 100,000 records, you would have to read the preceding 49,999 records first! Other data set organizations have been invented to support your TSO and on-line production work. We commonly use sequential data sets to house stable, unchanging historical data, including backups of important data sets. We don't use sequential data sets to contain either program or JCL statements.

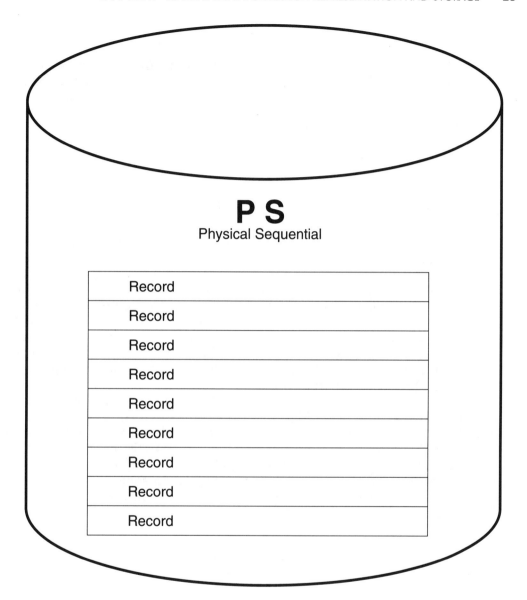

Figure 2.4   Sequential Data Set

A sequential data set is the simplest form of data set organization. You read records from it one by one, in the same sequence in which they were written. A sequential disk data set has a large minimum size of about 50,000 bytes, depending on the type of hard disk used. MVS identifies a sequential data set as type PS, which stands for ***Physical Sequential.***

2.13 Partitioned Data Sets

MVS allocates disk space in whole tracks only, so a data set always occupies this much disk space. This is about 50,000 bytes of space, depending on the model of hard disk your installation uses. Many JCL jobs and programs are much smaller than that. For this reason, IBM provides a way to divide up or "partition" the space in a sequential data set. IBM software engineers invented the *partitioned data set,* often called a PDS. Your TSO/ISPF libraries are really partitioned data sets.

2.14 The Partitioned Data Set Directory

To MVS, a partitioned data set is a special form of sequential data set. Every PDS includes a *directory* to keep track of how its allocated disk space, or *data space,* has been divided into parts, as shown in Figure 2.5. Each part is called a *member.* Each member acts like its own sequential data set.

Each member of a partitioned data set is represented by its name in the directory and an MVS-maintained pointer to its physical location. The directory also keeps track of statistics such as when each member was created, how many records it contained when it was created, how many records it has in it now, the date and time each member was last changed, and who (what TSO user-id) created it.

You allocate a partitioned data set to reserve space for it on disk. You can do this with TSO/ISPF function 3.2. At that time you have to decide how big its directory will be. You state this in terms of *directory blocks.* Each directory block holds information for five TSO-created members. You can't change the size of its directory after the partitioned data set is created, so you have to think about this in advance! In some installations the partitioned data sets you'll use for your TSO libraries are already allocated for you.

2.15 Compressing a Partitioned Data Set

Every time you change the contents of an existing partitioned data set member, MVS puts a new copy of it in its library's data space. MVS updates the library's directory to point to the location of the new copy of the member, but it doesn't delete or reclaim the space occupied by the old copy. You occasionally have to *compress* or reorganize the space in partitioned data sets as a form of housekeeping to reclaim this space. You compress a PDS with TSO/ISPF function 3.1 or by using JCL. A newer form of partitioned data set called the Partitioned Data Set Extended (PDSE) becomes available with MVS/ESA and the Storage Management Subsystem (SMS). A PDSE eliminates worrying about the size of the directory and compression.

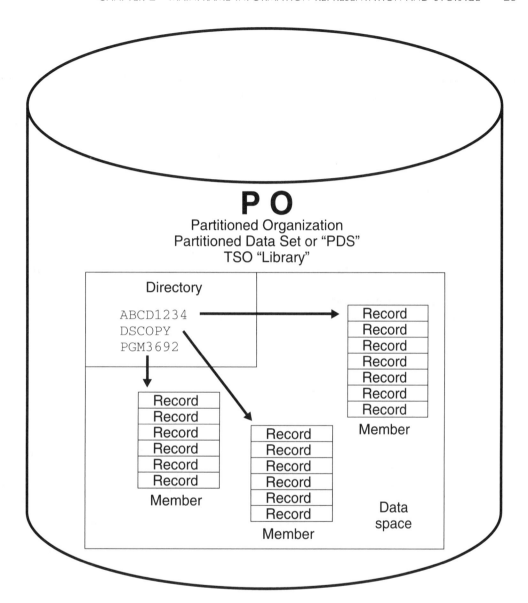

Figure 2.5 Partitioned Data Set

A partitioned data set (PDS) appears to MVS to be a special form of sequential data set. A PDS reserves a small area at its beginning for its directory, made up of *directory blocks.* These contain information about the names, origin, and location of the *members* of the partitioned data set. Your TSO libraries are actually partitioned data sets. The members of your libraries are individual JCL jobs or programs. PO stands for *Partitioned Organization.*

2.16 Your TSO Libraries

You will typically have at least two TSO libraries. You'll use one to house your program language statements (programs) and the other to house your JCL, as shown in Figure 2.6. The type part of the data set name for a JCL library is often CNTL, which stands for "control," but this is neither a TSO/ISPF or JCL requirement. The type part of the data set name will most likely be COBOL, PLI, FORTRAN, ASM, PASCAL, or C.

The TSO library names I've used here reflect the naming conventions of DePaul University:

CSCJGJ.CSC.CNTL   *My job control language library*
CSCJGJ.CSC.COBOL   *My program source code library*

The names you use for TSO libraries in your installation will be different because every installation can (and does) establish its own naming conventions.

A partitioned data set can only exist on disk. You can copy its contents to tape, but you can't directly access the data on tape. And a PDS can't straddle multiple disks; it must be contained on one disk only. But one disk device can hold hundreds and even thousands of different partitioned data sets.

2.17 The PDS Directory as Your Member Selection List

When you access one of your libraries using TSO/ISPF, you specify its name on the function 2 Edit-Entry screen. If you don't enter a specific member name there, TSO/ISPF presents the directory on the screen for you to choose a member.

MVS automatically keeps the entries in the directory of every partitioned data set in alphabetical order, regardless of the sequence in which you create the members. When you view a member selection list using TSO/ISPF, you'll always see the member names in this sequence.

2.18 Coding Member Names in JCL

To refer to a member of a data set using JCL, you code the data set name with the member name following in parentheses. Here is how I code data set name in my JCL when I have to refer to a job named EX1 in my CNTL library:

DSN=CSCJGJ.CSC.CNTL(EX1)

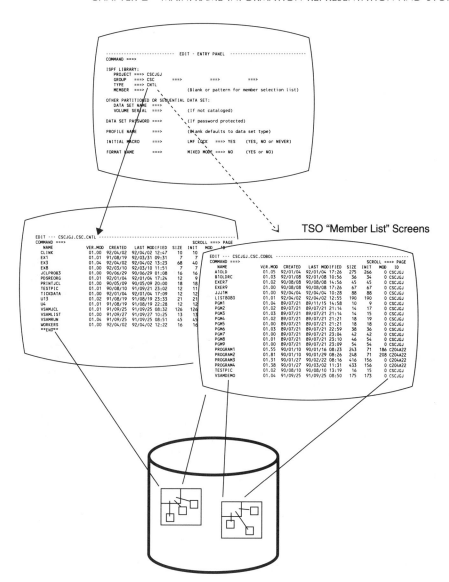

Figure 2.6 Your TSO/ISPF Libraries Are Partitioned Data Sets

Your programmer's libraries for job control language and program source code statements are partitioned data sets. You access each library through the TSO/ISPF function 2 Edit-Entry screen by name. The member selection list screen you get by leaving member name blank on the Edit-Entry screen is really the directory, formatted for easy reading on the screen. When you put an S in front of a member name on the member selection list screen and press <***Enter***>, TSO follows the information in the directory to obtain the member and lets you view and change it.

Using TSO/ISPF, you fill in the name on the screen this way:

```
PROJECT ===> CSCJGJ
GROUP   ===> CSC
TYPE    ===> CNTL
MEMBER  ===> EX1
```

2.19 Indexed Files: ISAM and VSAM

Indexed files are a more complex form of record storage than sequential organization. They provide not only sequential access to data but also direct access to individual records. Indexed files are suited only to disk storage. Although you can copy the data in them to tape to back them up, indexed files deliver their unique capabilities only on disk.

As I'll explain in Chapter 14, disk hardware lets the mechanism that writes and reads back information to physically get to any place on the disk recording surface. With the appropriate software, a program can obtain any record in an indexed file without having to read all of the other records in front of it in the data set. This is called **random access.** It's not random because the result is up to chance. Rather, the system sees this type of access as random because it can't predict what record your program will ask for next, unlike the case with a sequential file or member of a partitioned data set.

Indexed files are the modern way to harness the power of disk storage. There have been two types of indexed files in the IBM mainframe environment:

- ISAM (1968–87; now obsolete)
- VSAM (1973–present)

ISAM is obsolete and has been for a long time. I'm mentioning this only because you may still see references to ISAM in textbooks and manuals. Many books refer to any indexed file organization as ISAM because the letters stand for "indexed sequential access method," words that promise both indexed (random) and sequential access. All commercial computer systems have to support some form of indexed file to handle interactive (on-line) work. But technically, ISAM was and is a trademark of IBM for its first, now-obsolete way to provide indexed files.

VSAM stands for **Virtual Storage Access Method** and is IBM's contemporary way to implement indexed files. VSAM files are internally complex, as shown in Figure 2.7. Data is stored in a data component and the map to the data, called the index component, is stored elsewhere. VSAM data set internals are a complex subject entirely unrelated to JCL.

VSAM was developed a decade after the ancestor to the MVS operating system, and you need to use a special utility program named IDCAMS to

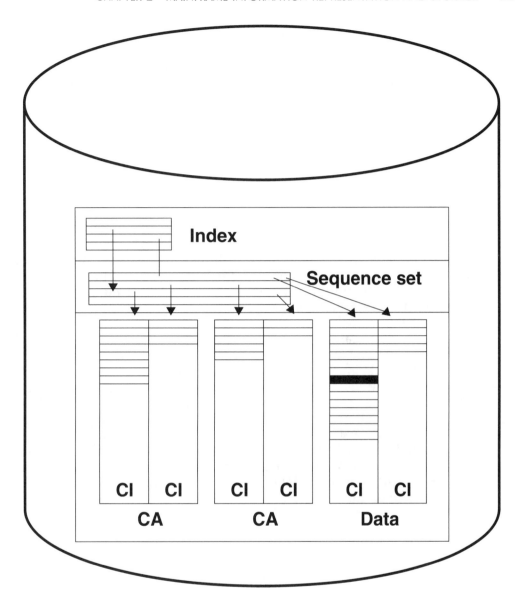

Figure 2.7   VSAM Data Set

A VSAM data set is internally complex. VSAM data sets house data accessed by interactive (CICS) programs; you don't use VSAM data sets to house your JCL or program statements. To create a VSAM data set you use the IDCAMS utility program, which you can execute via JCL or via TSO. VSAM stores data in Control Intervals (CI), which are grouped into Control Areas (CA). VSAM keeps a map to the data (its index) in two parts: the Index Set and the Sequence Set. Unless your installation has acquired and installed special software, you can't access VSAM data sets using TSO/ISPF.

create and manage VSAM data sets. Due to this complexity, you can't use TSO to access a VSAM data set directly, although various vendors supply software often attached to TSO to let you do this. You can accomplish reading of VSAM data sets through JCL just as with ordinary data sets.

2.20 Disk Volume Table of Contents

To work effectively with MVS, you need to understand how it keeps track of data sets. MVS uses two levels of "housekeeping" information above the level of your partitioned data set directory.

A mainframe might have hundreds of hard disk drives attached to it. The disk "volume" is the assembly of magnetic platters within a disk drive. Data sets (sequential, partitioned, and VSAM) each exist as recorded information on one or more disk volumes. Each disk volume provides hundreds of millions of bytes of storage capacity and has its own unique identifier. The identifier is called the *volume serial number* but could be any six characters such as CAR651.

Recorded on each disk volume is a Volume Table of Contents, or VTOC. This is a special data set managed by MVS to keep track of all of the data sets on the volume. Records in the VTOC point to data sets on the disk and keep important information about each data set, such as its organization. For your partitioned data sets (libraries), the VTOC points to the whole partitioned data set, and the partitioned data set's directory points to its individual members. A disk volume's VTOC knows only about the data sets on that disk volume.

Magnetic tapes have something analogous to a disk volume table of contents, and each tape has a unique volume serial number. It's recorded in the tape *label,* a small data set at the beginning of the tape, as I'll show you in Chapter 15.

2.21 The MVS System Catalog

MVS maintains a critical data set on a special disk volume. This is the *MVS system catalog.* Its purpose is simple: to keep information about where (on which disk volume) each data set resides, as shown in Figure 2.8. When MVS keeps information about a data set by keeping its name and location in the catalog, we say that the data set is *cataloged.* If MVS does not have the name of a data set in its catalog, the data set is *uncataloged.*

The internal layout of the MVS catalog has been changed by IBM throughout the years. The present form of the catalog is called the Integrated Catalog Facility (ICF). Your installation might break the catalog into subcatalogs, but its internal operation is usually hidden from programmers.

In a modern installation, all data sets, no matter whether they are on tape or disk, are cataloged. The cataloging process is automatic once you

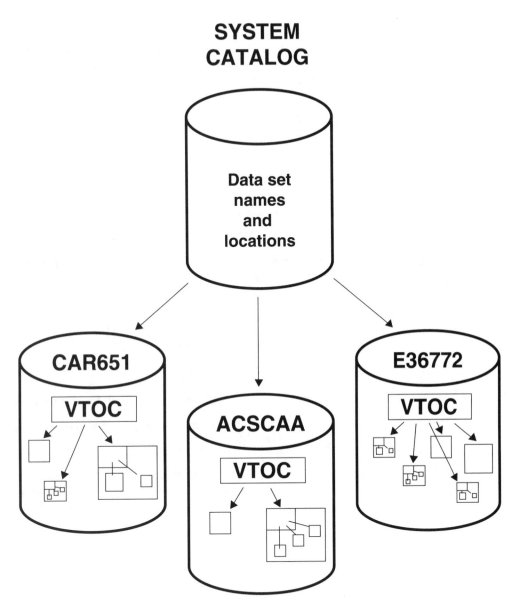

Figure 2.8 Volume Table of Contents and the MVS System Catalog

MVS uses two levels of "housekeeping" information above the level of the
partitioned data set directory: the disk **Volume Table of Contents** (VTOC) and the
MVS **system catalog.** The VTOC of a disk volume keeps track of all of the data sets
on the volume. For partitioned data sets, the VTOC points to the entire partitioned
data set, and the partitioned data set's directory points to its individual members.
The MVS system catalog keeps track of where (on which volume) each data set
resides. This makes it possible for you to access a data set by name alone, without
knowing on which disk volume it is.

specify that you want it for a data set. It's mandatory that TSO data sets be cataloged because this allows you to access a data set by name alone. And all VSAM data sets must be cataloged because the catalog stores all of the information describing them.

2.22 Creating Some Data Using TSO/ISPF

In the next several chapters I'll show you how to use JCL to run programs, read files, send material to the printer, and create or delete files. All of the examples I'll use will deal with the data shown in Figure 2.9. You will need to enter this data into your computer system. This data consists of 80-byte records. Data is usually stored separately from job control language, but as a convenience you can enter this as a member of your job control language library.

The data I've shown here is from a simple payroll system for a small department store. Each record contains these fields:

Positions	Number of Bytes	Field Contents
1–5	5	Employee I.D. number
6	1	Filler; blank
7–17	11	Employee last name
18–27	10	Employee first name
28–30	3	Hours worked this week as 99V9; for example, 402 is 40.2 hours
31–50	20	Name of department in which employee works
51–80	30	Filler; blank

You will often have to draw a **graphic record layout** to document the format of records in data files. A graphic record layout shows the starting position and length of each field in a record. Many IBM-supplied programs that you execute using JCL, such as the sort utility and printing utilities, require you to state fields in terms of starting position and actual byte length. I'll use some of those programs in the next several chapters to show you how to use JCL.

Here is the graphic record layout I prepared for this data. Notice that I drew each field as wide as I needed to accommodate the information to document the field. The number of bytes in a field doesn't dictate how it's drawn.

EMP-ID-NUMBER	Filler	EMP-EMPLOYEE-NAME		EMP-HRS-WORKED	EMP-DEPARTMENT	Filler
		EMP-LAST-NAME	EMP-FIRST-NAME			
X(5)	X(1)	X(11)	X(10)	99V9	X(20)	X(30)
1 5	6	7 17	18 27	28 30	31 50	51 80

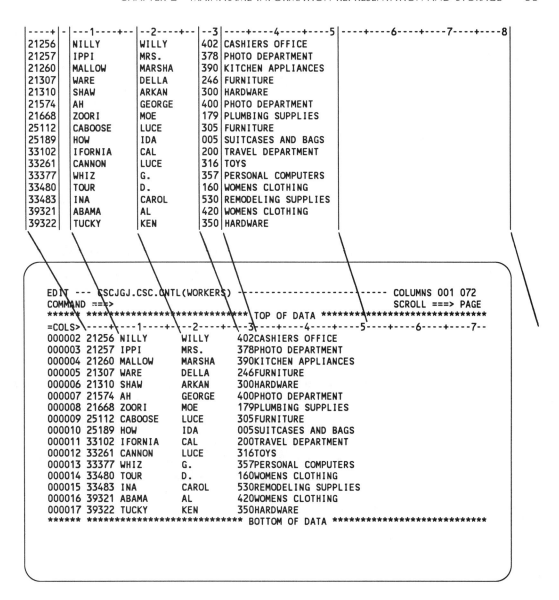

```
----+-|-|---1---+---|--2---+---|--3|----+----4----+----5|----+----6----+----7----+----8|
21256| NILLY    | WILLY    | 402| CASHIERS OFFICE
21257| IPPI     | MRS.     | 378| PHOTO DEPARTMENT
21260| MALLOW   | MARSHA   | 390| KITCHEN APPLIANCES
21307| WARE     | DELLA    | 246| FURNITURE
21310| SHAW     | ARKAN    | 300| HARDWARE
21574| AH       | GEORGE   | 400| PHOTO DEPARTMENT
21668| ZOORI    | MOE      | 179| PLUMBING SUPPLIES
25112| CABOOSE  | LUCE     | 305| FURNITURE
25189| HOW      | IDA      | 005| SUITCASES AND BAGS
33102| IFORNIA  | CAL      | 200| TRAVEL DEPARTMENT
33261| CANNON   | LUCE     | 316| TOYS
33377| WHIZ     | G.       | 357| PERSONAL COMPUTERS
33480| TOUR     | D.       | 160| WOMENS CLOTHING
33483| INA      | CAROL    | 530| REMODELING SUPPLIES
39321| ABAMA    | AL       | 420| WOMENS CLOTHING
39322| TUCKY    | KEN      | 350| HARDWARE
```

```
EDIT --- CSCJGJ.CSC.CNTL(WORKERS) --------------------------- COLUMNS 001 072
COMMAND ===>                                                  SCROLL ===> PAGE
****** **********************************TOP OF DATA *****************************
=COLS>----+----1----+---2----+---3----+----4----+----5----+----6----+----7--
000002 21256 NILLY    WILLY    402CASHIERS OFFICE
000003 21257 IPPI     MRS.     378PHOTO DEPARTMENT
000004 21260 MALLOW   MARSHA   390KITCHEN APPLIANCES
000005 21307 WARE     DELLA    246FURNITURE
000006 21310 SHAW     ARKAN    300HARDWARE
000007 21574 AH       GEORGE   400PHOTO DEPARTMENT
000008 21668 ZOORI    MOE      179PLUMBING SUPPLIES
000009 25112 CABOOSE  LUCE     305FURNITURE
000010 25189 HOW      IDA      005SUITCASES AND BAGS
000011 33102 IFORNIA  CAL      200TRAVEL DEPARTMENT
000012 33261 CANNON   LUCE     316TOYS
000013 33377 WHIZ     G.       357PERSONAL COMPUTERS
000014 33480 TOUR     D.       160WOMENS CLOTHING
000015 33483 INA      CAROL    530REMODELING SUPPLIES
000016 39321 ABAMA    AL       420WOMENS CLOTHING
000017 39322 TUCKY    KEN      350HARDWARE
****** *************************** BOTTOM OF DATA ******************************
```

Figure 2.9   Data for Your JCL Exercises

Exercises for this and the following chapters access the data shown here to demonstrate how you print things, create new data sets, and sort data. Data is usually stored in separate sequential data sets. But for convenience, enter these 16 records as member WORKERS of your job control language library so that you can run jobs with them.

Chapter 2 Review
Mini-Glossary

Bit   A single on-off value, the smallest unit of information

Byte   A group of eight bits, capable of storing one character

Catalog   The system's master locator of data sets, which keeps track of the disk volume on which each data set is stored

Data set   Mainframe term for file; where records are stored

Field   One or more bytes

File   A collection of zero or more records

Hexadecimal   A base-16 numbering system that provides a convenient shorthand for expressing the bit contents of bytes

Record   One or more fields

VTOC   Disk volume table of contents

Review Questions

1. Identify the pattern for data set name formation (including maximum length) and the characters valid in the name.
2. Explain what role a partitioned data set directory plays in storing and accessing information.
3. Describe the role played by disk VTOCs and the system catalog in managing information storage in the mainframe environment.

Exercises

A. The following is a character string expressed in hexadecimal. Convert this to ordinary characters using Appendix C:

    D1C3D34083829540828540C6E4D540A3964093858199955A

B. Identify which data set names are invalid and explain why:
    1. T.A00.JCL
    2. CSCJGJ\CSC\CNTL
    3. AJ1092.IMPORTANT.LIBRARY
    4. XYZ123.SAS$.DATA
    5. ACCTG.DATA.12MONTH
    6. CSCZMP.a00.COBOL

C. I need to create a TSO library that will house at least 100 JCL members. How many directory blocks should I specify?

Chapter Three

THE STRUCTURE OF JCL

Job control language is your way of telling the computer what *programs* you want to run, what *data sets* (files) these programs will use, and what "fate" or *disposition* the data sets will have when program execution ends. Your JCL will usually refer to more data sets than your two TSO libraries because actual data to be processed are usually stored in their own data sets.

You need to use JCL because the IBM mainframe is not arranged to listen to your requests to run programs one at a time. This is a lot different from your PC or a minicomputer like a VAX, which does process your commands one at a time. You may think that the mainframe likes to talk with you because you use TSO to deal with it interactively via a terminal or a PC acting as a terminal. But (review Figure 1.2) TSO is really just a program executed by MVS. TSO is a tool to get your programs and job control language into machine readable form; it's a giant word processor. TSO is just your messenger to MVS. *JCL is the only way you can talk to MVS!*

In this chapter I will show you how JCL is formed and the simple pattern that it follows. I told you in the preface that JCL can be easy to learn. Understanding the big picture I provide here will make this true for you. By the time you have finished this chapter, you will know the role and coding of each of the three most commonly used JCL statements. This foundation will enable you to feel confident enough to compose and run a simple set of JCL.

I wrap up this chapter by showing you several different types of error message reporting used by MVS. MVS is very fussy about the syntax of JCL. This chapter will help you to understand error reporting so that you can recognize why and how you get errors in your JCL.

3.1 JCL Executes Programs

Programs are sequences of logical instructions. When you write a program, you develop instructions in a high-level language such as COBOL, PL/I, FORTRAN, C, PASCAL, or Assembler. Your statements are converted to the machine language that the IBM mainframe understands and are stored in a disk data set called a *load module library.*

Executing a program means running it to accomplish what you intend it to do. To run, a program must

1. Be copied from disk into memory
2. Be hooked up with the files (data sets) it will use
3. Be given control of the computer system by MVS

To execute a program, you submit job control language that tells MVS to do these things for it.

3.2 How MVS Thinks About Programs

Programs are the smallest units of processing logic that MVS deals with. Regardless of the language you use to write a program, you can view the program (from MVS's point of view) as a box. Lines to and from the box indicate inputs (data sets) and outputs (data sets) that the program accesses when it executes. Arrowheads on these lines indicate the direction of information flow.

You can write programs and process them into machine language, and you'll no doubt do this as a programmer. But IBM also provides many programs with MVS that have already been written and processed into machine language. These are called *utilities* because they perform tasks that everyone usually needs to do often.

IEBGENER is one of the simplest utility programs already installed on your system. It is designed to copy the contents of a data set to another place. Figure 3.1 shows you how MVS views the IEBGENER program. The software engineers who coded IEBGENER followed an IBM convention in naming IEBGENER's four data set inputs and outputs, which are

SYSUT1	where IEBGENER expects to read its input data set
SYSUT2	where IEBGENER expects to write data
SYSIN	where IEBGENER expects to read any optional special instructions you might want to give it
SYSPRINT	where IEBGENER expects to write a simple report telling you what it did for you

These are strange names. They are not inherent to JCL. They are just symbolic identifiers used in this (IEBGENER) program. In Figure 3.2 you'll see how you use these names, which are hardcoded in IEBGENER, in the JCL that executes it.

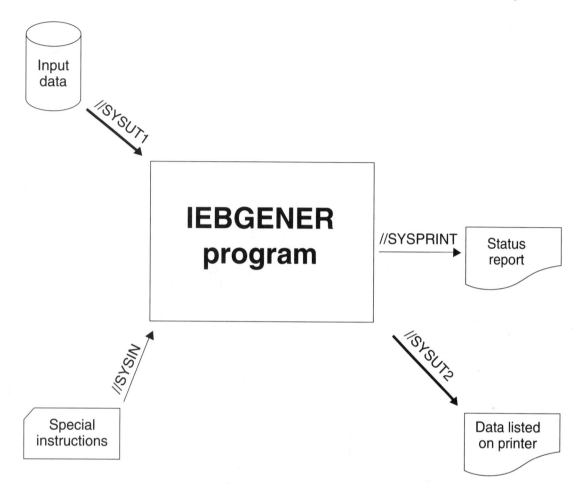

Figure 3.1   Inputs and Outputs of a Program

You use JCL to execute programs. From the JCL point of view, each program is a "black box" that receives input data sets and produces output data sets. You can draw the inputs and outputs of a program as lines with arrows. IBM supplies several utility programs such as IEBGENER along with MVS to make it easier for you to handle common processing tasks. IEBGENER is a "copy" utility. Its main job is to copy input from its //SYSUT1 and output it at its //SYSUT2, but IEBGENER also expects to receive instructions at //SYSIN and write a brief status report at //SYSPRINT.

3.3 JOB, EXEC, and DD Statements

JCL is simpler than you may think. Only eight different JCL statement types exist:

```
//name    JOB   parameters ...  ⎤
//name    EXEC  parameters ...  ⎬── You'll use these a lot!
//name    DD    parameters ...  ⎦

//name    PROC  parameters ...  ⎤  You'll use these only to
//name    PEND  parameters ...  ⎦  "package" JCL into procs

//*       comment              ⎤
/*        delimiter            ⎬── Optional
//        "null" ending statement ⎦
```

And JCL is even simpler because you'll use only three of these statements—JOB, EXEC, and DD—for almost all of your JCL. I focus on these three main statement types first in order to make you productive with JCL as fast as possible. I'll explain how you package JCL into procedures using PROC and PEND in Chapter 18.

Figure 3.2 shows you how I use JOB, EXEC, and DD statements to execute the IEBGENER program. This is a summarized picture of the statement types represented in my JCL, with most of the content omitted:

```
//CSCJGJA       JOB        parameters ...
//*
//STEP010       EXEC       parameters ...
//SYSUT1        DD         parameters ...
//SYSUT2        DD         parameters ...
//SYSPRINT      DD         parameters ...
//SYSIN         DD         parameters ...
//
```

Recognize the pattern! All of your JCL for a job will start with one JOB statement. The JCL for every program you want to execute will begin with an EXEC indicating the program name. And you'll code a separate DD statement (a **data device** statement) to associate every input or output of a program with an actual data set on the computer system.

The JCL in Figure 3.2 executes the IEBGENER program to copy the member named WORKERS from my CSCJGJ.CSC.CNTL library (created at the end of Chapter 2) to the system printer.

```
                 J E S 2   J O B   L O G   -- S Y S T E M   I B M 1   -- N O D E   N 1

16.23.31 JOB01515  IRR010I  USERID CSCJGJ   IS ASSIGNED TO THIS JOB.
16.23.31 JOB01515  ICH70001I CSCJGJ    LAST ACCESS AT 16:21:52 ON TUESDAY, SEPTEMBER 15, 1992
16.23.31 JOB01515  $HASP373 CSCJGJA  STARTED - INIT 1 - CLASS A - SYS IBM1
16.23.32 JOB01515  $HASP395 CSCJGJA  ENDED

------ JES2 JOB STATISTICS ------
     15 SEP 92 JOB EXECUTION DATE
         21 CARDS READ
         69 SYSOUT PRINT RECORDS
          0 SYSOUT PUNCH RECORDS
          4 SYSOUT SPOOL KBYTES
       0.01 MINUTES EXECUTION TIME

    1 //CSCJGJA   JOB  1,            ACCOUNTING INFORMATION            JOB01515
      //   'BIN 7--JANOSSY',         PROGRAMMER NAME AND DELIVERY BIN  00020000
      //   CLASS=A,                  INPUT QUEUE CLASS                 00030000
      //   MSGCLASS=X,               PRINT DESTINATION X A L N OR O    00040000
      //   MSGLEVEL=(1,1),           HOW MUCH MVS SYSTEM PRINT DESIRED 00050000
      //*  TYPRUN=SCAN,              UNCOMMENT IF WANT ONLY A JCL SCAN 00060000
      //   NOTIFY=CSCJGJ             WHO TO TELL WHEN JOB IS DONE      00070000
      //*                                                             00080000
      //* THIS JCL IS STORED AT CSCJGJ.CSC.CNTL(A2GENER)              00090000
      //*                                                             00100000
      //******************************************************************  00110000
      //*                                                             *     00120000
      //*   LIST THE WORKERS DATA WITHOUT FORMATTING IT FOR PRINT     *     00130000
      //*                                                             *     00140000
      //******************************************************************  00150000
    2 //STEP010   EXEC  PGM=IEBGENER                                  00160000
    3 //SYSUT1    DD    DSN=CSCJGJ.CSC.CNTL(WORKERS),  <=== //SYSUT1 IS INPUT 00170001
      // DISP=SHR                                                     00180000
    4 //SYSUT2    DD    SYSOUT=*                       <=== //SYSUT2 IS OUTPUT 00190001
    5 //SYSPRINT  DD    SYSOUT=*                                      00200000
    6 //SYSIN     DD    DUMMY                                         00210000

ICH70001I CSCJGJ    LAST ACCESS AT 16:21:52 ON TUESDAY, SEPTEMBER 15, 1992

IEF236I ALLOC. FOR CSCJGJA STEP010
IEF237I 111  ALLOCATED TO SYSUT1
IEF237I JES2 ALLOCATED TO SYSUT2
IEF237I JES2 ALLOCATED TO SYSPRINT
IEF237I DMY  ALLOCATED TO SYSIN
IEF142I CSCJGJA STEP010 - STEP WAS EXECUTED - | COND CODE 0000 |
IEF285I    CSCJGJ.CSC.CNTL
IEF285I    VOL SER NOS= USER00.
IEF285I    CSCJGJ.CSCJGJA.JOB01515.D0000101.?      SYSOUT
IEF285I    CSCJGJ.CSCJGJA.JOB01515.D0000102.?      SYSOUT
IEF373I STEP /STEP010 / START 92259.1623
IEF374I STEP /STEP010 / STOP  92259.1623 CPU    0MIN 00.13SEC SRB    0MIN 00.00SEC

IEF375I JOB /CSCJGJA / START 92259.1623
IEF376I JOB /CSCJGJA / STOP  92259.1623 CPU    0MIN 00.13SEC SRB    0MIN 00.00SEC

21256 NILLY      WILLY      402CASHIERS OFFICE
21257 IPPI       MRS.       378PHOTO DEPARTMENT
21260 MALLOW     MARSHA     390KITCHEN APPLIANCES
21307 WARE       DELLA      246FURNITURE
21310 SHAW       ARKAN      300HARDWARE
21574 AH         GEORGE     400PHOTO DEPARTMENT
21668 ZOORI      MOE        179PLUMBING SUPPLIES
25112 CABOOSE    LUCE       305FURNITURE
25189 HOW        IDA        005SUITCASES AND BAGS
33102 IFORNIA    CAL        200TRAVEL DEPARTMENT
33261 CANNON     LUCE       316TOYS
33377 WHIZ       G.         357PERSONAL COMPUTERS
33480 TOUR       D.         160WOMENS CLOTHING
33483 INA        CAROL      530REMODELING SUPPLIES
39321 ABAMA      AL         420WOMENS CLOTHING
39322 TUCKY      KEN        350HARDWARE
```

Every program can leave behind a COND CODE from 0000 through 4095. By convention 0000 means successful execution.

Output from IEBGENER's //SYSUT2 DD statement. This is the WORKERS data we asked IEBGENER to copy from a disk data set to the printer.

Figure 3.2   Execution of the IEBGENER Program

3.4 Your Framework for Learning JCL

You use these three types of JCL statements to form most of your JCL:

```
//name          JOB       parameters ...
//name          EXEC      parameters ...
//name          DD        parameters ...
```

On each of these statements the "name" —a label—starts immediately after the two slashes. You can form it with up to eight uppercase characters or numbers, but the first character of the name must be a letter. Each kind of JCL statement has a different set of parameters. Beyond learning the structure of JCL, you need to become familiar with what these parameters are, when you need to code them, and how to code them. Figure 3.3 shows you the JCL to execute the IEBGENER program.

Figure 3.4 will help you organize your thinking about the big three JCL statements. Here's what this chart says:

- JCL is made up mainly of JOB, EXEC, and DD statements
- JOB is easy to learn and use
- EXEC is easy to learn and use
- DD statements take three forms:
    DD statements to read a data set (easy)
    DD statements to print an output (easy)
    DD statements to create a new data set (hard!); to code this form of
        DD statement you have to learn how to use several complex
        parameters such as DISP, UNIT, DCB, SPACE, and others

You can accomplish a lot with JCL using JOB, EXEC, and just the two simpler forms of the DD statement (reading and printing data sets).

```
//CSCJGJA    JOB 1,'BIN 7 JANOSSY',MSGCLASS=X,MSGLEVEL=(1,1),
//  NOTIFY=CSCJGJ
//*
//STEP010     EXEC  PGM=IEBGENER
//SYSUT1      DD    DSN=CSCJGJ.CSC.CNTL(WORKERS),        Reading
//  DISP=SHR
//SYSUT2      DD    SYSOUT=*                             Printing
//SYSPRINT    DD    SYSOUT=*                             Shut off
//SYSIN       DD    DUMMY                                Shut off
//
```

Figure 3.3   Executing the IEBGENER Program

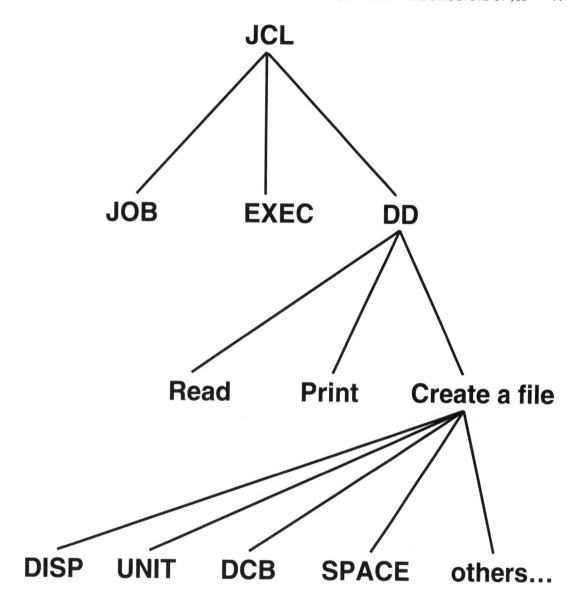

Figure 3.4   Your Framework for Learning JCL

3.5 Overview of the JOB Statement

You code the JOB statement first in any set of JCL. Its purpose is simple. It tells MVS who is submitting the series of program execution requests, where MVS should send the print output, how much reporting MVS should provide, and how important the job is in relation to other jobs in the system. You can also indicate memory and processing time limits on the JOB statement.

You code the JOB statement starting with a label that becomes the job name, in the general form:

```
//CSCJGJA    JOB ... other information
```

For almost all of your work as a programmer or end user, the name after the slashes is your TSO user-id *followed by a single letter*. If you don't supply the trailing letter on your JOB name, TSO asks you for it in the process of submitting your job. By making this letter different, you can give each of your job submissions a unique name. Jobs of the same name and CLASS are processed by MVS in sequence. MVS may process jobs with different names concurrently. If your jobs are quick running and you don't mind them following one another in execution, you can include the letter on the JOB statement (as I have indicated here) and make all your jobs have the same name.

The content of your JOB statement is usually very stable. Once you have established a JOB statement for yourself you can use it for most of your work. Your project leader or supervisor will usually give you the appropriate local account number to use, so that the resources used to run the job are charged to the appropriate budget account. (This example just uses "1" as the account number because we don't use a formal charge-back system on our training mainframe at DePaul University.)

In Figure 3.5a I've reproduced the JCL I use to submit IEBGENER print jobs. In Figure 3.5b I've coded the same JOB statement with one parameter on each line, and I've included documentary comments on the same line as each parameter. You can code any JCL statement in this way to make it easier to read and understand.

You may occasionally have to make some choices in the parameter coding that follows the accounting information because CLASS, MSGCLASS, and other parameters are subject to your installation's customization. Figure 3.5b is enough to answer most of your questions about JOB statement coding. In Chapter 6 I cover the JOB statement in detail. You can browse or skip that chapter as your needs dictate.

```
EDIT ---- CSCJGJ.CSC.CNTL(A3JOB) - 01.02 -------------------- COLUMNS 001 072
COMMAND ===>                                            SCROLL ===> PAGE
****** **************************** TOP OF DATA *******************************
000100 //CSCJGJA   JOB 1,'BIN 7--JANOSSY',CLASS=A,MSGCLASS=X,MSGLEVEL=(1,1),
000200 // NOTIFY=CSCJGJ
000300 //*
000400 //* THIS JCL IS STORED AT CSCJGJ.CSC.CNTL(A3JOB)
000500 //*
000600 //STEP010  EXEC  PGM=IEBGENER
000700 //SYSUT1     DD  DSN=CSCJGJ.CSC.CNTL(WORKERS),
000800 // DISP=SHR
000900 //SYSUT2     DD  SYSOUT=*
001000 //SYSPRINT   DD  SYSOUT=*
001100 //SYSIN      DD  DUMMY
001200 //
```

(a)

```
EDIT ---- CSCJGJ.CSC.CNTL(A4JOB) - 01.02 -------------------- COLUMNS 001 072
COMMAND ===>                                            SCROLL ===> PAGE
****** **************************** TOP OF DATA *******************************
000100 //CSCJGJA   JOB 1,            ACCOUNTING INFORMATION
000200 // 'BIN 7--JANOSSY',          PROGRAMMER NAME AND DELIVERY BIN
000300 // CLASS=A,                   INPUT QUEUE CLASS (WHICH INPUT QUEUE?)
000400 // MSGCLASS=X,                PRINTING CLASS (WHICH OUTPUT QUEUE?)
000500 // MSGLEVEL=(1,1),            HOW MUCH DETAIL DO YOU WANT IN MVS MESSAGES?
000600 // REGION=2048K,              MEMORY LIMIT FOR EACH STEP (2,048,000 BYTES)
000700 // TIME=(1,30),               MAX PROCESSING TIME FOR JOB (1.5 MINUTES)
000800 //* TYPRUN=SCAN,              UNCOMMENT IF WANT ONLY A JCL SCAN
000900 // NOTIFY=CSCJGJ              WHO SHOULD MVS TELL WHEN THE JOB FINISHES?
001000 //*
001100 //* THIS JCL IS STORED AT CSCJGJ.CSC.CNTL(A4JOB)
001200 //*
001300 //STEP010  EXEC  PGM=IEBGENER
001400 //SYSUT1     DD  DSN=CSCJGJ.CSC.CNTL(WORKERS),
001500 // DISP=SHR
001600 //SYSUT2     DD  SYSOUT=*
001700 //SYSPRINT   DD  SYSOUT=*
001800 //SYSIN      DD  DUMMY
001900 //
****** **************************** BOTTOM OF DATA *****************************
```

(b)

Figure 3.5 Two Styles of JOB Statement Coding

(a) You can code JCL with a compact JOB statement and put several parameters on one line. (b) An easier-to-read style is to code one parameter on each line, leaving room for same-line comments.

3.6 Overview of the EXEC Statement

You tell MVS the name of the program you want to execute (run) using an EXEC statement. A basic EXEC statement is

```
//STEP010    EXEC  PGM=IEBGENER
```

The name after the slashes is called the **step name.** It's a label that you can code as any eight characters or numbers; its first position must be a letter. Here are some important facts about the step name:

- Step name is optional. But if you omit coding it, your JCL is harder to read and you can't refer to the step in subsequent JCL. (This becomes important when you code jobs with more than one step, as I'll show you in Chapter 4.)
- You don't have to name a step starting with //STEP. You could, conceivably, name a step //BARBARA or //JOEY. But most people name steps as I show here because this makes things very clear in the JCL and in MVS reporting.

You can code optional parameters on the EXEC statement such as REGION, TIME, COND, PARM, and ACCT. I'll show you how to use each of these on an EXEC in Chapter 7. But in Figure 3.6a and 3.6b I've illustrated using REGION and TIME because these are the EXEC parameters you're most likely to need.

Compare Figure 3.5b to Figure 3.6a. You'll see that I have moved the REGION and TIME parameters down from the JOB statement to the EXEC at //STEP010. When you code REGION or TIME on the JOB statement, you set the memory limit for each step and the processing time for the entire job. But if you code REGION or TIME on an EXEC, you set the memory limit or processing time for the program executed at that step only. (If you code these on *both* JOB and EXEC, the coding on the JOB statement prevails.)

You can also use EXEC to execute a cataloged procedure:

```
//STEP010    EXEC  PROC=BT3506P1              PROC= coded
```

or

```
//STEP010    EXEC  BT3506P1                   PROC omitted
```

When you omit coding either PGM or PROC, MVS assumes you meant PROC. A **proc** is "canned" JCL. It's ordinary JCL that has been modified slightly and stored in a partitioned data set called a **procedure library,** or **proc lib**, so everyone can execute it. Procs are a handy way to allow everyone to perform standard functions, such as compiling, linking, and running programs. I'll show you how to execute a common proc in Chapter 5 and how to build procs in Chapter 18.

```
EDIT ---- CSCJGJ.CSC.CNTL(A5REGION) - 01.02 ----------------- COLUMNS 001 072
COMMAND ===>                                                 SCROLL ===> PAGE
****** **************************** TOP OF DATA ********************************
000100 //CSCJGJA   JOB  1,        ACCOUNTING INFORMATION
000200 //   'BIN 7--JANOSSY',     PROGRAMMER NAME AND DELIVERY BIN
000300 //   CLASS=A,              INPUT QUEUE CLASS (WHICH INPUT QUEUE?)
000400 //   MSGCLASS=X,           PRINTING CLASS (WHICH OUTPUT QUEUE?)
000500 //   MSGLEVEL=(1,1),       HOW MUCH DETAIL DO YOU WANT IN MVS MESSAGES?
000600 //* TYPRUN=SCAN,           UNCOMMENT IF WANT ONLY A JCL SCAN
000700 //   NOTIFY=CSCJGJ         WHO SHOULD MVS TELL WHEN THE JOB FINISHES?
000800 //*
000900 //* THIS JCL IS STORED AT CSCJGJ.CSC.CNTL(A5REGION)
001000 //*
001100 //STEP010  EXEC  PGM=IEBGENER,
001200 //   REGION=2048K,         LET STEP USE UP TO 2,048,000 BYTES
001300 //   TIME=(1,30)           LET STEP USE UP TO 1.5 MINUTES
001400 //SYSUT1     DD  DSN=CSCJGJ.CSC.CNTL(WORKERS),
001500 //   DISP=SHR
001600 //SYSUT2     DD  SYSOUT=*
001700 //SYSPRINT   DD  SYSOUT=*
001800 //SYSIN      DD  DUMMY
001900 //
```

(a)

```
EDIT ---- CSCJGJ.CSC.CNTL(A6REGION) - 01.00 ----------------- COLUMNS 001 072
COMMAND ===>                                                 SCROLL ===> PAGE
****** **************************** TOP OF DATA ********************************
000100 //CSCJGJA   JOB  1,
000200 //   'BIN 7--JANOSSY',
000300 //   CLASS=A,
000400 //   MSGCLASS=X,
000500 //   MSGLEVEL=(1,1),
000600 //* TYPRUN=SCAN,
000700 //   NOTIFY=CSCJGJ
000800 //*
000900 //* THIS JCL IS STORED AT CSCJGJ.CSC.CNTL(A6REGION)
001000 //*
001100 //STEP010  EXEC  PGM=IEBGENER,REGION=2048K,TIME=(1,30)
001200 //SYSUT1     DD  DSN=CSCJGJ.CSC.CNTL(WORKERS),
001300 //   DISP=SHR
001400 //SYSUT2     DD  SYSOUT=*
001500 //SYSPRINT   DD  SYSOUT=*
001600 //SYSIN      DD  DUMMY
001700 //
****** **************************** BOTTOM OF DATA *****************************
```

(b)

Figure 3.6   REGION and TIME on the EXEC Statement

(a) I moved REGION and TIME parameters down from the JOB statement to the EXEC in this JCL to give IEBGENER a limit of two megabytes and 1.5 minutes CPU time. (b) This JCL does the same thing as the JCL above, without on-the-line comments and without continuing the EXEC statement.

3.7 *Overview of the Three Kinds of DD Statements*

A program executed at a step can access zero, one, or multiple data sets (files). For every data set the program accesses, you must code a DD statement following the EXEC. There are only three general categories of DD statement:

1. A DD statement for a data set being read
2. A DD statement for lines (records) being printed
3. A DD statement for a data set being written (created)

MVS gives you flexibility because it frees a program from having to know the actual source of any of its inputs or the destination of any of its outputs. The program specifies in its source code the names that become DDnames for each of its inputs and outputs. These names are documented so that when you write JCL to execute the program, you know how to connect actual data sets and the printer with it.

In Figure 3.7 you see a DD statement of the first type being used to connect IEBGENER to a member WORKERS of a partitioned data set name CSCJGJ.CSC.CNTL for reading. The DDname //SYSUT1 is the coupling between the program and JCL. You could change the actual source of the data fed into IEBGENER by just changing the JCL.

I coded the DDname //SYSPRINT with a DD statement of the second type. SYSOUT=* is the most common way to send output to a printer. In Chapter 9 I'll show you more about this type of DD statement, including ways to use it to route output to different printers and to produce multiple printed copies.

IEBGENER expects to read instructions at DDname //SYSIN. It expects a few instructions telling it how you want to change the format of input records read at //SYSUT1 so that it writes them out at //SYSUT2 with fields in a different sequence or with a shorter or longer length. But to make IEBGENER do a "straight" copy, not changing the format of records it processes, you just don't give it any instructions at all. Coding DUMMY at //SYSIN simulates an empty file being read.

In the previous pages I've shown you the JCL to execute IEBGENER with //SYSUT2 directed to SYSOUT=*. This is a simple way to print records. At the bottom of Figure 3.7 you can also see what a DD statement of the third type looks like. If I coded //SYSUT2 with DSN, DISP, UNIT, DCB, and SPACE as shown, I could send the records read by IEBGENER at //SYSUT1 out to a newly created data set housed on disk named CSCJGJ. CSC.WORKERS2. In Chapter 10 I'll show you more about writing data sets.

You now know enough about JCL to code it for a program that reads records from one or more files and prints one or more reports! Let's now see how MVS reports errors in your JCL.

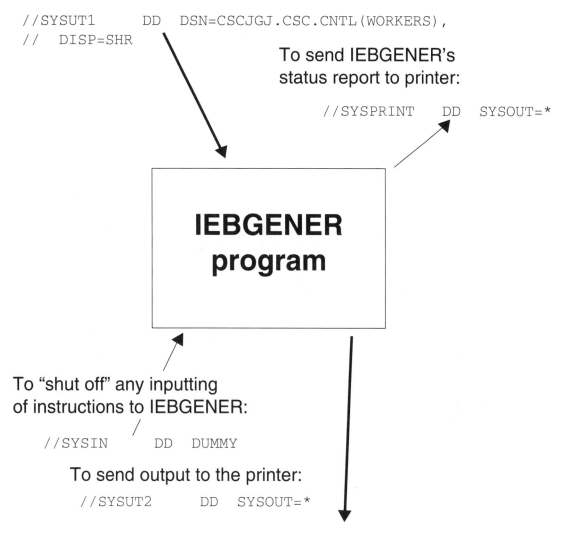

To read (input) a data set:

```
//SYSUT1      DD  DSN=CSCJGJ.CSC.CNTL(WORKERS),
//  DISP=SHR
```

To send IEBGENER's
status report to printer:

```
//SYSPRINT   DD  SYSOUT=*
```

**IEBGENER
program**

To "shut off" any inputting
of instructions to IEBGENER:

```
//SYSIN     DD  DUMMY
```

To send output to the printer:

```
//SYSUT2      DD  SYSOUT=*
```

To send output into (create) a new data set:

```
//SYSUT2       DD  DSN=CSCJGJ.CSC.WORKERS2,
//  DISP=(NEW,CATLG,DELETE),
//  UNIT=SYSDA,
//  DCB=(RECFM=FB,LRECL=80,BLKSIZE=6160),
//  SPACE=(TRK,1)
```

Figure 3.7 Reading, Printing, Writing, and Dummy DD Statements

3.8 A Common JCL Error: Using Column 72

It's always easy to make mistakes in coding JCL, because MVS is very fussy about the placement of every comma and space. But when you code JCL with several parameters on one line or use same-line comments, it's even easier to make a subtle mistake. *If you put something into column 72, MVS assumes that you are going to continue that line.*

In Figure 3.8a you see how the last "S" in the word SECONDS on line 001300 occupies column 72. This is at the end of my EXEC statement. It makes MVS think that I intend line 001400 to carry another parameter of the EXEC statement. But line 001400 is a new statement, a DD statement for //SYSUT1.

When I submit the JCL shown in Figure 3.8a, I receive a job number. But almost immediately, I receive notification from MVS that the job has failed due to a JCL error. Figure 3.8b shows you how MVS reports this JCL error. The job log at the top of the output clearly indicates that the job was not run. The MVS messages following the JCL indicate that the error is associated with statement 2—the EXEC statement. MVS expected a continuation but did not receive it, and it tells you so.

You will find that JCL errors like this are the easiest mistakes to interpret and resolve. You will encounter this same type of message when you incorrectly leave a space within the parameters of a statement, such as within a data set name (DSN). In responding to the printed MVS error message, keep in mind that MVS numbers your lines of JCL by whole statements, not by the individual lines making up a statement.

You've now seen several simple sets of JCL and the results they produce when processed by MVS. It's about time to summarize actual JCL coding rules for you.

3.9 Summary of Coding Rules for JCL Statements

A JCL statement can contain four parts; the fourth part, a comment, is optional:

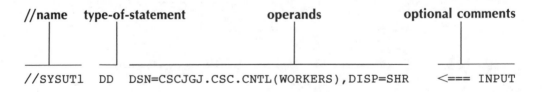

```
//name    type-of-statement           operands              optional comments
   |          |                           |                       |
   |          |                           |                       |
 __|__      __|__       _____|_____       __|__
//SYSUT1    DD    DSN=CSCJGJ.CSC.CNTL(WORKERS),DISP=SHR    <=== INPUT
```

```
EDIT ---- CSCJGJ.CSC.CNTL(A7ERROR) - 01.00 ------------------ COLUMNS 001 072
COMMAND ===> sub                                         SCROLL ===> PAGE
****** ***************************** TOP OF DATA ********************************
000100 //CSCJGJA   JOB  1,        ACCOUNTING INFORMATION
000200 //   'BIN 7--JANOSSY',     PROGRAMMER NAME AND DELIVERY BIN
000300 //   CLASS=A,              INPUT QUEUE CLASS (WHICH INPUT QUEUE?)
000400 //   MSGCLASS=X,           PRINTING CLASS (WHICH OUTPUT QUEUE?)
000500 //   MSGLEVEL=(1,1),       HOW MUCH DETAIL DO YOU WANT IN MVS MESSAGES?
000600 //*  TYPRUN=SCAN,          UNCOMMENT IF WANT ONLY A JCL SCAN
000700 //   NOTIFY=CSCJGJ         WHO SHOULD MVS TELL WHEN THE JOB FINISHES?
000800 //*
000900 //* THIS JCL IS STORED AT CSCJGJ.CSC.CNTL(A7ERROR)
001000 //*
001100 //STEP010  EXEC  PGM=IEBGENER,
001200 //   REGION=2048K,            I LET THIS STEP USE UP TO 2,048,000 BYTES
001300 //   TIME=(1,30)              I LET THIS STEP USE UP TO 1 MINUTE, 30 SECONDS
001400 //SYSUT1     DD  DSN=CSCJGJ.CSC.CNTL(WORKERS),
001500 //   DISP=SHR
001600 //SYSUT2     DD  SYSOUT=*
001700 //SYSPRINT   DD  SYSOUT=*
001800 //SYSIN      DD  DUMMY
001900 //
```

(a)

```
                    J E S 2   J O B   L O G  --  S Y S T E M   I B M 1  --  N O D E   N 1

  16.54.29 JOB01530  IRR010I  USERID CSCJGJ   IS ASSIGNED TO THIS JOB.
  16.54.30 JOB01530  IEFC452I CSCJGJA - | JOB NOT RUN - JCL ERROR |

  ------ JES2 JOB STATISTICS ------
            18 CARDS READ
            35 SYSOUT PRINT RECORDS
             0 SYSOUT PUNCH RECORDS
             2 SYSOUT SPOOL KBYTES
          0.00 MINUTES EXECUTION TIME

       1 //CSCJGJA   JOB  1,        ACCOUNTING INFORMATION                        JOB01530
         //   'BIN 7--JANOSSY',     PROGRAMMER NAME AND DELIVERY BIN              00020000
         //   CLASS=A,              INPUT QUEUE CLASS (WHICH INPUT QUEUE?)        00030000
         //   MSGCLASS=X,           PRINTING CLASS (WHICH OUTPUT QUEUE?)          00040000
         //   MSGLEVEL=(1,1),       HOW MUCH DETAIL DO YOU WANT IN MVS MESSAGES?  00050000
         //*  TYPRUN=SCAN,          UNCOMMENT IF WANT ONLY A JCL SCAN             00060000
         //   NOTIFY=CSCJGJ         WHO SHOULD MVS TELL WHEN THE JOB FINISHES?    00070000
         //*                                                                      00080000
         //* THIS JCL IS STORED AT CSCJGJ.CSC.CNTL(A7ERROR)                       00090000
         //*                                                                      00100000
       2 //STEP010  EXEC  PGM=IEBGENER,                                           00110000
         //   REGION=2048K,            I LET THIS STEP USE UP TO 2,048,000 BYTES  00120000
         //   TIME=(1,30)              I LET THIS STEP USE UP TO 1 MINUTE, 30 SECONDS00130000
       3 //SYSUT1     DD  DSN=CSCJGJ.CSC.CNTL(WORKERS),                           00140000
         //   DISP=SHR                                                            00150000
       4 //SYSUT2     DD  SYSOUT=*                                                     0000
       5 //SYSPRINT   DD  SYSOUT=*                                                 170000
       6 //SYSIN      DD  DUMMY                                                    180000

  STMT NO. MESSAGE
         2 IEFC621I EXPECTED CONTINUATION NOT RECEIVED
         3 IEFC019I MISPLACED DD STATEMENT
         4 IEFC019I MISPLACED DD STATEMENT
         5 IEFC019I MISPLACED DD STATEMENT
         6 IEFC019I MISPLACED DD STATEMENT
         6 IEFC607I JOB HAS NO STEPS
```

(b)

MVS interprets any character in column 72 (except a space there) as an indication that the JCL statement will be continued on the next line.

Figure 3.8 A Subtle JCL Error

(a) You can code a complete JCL statement only through column 71. Unintentionally using column 72 makes MVS think that you will continue the line; the second "S" in the word SECONDS in my same-line comment at line 001300 is a problem. (b) How MVS reports this JCL error.

You can continue a statement to another line (explicitly) by breaking it at a comma, and lines that are continued can still carry comments:

```
//SYSUT1  DD  DSN=CSCJGJ.CSC.CNTL(WORKERS),        <=== THIS IS
//  DISP=SHR                                        <=== INPUT
```

Most JCL statements carry a *name*, which is used to either identify the job, as in the case of the JOB statement, or to provide a label for the statement. You code the name as one to eight characters, beginning with a letter. The second and subsequent characters in the name may be numerals or @, $, or #. *Only uppercase letters are allowed!*

Type-of-statement is limited to one of a few statement types such as JOB, EXEC, DD, PROC, and PEND. MVS/ESA adds a few specialized statement types but continues to support all of the original ones, which really do the work of JCL.

Operands are called ***parameters***, and different ones exist for each type of JCL statement. Two types of parameters exist:

- *Keyword* parameters that are recognized by words such as DSN, DISP, UNIT, DCB, SPACE, VOL, and LABEL
- *Positional* parameters, which depend on positions within a list separated by commas, such as UNIT=(TAPE,,DEFER)

Except for the special purpose /* delimiter statement (discussed in Chapter 8), all JCL statements begin with // in positions 1 and 2. You have to code the type-of-statement no further to the right than column 16, or it will be treated as a comment. You can code same-line comments if you separate the comment from the last parameter on the line by at least one space. Columns 73–80 carry optional line numbers (applied automatically by TSO/ISPF). You'll get JCL errors if you violate these rules.

3.10 Misspelling a JCL Statement Type

In the JCL in Figure 3.9a I've misspelled the word EXEC on line 001000, making it EXXX. MVS does not know what EXXX means and complains about it in Figure 3.9b. But you also see other error messages here. Since I made the mistake in the only EXEC statement in this JCL, MVS doesn't see any EXEC statement at all in the JCL and complains that it has no steps.

```
EDIT ---- CSCJGJ.CSC.CNTL(A8ERROR) - 01.00 ------------------ COLUMNS 001 072
COMMAND ===> sub                                            SCROLL ===> PAGE
****** *************************** TOP OF DATA ********************************
000100 //CSCJGJA   JOB  1,        ACCOUNTING INFORMATION
000200 //  'BIN 7--JANOSSY',      PROGRAMMER NAME AND DELIVERY BIN
000300 //  CLASS=A,               INPUT QUEUE CLASS (WHICH INPUT QUEUE?)
000400 //  MSGCLASS=X,            PRINTING CLASS (WHICH OUTPUT QUEUE?)
000500 //  MSGLEVEL=(1,1),        HOW MUCH DETAIL DO YOU WANT IN MVS MESSAGES?
000600 //  NOTIFY=CSCJGJ          WHO SHOULD MVS TELL WHEN THE JOB FINISHES?
000700 //*
000800 //* THIS JCL IS STORED AT CSCJGJ.CSC.CNTL(A8ERROR)
000900 //*
001000 //STEP010 [EXXX] PGM=IEBGENER
001100 //SYSUT1    DD   DSN=CSCJGJ.CSC.CNTL(WORKERS),    <=== INPUT
001200 //  DISP=SHR
001300 //SYSUT2    DD   SYSOUT=*                         <=== OUTPUT
001400 //SYSPRINT  DD   SYSOUT=*
001500 //SYSIN     DD   DUMMY
001600 //
****** *************************** BOTTOM OF DATA *****************************

JOB CSCJGJA(JOB04698) SUBMITTED
11.32.11 JOB04698 $HASP165 CSCJGJA  ENDED AT N1 - JCL ERROR CN(INTERNAL)
***
```
(a)

```
                        J E S 2   J O B   L O G  --  S Y S T E M   I B M 1  --  N O D E   N 1
  11.32.11 JOB04698  IRR010I  USERID CSCJGJ   IS ASSIGNED TO THIS JOB.
  11.32.11 JOB04698  IEFC452I CSCJGJA [- JOB NOT RUN - JCL ERROR]

  ------ JES2 JOB STATISTICS ------
          15 CARDS READ
          32 SYSOUT PRINT RECORDS
           0 SYSOUT PUNCH RECORDS
           2 SYSOUT SPOOL KBYTES
        0.00 MINUTES EXECUTION TIME

     1 //CSCJGJA   JOB  1,        ACCOUNTING INFORMATION                      JOB04698
       //  'BIN 7--JANOSSY',      PROGRAMMER NAME AND DELIVERY BIN            00020000
       //  CLASS=A,               INPUT QUEUE CLASS (WHICH INPUT QUEUE?)      00030000
       //  MSGCLASS=X,            PRINTING CLASS (WHICH OUTPUT QUEUE?)        00040000
       //  MSGLEVEL=(1,1),        HOW MUCH DETAIL DO YOU WANT IN MVS MESSAGES? 00050000
       //  NOTIFY=CSCJGJ          WHO SHOULD MVS TELL WHEN THE JOB FINISHES?  00060000
       //*                                                                   00070000
       //* THIS JCL IS STORED AT CSCJGJ.CSC.CNTL(A8ERROR)                    00080000
       //*                                                                   00090000
     2 //STEP010 [EXXX] PGM=IEBGENER                                         00100000
     3 //SYSUT1    DD   DSN=CSCJGJ.CSC.CNTL(WORKERS),    <=== INPUT          00110000
       //  DISP=SHR                                                          00120000
     4 //SYSUT2    DD   SYSOUT=*                         <=== OUTPUT         00130000
     5 //SYSPRINT  DD   SYSOUT=*                                             00140000
     6 //SYSIN     DD   DUMMY                                                00150000

STMT NO. MESSAGE
     2 IEFC605I UNIDENTIFIED OPERATION FIELD
     3 IEFC019I MISPLACED DD STATEMENT
     4 IEFC019I MISPLACED DD STATEMENT
     5 IEFC019I MISPLACED DD STATEMENT
     6 IEFC019I MISPLACED DD STATEMENT
     6 IEFC607I JOB HAS NO STEPS
```
(b)

Figure 3.9 Misspelling Type-of-Statement Confuses MVS

(a) I misspelled the word EXEC, an "operation" field, at line 001000. (b) The lack of any identifiable EXEC statement make MVS see no work to be done, and it complains that the "job has no steps."

3.11 JOB ABEND (ABnormal ENDing) Reporting

It's possible for you to make a logical mistake—as opposed to a "syntax" error—in your JCL. When you omit a comma where you need it or put a comma where you shouldn't, MVS can catch the error very quickly as you submit the JCL. But when you code something that is correct in format yet logically invalid, MVS can't detect the problem until the job executes.

Several things qualify as logically invalid JCL. Misspelling a data set name that you want to read is a logical mistake, if what you code is legitimate in format. When your job executes, MVS will not be able to find the data set and will complain about this. In the same way, coding the name of a program that doesn't exist on an EXEC is a logical mistake.

MVS complains about your logical errors, serious program errors, and computer system malfunctions by using a mechanism called the **system completion code**, which is a three-position value expressed in hexadecimal. You can expect the code value to contain numerals and the letters A, B, C, D, E, or F. Over 500 different system completion codes exist. I have listed many of them for your convenience in Appendix E, along with explanations of what they mean.

Part of the problem in diagnosing the failure of a job (an ABEND) is simply finding the system completion code in the MVS system output! In Figure 3.10a I have intentionally made a mistake in spelling the name of the IEBGENER program, coding XEBGENER instead. The name has a valid format, but no such program exists! Figure 3.10b shows you how MVS reports the problem when the job executes. The job log, which is at the very top of the MVS system output, contains the word ABEND followed by S806. "S" just means "system." The system completion code in this case is 806. If you look it up in Appendix E, you will see that it means "program module not found."

Look at the last U0000 following the system completion code in Figure 3.10b. It's easy to confuse system completion code with the ordinary program communication called the **user return code** or COND CODE. You'll receive only one of these values at each step. If a step processes without abending, the MVS system output will show a four-digit COND CODE such as 0000 for the step but no system completion code. If you code a JCL logical error in the step or if the program at the step does something improper (such as attempting arithmetic on non-numeric data) you'll get a three-position system completion code such as 0C7 but no COND CODE. A non-zero COND CODE does not necessarily mean that a problem exists, but receiving a system completion code *always* indicates a problem.

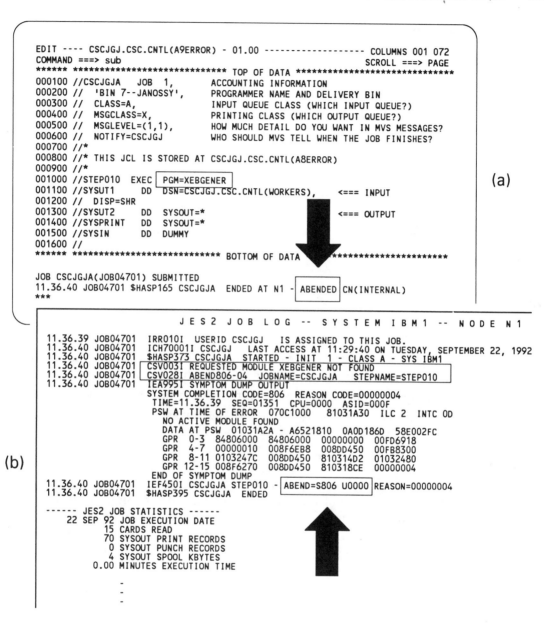

```
EDIT ---- CSCJGJ.CSC.CNTL(A9ERROR) - 01.00 ------------------ COLUMNS 001 072
COMMAND ===> sub                                             SCROLL ===> PAGE
****** ***************************** TOP OF DATA *********************************
000100 //CSCJGJA   JOB  1,        ACCOUNTING INFORMATION
000200 //    'BIN 7--JANOSSY',    PROGRAMMER NAME AND DELIVERY BIN
000300 //    CLASS=A,             INPUT QUEUE CLASS (WHICH INPUT QUEUE?)
000400 //    MSGCLASS=X,          PRINTING CLASS (WHICH OUTPUT QUEUE?)
000500 //    MSGLEVEL=(1,1),      HOW MUCH DETAIL DO YOU WANT IN MVS MESSAGES?
000600 //    NOTIFY=CSCJGJ        WHO SHOULD MVS TELL WHEN THE JOB FINISHES?
000700 //*
000800 //* THIS JCL IS STORED AT CSCJGJ.CSC.CNTL(A8ERROR)
000900 //*
001000 //STEP010  EXEC  PGM=XEBGENER                                        (a)
001100 //SYSUT1    DD  DSN=CSCJGJ.CSC.CNTL(WORKERS),    <=== INPUT
001200 //  DISP=SHR
001300 //SYSUT2    DD  SYSOUT=*                          <=== OUTPUT
001400 //SYSPRINT  DD  SYSOUT=*
001500 //SYSIN     DD  DUMMY
001600 //
****** *************************** BOTTOM OF DATA ****************************

JOB CSCJGJA(JOB04701) SUBMITTED
11.36.40 JOB04701 $HASP165 CSCJGJA  ENDED AT N1 - ABENDED CN(INTERNAL)
***
```

```
                   J E S 2   J O B   L O G  --  S Y S T E M   I B M 1  --  N O D E   N 1

      11.36.39 JOB04701   IRR010I  USERID CSCJGJ   IS ASSIGNED TO THIS JOB.
      11.36.40 JOB04701   ICH70001I CSCJGJ    LAST ACCESS AT 11:29:40 ON TUESDAY, SEPTEMBER 22, 1992
      11.36.40 JOB04701   $HASP373 CSCJGJA   STARTED - INIT  1 - CLASS A - SYS IBM1
      11.36.40 JOB04701   CSV003I REQUESTED MODULE XEBGENER NOT FOUND
      11.36.40 JOB04701   CSV028I ABEND806-04  JOBNAME=CSCJGJA    STEPNAME=STEP010
      11.36.40 JOB04701   IEA995I SYMPTOM DUMP OUTPUT
                          SYSTEM COMPLETION CODE=806  REASON CODE=00000004
                           TIME=11.36.39  SEQ=01351  CPU=0000  ASID=000F
                           PSW AT TIME OF ERROR  070C1000   81031A30  ILC 2  INTC 0D
                            NO ACTIVE MODULE FOUND
                            DATA AT PSW  01031A2A - A6521810  0A0D186D  58E002FC
                            GPR  0-3  84806000  84806000  00000000  00FD6918
                            GPR  4-7  00000010  008F6EB8  008DD450  00FB8300
                            GPR  8-11 0103247C  008DD450  810314D2  01032480
                            GPR 12-15 008F6270  008DD450  810318CE  00000004
                          END OF SYMPTOM DUMP
(b)   11.36.40 JOB04701   IEF450I CSCJGJA STEP010 - ABEND=S806 U0000 REASON=00000004
      11.36.40 JOB04701   $HASP395 CSCJGJA  ENDED

      ------ JES2 JOB STATISTICS ------
        22 SEP 92 JOB EXECUTION DATE
              15 CARDS READ
              70 SYSOUT PRINT RECORDS
               0 SYSOUT PUNCH RECORDS
               4 SYSOUT SPOOL KBYTES
            0.00 MINUTES EXECUTION TIME
                -
                -
                -
```

Figure 3.10   A System Completion Code Indicates an Abend

(a) Abend means "abnormal ending," a job failure, because in this case the EXEC at line 001000 indicates a nonexistent program name. (b) To resolve this type of problem you have to find the system completion code in this MVS output (806 here) and look up its meaning in Appendix E.

Chapter 3 Review

Mini-Glossary

ABEND   ABnormal ENDing, a program failure

System completion code   A three-position hexadecimal value printed in the job log by MVS to indicate the reason why a job had failed (ABnormally ENDed, or ABENDed)

COND CODE   A four-position value in the range 0000 through 4095 that is printed in the MVS system output for each step. The program executed at the step can control what appears as this value.

Parameter   One of the operands for a JCL statement, such as DSN, DISP, UNIT, DCB, SPACE, VOL, and LABEL

Review Questions

1. Explain the three things done to a program when it runs.
2. Figure 3.2 indicates that you need to code four DD statements to run the IEBGENER program. Explain why this is so.
3. Identify and describe the three most common JCL statements.
4. Describe the two "easy" types of DD statement.

Exercises

A. If you have not yet put the WORKERS data in Figure 2.9 into your CNTL library, enter it now. Arrange your JCL to access this data and print it using JCL similar to that in Figure 3.2. Then run the job and compare your system output to Figure 3.2. (Find out what the format of the JOB statement is in your installation and use it for this exercise.)

B. After completing Exercise A, modify your JCL so that you delete the coding for the DDname //SYSIN, which is presently coded with DUMMY. Run the job and see how MVS complains about your failure to provide a connection to this input desired by IEBGENER.

C. After completing Exercise A, misspell the member name of your input data to //SYSUT1. Run the job and use the system completion code and Appendix E to see how MVS reports the problem.

Chapter Four

MULTI-STEP JOB STREAMS

In Chapters 1 through 3 I have explained the structure of JCL to you. You now know that JCL serves these simple purposes:

1. Tells MVS what programs you want to run
2. Tells MVS what files these programs will use
3. Tells MVS what you want done with the files after the programs have used them

You also know that the three main statements of JCL are JOB, EXEC, and DD, and you have seen this pattern:

```
//jobname      JOB ... parameters
//stepname     EXEC ... parameters
//DDname       DD ... parameters
//DDname       DD ... parameters
//DDname       DD ... parameters
//DDname       DD ... parameters
//
```

But all you have seen up to this point is a set of JCL that executes one program using this pattern. In this chapter, I'll show you how we arrange JCL to execute more than one program, in series. It may seem a little silly, but the easiest way to picture how JCL works in this way is to think of a freight train. The JOB statement is the locomotive, each program to be run is a freight car, and the final null statement // is the caboose:

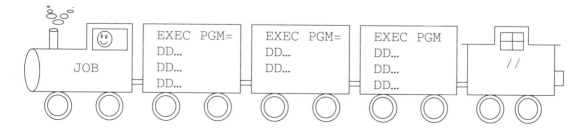

4.1 Flowchart Symbols and JCL

You use JCL to execute one program after another in sequence. Your JCL starts with a JOB statement and contains an EXEC statement for each program. Following each EXEC, you code the appropriate DD statements required by the program that the EXEC executes. At the end of your set of JCL you code a // null statement. JCL is as simple as that:

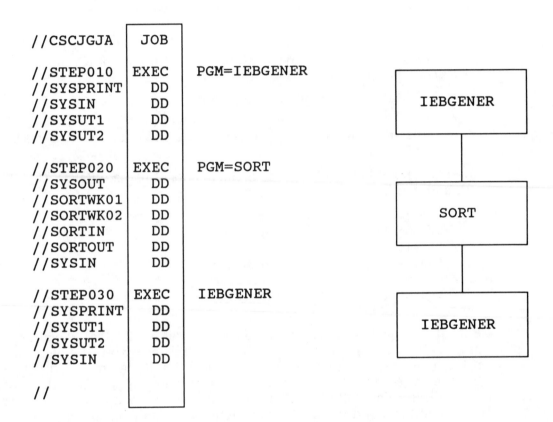

But it helps a lot to be able to graphically picture what a set of JCL will do (or does). Each program will read one or more data sets, produce one or more reports, and/or create one or more data sets. We can add the flow-charting symbols in Figure 4.1 to a simple diagram like the one above to show how data sets are accessed by programs and reports produced by them.

You've already seen how some of these symbols can depict what enters and leaves a program. In Figure 3.1, I pictured the IEBGENER program as

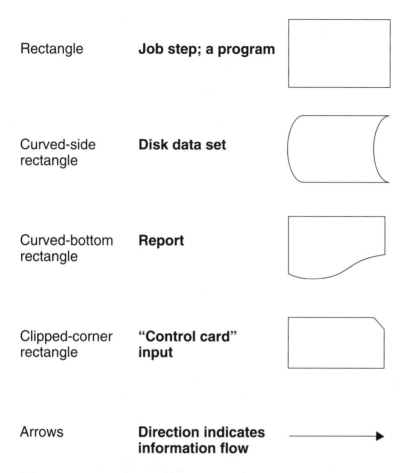

Rectangle	**Job step; a program**	
Curved-side rectangle	**Disk data set**	
Curved-bottom rectangle	**Report**	
Clipped-corner rectangle	**"Control card" input**	
Arrows	**Direction indicates information flow**	

Figure 4.1   JCL Flowcharting Symbols

You may already be familiar with flow charting symbols as a program logic mapping device. You'll notice a difference between JCL and program logic flowcharts: there is no diamond "decision" box here. JCL is not a programming language and therefore does not make decisions. When we use these symbols to map out what a set of JCL does, we list the program boxes vertically to represent simply that the execution of one program is followed by the execution of the next program.

a box with a disk data set entering at its //SYSUT1 and leaving at its //SYSUT2. Control statements entered the program at //SYSIN, and it produced a small status report at //SYSPRINT. Now you'll see how the JCL flowchart diagram of single program pictured in Figure 3.1 becomes just a building block of a larger, three-step job.

4.2 A Three-Step Job Stream

The flowchart in Figure 4.2 maps out a three-step process I would like to orchestrate using JCL. Since this job includes the execution of a series of programs, we usually call it a **job stream.** My intention is to

1. List the WORKERS data I put into a disk file in Chapter 2 (see Figure 2.9)
2. Sort the WORKER records so that they are arranged in ascending order of last name (the 11 bytes starting at position 7 in each record)
3. List the sorted WORKERS data, spreading apart the data fields so that the records are easier to read

The flowchart may seem complicated to you but if so, that's just because there are a lot of symbols and lines on it. Each box represents the execution of a program. There are as many arrows to and from a box (program) as there will be DD statements for the program. I have labeled each arrow with the DDname that needs to be coded in JCL to handle that input or output.

You can see that I have marked a large dashed-line "X" through the inputs or outputs I will "dummy" out. In the first step I will use DUMMY on //SYSIN and //SYSPRINT. In that step I don't care to give the IEBGENER program any special instructions (which it is set to receive at its //SYSIN). Neither do I care about the status report that IEBGENER produces at the DDname //SYSPRINT.

You can also see that I can execute the very same program more than once in a given set of JCL. Here I plan to run IEBGENER as the first step to do a straight copy of the raw WORKERS data. I also execute IEBGENER after the sort program, this time with special instructions to reformat the data it is sending to the printer. Every execution of a program is freestanding; there's no connection between the steps of the job stream just because I am executing the same program at different times.

Finally, notice that the steps of a job stream can share data. Two programs can read the same data set, as IEBGENER and the SORT do, one after another, with the WORKERS data. In addition, one program can output a data set—such as the //SORTOUT data set of the sort program here—and a program executed subsequently (like IEBGENER in step 3 here) can read that data as input.

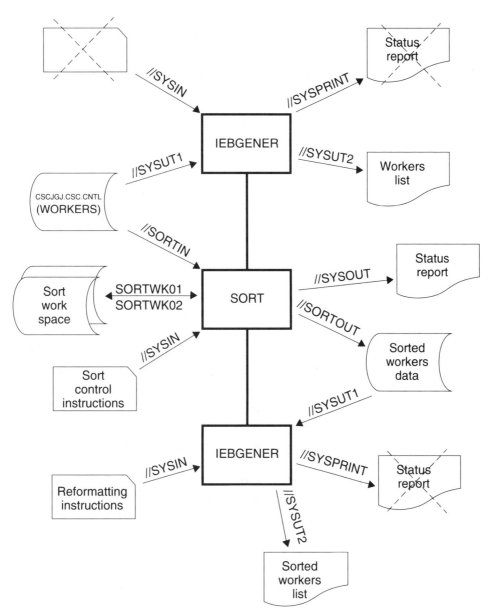

Figure 4.2   A Job Stream Flowchart

This flowchart shows how I plan to run three programs, one after another, in a single job. I'll print the data in CSCJGJ.CSC.CNTL(WORKERS) using the IEBGENER program, then sort the data into last name sequence, then print the sorted data using IEBGENER again. My JCL for this job will have three EXEC statements, one for each processing box.

4.3 Three-Step Job Stream JCL

Coding JCL from a job stream flowchart is really quite simple. You just follow the same pattern of JOB/EXEC/DDs that you would use in a single-step job, coding EXEC/DDs for each program. If you compare the JCL in Figure 4.3 to the job stream flowchart in Figure 4.2, you'll see this pattern.

In the first step IEBGENER's //SYSIN input is "capped off" with DUMMY, because I will not be giving it any special record reformatting instructions. I have also capped off its //SYSPRINT status report, electronically discarding it. IEBGENER will read the WORKERS data at its //SYSUT1 and output it at its //SYSUT2 to the printer.

My second step executes the SORT program to sort the WORKERS data into ascending sequence of last name. You see six DDnames here. Why? SORT program documentation indicates that it requires them:

- //SYSOUT is the DDname through which the sort wants to write a status report. Why isn't this name //SYSPRINT as with IEBGENER? The reason is simply that the software engineer who wrote the sort chose to call it //SYSOUT. DDnames are hardcoded in programs; that's what dictates how you code the JCL!
- //SORTWKnn are "working space" files that the sort needs.
- //SORTIN is where the sort reads the data to be sorted.
- //SORTOUT is where the sort writes the sorted data. Notice that this is one of that most difficult category of DD statement to compose, because a new file is being created.
- //SYSIN is where the sort program reads my instructions indicating the starting position of the field to sort on (the sort key), the length of the sort key, the format of the sort key (CH means character), and the sequence I want (A means ascending, D means descending).

My third step executes IEBGENER again to print the sorted WORKERS data, but you'll notice a difference from the first step. Now I am taking the opportunity to give some special instructions to IEBGENER to tell it to reformat the records it will print. Those instructions enter IEBGENER at its //SYSIN DDname. Notice that lines 005100 through 006200 *do not* start with slashes; *they are not JCL!* I'll explain more about those statements later in this chapter.

Study Figures 4.4 and 4.5 on the following pages. Figure 4.4 shows you the output of this JCL, and Figure 4.5 illustrates a problem revealed by COND CODE communication.

```
EDIT ---- CSCJGJ.CSC.CNTL(B1SORT) - 01.00 ------------------- COLUMNS 001 072
COMMAND ===>                                                SCROLL ===> PAGE
****** *************************** TOP OF DATA ***************************
000100 //CSCJGJA   JOB 1,'BIN 7 JANOSSY',CLASS=A,MSGCLASS=X,MSGLEVEL=(1,1),
000200 //  NOTIFY=CSCJGJ
000300 //*
000400 //*    THIS JCL IS STORED AT CSCJGJ.CSC.CNTL(B1SORT)
000500 //*
000600 //*    THIS IS A DEMONSTRATION JOB STREAM THAT SHOWS YOU HOW JCL IS
000700 //*    ARRANGED TO EXECUTE SEVERAL PROGRAMS IN SEQUENCE.
000800 //*
000900 //*******************************************************************
001000 //*                                                                 *
001100 //*    LIST THE WORKER DATA WITHOUT FORMATTING IT FOR PRINT         *
001200 //*                                                                 *
001300 //*******************************************************************
001400 //STEP010   EXEC  PGM=IEBGENER
001500 //SYSPRINT   DD   DUMMY
001600 //SYSIN      DD   DUMMY
001700 //SYSUT1     DD   DSN=CSCJGJ.CSC.CNTL(WORKERS),      <=== INPUT
001800 //  DISP=SHR
001900 //SYSUT2     DD   SYSOUT=*                           <=== OUTPUT
002000 //*******************************************************************
002100 //*                                                                 *
002200 //*    SORT WORKER DATA BY LAST NAME                                *
002300 //*                                                                 *
002400 //*******************************************************************
002500 //STEP020   EXEC  PGM=SORT
002600 //SYSOUT     DD   SYSOUT=*
002700 //SORTWK01   DD   UNIT=SYSDA,SPACE=(CYL,1)
002800 //SORTWK02   DD   UNIT=SYSDA,SPACE=(CYL,1)
002900 //SORTIN     DD   DSN=CSCJGJ.CSC.CNTL(WORKERS),      <=== INPUT
003000 //  DISP=SHR
003100 //SORTOUT    DD   DSN=&&WORKERS,                     <=== OUTPUT
003200 //  DISP=(NEW,PASS,DELETE),
003300 //  UNIT=SYSDA,
003400 //  DCB=(RECFM=FB,LRECL=80,BLKSIZE=3840),
003500 //  SPACE=(TRK,1)
003600 //SYSIN      DD   *                                  SORTING
003700      SORT FIELDS=(7,11,CH,A)                         <=== INSTRUCTIONS
003800 //*******************************************************************
003900 //*                                                                 *
004000 //*    LIST SORTED WORKER DATA                                      *
004100 //*    FIELDS ARE SPACED FOR EASIER READING USING INSTRUCTIONS      *
004200 //*    TO THE "IEBGENER" PROGRAM AT ITS //SYSIN DD STATEMENT        *
004300 //*                                                                 *
004400 //*******************************************************************
004500 //STEP030   EXEC  PGM=IEBGENER
004600 //SYSPRINT   DD   DUMMY
004700 //SYSUT1     DD   DSN=&&WORKERS,
004800 //  DISP=(OLD,DELETE)
004900 //SYSUT2     DD   SYSOUT=*
005000 //SYSIN      DD   *
005100    GENERATE  MAXFLDS=99,MAXLITS=80
005200      RECORD  FIELD=(5,1,,1),
005300              FIELD=(2,' ',,6),
005400              FIELD=(11,7,,8),
005500              FIELD=(2,' ',,17),
005600              FIELD=(10,18,,21),
005700              FIELD=(2,' ',,31),
005800              FIELD=(2,28,,33),
005900              FIELD=(1,'.',,35),
006000              FIELD=(1,30,,36),
006100              FIELD=(2,' ',,37),
006200              FIELD=(20,31,,39)
006300 //
```

These lines are not JCL but are "data" read by the IEBGENER program. These are usually called "control statements" and do not start with //.

Figure 4.3 JCL for a Three-Step Job Stream

This JCL contains 1 JOB statement, 3 EXEC statements, and 14 DD statements. Since I've indented my coding consistently, you can clearly see the pattern of JOB/ EXEC/DDs . . . EXEC/DDs constant throughout all JCL.

```
                    J E S 2   J O B   L O G   --   S Y S T E M   I B M 1   --   N O D E   N 1

10.16.47 JOB06308  IRR0101  USERID CSCJGJ    IS ASSIGNED TO THIS JOB.
10.16.48 JOB06308  ICH70001I CSCJGJ  LAST ACCESS AT 10:08:47 ON THURSDAY, SEPTEMBER 24, 1992
10.16.48 JOB06308  $HASP373 CSCJGJA  STARTED - INIT 1 - CLASS A - SYS IBM1
10.16.51 JOB06308  $HASP395 CSCJGJA  ENDED

------ JES2 JOB STATISTICS ------
   24 SEP 92 JOB EXECUTION DATE
          62 CARDS READ
         162 SYSOUT PRINT RECORDS
           0 SYSOUT PUNCH RECORDS
          11 SYSOUT SPOOL KBYTES
        0.05 MINUTES EXECUTION TIME

 1 //CSCJGJA   JOB 1,'BIN 7 JANOSSY',CLASS=A,MSGCLASS=X,MSGLEVEL=(1,1),             JOB06308
   //          NOTIFY=CSCJGJ                                                        00020000
   //*                                                                              00030000
   //*      THIS JCL IS STORED AT CSCJGJ.CSC.CNTL(B1SORT)                           00040000
   //*                                                                              00050000
   //*      THIS IS A DEMONSTRATION JOB STREAM THAT SHOWS YOU HOW JCL IS            00060000
   //*      ARRANGED TO EXECUTE SEVERAL PROGRAMS IN SEQUENCE.                       00070000
   //*                                                                              00080000
   //****************************************************************************   00090000
   //*                                                                          *   00100000
   //*      LIST THE WORKER DATA WITHOUT FORMATTING IT FOR PRINT                *   00110000
   //*                                                                          *   00120000
   //****************************************************************************   00130000
 2 //STEP010  EXEC PGM=IEBGENER                                                     00140000
 3 //SYSPRINT DD   DUMMY                                                            00150000
 4 //SYSIN    DD   DUMMY                                                            00160000
 5 //SYSUT1   DD   DSN=CSCJGJ.CSC.CNTL(WORKERS),        <=== INPUT                  00170000
   //         DISP=SHR                                                              00180000
 6 //SYSUT2   DD   SYSOUT=*                             <=== OUTPUT                 00190000
   //*                                                                              00200000
   //****************************************************************************   00210000
   //*                                                                          *   00220000
   //*      SORT WORKER DATA BY LAST NAME                                       *   00230000
   //*                                                                          *   00240000
   //****************************************************************************   00250000
 7 //STEP020  EXEC PGM=SORT                                                         00260000
 8 //SYSOUT   DD   SYSOUT=*                                                         00270000
 9 //SORTWK01 DD   UNIT=SYSDA,SPACE=(CYL,1)                                         00280000
10 //SORTWK02 DD   UNIT=SYSDA,SPACE=(CYL,1)                                         00290000
11 //SORTIN   DD   DSN=CSCJGJ.CSC.CNTL(WORKERS),        <=== INPUT                  00300000
   //         DISP=SHR                                                              00310000
12 //SORTOUT  DD   DSN=&&WORKERS,                       <=== OUTPUT                 00320000
   //         UNIT=SYSDA,                                                           00330000
   //         DISP=(NEW,PASS,DELETE),                                               00340000
   //         DCB=(RECFM=FB,LRECL=80,BLKSIZE=3840),                                 00350000
   //         SPACE=(TRK,1)                                                         00360000
13 //SYSIN    DD   *                                          SORTING               00370000
   //*                                                                          *   00380000
   //*      LIST SORTED WORKER DATA                                            *   00390000
   //*      FIELDS ARE SPACED FOR EASIER READING USING INSTRUCTIONS            *   00400000
   //*      TO THE "IEBGENER" PROGRAM AT ITS //SYSIN DD STATEMENT              *   00410000
   //****************************************************************************   00420000
   //                                                                              00430000
   //                                                                              00440000
```

MVS applies its own numbers to JCL statements. It refers to errors using these numbers. Notice that a single JCL statement can span many lines (card images).

62

```
                                                                                    00450000
                                                                                    00460000
                                                                                    00470000
                                                                                    00480000
                                                                                    00490000
                                                                                    00500000

14 //STEP030  EXEC  PGM=IEBGENER
15 //SYSPRINT DD    DUMMY
16 //SYSUT1   DD    DSN=&&WORKERS,
   //         DISP=(OLD,DELETE)
17 //SYSUT2   DD    SYSOUT=*
18 //SYSIN    DD    *

ICH70001I CSCJGJ   LAST ACCESS AT 10:08:47 ON THURSDAY, SEPTEMBER 24, 1992

IEF236I ALLOC. FOR CSCJGJ STEP010
IEF237I DMY ALLOCATED TO SYSPRINT
IEF237I 111 ALLOCATED TO SYSIN
IEF237I 111 ALLOCATED TO SYSUT1
IEF142I JES2 ALLOCATED TO SYSUT2
IEF142I CSCJGJA STEP010 - STEP WAS EXECUTED - COND CODE 0000
IEF285I CSCJGJ.CSC.CNTL
IEF285I VOL SER NOS= USER00.
IEF285I CSCJGJ.CSCJGJA.JOB06308.D0000103.?                     SYSOUT
IEF373I STEP /STEP010 / START 92268.1016
IEF374I STEP /STEP010 / STOP 92268.1016 CPU   0MIN 00.12SEC SRB   0MIN 00.00SEC

IEF236I ALLOC. FOR CSCJGJ STEP020
IEF237I JES2 ALLOCATED TO SYSOUT
IEF237I 117 ALLOCATED TO SORTWK01
IEF237I 115 ALLOCATED TO SORTWK02
IEF237I 116 ALLOCATED TO SORTIN
IEF237I 116 ALLOCATED TO SORTOUT
IEF142I JES2 ALLOCATED TO SYSIN
IEF142I CSCJGJA STEP020 - STEP WAS EXECUTED - COND CODE 0000
IEF285I CSCJGJ.CSCJGJA.JOB06308.D0000104.?                     DELETED
IEF285I SYS92268.T101648.RA000.CSCJGJA.R0009559               DELETED
IEF285I VOL SER NOS= USER03.
IEF285I SYS92268.T101648.RA000.CSCJGJA.R0009560               DELETED
IEF285I VOL SER NOS= USER01.
IEF285I CSCJGJ.CSC.CNTL                                        KEPT
IEF285I VOL SER NOS= USER00.                                   PASSED
IEF285I SYS92268.T101648.RA000.CSCJGJA.WORKERS
IEF285I VOL SER NOS= USER02.                                   SYSIN
IEF373I STEP /STEP020 / START 92268.1016
IEF374I STEP /STEP020 / STOP 92268.1016 CPU   0MIN 00.39SEC SRB   0MIN 00.01SEC

IEF236I ALLOC. FOR CSCJGJ STEP030
IEF237I DMY ALLOCATED TO SYSPRINT
IEF237I 116 ALLOCATED TO SYSIN
IEF237I JES2 ALLOCATED TO SYSUT2
IEF142I JES2 ALLOCATED TO SYSIN
IEF142I CSCJGJA STEP030 - STEP WAS EXECUTED - COND CODE 0000
IEF285I SYS92268.T101648.RA000.CSCJGJA.WORKERS
IEF285I VOL SER NOS= USER02.
IEF285I CSCJGJ.CSCJGJA.JOB06308.D0000105.?                     SYSOUT
IEF285I CSCJGJ.CSCJGJA.JOB06308.D0000102.?                     SYSIN
IEF373I STEP /STEP030 / START 92268.1016
IEF374I STEP /STEP030 / STOP 92268.1016 CPU   0MIN 00.13SEC SRB   0MIN 00.00SEC
IEF375I JOB /CSCJGJA / START 92268.1016
IEF376I JOB /CSCJGJA / STOP 92268.1016 CPU   0MIN 00.64SEC SRB   0MIN 00.01SEC
```

In reporting what was done in each of your job steps, MVS tells you what devices or facilities were "allocated" to each of your DD statements. The message labeled IEF236I begins MVS reporting for a step and the START/STOP lines end it. This reporting also tells you the name of every data set accessed in the step and the disk or tape VOL SER number where it is stored.

You get a COND CODE for each step (program) executed. The 0000 values you see in this run indicate that each program ran completely successfully.

Figure 4.4 Output from My Three-Step Job Stream

(continued)

```
21256 NILLY    WILLY      402CASHIERS OFFICE
21257 IPPI     MRS.       378PHOTO DEPARTMENT
21260 MALLOW   MARSHA     390KITCHEN APPLIANCES
21307 WARE     DELLA      246FURNITURE
21310 SHAW     ARKAN      300HARDWARE
21574 AH       GEORGE     400PHOTO DEPARTMENT
21668 ZOORI    MOE        179PLUMBING SUPPLIES
25112 CABOOSE  LUCE       305FURNITURE
25189 HOW      IDA        005SUITCASES AND BAGS
33102 IFORNIA  CAL        200TRAVEL DEPARTMENT
33261 CANNON   LUCE       316TOYS
33377 WHIZ     G.         357PERSONAL COMPUTERS
33480 TOUR     D.         160WOMENS CLOTHING
33483 INA      CAROL      530REMODELING SUPPLIES
39321 ABAMA    AL         420WOMENS CLOTHING
39322 TUCKY    KEN        350HARDWARE
```

This is the //SYSUT2 output of the first IEBGENER. It is a copy of the WORKERS data directed to the printer. The data is listed in the order in which it exists (it has not been sorted yet).

```
ICE143I 0 BLOCKSET    SORT  TECHNIQUE SELECTED

ICE000I 1 --- CONTROL STATEMENTS/MESSAGES ---- 5740-SM1 REL 11.1 ---- 10.16.49 SEP 24, 1992 --

                                  <=== INSTRUCTIONS  00370000

          SORT FIELDS=(7,11,CH,A)

ICE088I 1 CSCJGJA .STEP020 ,  INPUT LRECL = 80, BLKSIZE = 3840, TYPE = F
ICE093I 0 MAIN STORAGE = (MAX,4194304,4194304),NMAX = 13900
ICE156I 0 MAIN STORAGE ABOVE 16MB = (4141816,4141816)
ICE128I 0 OPTIONS: SIZE=4194304,MAXLIM=1048576,MINLIM=450560,EQUALS=N,LIST=Y,ERET=RC16,MSGDDN=SYSOUT
ICE129I 0 OPTIONS: VIO=N,RESDNT=ALL ,SMF=NO ,WRKSEC=Y,OUTSEC=Y,VERIFY=N,CHALT=N,DYNALOC=N ,ABCODE=MSG
ICE130I 0 OPTIONS: RESALL=4096,RESINV=0,SVC=109 ,CHECK=Y,WRKREL=Y,OUTREL=Y,CKPT=N,STIMER=Y,COBEXIT=COB1
ICE131I 0 OPTIONS: TMAXLIM=4194304,ARESALL=0,ARESINV=0,OVERRGN=65536,EXCPVR=NONE ,CINV=Y,CFW=Y
ICE132I 0 OPTIONS: VLSHRT=N,ZDPRINT=N,IEXIT=N,TEXIT=N,LISTX=N,EFS=NONE  ,EXITCK=S,PARMDDN=DFSPARM ,FSZEST=N
ICE133I 0 OPTIONS: HIPRMAX=OPTIMAL
ICE084I 0 EXCP ACCESS METHOD USED FOR SORTOUT
ICE084I 0 EXCP ACCESS METHOD USED FOR SORTIN
ICE090I 0 OUTPUT LRECL = 80, BLKSIZE = 3840, TYPE = F
ICE080I 0 IN MAIN STORAGE SORT
ICE055I 0 INSERT 0, DELETE 0
ICE054I 0 RECORDS - IN: 16, OUT: 16
ICE134I 0 NUMBER OF BYTES SORTED: 1280
ICE165I 0 TOTAL WORK DATA SET TRACKS ALLOCATED: 30 , TRACKS
ICE180I 0 HIPERSPACE STORAGE USED = 0K BYTES
ICE052I 0 END OF DFSORT
```

These are messages from the sort utility, output at its //SYSOUT DD statement. In addition to echoing the sort control statement (which I have documented as "instructions" in the JCL) these messages tell you how the sort chose to do its work, the resources it used, and how many records it read IN and wrote OUT. IEBGENER would produce status messages too, if I had not coded DUMMY at its //SYSPRINT DD statement in the third step.

Sorted

39321	ABAMA	AL	42.0 WOMENS CLOTHING
21574	AH	GEORGE	40.0 PHOTO DEPARTMENT
25112	CABOOSE	LUCE	30.5 FURNITURE
33261	CANNON	LUCE	31.6 TOYS
25189	HOW	IDA	00.5 SUITCASES AND BAGS
33102	IFORNIA	CAL	20.0 TRAVEL DEPARTMENT
33483	INA	CAROL	53.0 REMODELING SUPPLIES
21257	IPPI	MRS.	37.8 PHOTO DEPARTMENT
21260	MALLOW	MARSHA	39.0 KITCHEN APPLIANCES
21256	NILLY	WILLY	40.2 CASHIERS OFFICE
21310	SHAW	ARKAN	30.0 HARDWARE
33480	TOUR	D.	16.0 WOMENS CLOTHING
39322	TUCKY	KEN	35.0 HARDWARE
21307	WARE	DELLA	24.6 FURNITURE
33377	WHIZ	G.	35.7 PERSONAL COMPUTERS
21668	ZOORI	MOE	17.9 PLUMBING SUPPLIES

Formatted

This is the output from the second execution of IEBGENER. It has read the sorted data at its //SYSUT1 DD statement and output it according to my control statement formatting instructions at its //SYSUT2 DD statement. I have sent the records emerging at //SYSUT2 to the printer, and you see them here. If I had not coded DUMMY at the //SYSPRINT DD statement of the third step, IEBGENER would have echoed back my formatting control statements here. Generally speaking, you should not dummy out utility program status reporting as I did in this example, because a utility program gives you error messages about control statements in its status report!

Look at the IEBGENER formatting control statements in Figure 4.3. Notice that in this listing I have formatted the records differently than they originally exist. I have spread the fields apart and I have inserted a period to serve as a decimal point in the "hours worked this week" field. *I give you a one-page quick reference showing you how to code formatting control statements in Figure 4.8.*

Figure 4.4 *(Continued)*

```
EDIT ---- CSCJGJ.CSC.CNTL(B2COND) - 01.01 ------------------- COLUMNS 001 072
COMMAND ===>                                            SCROLL ===> PAGE
002500 //STEP020   EXEC  PGM=SORT
002600 //*YSOUT     DD    SYSOUT=*
       //SORTWK01   DD    UNIT=SYSDA,SPACE=(CYL,1)
       //SORTWK02   DD    UNIT=SYSDA,SPACE=(CYL,1)
       //SORTIN     DD    DSN=CSCJGJ.CSC.CNTL(WORKERS),      <=== INPUT
 .00L  //  DISP=SHR
 03100 //SORTOUT    DD    DSN=&&WORKERS,                     <=== OUTPUT
003200 //  DISP=(NEW,PASS,DELETE),
003300 //  UNIT=SYSDA,
003400 //  DCB=(RECFM=FB,LRECL=80,BLKSIZE=3840),
003500 //  SPACE=(TRK,1)
003600 //SYSIN      DD    *                                 SORTING
003700      SORT FIELDS=(7,11,CH,A)                         <=== INSTRUCTIONS
```

```
            J E S 2   J O B   L O G  --  S Y S T E M   I B M 1  --  N O D E   N 1

14.27.11 JOB06499  IRR010I  USERID CSCJGJ   IS ASSIGNED TO THIS JOB.
14.27.12 JOB06499  ICH70001I CSCJGJ   LAST ACCESS AT 14:24:22 ON THURSDAY, SEPTEMBER 24, 1992
14.27.12 JOB06499  $HASP373 CSCJGJA  STARTED - INIT  1 - CLASS A - SYS IBM1
14.27.13 JOB06499  +ICE158A 0 CSCJGJA .STEP020  SYSOUT DD STATEMENT MISSING
14.27.14 JOB06499  $HASP395 CSCJGJA  ENDED

------ JES2 JOB STATISTICS ------
    24 SEP 92 JOB EXECUTION DATE
           62 CARDS READ
          136 SYSOUT PRINT RECORDS
            0 SYSOUT PUNCH RECORDS
            9 SYSOUT SPOOL KBYTES
         0.04 MINUTES EXECUTION TIME

IEF236I ALLOC. FOR CSCJGJA STEP010
IEF237I DMY  ALLOCATED TO SYSPRINT
IEF237I DMY  ALLOCATED TO SYSIN
IEF237I 111  ALLOCATED TO SYSUT1
IEF237I JES2 ALLOCATED TO SYSUT2
IEF142I CSCJGJA STEP010 - STEP WAS EXECUTED
IEF285I     CSCJGJ.CSC.CNTL
IEF285I     VOL SER NOS= USER00.
IEF285I     CSCJGJ.CSCJGJA.JOB06499.D0000103.?
IEF373I STEP /STEP010 / START 92268.1427
IEF374I STEP /STEP010 / STOP  92268.1427 CPU

IEF236I ALLOC. FOR CSCJGJA STEP020
IEF237I 115  ALLOCATED TO SORTWK01
IEF237I 116  ALLOCATED TO SORTWK02
IEF237I 111  ALLOCATED TO SORTIN
IEF237I 112  ALLOCATED TO SORTOUT
IEF237I JES2 ALLOCATED TO SYSIN
IEF142I CSCJGJA STEP020 - STEP WAS EXECUTED - COND CODE 0020
```

I commented out //SYSOUT in the second step, a DD statement at which the sort utility writes its status report. The sort utility puts a clear message about this in the MVS job log. It also issues COND CODE 0020 to communicate the problem. Not all utilities issue plain messages like this, but *all* utilities use COND CODE reporting. I included Appendix D in this book to give you a convenient way to look up the meaning of COND CODEs issued by the most commonly used IBM utility programs.

Figure 4.5 COND CODE Error Reporting

I introduced an intentional error in my JCL to show you how COND CODE reporting works.

4.4 Temporary Data Set Names

You can code a temporary data set name using two ampersands and any eight-character name that begins with a letter, such as &&WORKERS. I've done this in //STEP020 at line 003100 to name the data set that will contain the records output by the sort. You create temporary data sets to pass data from one program to another. They give you these advantages:

- A temporary data set is deleted automatically by MVS when your job finishes. (You can eliminate the data set even sooner in the job yourself but if you don't, it's taken care of.)
- MVS keeps information about the passed data set handy. This makes subsequent access to it slightly more efficient.

You can access a temporary data set in any number of subsequent steps. Each subsequent step can open a passed data set *once*.

4.5 Data Set Name Referbacks

MVS accumulates and retains information needed to process each job step as it executes your job stream. You can tell MVS to refer back to an earlier step to pick up and use some of the same information at another step. In Figure 4.6 I show you how to use one of the most common **referbacks**, for data set name.

At line 001700, the //SYSUT1 DDname of IEBGENER accesses a data set to read it. This is CSCJGJ.CSC.CNTL(WORKERS). The same data set is accessed by //SORTIN at line 002900 in the second step. In earlier versions of my three-step job stream, I coded the data set name at both of these "reading" DD statements. But now I've coded a data set name referback at line 002900:

```
//SORTIN     DD  DSN=*.STEP010.SYSUT1,
//  DISP=SHR
```

A DSN referback starts with the asterisk followed by a period. You then code the name of a prior step, a period, and the DDname of the DD statement to which you want to refer back. When it interprets your JCL, MVS brings the data set name you coded at the earlier DD statement into the place occupied by the DSN referback. I also coded a DSN referback at line 004700 to access the //SORTOUT data set. Your referbacks can refer back many steps, but only within the same set of JCL. You can also refer back for other parameters as I'll show you in later chapters.

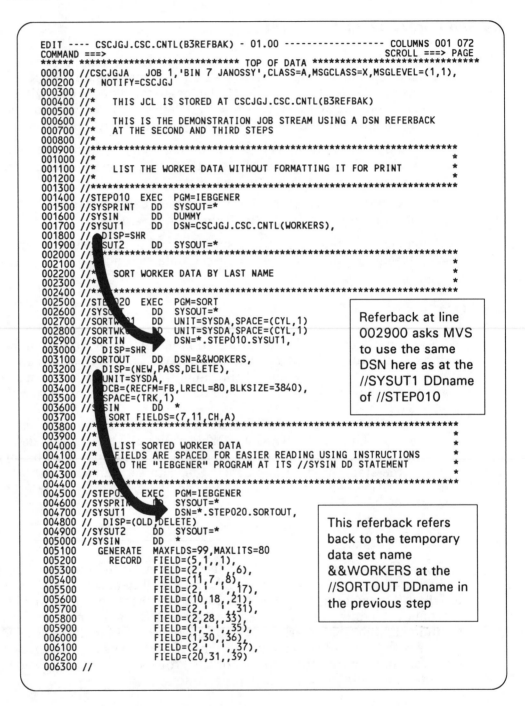

```
EDIT ---- CSCJGJ.CSC.CNTL(B3REFBAK) - 01.00 ----------------- COLUMNS 001 072
COMMAND ===>                                              SCROLL ===> PAGE
****** ************************ TOP OF DATA ***************************
000100 //CSCJGJA   JOB 1,'BIN 7 JANOSSY',CLASS=A,MSGCLASS=X,MSGLEVEL=(1,1),
000200 //   NOTIFY=CSCJGJ
000300 //*
000400 //*    THIS JCL IS STORED AT CSCJGJ.CSC.CNTL(B3REFBAK)
000500 //*
000600 //*    THIS IS THE DEMONSTRATION JOB STREAM USING A DSN REFERBACK
000700 //*    AT THE SECOND AND THIRD STEPS
000800 //*
000900 //****************************************************************
001000 //*                                                             *
001100 //*    LIST THE WORKER DATA WITHOUT FORMATTING IT FOR PRINT      *
001200 //*                                                             *
001300 //****************************************************************
001400 //STEP010   EXEC  PGM=IEBGENER
001500 //SYSPRINT  DD    SYSOUT=*
001600 //SYSIN     DD    DUMMY
001700 //SYSUT1    DD    DSN=CSCJGJ.CSC.CNTL(WORKERS),
001800 //   DISP=SHR
001900 //SUT2      DD    SYSOUT=*
002000 //****************************************************************
002100 //*                                                             *
002200 //*    SORT WORKER DATA BY LAST NAME                            *
002300 //*                                                             *
002400 //****************************************************************
002500 //STEP020   EXEC  PGM=SORT
002600 //SYSOUT    DD    SYSOUT=*
002700 //SORTWK01  DD    UNIT=SYSDA,SPACE=(CYL,1)
002800 //SORTWK02  DD    UNIT=SYSDA,SPACE=(CYL,1)
002900 //SORTIN    DD    DSN=*.STEP010.SYSUT1,
003000 //   DISP=SHR
003100 //SORTOUT   DD    DSN=&&WORKERS,
003200 //   DISP=(NEW,PASS,DELETE),
003300 //   UNIT=SYSDA,
003400 //   DCB=(RECFM=FB,LRECL=80,BLKSIZE=3840),
003500 //   SPACE=(TRK,1)
003600 //SYSIN     DD    *
003700    SORT FIELDS=(7,11,CH,A)
003800 //****************************************************************
003900 //*                                                             *
004000 //*    LIST SORTED WORKER DATA                                  *
004100 //*    FIELDS ARE SPACED FOR EASIER READING USING INSTRUCTIONS  *
004200 //*    TO THE "IEBGENER" PROGRAM AT ITS //SYSIN DD STATEMENT     *
004300 //*                                                             *
004400 //****************************************************************
004500 //STEP030   EXEC  PGM=IEBGENER
004600 //SYSPRINT  DD    SYSOUT=*
004700 //SYSUT1    DD    DSN=*.STEP020.SORTOUT,
004800 //   DISP=(OLD,DELETE)
004900 //SYSUT2    DD    SYSOUT=*
005000 //SYSIN     DD    *
005100    GENERATE  MAXFLDS=99,MAXLITS=80
005200       RECORD  FIELD=(5,1,,1),
005300               FIELD=(2,' ',,6),
005400               FIELD=(11,7,,8),
005500               FIELD=(2,' ',,17),
005600               FIELD=(10,18,,21),
005700               FIELD=(2,' ',,31),
005800               FIELD=(2,28,,33),
005900               FIELD=(1,' ',,35),
006000               FIELD=(1,30,,36),
006100               FIELD=(2,' ',,37),
006200               FIELD=(20,31,,39)
006300 //
```

> Referback at line 002900 asks MVS to use the same DSN here as at the //SYSUT1 DDname of //STEP010

> This referback refers back to the temporary data set name &&WORKERS at the //SORTOUT DDname in the previous step

Figure 4.6 Temporary Data Set Names and DSN Referbacks

Input at //SORTIN:

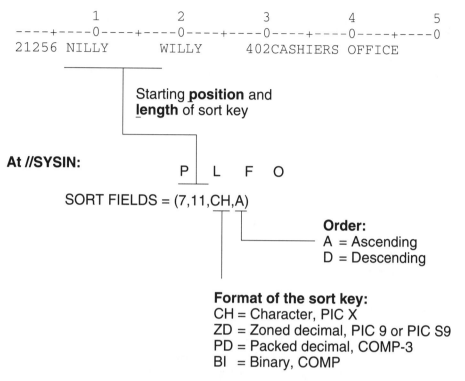

```
            1          2          3          4          5
----+----0----+----0----+----0----+----0----+----0
21256 NILLY    WILLY      402CASHIERS OFFICE
```

Starting **position** and
length of sort key

At //SYSIN:

P   L   F   O

SORT FIELDS = (7,11,CH,A)

Order:
A = Ascending
D = Descending

Format of the sort key:
CH = Character, PIC X
ZD = Zoned decimal, PIC 9 or PIC S9
PD = Packed decimal, COMP-3
BI = Binary, COMP

You can use a secondary sort key to control the sort sequence when two or more records have the same primary sort key. Just repeat the pattern of **position, length, format,** and **order.** For example, to sort the WORKERS data ascending by department and within this by last name, you would code:

Primary sort key (department)

P   L   F O

SORT FIELDS = (31,20,CH,A,7,11,CH,A)

P   L   F O

Secondary sort key (employee last name)

Figure 4.7   SORT Control Statement Quick Reference
From ***Practical MVS JCL Examples*** © 1993 James G. Janossy (John Wiley & Sons, Inc., 1993)

4.6 SORT and IEBGENER Quick References

I've used the sort and IEBGENER utility programs in this chapter to show you a multi-step job stream. You can begin experimenting with these programs in your own JCL. To help you code the control statements for them I've included quick references for each, as Figures 4.7 and 4.8.

Input at //SYSUT1:

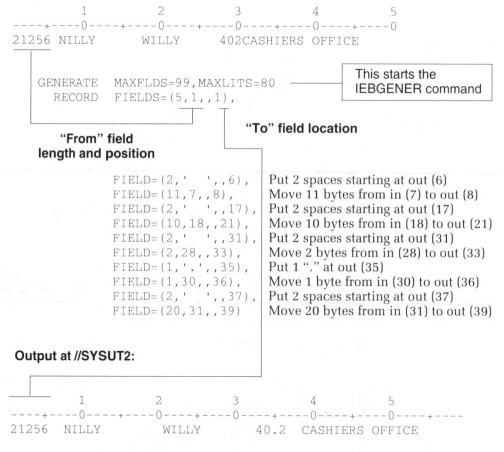

```
           1         2         3         4         5
----+----0----+----0----+----0----+----0----+----0
21256 NILLY     WILLY      402CASHIERS OFFICE
```

```
GENERATE   MAXFLDS=99,MAXLITS=80
RECORD     FIELDS=(5,1,,1),
```

This starts the IEBGENER command

**"From" field
length and position**

"To" field location

FIELD=(2,' ',,6),	Put 2 spaces starting at out (6)
FIELD=(11,7,,8),	Move 11 bytes from in (7) to out (8)
FIELD=(2,' ',,17),	Put 2 spaces starting at out (17)
FIELD=(10,18,,21),	Move 10 bytes from in (18) to out (21)
FIELD=(2,' ',,31),	Put 2 spaces starting at out (31)
FIELD=(2,28,,33),	Move 2 bytes from in (28) to out (33)
FIELD=(1,'.',,35),	Put 1 "." at out (35)
FIELD=(1,30,,36),	Move 1 byte from in (30) to out (36)
FIELD=(2,' ',,37),	Put 2 spaces starting at out (37)
FIELD=(20,31,,39)	Move 20 bytes from in (31) to out (39)

Output at //SYSUT2:

```
           1         2         3         4         5
----+----0----+----0----+----0----+----0----+----
21256  NILLY      WILLY       40.2  CASHIERS OFFICE
```

Figure 4.8 IEBGENER Quick Reference
From *Practical MVS JCL Examples* © 1993 James G. Janossy (John Wiley & Sons, Inc., 1993)

This illustration shows you enough about the control statement format for the simple IEBGENER utility to enable you to use it easily. If you use DUMMY at its //SYSIN input, it will copy a data set from //SYSUT1 to //SYSUT2 unchanged. But if you feed IEBGENER correctly formed instructions such as these, it will reformat the input according to your specifications as a part of the copying process.

Chapter 4 Review

Mini-Glossary

JCL flowchart   A diagram that uses flowchart symbols for programs and data sets, used to plan and document JCL

Multi-step job stream   A set of JCL having more than one EXEC

Sort utility   A program already available on the computer system that you can use to create new data sets containing records rearranged in a desired sequence

Control statements   80-byte records that you code with instructions to a utility program

Temporary data set   A data set named with ampersands (&&) followed by up to eight characters; it's automatically deleted by MVS when your job ends.

Review Questions

1. Explain how a job stream is like a freight train.
2. Why don't IEBGENER control statements start with slashes?
3. Explain the uses of a temporary data set.
4. Explain how and why a data set name referback can be useful.

Exercises

A. Look at the WORKERS data pictured in Figure 2.9. Map out a job stream flowchart for a two-step job stream that sorts this data in *descending* sequence of employee id number and lists it with IEBGENER.

B. Use Figure 4.3 as a guide to arrange JCL for a two-step job stream. The first step should sort the WORKERS records into descending (high to low) sequence of the employee id number field (positions 1 through 5). Put the sorted records into a temporary data set named &&HOWDY. The second step should execute the IEBGENER program to reformat and list four fields of your sorted WORKERS data as shown below. (The first two lines here are a column ruler to show you what columns to put fields into; don't try to print the column ruler!):

```
              1         2         3         4         5         6
----+----0----+----0----+----0----+----0----+----0----+----0
WILLY         NILLY         CASHIERS OFFICE         21256
```

Chapter Five

COMPLETING YOUR OVERVIEW: COMPILING WITH A PROC

In Chapters 1 through 4 I have explained to you a lot about the IBM main-frame environment. You can see how the MVS operating system is the supervisor of the mainframe and how TSO/ISPF is your tool to create programs and JCL. You have already seen (and hopefully completed) several exercises in which you submitted JCL to execute programs such as IEBGE-NER and the SORT utility. And you have seen how you can use TSO/ISPF to view the output of your jobs.

The programs we have executed thus far have been supplied by IBM along with MVS itself. IEBGENER, for example, was written in Assembler language by an IBM employee in 1964 and was processed into machine language. When we execute it, we don't have to process it into machine language again and again; its load module is already present on the system.

What I haven't shown you yet is how you, yourself, can compose a program in a language such as COBOL, PL/I, FORTRAN, C, Pascal, or Assembler, process it into machine language, and then execute it—all on your own. In Chapter 5 I'll complete your overview of the mainframe environment by showing you how to compile, linkage edit, and execute a program that you originate yourself. I'll demonstrate this with a very simple COBOL program and show you how the process works, using JCL packaged in procs. A similar process is used for any programming language.

Procs are an advanced subject, but they simplifiy the use of JCL. In this chapter, I'll give you the "big picture" of what procs are and how you use them. Once you understand procs, you can easily use them even though you will not yet know how to create them. In Chapter 18 I'll show you how to originate procs too, after you have become familiar with the subtleties and capabilities of JCL.

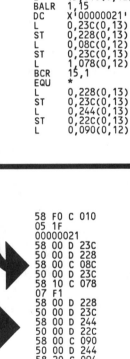

```
0000-MAINLINE.
    PERFORM 1000-BEGIN-JOB.
    PERFORM 2000-PROCESS-A-RECORD
      UNTIL WS-FLAG = 'E'.
    PERFORM 3000-END-JOB.
    STOP RUN.
```

COBOL and **C** are third generation languages. Each instruction such as PERFORM causes *several* machine language instructions to be generated.

```
START    EQU    *
L        15,010(0,12)
BALR     1,15
DC       X'00000021'
L        0,23C(0,13)
ST       0,228(0,13)
L        0,08C(0,12)
ST       0,23C(0,13)
L        1,078(0,12)
BCR      15,1
EQU      *
L        0,228(0,13)
ST       0,23C(0,13)
L        0,244(0,13)
ST       0,22C(0,13)
L        0,090(0,12)
```

Assembler is a second generation language. Each instruction stands for *one* machine language instruction. The assembler that processes this code takes care of memory addresses and eases the burden of the programmer.

```
58 F0 C 010
05 1F
00000021
58 00 D 23C
50 00 D 228
58 00 C 08C
50 00 D 23C
58 10 C 078
07 F1
58 00 D 228
50 00 D 23C
58 00 D 244
50 00 D 22C
58 00 C 090
50 00 D 244
58 20 C 094
```

Machine language is the language of the logic circuits making up the computer. This is the only language the computer actually understands. You see here a part of a **load module** expressed in hexadecimal, a handy abbreviation for binary on/off values. Machine language is really stored as binary values (0's and 1's).

Figure 5.1   Hierarchy of Programming Languages

Machine language is expressd in electronic on-off signals, (binary 0s and 1s) abbreviated in hexadecimal. It's the only language that computers actually understand. You use software to turn Assembler or higher-level languages like COBOL into machine language. Assembling or compiling programs is so common that we provide especially easy ways to do it using JCL.

5.1 Evolution of Programming Languages

The magic of computers comes about because engineers and scientists figured out how to make programmable switches and "gates." What's a programmable switch? It's an electronic device that can send a signal based on an instruction expressed as a signal. A gate is a logic circuit that can combine a set of signals into a new signal. In the early days of computing, the switches and gates that make up computer logic circuitry were built with vacuum tubes. Modern computers use transistors instead, packaged in very dense arrangements on silicon chips.

Instructions to computer circuitry are series of binary 0s and 1s—on and off electronic charges. The circuitry does not understand COBOL, PL/I, FORTRAN, C, Assembler, or any other "higher-level" programming language. The actual instructions of the circuitry are called *machine language.*

You could compose programs in machine language but you would find this extremely tedious and error prone. Machine language is at the bottom of the hierarchy of programming language, as you can see in Figure 5.1. Expressed in the hexadecimal abbreviation of binary values, machine language looks like a collection of numbers and letters. Besides its other drawbacks for programming, machine language is very dependent on the circuitry of each specific model of computer. You can't take machine language from one type of computer and run it on a different computer.

Instead of trying to program directly in machine language, tools have been developed to transform easier-to-code instructions into machine language for us. The first higher-level language was Assembler. I've shown it in Figure 5.1 on the level above machine language. Assembler looks cryptic, and it takes a long time to learn to code it well. But it's faster to write and a little more portable than machine language. Assembler is "assembled" into machine language by a software product called (very appropriately) an *assembler*.

COBOL, PL/I, FORTRAN, Pascal, and C are a level above Assembler in the hierarchy of programming languages. To use one of these third generation languages, you need to understand its *syntax* (grammar). To generate machine language from it, you send it through a software product called a *compiler*.

In Figure 5.1 I show you the Assembler and machine language equivalents of the COBOL code fragment you see at the top of the page. If you write programs in anything except machine language, you will need to process your programs into machine language to run them. That process is so common that we arrange easy ways for people to do it. I'll show you how it's done for COBOL programs. You'll use almost identical steps to process programs you write in any language.

```
EDIT --- CSCJGJ.CSC.COBOL(COPYIT) - 01.01 ----------------- COLUMNS 007 078
COMMAND ===>                                                SCROLL ===> PAGE
****** *************************** TOP OF DATA *****************************
000100  IDENTIFICATION DIVISION.
000200  PROGRAM-ID.     COPYIT.                    ┌─────────────────┐
000300  AUTHOR.         J JANOSSY.                 │ Documentation   │
000400 *                                           └─────────────────┘
000500 *REMARKS.        SIMPLE PROGRAM TO READ AND PRINT 80 BYTE RECORDS.
000600 *
────────────────────────────────────────────────────────────────────────
000700  ENVIRONMENT DIVISION.
000800  INPUT-OUTPUT SECTION.                      ┌─────────────────┐
000900  FILE-CONTROL.                              │ Interface to JCL│
001000      SELECT INPUT-FILE   ASSIGN TO ┌COPYIN.  │ DDnames        │
001100      SELECT OUTPUT-FILE  ASSIGN TO └COPYOUT. └─────────────────┘
001200 *
────────────────────────────────────────────────────────────────────────
001300  DATA DIVISION.
001400  FILE SECTION.
001500  FD  INPUT-FILE
001600      LABEL RECORDS ARE STANDARD
001700      RECORD CONTAINS 80 CHARACTERS
001800      BLOCK CONTAINS 0 RECORDS.
001900  01  INPUT-RECORD                PIC X(80).
002000 *
002100  FD  OUTPUT-FILE                            ┌─────────────────┐
002200      LABEL RECORDS ARE OMITTED              │ Memory field    │
002300      RECORD CONTAINS 80 CHARACTERS          │ declarations    │
002400      BLOCK CONTAINS 0 RECORDS.              └─────────────────┘
002500  01  OUTPUT-RECORD               PIC X(80).
002600 /
002700  WORKING-STORAGE SECTION.
002800  01  WS-FLAG                     PIC X(1)  VALUE 'M'.
002900  01  WS-COUNT                    PIC 9(5)  VALUE 0.
003000  01  WS-COUNT-Z                  PIC ZZ,ZZ9.
003100 /
────────────────────────────────────────────────────────────────────────
003200  PROCEDURE DIVISION.
003300  0000-MAINLINE.
003400      PERFORM 1000-BEGIN-JOB.
003500      PERFORM 2000-PROCESS-A-RECORD UNTIL WS-FLAG = 'E'.
003600      PERFORM 3000-END-JOB.
003700      STOP RUN.
003800 *
003900  1000-BEGIN-JOB.
004000      OPEN  INPUT  INPUT-FILE   OUTPUT  OUTPUT-FILE.
004100      MOVE '*** START OF COPYIT LISTING' TO OUTPUT-RECORD.
004200      WRITE OUTPUT-RECORD.
004300      PERFORM 2700-READ-A-RECORD.
004400 *
004500  2000-PROCESS-A-RECORD.
004600      MOVE INPUT-RECORD TO OUTPUT-RECORD.   ┌─────────────────┐
004700      WRITE OUTPUT-RECORD.                  │ Logic statements to│
004800      ADD 1 TO WS-COUNT.                    │ manipulate memory  │
004900      PERFORM 2700-READ-A-RECORD.           │ fields and specify │
005000 *                                          │ input/output actions│
005100  2700-READ-A-RECORD.                       └─────────────────┘
005200      READ INPUT-FILE
005300         AT END MOVE 'E' TO WS-FLAG.
005400 *
005500  3000-END-JOB.
005600      MOVE WS-COUNT TO WS-COUNT-Z.
005700      MOVE SPACES TO OUTPUT-RECORD.
005800      STRING '*** END OF LISTING, RECORDS = ', WS-COUNT-Z
005900         DELIMITED BY SIZE  INTO OUTPUT-RECORD.
006000      WRITE OUTPUT-RECORD.
006100      CLOSE  INPUT-FILE  OUTPUT-FILE.
```

Figure 5.2   COBOL Source Code for the COPYIT Program

This simple COBOL program copies records from an input data set to an output destination. The program has to be turned into machine language to run it.

5.2 COBOL Source Code for a Simple Program

COBOL (COmmon Business Oriented Language) is one of several high-level languages. It's often associated with JCL because both COBOL and JCL have been heavily used on IBM mainframes since 1964. As with any language you might use to develop programs on a mainframe, you compose COBOL "source code" using TSO/ISPF. You store your program source code in a library (partitioned data set). If your installation follows an IBM naming convention, the name of your COBOL library will be similar to my library name CSCJGJ.CSC.COBOL. The ending part of the name is usually COBOL.

Figure 5.2 shows you the COBOL source code I wrote for the COPYIT program. COPYIT accomplishes a simple record-copying process. It will copy the WORKERS records from disk to paper. The result will be printed output that looks a lot like the output of the IEBGENER jobs I showed you in Chapters 3 and 4:

```
*** START OF COPYIT LISTING
21256      NILLY       WILLY       402CASHIERS OFFICE
21257      IPPI        MRS.        378PHOTO DEPARTMENT
21260      MALLOW      MARSHA      390KITCHEN APPLIANCES
21307      WARE        DELLA       246FURNITURE
21310      SHAW        ARKAN       300HARDWARE
21574      AH          GEORGE      400PHOTO DEPARTMENT
21668      ZOORI       MOE         179PLUMBING SUPPLIES
25112      CABOOSE     LUCE        305FURNITURE
25189      HOW         IDA         005SUITCASES AND BAGS
33102      IFORNIA     CAL         200TRAVEL DEPARTMENT
33261      CANNON      LUCE        316TOYS
33377      WHIZ        G.          357PERSONAL COMPUTERS
33480      TOUR        D.          160WOMENS CLOTHING
33483      INA         CAROL       530REMODELING SUPPLIES
39321      ABAMA       AL          420WOMENS CLOTHING
39322      TUCKY       KEN         350HARDWARE
*** END OF LISTING, RECORDS =     16
```

Just about the only difference between IEBGENER and COPYIT output are the message lines COPYIT prints before and after the data.

There isn't much reason to write a program like COPYIT; you could execute IEBGENER to do a simple copy. But you could enhance COPYIT to make it do more things. You could include logic to add up the "hours worked" field, or add logic to compute the pay for each worker based on the number of hours he or she worked. I'll use COPYIT in its present form to show you how to compile, linkage edit, and run a program.

Notice the SELECT/ASSIGN statements in COPYIT. The right side of these statements is where you hardcode the names like COPYIN and COPYOUT that you have to use in your JCL as **DDnames** for data sets. Other programming languages have statements similar in purpose.

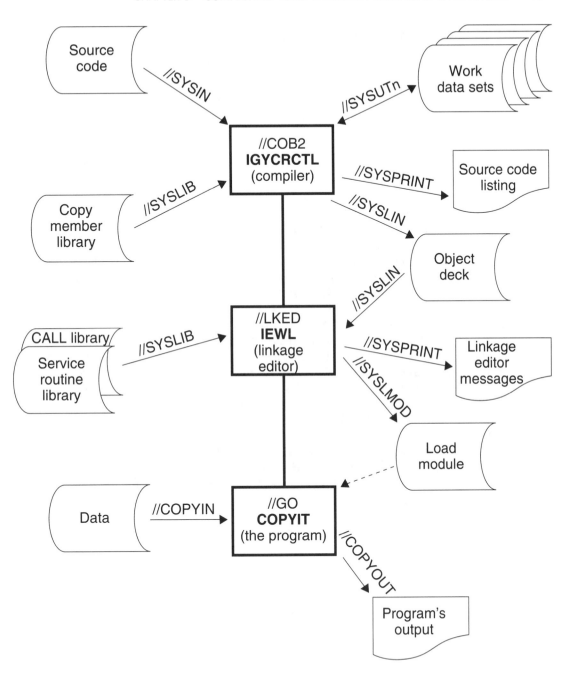

Figure 5.3 Compile, Linkage Edit, and "Go" JCL Flowchart

This JCL flowchart shows you the three steps involved in transforming program source code into machine language (load module) and running it.

5.3 Job Stream to Compile, Linkage Edit, and Run

To transform your source code for a program written in COBOL, PL/I, FORTRAN, Pascal, or C into machine language, you have to send it through a two-part process. The first part of the process is done by the language **compiler**. The second part of the process is handled by the **linkage editor**. The result is machine language that does what your program statements indicate you want done.

The compiler translates much of your source code into machine language. But it leaves some code for input/output actions untranslated. It limits its work to your computations, comparisons, and other logic because translating these doesn't depend on the configuration of devices attached to your computer system. Input/output actions do depend on your local equipment complement. The compiler produces two major outputs: a listing of your source code and an **object file**. The object file consists of 80-byte punch card images (records) that can be read by the linkage editor.

The linkage editor is like a magazine editor who gathers and arranges all of the articles that will appear in a given edition of a magazine. The linkage editor reads the object file output by the compiler, it reads standard input/output service routines, and it combines all of this machine language to produce a single executable "module" of machine language. The linkage editor's primary output is this **load module.** As a minor output it also produces a small report that tells you that it functioned. (Incidentally, all IBM compilers produce the same format of object file. You process your program with the same linkage editor no matter what program language you work in.)

Once your program has been compiled and linkage edited, you can execute its load module. Executing the load module has traditionally been called the "go" step. You can see that compile, linkage edit, and "go" amount to three program executions. You can map out these software executions using a JCL flowchart. I've done this in Figure 5.3. It's just a coincidence that this compile/link/go job stream has three steps like my earlier examples. A job stream can have any number of steps to do whatever it needs to do.

To accomplish compile, linkage edit, and "go" program execution, you could code a three-step JCL job stream from my flowchart. If you did that, you would need to refer to documentation about the compiler and linkage editor to know more about every one of their inputs and outputs. If you coded that JCL, it would look a lot like Figure 5.4.

```
EDIT ---- SYS1.PROCLIB(COB2J) - 01.01 --------------------- COLUMNS 001 072
COMMAND ===>                                                 SCROLL ===> PAGE
****** ******************************* TOP OF DATA ********************************
000100 //COB2J    PROC PDS='***',       NAME OF SOURCE CODE LIBRARY
000200 //     MEMBER='***',             NAME OF PROGRAM MEMBER TO COMPILE
000300 //     PRINTAT='*',              PRINT DESTINATION
000400 //*-------------------------------------------------------------------
000500 //*    DEPAUL UNIVERSITY  DEPT OF COMPUTER SCIENCE AND INFO SYSTEMS
000600 //*    ROOM 450, 243 S. WABASH AVE., CHICAGO, ILLINOIS 60604
000700 //*    COMPILE, LINK, GO USING VS COBOL II     IBM ES/9000 MVS/ESA
000800 //*-------------------------------------------------------------------
001000 //*
001100 //*
001200 //*    VS COBOL II COMPILE
001300 //*
001400 //COB2     EXEC PGM=IGYCRCTL,  ********************************************
001500 //    REGION=2048K,             ALLOW 2 MB FOR COMPILER      **          **
001600 //    TIME=(,6),                ALLOW UP TO 6 SECONDS        **          **
001700 //    PARM=('NOADV',            PGM RESERVES CC BYTE COL 1   **          **
001800 //          'FDUMP',            FORMATTED DUMP IF ABEND      **          **
001900 //          'NUMPROC(PFD)',     PREFERRED SIGN HANDLING      **          **
002000 //          'FLAG(I,E)',        ALL MSGS: IMBED ERROR MSGS   **          **
002100 //          'DYN',              USE DYNAMIC LOADING          **          **
002200 //          'LANGUAGE(UE)',     HEADING/MSGS UPPERCASE       **          **
002300 //          'APOST',            USE APOSTROPHE AS QUOTE      **          **
002400 //          'FDUMP',            GIVE FORMATTED ABEND DUMP    **          **
002500 //          'LIB',              COPY LIBRARY OK              **          **
002600 //          'NOMAP',            NO IMBEDDED CELL REFS        **          **
002700 //          'OBJ',              PRODUCE OBJECT CODE          **          **
002800 //          'RES',              MAKE CODE DYN RESIDENT       **          **
002900 //          'NOOPT',            NOOPT GIVES LINE# ON ABEND   **          **
003000 //          'XREF')             PROVIDE IMBEDDED CROSS REF   ** COMPILE  **
003100 //STEPLIB  DD  DSN=SYS1.COB2COMP,DISP=SHR                    **          **
003200 //SYSIN    DD  DSN=&PDS(&MEMBER),DISP=SHR
003300 //SYSLIB   DD  DSN=&PDS,DISP=SHR
003400 //SYSPRINT DD  SYSOUT=&PRINTAT
003500 //SYSLIN   DD  DSN=&&LOADSET,
003600 //    DISP=(NEW,PASS),
003700 //    UNIT=VIO,
003800 //    SPACE=(TRK,(3,3),RLSE),
003900 //    DCB=(RECFM=FB,LRECL=80,BLKSIZE=3120)
004000 //SYSUT1   DD  UNIT=VIO,SPACE=(CYL,(1,1))
004100 //SYSUT2   DD  UNIT=VIO,SPACE=(CYL,(1,1))
004200 //SYSUT3   DD  UNIT=VIO,SPACE=(CYL,(1,1))
004300 //SYSUT4   DD  UNIT=VIO,SPACE=(CYL,(1,1))
004400 //SYSUT5   DD  UNIT=VIO,SPACE=(CYL,(1,1))
004500 //SYSUT6   DD  UNIT=VIO,SPACE=(CYL,(1,1))
004600 //SYSUT7   DD  UNIT=VIO,SPACE=(CYL,(1,1))
004700 //*
004800 //*    LINKAGE EDIT
004900 //*
005000 //LKED     EXEC PGM=IEWL,   *********************************************
005100 //    COND=(4,LT,COB2),         SHUT OFF IF BAD COMPILE      **          **
005200 //    TIME=(,6),                ALLOW 6 SECONDS              **          **
005300 //    PARM=('SIZE=2048K')       ALLOW 2 MB FOR LINKAGE ED.   **          **
005400 //SYSLIN   DD  DSN=&&LOADSET,                                **          **
005500 //    DISP=(OLD,DELETE)                                      **          **
005600 //SYSLMOD  DD  DSN=&&GOSET(YOURPGM),                         ** LINK     **
005700 //    DISP=(NEW,PASS),                                       **          **
005800 //    UNIT=VIO,                                              **          **
005900 //    SPACE=(CYL,(1,1,1))                                    **          **
006000 //SYSLIB   DD  DSN=SYS1.COB2LIB,DISP=SHR                     **          **
006100 //SYSUT1   DD  UNIT=VIO,SPACE=(CYL,(1,1))                    **          **
006200 //SYSPRINT DD  SYSOUT=&PRINTAT  *********************************************
006300 //*
006400 //*    EXECUTE THE PROGRAM
006500 //*
006600 //GO       EXEC PGM=*.LKED.SYSLMOD,  ***************************************
006700 //    COND=((4,LT,COB2),(4,LT,LKED)), NO RUN IF BAD C OR L   **          **
006800 //    REGION=2048K,             ALLOW PGM 2 MB               **          **
006900 //    TIME=(,6)                 ALL PGM 6 SECONDS            **          **
007000 //STEPLIB  DD  DSN=SYS1.COB2LIB,   VS COBOL II ROUTINES      **          **
007100 //    DISP=SHR                                               **          **
007200 //SYSOUT   DD  SYSOUT=&PRINTAT   DISPLAY OUTPUT              ** GO       **
007300 //SYSABOUT DD  SYSOUT=&PRINTAT   ABEND INFO                  **          **
007400 //SYSDBOUT DD  SYSOUT=&PRINTAT   FDUMP INFO                  **          **
007500 //SORTWK01 DD  UNIT=VIO,SPACE=(TRK,5)                        **          **
007600 //SORTWK02 DD  UNIT=VIO,SPACE=(TRK,5)                        **          **
007700 //SORTWK03 DD  UNIT=VIO,SPACE=(TRK,5)    *********************************
```

This "proc" tells MVS to do the processing shown in Figure 5.3. I'll show you how to package JCL into a proc in Chapter 18, once you know how to write "raw" JCL.

Figure 5.4   Compile, Linkage Edit, and "Go" Proc COB2J

This job control language tells MVS to do the processing pictured in the JCL flowchart of Figure 5.3. It's my locally-customized version of IBM's standard proc COB2UCLG.

5.4 JCL for Compile, Linkage Edit, and Go

Figure 5.3 showed you a JCL flowchart for the compile, linkage edit, and "go" (program execution) processes. The compiler and linkage editor might sound to you like machines, but they are really programs. These programs were written by IBM software engineers and are already available on your computer system. You have to tell MVS to run these programs to process your locally written COBOL, PL/I, FORTRAN, Pascal, or C programs. You tell MVS to do this using JCL!

The JCL you see in Figure 5.4 looks a little different to you than earlier JCL examples. Notice that there is no JOB statement at the top; instead, there is a PROC statement. Notice that rather strange "placeholder" names exist in the JCL, such as &PDS and &MEMBER. And notice that there is no null // statement at the end. Aside from these differences, though, you can probably understand how this JCL implements what my JCL flowchart in Figure 5.3 indicates.

The JCL in Figure 5.3 is a "procedure"; it's "packaged" JCL in a library named SYS1.PROCLIB, which I (and almost all programmers) can't directly change. This JCL is available to everyone on the system, and as a proc it can be used (executed) very easily. Procs provide the way for JCL to be stored and run in a consistent and convenient way.

The COBOL compiler executed by this JCL is for VS COBOL II. This compiler expects to read your source code at DDname //SYSIN, coded here at line 003200. The &PDS and &MEMBER at that line are placeholders called *symbolic parameters*. You can substitute your actual library name and member name for these when you run this JCL. I show you how to run this proc in Figure 5.5. You'll see that even though compiling, linkage editing, and running a program requires about 77 lines of JCL, executing this packaged JCL takes only a few lines. Compile/link/go procs like this exist to make your work as a programmer or end user much easier.

5.5 JCL to Submit a Compile/Link/Go Proc

A proc (procedure) represents "canned" JCL that you can execute by name. The name of a proc is the name under which it is stored in a procedure library. There's nothing mysterious about a procedure library: it's just a partitioned data set. You can see in my execution JCL in Figure 5.5 that I want to execute COB2J, the compile/link/go proc in Figure 5.4. COB2J is just a member of SYS1.PROCLIB.

```
EDIT ---- CSCJGJ.CSC.CNTL(C1COMPGO) - 01.00 ---------------- COLUMNS 001 072
COMMAND ===> sub                                          SCROLL ===> PAGE
****** ************************** TOP OF DATA ******************************
000100 //CSCJGJA  JOB 1,'BIN 7 JANOSSY',CLASS=A,MSGCLASS=X,MSGLEVEL=(1,1),
000200 //  NOTIFY=CSCJGJ
000300 //*
000400 //*    THIS JCL IS STORED AT CSCJGJ.CSC.CNTL(C1COMPGO)
000500 //*
000600 //STEPA    EXEC  PROC=COB2J,
000700 //         PDS='CSCJGJ.CSC.COBOL',
000800 //   MEMBER='COPYIT'
000900 //GO.COPYIN   DD  DSN=CSCJGJ.CSC.CNTL(WORKERS),DISP=SHR
001000 //GO.COPYOUT  DD  SYSOUT=*
001100 //
****** ************************** BOTTOM OF DATA **************************

JOB CSCJGJA(JOB07913) SUBMITTED
11.17.33 JOB07913 $HASP165 CSCJGJA  ENDED AT N1 CN(INTERNAL)
***
```

Figure 5.5   Submitting a Job Using a Proc

To submit a job using a proc, you code a JOB statement, then an EXEC naming the PROC. If you don't code PROC= and don't code PGM= either, MVS assumes you are trying to execute a proc. The "GO." DD statements supply DD statements needed by the COPYIT program at the //GO step.

When you execute a proc as I'm doing here, you get a chance to substitute any values you like for the placeholder names coded in the proc. In Figure 5.5 I'm substituting CSCJGJ.CSC.COBOL for the placeholder PDS and COPYIT for the placeholder MEMBER. These are coded with a prefacing ampersand & in the proc. But you don't use the ampersands in your JCL to execute a proc. And notice that in my proc EXEC statement, I'm dealing purely with character string substitution. This means that I have to use IBM quotes (apostrophes) around 'CSCJGJ.CSC.COBOL' and 'COPYIT'.

Lines 000900 and 001000 of my execution JCL may look a little strange to you. They are coded

```
//GO.COPYIN    DD    DSN=CSCJGJ.CSC.CNTL(WORKERS),DISP=SHR
//GO.COPYOUT   DD    SYSOUT=*
```

These are "added" DD statements. If you look in the compile/link/go proc, you won't see DD statements //COPYIN and //COPYOUT at the //GO step. How could I reasonably expect the proc to contain these? I'll need those DDnames in the //GO step only when I process and run the COPYIT program.

The author of the proc couldn't possibly anticipate that I would use DDnames //COPYIN and //COPYOUT in my program. So I must add them when I execute the proc. The "GO." in front of these DDnames tells MVS to add them into the //GO step. (If I forgot to code GO. on these DDnames, MVS would add these DD statements to the first step of the proc, which would not be the right place for them.) And notice this: In "real" DD statements, such as lines 009000 and 001000, you *don't* use IBM quotes (apostrophes) around the data set name, because these are not character string substitution statements.

When I submit the JCL I've shown in Figure 5.5, I get a job number from MVS. Behind the scenes, MVS accesses SYS1.PROCLIB, brings a copy of COB2J into memory, replaces the character strings at placeholders PDS and MEMBER, and checks out the resulting JCL. If the resulting JCL is valid in format, MVS accepts it for processing.

5.6 What Happens When You Submit a Proc?

When you submit a proc, you get essentially the same response from MVS as when you submit "raw" JCL. MVS issues a unique job number to you. Eventually, MVS sends you a message indicating that your job has finished (assuming that you have coded a valid NOTIFY on your JOB statement).

But behind the scenes, MVS handles non-proc ("raw" JCL) and proc execution differently. When you submit raw JCL, the JCL is already complete with EXEC and DD statements for the programs you want to execute. The sequence of events proceeds as shown in Figure 5.6a.

When you submit JCL that invokes a proc, events proceed as I've shown in Figure 5.6b. You receive a job number, but MVS also accesses the proc library to retrieve the "canned" JCL stored there under the proc name. MVS puts your submitted JCL into memory, and inserts the proc JCL into it there. MVS also edits the resulting JCL in memory to make the symbolic

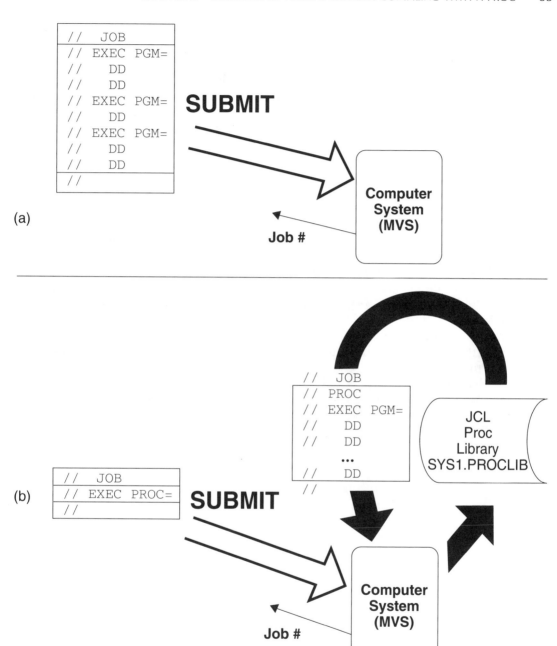

Figure 5.6   Comparing Raw JCL and Proc Execution

(a) Raw JCL is self-contained and includes JOB, EXEC, and DD statements.
(b) When you execute a proc, you invoke "packaged" JCL already housed in a library, and MVS merges your JCL with the proc.

parameter character string substitutions that you coded on any EXEC statements that invoke procs. When all of this work is done, MVS accepts the
edited JCL for processing.

Proc execution is very flexible. You could code several steps in the raw
JCL you submit. More than one of those steps could invoke a proc. You
could invoke the same proc several times or invoke different procs in your
steps. You could intersperse your execution of procs between raw JCL steps
in which you execute programs. Regardless of these or other possible variations, MVS sees the raw JCL you submit and the JCL put together with
it as one set of JCL. To MVS, this all becomes one job.

Procs do have some limitations. Within a proc, you can't execute another
proc—that is, procs can't be nested. (This limitation disappears in Release
4 of MVS/ESA.) And you can't house "instream data," which I'll explain
to you in Chapter 8, in a proc. I'll give you complete guidance on creating
procs in Chapter 18.

You should also realize that while procs simplify the submission of JCL,
they don't make the reading of your system output any simpler. When you
see the MVS system output resulting from your submission of a proc, you
will see a listing of all of the final edited JCL that MVS processed, including
the JCL contained in the proc. Unless you are aware of what MVS does to
execute a proc, you might find it mysterious that more JCL comes out than
you put in!

I've listed in Figure 5.7 the MVS/ESA system output from my submission of the COB2J proc for my COPYIT program. The annotations I have
put on Figure 5.7 explain a lot about the operation of MVS and the VS
COBOL II compiler.

Figure 5.7   Output of Compile/Link/Go Job →

Figure 5.7 shows you the output produced when I submit the JCL
shown in Figure 5.5. Turn your book sideways to look at this output
and you will see that it is printed here very much like the way you
will see it as a computer printout.

Chapter 5 Review follows on page 92.

J E S 2   J O B   L O G   - -   S Y S T E M   I B M 1   - -   N O D E   N 1

```
11.17.28 JOB07913 IRR010I USERID CSCJGJ  IS ASSIGNED TO THIS JOB.
11.17.29 JOB07913 ICH70001I CSCJGJ  LAST ACCESS AT 11:13:50 ON SATURDAY, SEPTEMBER 26, 1992
11.17.29 JOB07913 $HASP373 CSCJGJA  STARTED - INIT  1 - CLASS A - SYS IBM1
11.17.33 JOB07913 $HASP395 CSCJGJA  ENDED

----- JES2 JOB STATISTICS -----
 26 SEP 92 JOB EXECUTION DATE
         10 CARDS READ
        376 SYSOUT PRINT RECORDS
          0 SYSOUT PUNCH RECORDS
         23 SYSOUT SPOOL KBYTES
       0.06 MINUTES EXECUTION TIME
```

Text box (right side):

What You Get When You Execute a Compile/Link/Go Proc

I executed a proc named **COB2J** to compile, linkage edit, and run my program COPYIT using the JCL in Figure 5.5. Here you see the *"expansion"* of this proc. MVS has copied the proc in from a proc library named SYS1.PROCLIB; the proc is actually *member* COB2J of this library. IBM provides many procs containing JCL to process programs. Most installations (such as ours at DePaul University) customize the standard procs to tailor them for local use. MVS changes the leading // to XX when it lists the JCL of a proc in its reporting.

```
1 //CSCJGJA  JOB 1,'BIN 7 JANOSSY',CLASS=A,MSGCLASS=X,MSGLEVEL=(1,1),         JOB07913
   //         NOTIFY=CSCJGJ                                                   00020000
   //*                                                                        00030000
   //*      THIS JCL IS STORED AT CSCJGJ.CSC.CNTL(C1COMPGO)                    00040000
   //*                                                                        00050000
2 //STEPA    EXEC  PROC=COB2J,                                                00060000
   //        PDS='CSCJGJ.CSC.COBOL',   NAME OF SOURCE CODE LIBRARY            00070000
   //        MEMBER='COPYIT'           NAME OF PROGRAM MEMBER TO COMPILE      00080000
3 XXCOB2J   PROC PDS='****',           NAME OF PROGRAM MEMBER TO COMPILE      00010014
   XX        MEMBER='****',            PRINT DESTINATION                      00020014
   XX        PRINTAT='*',                                                     00030014
   XX*----------------------------------------------------------------       00040024
   XX*      DEPAUL UNIVERSITY DEPT OF COMPUTER SCIENCE AND INFO SYSTEMS       00050024
   XX*      ROOM 450, 243 S. WABASH AVE., CHICAGO, ILLINOIS 60604             00060024
   XX*                                            IBM ES/9000 MVS/ESA         00070024
   XX*      COMPILE, LINK, GO USING VS COBOL II      JIM JANOSSY  9/10/92     00080024
   XX*      (COMPILE/LINK PROC IS COB2CLJ)                                    00090024
   XX*                                                                        00100024
   XX*                                                                        00110005
   XX*     VS COBOL II COMPILE                                                00120005
   XX*                                                                        00130005
4 XXCOB2    EXEC PGM=IGYCRCTL,        ***************************************  00140023
   XX       REGION=2048K,              ALLOW 2 MB FOR COMPILER           **   00150023
   XX       TIME=(,6),                 ALLOW UP TO 6 SECONDS             **   00160017
   XX       PARM=('NOADV',             PGM RESERVES CC BYTE COL 1        **   00170017
   XX             'FDUMP',             FORMATTED DUMP IF ABEND           **   00180020
   XX             'NUMPROC(PFD)',      PREFERRED SIGN HANDLING           **   00190012
   XX             'FLAG(I,E)',         ALL MSGS; IMBED ERROR MSGS        **   00200016
   XX             'DYN',               USE DYNAMIC LOADING               **   00210012
   XX             'LANGUAGE(UE)',      HEADING/MSGS UPPERCASE            **   00220012
   XX             'APOST',             USE APOSTROPHE AS QUOTE           **   00230012
   XX             'FDUMP',             GIVE FORMATTED ABEND DUMP         **   00240012
   XX             'LIB',               COPY LIBRARY OK                   **   00250012
   XX             'NOMAP',             NO IMBEDDED CELL REFS             **   00260012
   XX             'RES',               PRODUCE OBJECT CODE               **   00270012
   XX             'OBJ',               MAKE CODE DYN RESIDENT            **   00280012
   XX             'NOOPT,               NOOPT GIVES LINE# ON ABEND       **   00290025
   XX             'XREF')              PROVIDE IMBEDDED CROSS REF ** COMPILE  00300023
5 XXSTEPLIB DD DSN=SYS1.COB2COMP,DISP=SHR                                     00310011
6 XXSYSIN   DD DSN=&PDS(&MEMBER),DISP=SHR                                     00320018
   IEFC653I SUBSTITUTION JCL - DSN=CSCJGJ.CSC.COBOL(COPYIT),DISP=SHR
```

Figure 5.7 Output of Compile/Link/Go Job

(continued)

85

At several places in this MVS system reporting for your compile/link/go proc you will see *substitution JCL.* These are the lines in the proc which are affected by the specific values such as data set names which you supply in your execution JCL. For example, in my execution JCL in Figure 5.5, I stated that my COBOL library (PDS) was named **CSCJGJ.CSC.COBOL** and that I wanted to compile a program (MEMBER) named **COPYIT**. This affects JCL statements 6 and 7. See if you can find the other JCL substitutions reported in this MVS system output.

```
  7 XXSYSLIB   DD  DSN=&PDS,DISP=SHR                                    **  00330018
    IEFC653I SUBSTITUTION JCL - DSN=CSCJGJ.CSC.COBOL,DISP=SHR           **  00340012
  8 XXSYSPRINT DD  SYSOUT=&PRINTAT                                      **  00350011
    IEFC653I SUBSTITUTION JCL - SYSOUT=*                                **  00360011
  9 XXSYSLIN   DD  DSN=&&LOADSET,                                       **  00370011
    XX         DISP=(NEW,PASS),                                         **  00380011
    XX         UNIT=VIO,                                                **  00390011
    XX         SPACE=(TRK,(3,3),RLSE),                                  **  00400011
    XX         DCB=(RECFM=FB,LRECL=80,BLKSIZE=3120)                     **  00410011
 10 XXSYSUT1   DD  UNIT=VIO,SPACE=(CYL,(1,1))                           **  00420011
 11 XXSYSUT2   DD  UNIT=VIO,SPACE=(CYL,(1,1))                           **  00430011
 12 XXSYSUT3   DD  UNIT=VIO,SPACE=(CYL,(1,1))                           **  00440011
 13 XXSYSUT4   DD  UNIT=VIO,SPACE=(CYL,(1,1))                           **  00450011
 14 XXSYSUT5   DD  UNIT=VIO,SPACE=(CYL,(1,1))                           **  00460011
 15 XXSYSUT6   DD  UNIT=VIO,SPACE=(CYL,(1,1))                           **  00470005
 16 XXSYSUT7   DD  UNIT=VIO,SPACE=(CYL,(1,1))                           **  00480005
    XX* LINKAGE EDIT  ****************************************************   00490005
 17 XXLKED  EXEC PGM=IEWL,      SHUT OFF IF BAD COMPILE    **           **  00500023
    XX  COND=(4,LT,COB2),       ALLOW 6 SECONDS            **           **  00510023
    XX  TIME=(,6),              ALLOW 2 MB FOR LINKAGE ED. **           **  00520023
    XX  PARM=('SIZE=2048K')                                **           **  00530023
 18 XXSYSLIN   DD  DSN=&&LOADSET,                          **           **  00540023
    XX  DISP=(OLD,DELETE),                                 **           **  00550023
 19 XXSYSLMOD  DD  DSN=&&GOSET(YOURPGM),        LINK       **           **  00560023
    XX  DISP=(NEW,PASS),                                   **           **  00570011
    XX  UNIT=VIO,                                          **           **  00580023
    XX  SPACE=(CYL,(1,1))                                  **           **  00590011
 20 XXSYSLIB   DD  DSN=SYS1.COB2LIB,DISP=SHR               **           **  00600011
 21 XXSYSUT1   DD  UNIT=VIO,SPACE=(CYL,(1,1))              **           **  00610011
 22 XXSYSPRINT DD  SYSOUT=&PRINTAT  ************************           **  00620023
    XX* EXECUTE THE PROGRAM                                              **  00630005
    IEFC653I SUBSTITUTION JCL - SYSOUT=*                                 **  00640005
    ****************************************************************        00650005
 23 XXGO  EXEC PGM=*.LKED.SYSLMOD,    NO RUN IF BAD C OR L **           **  00660023
    XX  COND=((4,LT,COB2),(4,LT,LKED)),   ALLOW PGM 2 MB   **           **  00670023
    XX  REGION=2048K,               ALLOW PGM 6 SECONDS    **           **  00680023
    XX  TIME=(,6)                   VS COBOL II ROUTINES   **           **  00690023
 24 XXSTEPLIB  DD  DSN=SYS1.COB2LIB,                       **           **  00700023
    XX  DISP=SHR                                           **           **  00710023
 25 XXSYSOUT   DD  SYSOUT=&PRINTAT      DISPLAY OUTPUT     **       GO  **  00720023
    IEFC653I SUBSTITUTION JCL - SYSOUT=*                                 **  00730023
 26 XXSYSABOUT DD  SYSOUT=&PRINTAT      ABEND INFO         **           **  00740023
    IEFC653I SUBSTITUTION JCL - SYSOUT=*
 27 XXSYSDBOUT DD  SYSOUT=&PRINTAT      FDUMP INFO         **           **  00750011
    IEFC653I SUBSTITUTION JCL - SYSOUT=*  ***********************        **  00760019
 28 XXSORTWK01 DD  UNIT=VIO,SPACE=(TRK,5)                  **           **  00770023
 29 XXSORTWK02 DD  UNIT=VIO,SPACE=(TRK,5)                  **           **  00090000
 30 XXSORTWK03 DD  UNIT=VIO,SPACE=(TRK,5)                                   00100000
 31 //GO.COPYIN   DD  DSN=CSCJGJ.CSC.CNTL(WORKERS),DISP=SHR
 32 //GO.COPYOUT  DD  SYSOUT=*

STMT NO. MESSAGE
    2 IEFC001I PROCEDURE COB2J WAS EXPANDED USING SYSTEM LIBRARY SYS1.PROCLIB
```

```
ICH70001I CSCJGJ    LAST ACCESS AT 11:13:50 ON SATURDAY, SEPTEMBER 26, 1992

IEF236I ALLOC. FOR CSCJGJA COB2 STEPA
IEF237I 110 ALLOCATED TO STEPLIB
IEF237I 111 ALLOCATED TO SYSIN
IEF237I 111 ALLOCATED TO SYSLIB
IEF237I JES2 ALLOCATED TO SYSPRINT
IEF237I VIO ALLOCATED TO SYSLIN
IEF237I VIO ALLOCATED TO SYSUT1
IEF237I VIO ALLOCATED TO SYSUT2
IEF237I VIO ALLOCATED TO SYSUT3
IEF237I VIO ALLOCATED TO SYSUT4
IEF237I VIO ALLOCATED TO SYSUT5
IEF237I VIO ALLOCATED TO SYSUT6
IEF237I VIO ALLOCATED TO SYSUT7
IEF142I CSCJGJA COB2 STEPA - STEP WAS EXECUTED - COND CODE 0000
IEF285I    SYS1.COB2COMP                               KEPT
IEF285I    VOL SER NOS= ACSRES.
IEF285I    CSCJGJ.CSC.COBOL                            KEPT
IEF285I    VOL SER NOS= USER00.
IEF285I    CSCJGJ.CSC.COBOL
IEF285I    VOL SER NOS= USER00.
IEF285I    CSCJGJA.JOB07913.D0000101.?                 SYSOUT
IEF285I    CSCJGJ.CSCJGJA.LOADSET                       PASSED
IEF285I    SYS92270.T111729.RA000.CSCJGJA.R0015228      DELETED
IEF285I    SYS92270.T111729.RA000.CSCJGJA.R0015229      DELETED
IEF285I    SYS92270.T111729.RA000.CSCJGJA.R0015230      DELETED
IEF285I    SYS92270.T111729.RA000.CSCJGJA.R0015231      DELETED
IEF285I    SYS92270.T111729.RA000.CSCJGJA.R0015232      DELETED
IEF285I    SYS92270.T111729.RA000.CSCJGJA.R0015233      DELETED
IEF285I    SYS92270.T111729.RA000.CSCJGJA.R0015234      DELETED
IEF373I STEP /COB2    / START 92270.1117
IEF374I STEP /COB2    / STOP  92270.1117 CPU  0MIN 00.73SEC SRB  0MIN 00.01SEC VIRT  2048K SYS  260K EXT  32740K

IEF236I ALLOC. FOR CSCJGJA LKED STEPA
IEF237I VIO ALLOCATED TO SYSLIN
IEF237I VIO ALLOCATED TO SYSLMOD
IEF237I VIO ALLOCATED TO SYSLIB
IEF237I VIO ALLOCATED TO SYSUT1
IEF142I JES2 ALLOCATED TO SYSPRINT
IEF142I CSCJGJA LKED STEPA - STEP WAS EXECUTED - COND CODE 0000
IEF285I    SYS92270.T111729.RA000.CSCJGJA
IEF285I    SYS92270.T111729.RA000.CSCJGJA.GOSET         KEPT
IEF285I    SYS1.COB2LIB
IEF285I    VOL SER NOS= ACSRES.
IEF285I    SYS92270.T111729.RA000.CSCJGJA.R0015235      DELETED
IEF285I    CSCJGJ.CSCJGJA.JOB07913.D0000102.?           SYSOUT
IEF373I STEP /LKED    / START 92270.1117
IEF374I STEP /LKED    / STOP  92270.1117 CPU  0MIN 00.22SEC SRB  0MIN 00.00SEC VIRT  1024K SYS  276K EXT  4K

IEF236I ALLOC. FOR CSCJGJA GO STEPA
IEF237I VIO ALLOCATED TO PGM=*.DD
IEF237I 110 ALLOCATED TO STEPLIB
IEF237I JES2 ALLOCATED TO SYSOUT
IEF237I JES2 ALLOCATED TO SYSABOUT
IEF237I JES2 ALLOCATED TO SYSDBOUT
```

This MVS system reporting shows you the *devices* and *facilities* allocated to service the DD statements of each step and the final disposition of the data sets accessed. The allocations are listed by *device address* (such as 110) first within each step. Then you see the **COND CODE** left behind by the program executed at the step. Finally, you see the name of each data set accessed by the program that ran in this step. Listed to the right of the data set name is a word like **KEPT**, indicating what has been done with it. On the line following the data set name is the *volume serial number* of the disk or tape on which it is located.

Figure 5.7 *(Continued)*

(continued)

```
IEF237I VIO  ALLOCATED TO SORTWK01
IEF237I VIO  ALLOCATED TO SORTWK02
IEF237I VIO  ALLOCATED TO SORTWK03
IEF237I 111  ALLOCATED TO COPYIN
IEF237I JES2 ALLOCATED TO COPYOUT
IEF142I CSCJGJA GO STEPA - STEP WAS EXECUTED -  COND CODE 0000
IEF285I   SYS92270.T111729.RA000.CSCJGJA
IEF285I   SYS1.COB2LIB
IEF285I   VOL SER NOS= ACSRES.
IEF285I   CSCJGJ.CSCJGJA.JOB07913.D0000103.?         SYSOUT
IEF285I   CSCJGJ.CSCJGJA.JOB07913.D0000104.?         SYSOUT
IEF285I   CSCJGJ.CSCJGJA.JOB07913.D0000105.?         SYSOUT
IEF285I   SYS92270.T111729.RA000.CSCJGJA.R0015236    DELETED
IEF285I   SYS92270.T111729.RA000.CSCJGJA.R0015237    DELETED
IEF285I   SYS92270.T111729.RA000.CSCJGJA.R0015238    DELETED
IEF285I   CSCJGJ.CSC.CNTL                            KEPT
IEF285I   VOL SER NOS= USER00.
IEF285I   CSCJGJ.CSCJGJA.JOB07913.D0000106.?         SYSOUT
IEF373I STEP /GO     / START 92270.1117
IEF374I STEP /GO     / STOP  92270.1117 CPU    0MIN 00.16SEC SRB    0MIN 00.01SEC VIRT  288K SYS  264K EXT  4K
IEF285I   SYS92270.T111729.RA000.CSCJGJA.GOSET       DELETED

IEF375I JOB /CSCJGJA / START 92270.1117
IEF376I JOB /CSCJGJA / STOP  92270.1117 CPU    0MIN 01.11SEC SRB    0MIN 00.02SEC
```

MVS system reporting ends with IEF375I and IEF376I messages indicating the overall job start and stop time in the form **YYDDD.HHMM**, in other words, as the Julian date and the hour and minute. You also see the CPU time, which is the amount of time that the job actually was active. After this point in your output you see the print output produced by the programs you have executed. The compiler is the first program I executed in this job stream, and its print output comes next.

```
PP 5668-958 IBM VS COBOL II RELEASE 3.2 09/05/90                 DATE 09/26/92  TIME 11:17:30  PAGE  1

INVOCATION PARAMETERS:
NOADV,FDUMP,NUMPROC(PFD),FLAG(I,E),DYN,LANGUAGE(UE),APOST,FDUMP,LIB,NOMAP,OBJ,RES,NOOPT,XREF

OPTIONS IN EFFECT:
 NOADV
    APOST
 NOAMO
    BUFSIZE(4096)
 NOCMPR2
 NOCOMPILE(S)
    DATA(31)
 NODBCS
 NODECK
 - -
 - -
```

This is the start of print output from the VS COBOL II compiler. This emerges at its //SYSPRINT DD statement. The compiler first lists for you the way its options were set for this run. With VS COBOL II you can adjust over 40 option settings! Some of these activate program listing features, others invoke debugging aids, and still others change the way the compiled program will handle arithmetic and memory addressing. For more information on the option settings of the VS COBOL II compiler, you can look in another of my books, *VS COBOL II: Highlights and Techniques* (Wiley, 1992).

```
LINEID  PL SL  ----+--*A-1-B--+----2----+----3----+----4----+----5----+----6----+----7-|--+----8   MAP AND CROSS REFERENCE
000001         000100 IDENTIFICATION DIVISION.
000002         000200 PROGRAM-ID.    COPYIT.
000003         000300 AUTHOR.        J JANOSSY.
000004         000400*
000005         000500*REMARKS.         SIMPLE PROGRAM TO READ AND PRINT 80 BYTE RECORDS.
000006         000600*
000007         000700 ENVIRONMENT DIVISION.
000009         000800 INPUT-OUTPUT SECTION.
000009         000900 FILE-CONTROL.
000010         001000     SELECT INPUT-FILE    ASSIGN TO  COPYIN.
000011         001100     SELECT OUTPUT-FILE   ASSIGN TO  COPYOUT.
000012         001200*
000013         001300 DATA DIVISION.
000014         001400 FILE SECTION.
000015         001500 FD  INPUT-FILE
000016         001600     LABEL RECORDS ARE STANDARD
000017         001700     RECORD CONTAINS 80 CHARACTERS
000018         001800     BLOCK CONTAINS 0 RECORDS.
000019         001900 01  INPUT-RECORD                              PIC X(80).
000021         002000*
000021         002100 FD  OUTPUT-FILE
000022         002200     LABEL RECORDS ARE OMITTED
000023         002300     RECORD CONTAINS 80 CHARACTERS
000024         002400     BLOCK CONTAINS 0 RECORDS.
000025         002500 01  OUTPUT-RECORD                             PIC X(80).
000026         002600/
000027         002700 WORKING-STORAGE SECTION.
000028         002800 01  WS-FLAG               PIC X(1)  VALUE 'M'.        39
000029         002900 01  WS-COUNT              PIC 9(5)  VALUE 0.          45  28
000030         003000 01  WS-COUNT-Z            PIC ZZ,ZZ9.                 55
000031         003100/
000032         003200 PROCEDURE DIVISION.
000033         003300 0000-MAINLINE.
000034         003400     PERFORM 1000-BEGIN-JOB.                           15  21
000035         003500     PERFORM 2000-PROCESS-A-RECORD UNTIL WS-FLAG = 'E'. 25
000036         003600     PERFORM 3000-END-JOB.                            51
000037         003700     STOP RUN.
000038         003800*
000039         003900 1000-BEGIN-JOB.
000040         004000     OPEN INPUT  INPUT-FILE  OUTPUT  OUTPUT-FILE.
000041         004100     MOVE '*** START OF COPYIT LISTING' TO OUTPUT-RECORD.
000042         004200     WRITE OUTPUT-RECORD.
000043         004300     PERFORM 2700-READ-A-RECORD.
000044         004400*
000045         004500 2000-PROCESS-A-RECORD.                               19  25
000046         004600     MOVE INPUT-RECORD TO OUTPUT-RECORD.              25
000047         004700     WRITE OUTPUT-RECORD.                             29
000048         004800     ADD 1 TO WS-COUNT.                               51
000049         004900     PERFORM 2700-READ-A-RECORD.
000050         005000*
```

The VS COBOL II compiler lists the **source code** of the program you asked it to process. This source code enters the compiler at its //SYSIN DD statement. The numbers listed at the right are an imbedded *cross reference.* For PERFORM statements, these numbers show you where the PERFORMed paragraph is, by its compiler-assigned line number. (Compiler-assigned line numbers are in the leftmost column.) For data names, the cross reference shows you where in the program the data name is defined.

(continued)

Figure 5.7 *(Continued)*

```
000051          005100 2700-READ-A-RECORD.
000052          005200        READ INPUT-FILE
000053        1 005300            AT END MOVE 'E' TO WS-FLAG.
000054          005400*
000055          005500 3000-END-JOB.
000056          005600        MOVE WS-COUNT TO WS-COUNT-Z.
000057          005700        MOVE SPACES TO OUTPUT-RECORD.
000058          005800        STRING '*** END OF LISTING, RECORDS = ', WS-COUNT-Z
000059          005900            DELIMITED BY SIZE INTO OUTPUT-RECORD.
000060          006000        WRITE OUTPUT-RECORD.
000061          006100        CLOSE INPUT-FILE OUTPUT-FILE.
```

```
                                                  15
                                                  28

                                                  29 30
                                                  IMP 25
                                                  30
                                                  25
                                                  15 21
```

PP 5668-958 IBM VS COBOL II RELEASE 3.2 09/05/90   COPYIT   DATE 09/26/92   TIME 11:17:30   PAGE   5

AN "M" PRECEDING A DATA-NAME REFERENCE INDICATES THAT THE DATA-NAME IS MODIFIED BY THIS REFERENCE.

```
DEFINED  CROSS-REFERENCE OF DATA NAMES      REFERENCES

   15    INPUT-FILE. . . . . . . . . :     10 40 52 61
   19    INPUT-RECORD. . . . . . . . :     46
   21    OUTPUT-FILE . . . . . . . . :     11 40 61
   25    OUTPUT-RECORD . . . . . . . :     M41 42  M46 47 M57 M59 60
   29    WS-COUNT. . . . . . . . . . :     M48 56
   30    WS-COUNT-Z. . . . . . . . . :     M56 58
   28    WS-FLAG . . . . . . . . . . :     35 M53
```

> You get this cross reference when you activate the **XREF** compiler option. Here you see the data names defined in the program, listed in *alphabetical sequence*. **REFERENCES** shows you the line numbers where each data name is mentioned.

PP 5668-958 IBM VS COBOL II RELEASE 3.2 09/05/90   COPYIT   DATE 09/26/92   TIME 11:17:30   PAGE   6

CONTEXT USAGE IS INDICATED BY THE LETTER PRECEDING A PROCEDURE-NAME REFERENCE.
THESE LETTERS AND THEIR MEANINGS ARE:

```
A = ALTER (PROCEDURE-NAME)
D = GO TO (PROCEDURE-NAME) DEPENDING ON
E = END OF RANGE OF (PERFORM) THROUGH (PROCEDURE-NAME)
G = GO TO (PROCEDURE-NAME)
P = PERFORM (PROCEDURE-NAME)
T = (ALTER) TO PROCEED TO (PROCEDURE-NAME)
U = USE FOR DEBUGGING (PROCEDURE-NAME)
```

```
DEFINED  CROSS-REFERENCE OF PROCEDURES      REFERENCES

   33    0000-MAINLINE
   39    1000-BEGIN-JOB. . . . . . . :     P34
   45    2000-PROCESS-A-RECORD . . . :     P35
   51    2700-READ-A-RECORD. . . . . :     P43 P49
   55    3000-END-JOB. . . . . . . . :     P36
```

> This cross reference (also produced by **XREF**) shows you the paragraphs ("procedures") of the program and the line number where each starts.

90

```
PP 5668-958 IBM VS COBOL II RELEASE 3.2 09/05/90          COPYIT      DATE 09/26/92  TIME 11:17:30  PAGE   8

LINEID MESSAGE CODE  MESSAGE TEXT

    15 IGYGR1216-I    A "RECORDING MODE" OF "F" WAS ASSUMED FOR FILE "INPUT-FILE".

    21 IGYGR1216-I    A "RECORDING MODE" OF "F" WAS ASSUMED FOR FILE "OUTPUT-FILE".

MESSAGES    TOTAL        INFORMATIONAL    WARNING    ERROR    SEVERE    TERMINATING
PRINTED:      2               2

*  STATISTICS FOR COBOL PROGRAM COPYIT:
*     SOURCE RECORDS = 61
*     DATA DIVISION STATEMENTS = 5
*     PROCEDURE DIVISION STATEMENTS = 19

END OF COMPILATION 1,  PROGRAM COPYIT,  HIGHEST SEVERITY 0.
RETURN CODE 0
```

This is the end of the compiler's //SYSPRINT listing. I set the compiler options to list *informational messages* here only. Error messages will list after each line with a problem, and here also. The **RETURN CODE** listed as the last item here is the same as the **COND CODE** for your compile step.

```
MVS/DFP VERSION 3 RELEASE 3 LINKAGE EDITOR      11:17:31  SAT  SEP 26, 1992
JOB CSCJGJA      STEP STEPA        PROCEDURE LKED
INVOCATION PARAMETERS - SIZE=2048K
ACTUAL  SIZE=(962560,86016)
OUTPUT DATA SET SYS92270.T111729.RA000.CSCJGJA.GOSET IS ON VOLUME
** YOURPGM DID NOT PREVIOUSLY EXIST BUT WAS ADDED AND HAS AMODE ANY
** LOAD MODULE HAS RMODE 31
** AUTHORIZATION CODE IS              0.
```

These messages are from the *linkage editor* step. You usually don't have to pay much attention to these messages.

```
*** START OF COPYIT LISTING
21256 NILLY      WILLY     402CASHIERS OFFICE
21257 IPPI       MRS.      378PHOTO DEPARTMENT
21260 MALLOW     MARSHA    390KITCHEN APPLIANCES
21307 WARE       DELLA     246FURNITURE
21310 SHAW       ARKAN     300HARDWARE
21574 AH         GEORGE    400PHOTO DEPARTMENT
21668 ZOORI      MOE       179PLUMBING SUPPLIES
25112 CABOOSE    LUCE      305FURNITURE
25189 HOW        IDA       005SUITCASES AND BAGS
33102 IFORNIA    CAL       200TRAVEL DEPARTMENT
33261 CANNON     LUCE      316TOYS
33377 WHIZ       G.        357PERSONAL COMPUTERS
33480 TOUR       D.        160WOMENS CLOTHING
33483 INA        CAROL     530REMODELING SUPPLIES
39321 ABAMA      AL        420WOMENS CLOTHING
39322 TUCKY      KEN       350HARDWARE
*** END OF LISTING, RECORDS =   16
```

Finally! Here is the output of my //GO step -- the printlines written by my **COPYIT** program at its //COPYOUT DD statement. The program read these records from the **WORKERS** member of my **CSCJGJ.CSC.CNTL** library. With appropriate programming I could produce a much fancier report of this data.

Figure 5.7 *(Continued)*

91

Chapter 5 Review

Mini-Glossary

Machine language The binary (0s and 1s) language understood by the electronic switches and gates of computer circuitry

Source code Program language statements of a language such as COBOL, PL/I, FORTRAN, Pascal, or C

Compiler A program that does part of the work of transforming source code into machine language, creating an object file

Linkage editor A program that accepts the compiler-produced object file and creates a machine language load module

Execution JCL JCL starting with a JOB statement that you can submit to MVS to initiate work; it may invoke a proc.

Proc "Packaged" JCL for a common process, housed in a library, that you can execute with EXEC PROC=name or EXEC name

Review Questions

1. Briefly compare first generation programming languages, second generation languages, and third generation languages.

2. Explain in your own words what a compiler does.

3. Explain why you need only one linkage editor on a computer system even if multiple programming languages are used.

4. Describe the differences between execution JCL and a proc.

Exercise

A. Listed below is the smallest valid COBOL program that you can write. Enter it into a member of your COBOL or CNTL library named LITTLE1, putting your name in it where you see hyphens in line 000600. Then use your installation's VS COBOL or VS COBOL II compile/link/go proc to process and run it and compare your output to Figure 5.7.

```
000100    IDENTIFICATION DIVISION.
000200    PROGRAM-ID.    LITTLE1.
000300    ENVIRONMENT DIVISION.
000400    DATA DIVISION.
000500    PROCEDURE DIVISION.
000600        DISPLAY 'JCL IS FUN SAYS ---------'.
000700        STOP RUN.
```

Chapter Six

THE JOB STATEMENT IN DETAIL

You must start every set of your JCL with a JOB statement and should end the JCL with a null // statement. I have already shown you the most important things about JOB in the overview of Figures 3.5a and 3.5b in Chapter 3. But here I'll give you more details of the parameters you can code with JOB. Perhaps you have already composed a job statement suited to your local conditions and used it to run some exercises. If so, you can browse this chapter and regard it as a reference for your later work.

I'll cover the most commonly used JOB parameters first. You'll use many of the JOB parameters only rarely, if at all. Some of the parameters serve special purposes for systems programmers, communicate with IBM's own software security system (RACF), or are used only when you have to restart a job that was interrupted.

A word of warning! Since MVS needs the JOB statement to identify you as the originator of a job, it's especially frustrating to make a mistake coding JOB. A syntax error on JOB often means that MVS doesn't recognize who you are and therefore can't send you error messages. If you submit a job with an incorrect JOB statement, you will be given a job number but will probably never see anything of the job again!

6.1 What Does JOB Do?

The JOB statement provides more than 20 parameters that

- give the job a name and identify who submitted it
- indicate where the print output is to be sent
- tell who (that is, which account) will pay for the memory and computer time that the job uses
- tell MVS the importance of the job relative to other jobs

The general form of the JOB statement is similar from one IBM installation to another, but your installation's system programmers and managers decide a lot about what job statement parameters you need to code. You'll have to code your JOB statements according to rules documented locally by your installation. In Figure 6.1a you see a compact (but hard to read) JOB statement. You can code a clearer self-documenting JOB statement to tell MVS the very same things about your job, as I've done in Figure 6.1b. I'll explain how to use each of the parameters I've coded here in the sections that follow.

I'd encourage you to collect some samples of JOB statements from jobs run in your shop and compare them to these examples. This will help you get a precise idea of what parameters are usually coded in your environment and their locally preferred coding format.

```
EDIT --- CSCJGJ.CSC.CNTL(D1JOB) - 01.00 -------------------- COLUMNS 001 072
COMMAND ===>                                                  SCROLL ===> PAGE
****** **************************** TOP OF DATA ****************************
000100 //CSCJGJA  JOB  WCWC13DT,'BIN 7-JANOSSY',CLASS=E,MSGCLASS=X,
000200 //  MSGLEVEL=(1,1),PRTY=6,REGION=2048K,TIME=(2,30),
000300 //  NOTIFY=CSCJGJ,TYPRUN=SCAN
000400 //*
```
(a)

```
EDIT --- CSCJGJ.CSC.CNTL(D2JOB) - 01.00 -------------------- COLUMNS 001 072
COMMAND ===>                                                  SCROLL ===> PAGE
****** **************************** TOP OF DATA ****************************
000100 //CSCJGJA  JOB WCWC13DT,       Job name and account to be charged
000200 //  'BIN 7-JANOSSY',           How to label the print output
000300 //  CLASS=E,                   Input "job class"
000400 //  MSGCLASS=X,                Where and how to print MVS output
000500 //  MSGLEVEL=(1,1),            How much MVS output should print?
000600 //  PRTY=6,                    What is job priority (0-15)?
000700 //  REGION=2048K,              Allow job to use 2 megabytes memory
000800 //  TIME=(2,30),               Allow job to use 2 minutes, 30 seconds
000900 //* TYPRUN=SCAN,               MVS should check JCL, but not run it
001000 //  NOTIFY=CSCJGJ              Tell TSO user CSCJGJ when job is done
001100 //*                           (a comment statement)
****** **************************** BOTTOM OF DATA ****************************
```
(b)

Figure 6.1 JOB Statements

(a) This JOB statement shows you the typical format for coding commonly used JOB parameters. The accounting information and the specific parameters used vary from installation to installation. (b) If you code your JOB statement with a single parameter on each line, you can deactivate TYPRUN=SCAN, just by putting an asterisk after its slashes.

6.2 JOB Name and Account

When you run a job, MVS is set to print the messages it generates. The most commonly used JOB parameters are those that label your job's printed output.

```
//CSCJGJA JOB WCWC13DT,        Job name and account to be charged
// 'BIN 7-JANOSSY',            How to label the print output
```

Your printed output begins with one or more "separator pages" labeled with job name. You won't see these pages when you view your output using TSO/ISPF. They appear only to help personnel physically separate your job output from the output of other jobs at the printer. Here are some job name and accounting details:

//CSCJGJA   *Job name* is mandatory. The one to eight letters following the slashes will be printed on the separator page in large block letters. Generally (but not always—check your installation guidelines) when you submit a job via TSO, you code this name as your TSO user id (my TSO user id at DePaul University, for example, is CSCJGJ). In cases where you do not use your TSO user id as the job name, you must start the job name with a letter or @, $, or #; you can then use numbers, letters, or the symbols @, $, or # for the remaining seven characters of the job name.

   Notice that I coded a final letter ("A" in this case) after CSCJGJ, my TSO identifier. If you don't code this on the JOB statement, TSO will ask you to supply it when you submit the job. By changing this final letter you can make each job name different. That's important if you want to submit several jobs to run at the same time because MVS can execute only one job of a given name at a time (within a CLASS; see Section 6.5).

WCWC13DT   *Account.* MVS regards what you put here as optional, but local standards usually require you to code it a certain way. You may have to code a different account for jobs that you run for different work assignments or projects. The account information you code here is captured within the MVS System Management Facility (SMF), which logs everything done by MVS. Account can be made up of 1 to 142 bytes as determined by your installation.

'BIN 7-JANOSSY'   *Labeling and/or routing information.* This is optional to MVS, but you usually have to code it for practical reasons. For example, at DePaul University we provide 150 "bins" for print output. By putting "BIN 7" in my JOB labeling field, I am telling MVS to print "BIN 7" at the bottom of my job separator pages. The personnel running the mainframe printer will know to put my output in bin 7, where I will look for it. Each installation uses its own coding scheme for labeling/routing.

6.3 MVS Input and Output Queues

In the old days of the 1970s when I learned data processing, we prepared JCL on punch cards. Back then, submitting a job meant physically putting a deck of cards into a hopper and pressing a button to start feeding them through the "reader." The computer received a coded stream of electronic signals generated from the holes punched in the cards. The card reader could process only a few hundred cards a minute. This was much slower than the computer system itself could actually process the information (even then!), so information was read into a disk data set first. The system would quickly pick up the incoming JCL from the disk staging area after several jobs had been read in.

Now, using TSO, you submit your JCL for processing just by putting SUB on the command line while you are editing it. But as I showed you in Figure 1.1, the JCL still goes into a disk data set rather than being processed by MVS immediately. The disk data set is called the *input queue.* Everyone's JCL goes there first when it's submitted, and MVS quickly scans each set of JCL for syntax errors. JCL that's correct in syntax remains in the input queue; JCL with errors goes immediately to a different staging area called the *output queue,* which also contains the print output of successfully executed jobs.

The input and output queues are managed by software called Job Entry Subsystem (JES). JES comes in two versions: JES2, which most MVS computer systems use, and JES3, which is used by the very largest networks of mainframes. You can think of JES as a layer of software around MVS. You can give commands directly to JES using special control statements that you code before or after the JOB statement. I'll show you some of the JES2 and JES3 control statements at the end of this chapter. I'll discuss others in Chapter 9 when we look at printing features.

6.4 How MVS Picks Jobs for Execution

In a typical mainframe installation, hundreds or even thousands of sets of JCL (jobs) are usually submitted during the course of a day by perhaps hundreds of people located in different places. JCL that is syntactically correct remains in the input queue until MVS "picks it" for processing. MVS picks jobs for execution according to the CLASS you code on the JOB statement, such as CLASS=E. Coding job class is actually optional as far as MVS is concerned. If you omit it from your JOB statement, it defaults to CLASS=A. But what do these class letters mean?

Look at Figure 6.2. In it I show you how the input queue is actually segregated into different categories of jobs awaiting processing. The different categories are each identified by a single character code. This code is the CLASS.

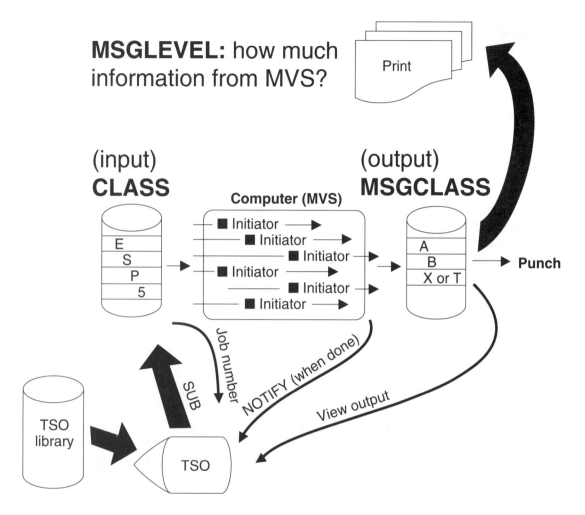

Figure 6.2   Input and Output Queues and Program Initiators

Jobs that you submit to MVS are "staged" in a disk data set called the ***input queue***. This queue is separated into categories by job CLASS, a locally established single-character code. A job in the input queue waits until it is picked up for execution by one of several program initiators. Print output from a job is staged to the ***output queue***, another disk data set. You can view output using TSO/ISPF function 3.8, SDSF, or other interactive software such as the "Flasher" utility.

6.5 CLASS and Program Initiators

Your installation establishes different class codes based on whatever criteria it chooses. Most installations establish a class like "E" for "express" jobs that use little computer time and only disk data sets. These jobs can be processed very quickly because they require no human intervention to find and mount tapes, so MVS can be set to give this class "picking" preference for execution.

Installations usually define other job CLASSes for large-scale jobs that require lots of processing time, jobs that use a few tapes, jobs that use many tapes, jobs that run CICS or IMS system software, and jobs that can be run during the night shift. The CLASS codes for these differ from one installation to another. As a programmer or end user new to an installation, one of the first things you will be given is a list of the job classes in local use. CLASS=A (the default if you don't code CLASS) may not even be a legitimate job class in your installation.

The job class mechanism works because of how MVS actually picks jobs for execution. MVS uses special programs called *program initiators* to do job picking. As a programmer or end user you can't control how many initiators MVS uses at any moment or what the initiators do. But it helps for you to understand what an initiator is and how the job picking process works.

6.6 Why Each Program Initiator Is Like a Nanny

In England you may see each child in some parks accompanied by a full time babysitter called a nanny. The nanny pushes a smaller child in a perambulator (a "pram," or stroller). When the child grows older and starts to walk, the nanny will surely hold his or her hand to cross major boulevards.

Each MVS program initiator shown in Figure 6.2 is a nanny. It "holds hands" with a program to get it through processing. A job on the input queue can't begin processing until an initiator picks it up. The initiator holds hands with the job it has picked for execution until that job finishes. Then the initiator becomes "free" and can go back to the input queue to pick up another job.

At any given time, MVS may be "running" 15 or more initiators, each holding hands or seeking to hold hands with one program at a time. Each initiator is governed by its own list of job classes from which it preferentially picks jobs for execution from the input queue.

For example, if initiator 1 becomes free, it consults its class list, which might be "EPASQ." This initiator will first look for a class E job awaiting processing. If no class E jobs are waiting, it will look for a class P job. If no class P jobs are waiting, it will look for a class A job. You can see that if no initiator carries a given job class in its selection list, a job in the input queue coded with that class will not be picked for execution. For example, if you code CLASS=C and there is no job class C defined in your installation, your job will just sit in the input queue forever.

Within a given class, initiators pick jobs for execution in descending order of their PRTY (priority), another job statement parameter.

6.7 The Computer Operator Manages Initiators

MVS expects a computer operator to be present at a special terminal near the system, called the "console." The computer operator manages the job mix on the system by managing the quantity and action of the program initiators. The computer operator can change the job class list for any initiator, allowing it to favor or discriminate against jobs of different classes. This is called "reconfiguring" the initiators. If the operator tells the initiators to stop picking more jobs from the input queue as they become free, the operator is "draining" the initiators.

Programmers and end users are not usually given access to the system console commands that reconfigure initiators. You probably can't even view the initiator class lists. The computer operator can change the CLASS of a job even after it's been submitted. Several initiators are typically set to pick first a high-priority job class code that is not widely publicized in an installation. The computer operator alone can switch an especially "hot" job into this class to make it start execution as soon as possible.

6.8 MSGCLASS: Print Classes and the Output Queue

From the discussion above, you know that CLASS divides the input queue into different categories. An analogous (but entirely unrelated) set of single-character codes also exists to divide the output queue into categories. On the JOB statement this is called MSGCLASS. You code MSGCLASS to tell MVS (and JES2/JES3) where and how you want your reporting from MVS to be printed. MSGCLASS=A traditionally sends your system output directly to the printer "local" to the computer system. Installations create for themselves other print class codes for different locations or different types of laser or impact printers. You usually code MSGCLASS=X or T (check your local standards) to hold system output in the output queue without printing so that you can view it using TSO.

6.9 MSGLEVEL

You can code MSGLEVEL to tell MVS how much of its reporting you want the system output to contain. The pattern for MSGLEVEL is MSGLEVEL= (a,b) and an example is MSGLEVEL=(1,1). The first number specifies what JCL statements are listed, and the second number indicates what types of allocation/deallocation messages are printed.

a = JCL statement printing:
  0 Print only the JOB statement
  1 Print JOB statement, JCL, and invoked proc JCL
  2 Print JOB statement and JCL only, no invoked procs

b = System messages:
  0 Print system messages only if the job abends
  1 Always print all messages

If you code MSGLEVEL=(1,1), you receive the maximum amount of MVS print. If you don't code MSGLEVEL, it defaults to an installation-defined value, often (1,1). You can code a shortened form, MSGLEVEL=1, if you just want to affect JCL statement printing.

6.10 PRTY and DPRTY (Priority)

Priority dictates the sequence in which MVS picks jobs for execution within their job class in the input queue. This is coded as PRTY=n, where "n" ranges from 0 to 15 if your installation uses JES2 or 0 to 14 under JES3. Priority 15 is at the "immediate attention" end of the spectrum for initiation, whereas 0 is given attention only after all other jobs with the same CLASS carrying higher priorities have been run.

PRTY just deals with job picking, not with the attention your job will get from MVS as it runs. Another parameter named DPRTY (*dispatch priority*) governs the way MVS allocates time to jobs that are executing. DPRTY is almost never available to programmers or end users. (DPRTY coding follows arcane rules, and I don't cover it. I'd suggest that you consult another Wiley book, *System 370/390 JCL* by Gary Brown, if you need more information about DPRTY.)

Installations often prohibit people from coding PRTY on the JOB statement; some even install extra JCL-scanning software to find it on their submitted JCL and cancel jobs on which it is coded. If you are permitted to code it, local guidelines usually exist concerning its use. Generally speaking, the higher priority you request for a job, the more you (or your corporate budget) will be billed for the job. Here is a typical service delivery and charging table from a commercial installation:

Priority	Guaranteed Initiation Time	Cost Charging Factor
2	1 week	.20
3	4 days	.30
4	2 days	.50
5	1 day	.70
6	6 hours	1.00
7	1 hour	2.00
8	30 minutes	3.00
9	15 minutes	4.00

For example, if processing costs $2.50 per second (this sounds like a lot, but it's pretty typical since a huge amount of work can be done in a second!), you would pay $2.50 per second for a job submitted with PRTY=6. You would expect to get this job to run within 6 hours. If you coded PRTY=7 on this job, it would start within one hour, but you would be billed $2.50 x 2.00 = $5.00 for each second of computer time it used.

MVS itself often automatically increases the priority of jobs waiting a long time in the input queue to give them a better chance of starting. You are ordinarily not billed for these types of priority increases because they are a part of the system's internal operation.

6.11 REGION

By default MVS establishes a limit as to how much memory any step of your job can use, often 1,024,000 bytes. You can change this by coding such as REGION=2048K. The "K" means "thousands of bytes," so this requests 2,048,000 bytes (two megabytes). You could also code REGION=2M to request two megabytes. If the software you are executing needs more memory than this limit, the step abends with a system completion code of 804 or 80A.

You don't ordinarily need to code REGION unless documentation for the software you are running tells you that it's necessary. In older times, we coded REGION to use less than the system default so more memory remained for other programs. Since 1973, when IBM began providing virtual storage memory management, each program has 16 megabytes or even much more memory available to it, without taking this away from other programs. Modern software often makes use of huge amounts of memory. You'll now see REGION coded more often for large values. The largest you can code it, on IBM's largest MVS/ESA systems, is REGION=2047M, which is 2,047,000,000 bytes!

You can also code REGION on individual EXEC statements. Coding on EXEC is more common. If you code REGION on both JOB and EXEC, what you put on the JOB statement limits the REGION parameter coded on any EXEC.

6.12 TIME

You can code TIME=(m,s) on the JOB statement, where "m" is minutes and "s" is seconds, to establish a time limit for the entire job. For example, TIME=(1,30) indicates a time limit of 1 minute 30 seconds. This is central processor time, not "wall" (elapsed) time, which can be much longer due to the slow pace of I/O operations and the sharing of the system with other jobs. To establish a time limit of less than a minute, you code TIME as TIME=(,s) which sets "s" seconds as the limit. The limit is approximate because MVS checks accumulated CPU time at intervals of several seconds.

There are two reasons why you might code TIME. One reason is to use it as a safeguard when you are testing a new program. If the program goes into a loop, it can run forever unless it is "timed out." Because CPU time costs about $2.50 or more per second, you can see that a program running wild during a test can really be an expensive mistake! Putting TIME on the EXEC for this program is usually better than putting it on JOB.

The second reason for coding TIME applies only to very special jobs, such as those that initiate TSO or CICS. Coding TIME=1440 takes off any MVS-monitored time limit and lets these jobs run continuously. *Don't code this!* If you run a job that enters a "wait state" and performs no activity for 30 minutes, it will be timed out with a system completion code of 522. TIME=1440 abandons wait state inactivity checking too.

6.13 TYPRUN

You can have MVS give your JCL a syntax check without having it attempt to run the job by coding TYPRUN=SCAN. You'll get all of the same error messages that you would in a real run. I've shown you this in Figure 6.1.

By coding parameters on separate lines, you can comment out this parameter or make it active very easily, as you see here:

```
//CSCJGJA JOB WCWC13DT,
//   'BIN 7-JANOSSY',
//   CLASS=E,
//   MSGCLASS=X,
//   MSGLEVEL=(1,1),
//   PRTY=6,
//   REGION=2048K,
//   TIME=(2,30),
//*  TYPRUN=SCAN,              the * "comments out" this parameter
//   NOTIFY=CSCJGJ
```

Some installations build or acquire JCL syntax-scanning software that does checking much like TYPRUN=SCAN. If you use TYPRUN=SCAN, just remember to make it inactive when you really do want to run the job. When you check valid JCL with TYPRUN=SCAN, it appears to finish execution in exactly the same way as JCL that was actually run!

6.14 NOTIFY

At your option you can code NOTIFY to have MVS send you a message when your job finishes. You code this in the form NOTIFY=CSCJGJ, where CSCJGJ is your TSO user-id. *Notice that here, unlike for the job name, you don't code any extra letter after your user-id.* To send this message MVS uses the ordinary TSO "send" facility, a crude and limited form of electronic mail.

6.15 Security Software Parameters

IBM designed some parameters of the JOB statement specifically for its own security software Resource Acquisition Control Facility (RACF). PASSWORD is used by competing security software also.

USER=   identifies a RACF "userid".

GROUP=   specifies a RACF security "group".

PASSWORD=   specifies a security system password; this is meaningful only for non-TSO submitted batch jobs and varies depending on the type of security software your installation uses.

6.16 JOB Parameters for Restarting a Failed Job

In addition to the commonly used JOB parameters, you may occasionally see or have to use certain others on the JOB statement when a job has failed and you have to restart it. Restarting a failed job involves some potentially tricky arrangements. I cover RESTART and RD in *Advanced MVS/ESA JCL Examples*, a companion to this book (John Wiley & Sons, Inc., 1993).

6.17 Rarely Used JOB Statement Parameters

As a programmer or end user you'll see the following JOB statement parameters infrequently or not at all, because they serve highly specialized purposes. You can skip over this section if you have limited time:

ADDRSPC=VIRT or ADDRSPC=REAL requests either virtual memory or real memory. The default is virtual memory—that is, a combination of real memory and high-speed disk storage. MVS manages virtual storage entirely on its own to make a program think it is always entirely in real memory. Virtual memory is not as fast as real memory but delivers satisfactory performance to almost all jobs. The use of REAL is usually prohibited to all but time-critical support software such as CICS.

COND=(0,LT) sets up a blanket condition code test that will be applied to each step of the job in advance of the COND testing coded on the steps. The condition is automatically tested before each step is allowed to execute; if the test is satisfied, the step is prevented from running. You'll more typically use COND on individual EXEC statements, as I explain in Chapter 7.

PERFORM=nnn is a value from 1 to 999 that puts the job into a specified "performance group." Performance groups segregate job processing to balance the workload of the system. Omitting this parameter lets it default to a locally defined value set by systems programmers, which is highly desired in almost all cases.

6.18 JES Control Statements

Your installation will use either JES2 or JES3 as an input/output handling subsystem associated with MVS. JCL was designed to communicate with MVS. As a feature grafted onto JCL, you can use a certain syntax of nonfunctional JCL statement to communicate to JES2 and JES3. The specific way in which you might use some of these statements varies from installation to installation according to locally established computer site names and print destinations. In this section I will give you a general overview of JES control statements so you will know how to recognize and interpret your local documentation.

Statement format varies between JES2 and JES3, but the idea is much the same. JES commands let you give instructions to the input/output subsystem, dealing with the computers in a network, input handling, and the handling of your job output.

6.19 JES2 Control Statement Overview

JES2 control statements start with /* followed by a special word. If you use the first two of these JES2 statements you have to put them before the JOB statement:

```
/*$COMMAND ...                  Issues a JES2 operator command
/*PRIORITY 6                    Same as coding PRTY=6 on JOB
//CSCJGJA JOB WCWC13DT,        ⎤
//   'BIN 7-JANOSSY',          ⎟
//   CLASS=E,                  ⎟
//   MSGCLASS=X,               ⎟
//   MSGLEVEL=(1,1),            ⎬  Ordinary JOB statement
//   PRTY=6,                   ⎟
//   REGION=2048K,             ⎟
//   TIME=(2,30),              ⎟
//*  TYPRUN=SCAN,              ⎟
//   NOTIFY=CSCJGJ             ⎦
/*JOBPARM PROCLIB=PROC08        Special proc library to use
/*MESSAGE HELLO WORLD           Message to operator when job is read in
/*ROUTE   PRINT R14             Sends job output to remote 14
/*SETUP   045361,087586         Asks library to find tapes to be used
```

Most JES2 statements have to come right after the JOB statement, and before any EXECs, and you can't continue them from one line to another. It helps to understand why the format of JES2 statements is a little fussy. Notice that the /* followed by the "magic word" used to recognize each statement consumes at the most ten bytes at the front of a statement (/*PRIORITY is the longest, at ten bytes). The system software that analyzes these statements looks at position 11 and beyond for whatever parameters you code on a JES2 control statement. Some of the other JES2 commands you might encounter include:

/*XEQ	node	*Routes the job to a different computer*
/*XMIT	node name	*Routes data to a different computer*
/*NETACCT	account	*Account number for this job*
/*OUTPUT	option	*Specifies up to 20 printing options*
/*NOTIFY	user-id	*Much like NOTIFY on the JOB statement*
/*SIGNON	...	*Remote station number in column 16*
/*SIGNOFF		*Disconnects a remote session*

You may not have to use any JES2 control statements in your JCL. I'll show you more about the common JES2 statements in Chapter 9 (printing).

6.20 JES3 Control Statement Overview

JES3 is a more complex subsystem than JES2. It's used to manage the work of up to eight mainframe computers. One of these machines acts as the global processor to schedule the work of all machines. The other machines are called main processors.

JES3 control statements start with //* and so appear to be ordinary comments. Except for the command entry JES3 statement //** you code them after the JOB statement. You can continue a JES3 statement from one line to another by using a comma at the end of a continued line, but unlike JCL you don't indent the subsequent lines:

```
//**VARY,54B,ONLINE                          |  A JES3 command statement
//CSCJGJA JOB WCWC13DT,
//    'BIN 7-JANOSSY',
//    CLASS=E,
//    MSGCLASS=X,
//    MSGLEVEL=(1,1),                            Ordinary JOB statement
//    PRTY=6,
//    REGION=2048K,
//    TIME=(2,30),
//*   TYPRUN=SCAN,
//    NOTIFY=CSCJGJ
//*MAIN ORG=BILOXI
//*FORMAT PR,                                 |  Single-line JES3 statement
```

```
//*DDNAME=STEP030.REPORT1,
//*DEST=BOSTON,
//*FORMS=1774,
//*COPIES=2
```

*A long JES3 control
statement continued
with commas*

As is the case with JES2, a lot of what you might have to code in the way of JES3 control statements depends on your installation. Here is a list of JES3 control statements:

`//*NETACCT ...`	*Account number for this job*
`//*ROUTE XEQ ...`	*Destination of the job for execution*
`//*MAIN ...`	*Processor requirements for job*
`//*FORMAT ...`	*Special requests for print handling*
`//*NET ...`	*Establishes dependencies between jobs*
`//*DATASET ...`	*Instream data to be spooled for a step*
`//*ENDATASET ...`	*Marks the end of instream data*
`//*PROCESS ...`	*Starts special processing requirements*
`//*ENDPROCESS ...`	*End of special processing requirements*
`//*OPERATOR ...`	*Lets you send a message to the operator*
`//*SIGNON ...`	*Begins a remote session*
`//*SIGNOFF`	*Ends a remote session*
`//*XMIT ...`	*Sends a job to another computer (node) but does not execute it*

Several JES3 control statements, such as //*MAIN, //*FORMAT, and //*NET, each have dozens of parameters and are commonly used in JES3 installations, whereas others, such as //*PROCESS, are used less often. If you need to code JES3 statements, check your locally generated installation documentation for specific computer site (node) names to be used and details of how to code them.

Chapter 6 Review
Mini-Glossary

CLASS= JOB class you want for MVS system output

MSGCLASS= Print class you want for MVS system output

TIME= JOB parameter to specify a processing time limit

REGION= JOB parameter to specify a memory limit

TYPRUN=SCAN An optional parameter that tells MVS to check your JCL for syntax but not execute it

JES2/JES3 Job Entry Subsystem version 2 or 3, which manages input and output functions on one or multiple computers

JES control statements Non-JCL statements starting with /* or //* that are used to communicate with the Job Entry Subsystem

Review Questions

1. Explain the four main things that a JOB statement does.
2. Explain how you will normally form your job name, including the purpose of the final job name letter.
3. Describe how the input queue is divided into categories and how you code one of these on the JOB statement.
4. Describe how the output queue is divided into categories and how you code one of these on the JOB statement.

Exercises

A. Take any JCL you have already used to run an exercise. Put TYPRUN=SCAN on its JOB statement and submit it. Examine the system output and explain what it tells you.

B. Code MSGLEVEL=(1,1) on the JOB statement in a previous exercise and run the job. Then change this to MSGLEVEL=(1,0) and compare the difference in system output between the runs. Make a third run with MSGLEVEL=(0,0) and compare its output to the first two runs.

Chapter Seven

THE EXEC STATEMENT IN DETAIL

You code one EXEC statement for each step of a job stream. The primary EXEC parameter is either PGM or PROC, which indicates what you want to execute at a given step. But a dozen other EXEC statement parameters also exist. Of these, you'll commonly find only REGION, TIME, COND, and PARM useful. In this chapter I'll show you how to use each of these, and I'll also explain what the less-useful EXEC parameters do.

7.1 Stepname on EXEC

An EXEC statement begins with a name of up to eight characters, the first of which must be a letter:

```
//STEP010   EXEC   PGM=IEBGENER
```

By convention, step names are often formed starting with the letters STEP followed by a three- or four-digit number. It's also common to increment the number by tens so that steps can be inserted into JCL later if necessary. Under another popular convention some people code step names as letters, for example:

```
//STEPA    EXEC   PGM=IEBGENER
```

Either of these conventions makes it easier to find information about your steps in MVS job reporting. The step name is also important because subsequent steps use it to refer back to earlier steps.

7.2 EXEC PGM or PROC?

The simplest EXEC statement has just a step name and uses either PGM=
or PROC=. You can code either PGM or PROC, not both, on a given EXEC:

```
//STEP010   EXEC   PGM=IEBGENER      Execute a program
//STEP010   EXEC   PROC=COBUCLG      Execute a cataloged procedure
//STEP010   EXEC   COBUCLG           Execute a cataloged procedure
```

If you don't code PGM= or PROC=, MVS acts as if you had coded PROC=.
Figure 7.1 helps you realize that the thing you are trying to execute is
always a member of a library.

7.3 When You Code EXEC PGM=...

The name you code after PGM= is the name under which the machine
language for a program is stored in a machine language (load module) library. When you are executing a utility program, you don't have to take
any special action to tell MVS the name of the library where the program
load module is housed. The default load module library is named
SYS1.LINKLIB, and IBM utility programs are usually stored there. Like most
installations, your installation has probably also created additional load
module libraries and made MVS aware of them.

It's not often of interest, but you can also create a load module library of your own. In Figure 7.1,
you see a simplified picture of my own load module library, named
CSCJGJ.CSC.LOADLIB. In Chapter 16 I explain how you can create such a
library and how you tell MVS about it using a //JOBLIB or //STEPLIB
statement in your job.

It's not often of interest, but you can also use a referback to specify
program name on an EXEC. In this case, for example, the EXEC indicates
that the machine language module to be executed was created in prior step
//LKED at DDname //SYSLMOD:

```
//GO   EXEC   PGM=*.LKED.SYSLMOD
```

You will see this technique used in compile/link/go procs.

7.4 When You Code EXEC PROC=...

When you code PROC=name (or omit PGM= and PROC=), the name you
code is the name under which "packaged" JCL is stored in a JCL (procedure)
library. The default procedure library is SYS1.PROCLIB. IBM-supplied
procs for common processes such as compile/link/go are usually stored

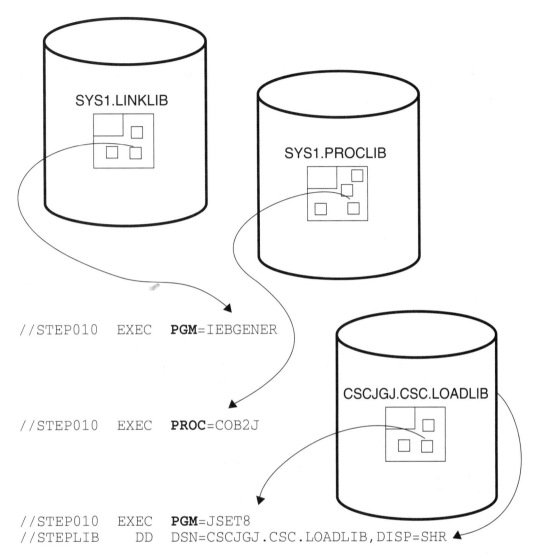

Figure 7.1 EXEC Always Cites a Member Name

When you execute a program by coding EXEC **PGM**=**name** you cite a member of a load module library (partitioned data set) such as SYS1.LINKLIB. When you execute a procedure ("canned" JCL) by coding EXEC **PROC**=**name** or simply EXEC **name** you cite a member of a procedure library such as SYS1.PROCLIB.

there. Your installation has probably created additional proc libraries and made MVS aware of them.

You may be able to create a proc library of your own. In Chapter 18 I'll show you how to tell MVS about such a "private" proc library using the /*JOBPARM PROC (JES2) or //*MAIN PROC (JES3) statements. MVS/ESA Release 4 gives you the new statement type JCCLIB to do this, as Chapter 18 also demonstrates.

7.5 TIME: Time Limit for the Step

Coding TIME on an EXEC is optional. If you code it, it's usually for safety, to set an upper limit on the amount of processing time a program can use. For example, this sets a limit of six seconds on the execution of a program named SUMITUP:

```
//STEP030   EXEC   PGM=SUMITUP,TIME=(,6)
```

You code TIME on an EXEC in exactly the same format as on the JOB statement: TIME=(m,s), where "m" is minutes and "s" is seconds. On a modern mainframe, a huge amount of processing can be done in six seconds. A malfunctioning program in an endless loop involving printing can output 50,000 or more lines in this relatively short period of time. If you omit coding TIME, each step may run up to a time limit defined by your installation for the job class used for the job, or the time limit coded on the JOB statement. Your installation default time allocation might be five minutes or more.

If a program runs long enough to exceed its time limit (regardless of whether the limit is due to your coding TIME or your installation's default time limit), the step fails with a system completion code of 322 (see Appendix E).

7.6 REGION: Memory Limit for the Step

You code REGION on an EXEC to tell MVS how much memory the program you are executing can use:

```
//STEP030   EXEC   PGM=SUMITUP,TIME=(,6),REGION=2048K
```

"K" stands for kilobytes (thousands of bytes) while "M" means megabytes. This says the same thing as above:

```
//STEP030   EXEC   PGM=SUMITUP,TIME=(,6),REGION=2M
```

If you don't code REGION, MVS uses an installation-defined default value such as 1024K. If you code REGION on the JOB statement and on EXECs, the JOB limit overrides any REGION that's larger.

In earlier days it was common to code REGION smaller than 1024K to avoid acquiring more memory than a program actually needed. But coding REGION to minimize memory use had relevance only before 1973, when virtual storage became a feature of MVS. You now generally don't code REGION unless a particular step uses especially large input/output buffers due to large block sizes, specifies several I/O buffers, or uses an internal sort. If a program can't get as much memory as it needs, the step fails with a system completion code of 804 or 80A, as I documented in Appendix E.

7.7 PARM and COND Overview

Two parameters of EXEC—PARM and COND—are especially useful. But each of these requires more than a brief explanation. In the following sections I demonstrate both of these to you. Before doing that, however, I think it's useful for you to see an example of real JCL that reviews things I've already told you about EXEC and also demonstrates PARM and COND in actual use.

Figure 7.2 is the COB2J procedure that you have already seen in Chapter 5. In this copy of it I have highlighted the EXEC statements at its three steps: //COB2 (compile), //LKED (linkage edit), and //GO (program execution). I'll refer to this figure in connection with both PARM and COND.

7.8 What PARM Does and How It Does It

PARM stands for "parameter." This word means "an input value that controls something." PARM gives you the ability to feed up to 100 bytes of information to a program by putting it on the EXEC statement. The information is usually used by the program to control some aspect of its operation.

When, for example, you code PARM='ABCDEFG' on an EXEC statement, MVS allocates a special 102-byte segment of memory. It parses the characters you have coded between the apostrophes after PARM= and counts them. MVS then expresses this count as a 16-bit signed binary number and puts that count into the first 2 bytes of the 102-byte memory segment. It copies the characters (ABCDEFG in this case) into the memory segment starting at the third byte, after the character count. Finally, MVS makes available to the program being executed the address at which the

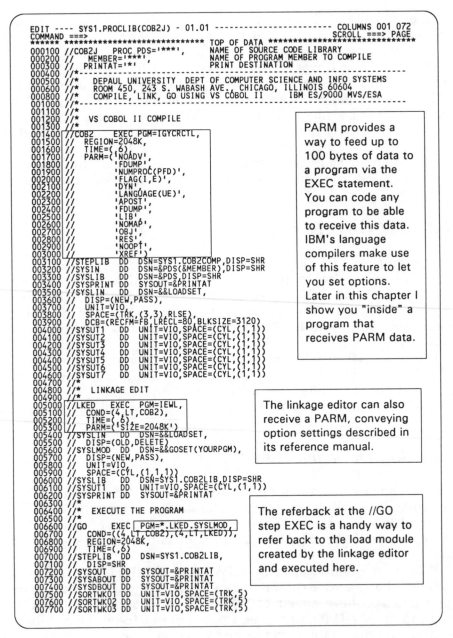

```
EDIT ---- SYS1.PROCLIB(COB2J) - 01.01 --------------------- COLUMNS 001 072
COMMAND ===>                                                  SCROLL ===> PAGE
****** *********************************** TOP OF DATA ***********************
000100 //COB2J    PROC PDS='***',          NAME OF SOURCE CODE LIBRARY
000200 //    MEMBER='***',                 NAME OF PROGRAM MEMBER TO COMPILE
000300 //    PRINTAT='*',                  PRINT DESTINATION
000400 //*-----------------------------------------------------------------
000500 //*    DEPAUL UNIVERSITY DEPT OF COMPUTER SCIENCE AND INFO SYSTEMS
000600 //*    ROOM 450, 243 S. WABASH AVE.  CHICAGO, ILLINOIS 60604
000800 //*    COMPILE, LINK, GO USING VS COBOL II    IBM ES/9000 MVS/ESA
001000 //*-----------------------------------------------------------------
001100 //*
001200 //*    VS COBOL II COMPILE
001300 //*
001400 //COB2     EXEC PGM=IGYCRCTL,
001500 //    REGION=2048K,
001600 //    TIME=(,6),
001700 //    PARM=('NOADV',
001800 //          'FDUMP',
001900 //          'NUMPROC(PFD)',
002000 //          'FLAG(I,E)',
002100 //          'DYN',
002200 //          'LANGUAGE(UE)',
002300 //          'APOST',
002400 //          'FDUMP',
002500 //          'LIB',
002600 //          'NOMAP',
002700 //          'OBJ',
002800 //          'RES',
002900 //          'NOOPT',
003000 //          'XREF'),
003100 //STEPLIB  DD  DSN=SYS1.COB2COMP,DISP=SHR
003200 //SYSIN    DD  DSN=&PDS(&MEMBER),DISP=SHR
003300 //SYSLIB   DD  DSN=&PDS,DISP=SHR
003400 //SYSPRINT DD  SYSOUT=&PRINTAT
003500 //SYSLIN   DD  DSN=&&LOADSET,
003600 //    DISP=(NEW,PASS),
003700 //    UNIT=VIO,
003800 //    SPACE=(TRK,(3,3),RLSE),
003900 //    DCB=(RECFM=FB,LRECL=80,BLKSIZE=3120)
004000 //SYSUT1   DD  UNIT=VIO,SPACE=(CYL,(1,1))
004100 //SYSUT2   DD  UNIT=VIO,SPACE=(CYL,(1,1))
004200 //SYSUT3   DD  UNIT=VIO,SPACE=(CYL,(1,1))
004300 //SYSUT4   DD  UNIT=VIO,SPACE=(CYL,(1,1))
004400 //SYSUT5   DD  UNIT=VIO,SPACE=(CYL,(1,1))
004500 //SYSUT6   DD  UNIT=VIO,SPACE=(CYL,(1,1))
004600 //SYSUT7   DD  UNIT=VIO,SPACE=(CYL,(1,1))
004700 //*
004800 //*    LINKAGE EDIT
004900 //*
005000 //LKED     EXEC PGM=IEWL,
005100 //    COND=(4,LT,COB2),
005200 //    TIME=(,6)
005300 //    PARM=('SIZE=2048K',
005400 //SYSLIN   DD  DSN=&&LOADSET,
005500 //    DISP=(OLD,DELETE),
005600 //SYSMOD   DD  DSN=&&GOSET(YOURPGM),
005700 //    DISP=(NEW,PASS),
005800 //    UNIT=VIO,
005900 //    SPACE=(CYL,(1,1,1))
006000 //SYSLIB   DD  DSN=SYS1.COB2LIB,DISP=SHR
006100 //SYSUT1   DD  UNIT=VIO,SPACE=(CYL,(1,1))
006200 //SYSPRINT DD  SYSOUT=&PRINTAT
006300 //*
006400 //*    EXECUTE THE PROGRAM
006500 //*
006600 //GO       EXEC PGM=*.LKED.SYSLMOD,
006700 //    COND=((4,LT,COB2),(4,LT,LKED)),
006800 //    REGION=2048K,
006900 //    TIME=(,6)
007000 //STEPLIB  DD  DSN=SYS1.COB2LIB,
007100 //    DISP=SHR
007200 //SYSOUT   DD  SYSOUT=&PRINTAT
007300 //SYSABOUT DD  SYSOUT=&PRINTAT
007400 //SYSDBOUT DD  SYSOUT=&PRINTAT
007500 //SORTWK01 DD  UNIT=VIO,SPACE=(TRK,5)
007600 //SORTWK02 DD  UNIT=VIO,SPACE=(TRK,5)
007700 //SORTWK03 DD  UNIT=VIO,SPACE=(TRK,5)
```

PARM provides a way to feed up to 100 bytes of data to a program via the EXEC statement. You can code any program to be able to receive this data. IBM's language compilers make use of this feature to let you set options. Later in this chapter I show you "inside" a program that receives PARM data.

The linkage editor can also receive a PARM, conveying option settings described in its reference manual.

The referback at the //GO step EXEC is a handy way to refer back to the load module created by the linkage editor and executed here.

Figure 7.2 How the COB2J Proc Uses PARM, COND, and TIME

COB2J is my locally customized version of COB2UCLG, the IBM compile/link/go proc for VS COBOL II. I installed this at DePaul University, and we use it for several COBOL programming courses. PARM is used to send controlling data into programs such as a compiler.

102-byte segment of memory is located. If the program being executed has been coded with appropriate logic to receive the address of the PARM data segment in memory, it can examine this memory. The program can make any use of the passed data that it wishes.

Compiler programs make extensive use of the PARM feature because each compiler has a number of settings you can turn on to produce cross-references and other debugging and documentation aids. In Figure 7.2 you see my coding for several VS COBOL II compiler parameters in my COB2J proc. These tell the compiler to produce a sorted cross-reference and activate other features. The PARM feature is just an "information pipe" into a program such as the compiler.

MVS doesn't know or care what you code as the PARM string on any EXEC. But MVS is fussy about the way you continue PARM coding! Figure 7.2 shows you the correct syntax. The parentheses around the apostrophes in the PARM aren't really required unless you have to continue a PARM string to a second line.

7.9 A Practical PARM Example

The WORKERS data listed in Figure 2.9 contains one record for each employee of a department store. I'm now going to use this data with a COBOL program named PARMDEMO. This program reads the data and lists just the records carrying an "hours worked" value within a specified range. But the selection range is not hardcoded in the program. The low and high ends of the "hours worked" range come into the program via a PARM, and so does the title to be used on the report the program produces!

Figure 7.3 shows you a job stream that sorts the WORKERS data into descending order of hours worked. Then, at //STEP020, the job stream executes the COB2J proc to compile, link, and run PARMDEMO with an hours worked range of 40.1 through 99.9. This is a listing of employees who worked more than 40 hours and are being paid overtime. Finally, //STEP030 does the compile, link, and run again, this time with an hours worked range of 5 to 30 hours. (It's inefficient to recompile and re-link the program, but I haven't yet shown you how to save the machine language load module of a program for re-execution. I'll show you how to do that in Chapter 16.)

Figure 7.4 lists the source code of PARMDEMO. Use this as a model for similar applications of your own. If you work in PL/I, C, or Assembler, you can find similar examples in *Advanced MVS/ESA JCL Examples* (Jim Janossy, John Wiley & Sons, Inc., 1993).

```
EDIT ---- CSCJGJ.CSC.CNTL(E1PARM) - 01.00 -------------------- COLUMNS 001 072
COMMAND ===>                                                SCROLL ===> HALF
***** ********************************* TOP OF DATA *********************************
000100 //CSCJGJA   JOB 1,'BIN 7 JANOSSY',CLASS=A,MSGCLASS=X,MSGLEVEL=(1,1),
000200 //   NOTIFY=CSCJGJ
000300 //*
000400 //*   THIS JCL IS STORED AT CSCJGJ.CSC.CNTL(E1PARM)
000500 //*
000600 //*************************************************************************
000700 //*                                                                      *
000800 //*   SORT WORKER DATA DESCENDING BY HOURS WORKED                        *
000900 //*                                                                      *
001000 //*************************************************************************
001100 //STEP010   EXEC  PGM=SORT
001200 //SYSOUT      DD   SYSOUT=*
001300 //SORTWK01    DD   UNIT=SYSDA,SPACE=(CYL,1)
001400 //SORTWK02    DD   UNIT=SYSDA,SPACE=(CYL,1)
001500 //SORTIN      DD   DSN=CSCJGJ.CSC.CNTL(WORKERS),DISP=SHR
001600 //SORTOUT     DD   DSN=&&WORKERS,
001700 //   UNIT=SYSDA,
001800 //   DISP=(NEW,PASS,DELETE),
001900 //   DCB=(RECFM=FB,LRECL=80,BLKSIZE=3840),
002000 //   SPACE=(TRK,1)
002100 //SYSIN       DD   *                              SORTING
002200     SORT FIELDS=(28,3,ZD,D)                <=== INSTRUCTIONS
002300 /*
002400 //*
002500 //*************************************************************************
002600 //*                                                                      *
002700 //*   COMPILE, LINK, AND RUN PARMDEMO LISTING PROGRAM                     *
002800 //*                                                                      *
002900 //*************************************************************************
003000 //STEP020   EXEC  COB2J,
003100 //   PDS='CSCJGJ.CSC.COBOL',
003200 //   MEMBER='PARMDEMO'
003300 //   PARM.GO='401-999,OVERTIME REPORT'           ⟵ a
003400 //GO.WORKERS   DD  DSN=&&WORKERS,DISP=SHR
003500 //GO.WORKREPT  DD  SYSOUT=*
003600 //*
003700 //*************************************************************************
003800 //*                                                                      *
003900 //*   RUN ANOTHER (DIFFERENT) REPORT USING A DIFFERENT PARM              *
004000 //*                                                                      *
004100 //*************************************************************************
004200 //STEP030   EXEC  COB2J,
004300 //   PDS='CSCJGJ.CSC.COBOL',
004400 //   MEMBER='PARMDEMO'
004500 //   PARM.GO='050-300,5 HR TO 30 HR WORKERS'     ⟵ b
004600 //GO.WORKERS   DD  DSN=&&WORKERS,DISP=SHR
004700 //GO.WORKREPT  DD  SYSOUT=*
004800 //
```

```
**********************************************************
OVERTIME REPORT              LO=40.1  HI=99.9    PAGE    1
**********************************************************

a  33483  CAROL INA          53.0  REMODELING SUPPLIES
   39321  AL ABAMA           42.0  WOMENS CLOTHING
   21256  WILLY NILLY        40.2  CASHIERS OFFICE

   RECORDS READ        16
   RECORDS LISTED       3
```

```
**********************************************************
5 HR TO 30 HR WORKERS        LO=05.0  HI=30.0    PAGE    1
**********************************************************

b  21310  ARKAN SHAW         30.0  HARDWARE
   21307  DELLA WARE         24.6  FURNITURE
   33102  CAL IFORNIA        20.0  TRAVEL DEPARTMENT
   21668  MOE ZOORI          17.9  PLUMBING SUPPLIES
   33480  D. TOUR            16.0  WOMENS CLOTHING

   RECORDS READ        16
   RECORDS LISTED       5
```

Figure 7.3 Output of a PARM-Driven Reporting Program

```
000100 IDENTIFICATION DIVISION.
000200 PROGRAM-ID.     PARMDEMO.
000300 AUTHOR.         J JANOSSY.
000400*REMARKS.        READS WORKERS DATA AND LIST RECORDS MEETING
000500*                SELECTION CRITERIA CONVEYED ON PARM:
000600*
000700*                PARM='HHH-HHH,REPORT TITLE              '
000800*                      === === ----------------------------
000900*                      LO  HI      28 CHARACTER TITLE
001000*                      ----------------
001100*                      HRS WORKED RANGE
001200*
001300 ENVIRONMENT DIVISION.
001400 INPUT-OUTPUT SECTION.
001500 FILE-CONTROL.
001600     SELECT WORKERS-FILE         ASSIGN TO WORKERS.
001700     SELECT WORKERS-REPORT       ASSIGN TO WORKREPT.
001800*
001900 DATA DIVISION.
002000 FILE SECTION.
002100*
002200 FD  WORKERS-FILE
002300     BLOCK CONTAINS O RECORDS
002400     RECORD CONTAINS 80 CHARACTERS.
002500 01  WORKERS-REC.
002600     05 WR-EMP-ID-NUMBER          PIC X(5).
002700     05 FILLER                    PIC X(1).
002800     05 WR-EMPLOYEE-NAME.
002900        10 WR-EMP-LAST-NAME       PIC X(11).
003000        10 WR-EMP-FIRST-NAME      PIC X(10).
003100     05 WR-HOURS-WORKED           PIC 99V9.
003200     05 WR-DEPARTMENT             PIC X(20).
003300     05 FILLER                    PIC X(30).
003400*
003500 FD  WORKERS-REPORT
003600     BLOCK CONTAINS O RECORDS
003700     RECORD CONTAINS 133 CHARACTERS.
003800 01  WORKERS-REPORT-LINE          PIC X(133).
003900*
004000 WORKING-STORAGE SECTION.
004100 01  WS-EOF-FLAG                  PIC X(1)  VALUE 'M'.
004200     88 WS-END-OF-FILE                      VALUE 'E'.
004300 01  WS-RECORDS-READ              PIC S9(5) VALUE +0.
004400 01  WS-RECORDS-LISTED            PIC S9(5) VALUE +0.
004500 01  WS-PAGE-COUNT                PIC S9(5) VALUE +0.
004600 01  WS-LINES-REMAINING           PIC S9(5).
004700*
004800 01  R1-BORDER                    PIC X(61) VALUE ALL '*'.
004900*
005000 01  R1-PAGEINFO-LINE.
005100     05 FILLER                    PIC X(1).
005200     05 R1-PAGEINFO-TITLE         PIC X(28).
005300     05 FILLER                    PIC X(5)  VALUE ' LO='.
005400     05 R1-PAGEINFO-LO            PIC 99.9.
005500     05 FILLER                    PIC X(5)  VALUE ' HI='.
005600     05 R1-PAGEINFO-HI            PIC 99.9.
005700     05 FILLER                    PIC X(4)  VALUE SPACES.
005800     05 FILLER                    PIC X(5)  VALUE 'PAGE '.
005900     05 R1-PAGEINFO-PAGE-NUM      PIC ZZZZ9.
006000*
006100 01  REPORT-LINE.
006200     05 FILLER                    PIC X(1).
006300     05 RL-EMP-ID-NUMBER          PIC X(5).
006400     05 FILLER                    PIC X(2)  VALUE SPACES.
006500     05 RL-EMPLOYEE-NAME          PIC X(22).
006600     05 FILLER                    PIC X(2)  VALUE SPACES.
006700     05 RL-HOURS-WORKED           PIC ZZ.9.
006800     05 FILLER                    PIC X(2)  VALUE SPACES.
006900     05 RL-DEPARTMENT             PIC X(20).
007000*
007100 01  SUMMARY-LINE.
007200     05 FILLER                    PIC X(1)  VALUE SPACE.
007300     05 SL-MESSAGE                PIC X(15).
007400     05 SL-COUNT                  PIC ZZ,ZZ9.
007500
007600 LINKAGE SECTION.
007700 01  USER-PARM.
007800     05 UP-LENGTH                 PIC S9(4) COMP.
007900     05 UP-DATA.
008000        10 UP-HRS-LO-RANGE        PIC 99V9.
008100        10 FILLER                 PIC X(1).
008200        10 UP-HRS-HI-RANGE        PIC 99V9.
008300        10 FILLER                 PIC X(1).
008400        10 UP-TITLE               PIC X(28).
```

These comments document the nature of the PARM data that the program expects to receive from MVS via the EXEC statement

You define in the LINKAGE SECTION the nature of the PARM data to be received by the program from MVS

Figure 7.4 PARMDEMO: A Program That Receives and Uses a PARM

```
008500/
008600 PROCEDURE DIVISION USING USER-PARM.
008700 0000-MAINLINE.
008800     PERFORM 1000-BOP.
008900     PERFORM 2000-PROCESS
009000        UNTIL WS-END-OF-FILE.
009100     PERFORM 3000-EOJ.
009200     STOP RUN.
009300*
009400 1000-BOP.
009500     IF UP-LENGTH = +0
009600        DISPLAY '*** PARM MISSING ON EXEC, REPORTED ABORTED! ***'
009700        STOP RUN.
009800     IF UP-HRS-LO-RANGE NOT NUMERIC
009900     OR UP-HRS-HI-RANGE NOT NUMERIC
010000        DISPLAY UP-DATA
010100        DISPLAY '*** BAD PARM DATA ON EXEC, REPORT ABORTED! ***'
010200        STOP RUN.
010300*
010400     MOVE UP-HRS-LO-RANGE TO R1-PAGEINFO-LO.
010500     MOVE UP-HRS-HI-RANGE TO R1-PAGEINFO-HI.
010600     MOVE UP-TITLE TO R1-PAGEINFO-TITLE.
010700*
010800     OPEN  INPUT WORKERS-FILE  OUTPUT WORKERS-REPORT.
010900     PERFORM 2900-NEWPAGE.
011000     PERFORM 2700-READ.
011100*
011200 2000-PROCESS.
011300     IF WR-HOURS-WORKED NOT < UP-HRS-LO-RANGE
011400     AND WR-HOURS-WORKED NOT > UP-HRS-HI-RANGE
011500        PERFORM 2100-LIST-THE-RECORD.
011600     PERFORM 2700-READ.
011700*
011800 2100-LIST-THE-RECORD.
011900     MOVE WR-EMP-ID-NUMBER      TO RL-EMP-ID-NUMBER.
012000     MOVE SPACES TO RL-EMPLOYEE-NAME.
012100     STRING WR-EMP-FIRST-NAME  DELIMITED BY SPACE
012200        ' '                    DELIMITED BY SIZE
012300        WR-EMP-LAST-NAME       DELIMITED BY SPACE
012400        INTO RL-EMPLOYEE-NAME.
012500     MOVE WR-HOURS-WORKED      TO RL-HOURS-WORKED.
012600     MOVE WR-DEPARTMENT        TO RL-DEPARTMENT.
012700     IF WS-LINES-REMAINING < +1
012800        PERFORM 2900-NEWPAGE.
012900     WRITE WORKERS-REPORT-LINE FROM REPORT-LINE
013000        AFTER ADVANCING 1 LINES.
013100     ADD +1 TO WS-RECORDS-LISTED.
013200     SUBTRACT +1 FROM WS-LINES-REMAINING.
013300*
013400 2700-READ.
013500     READ WORKERS-FILE
013600        AT END
013700           SET WS-END-OF-FILE TO TRUE
013800        NOT AT END
013900           ADD +1 TO WS-RECORDS-READ.
014000*
014100 2900-NEWPAGE.
014200     ADD +1 TO WS-PAGE-COUNT.
014300     MOVE WS-PAGE-COUNT TO R1-PAGEINFO-PAGE-NUM.
014400     WRITE WORKERS-REPORT-LINE FROM R1-BORDER
014500        AFTER ADVANCING PAGE.
014600     WRITE WORKERS-REPORT-LINE FROM R1-PAGEINFO-LINE
014700        AFTER ADVANCING 1 LINES.
014800     WRITE WORKERS-REPORT-LINE FROM R1-BORDER
014900        AFTER ADVANCING 1 LINES.
015000     MOVE SPACES TO WORKERS-REPORT-LINE.
015100     WRITE WORKERS-REPORT-LINE
015200        AFTER ADVANCING 2 LINES.
015300     MOVE 50 TO WS-LINES-REMAINING.
015400*
015500 3000-EOJ.
015600     MOVE 'RECORDS READ'     TO SL-MESSAGE
015700     MOVE WS-RECORDS-READ    TO SL-COUNT.
015800     WRITE WORKERS-REPORT-LINE FROM SUMMARY-LINE
015900        AFTER ADVANCING 2 LINES.
016000*
016100     MOVE 'RECORDS LISTED'   TO SL-MESSAGE
016200     MOVE WS-RECORDS-LISTED  TO SL-COUNT.
016300     WRITE WORKERS-REPORT-LINE FROM SUMMARY-LINE
016400        AFTER ADVANCING 1 LINES.
016500*
016600     CLOSE  WORKERS-FILE  WORKERS-REPORT.
```

This gains "addressability" to the LINKAGE SECTION

Validate the PARM data

If the PARM data is good, use it

These statements are the "filter" that selects records based on PARM data

SET (condition name) and **NOT AT END** are 1985 COBOL features provided by VS COBOL II. For more information on them, see *VS COBOL II Highlights and Techniques* (Janossy, John Wiley & Sons, Inc., 1992)

Figure 7.4   *(Continued)*

7.10 Sending a PARM Into a Program Through a Proc

When you execute a program load module (machine language) directly and supply a PARM to it, you code just the word PARM on the EXEC, followed by the PARM data:

```
//STEP020  EXEC  PGM=PARMDEMO,
//  PARM='401-999,OVERTIME REPORT'
```

In Figure 7.3, you see the PARM coded a bit differently. Here I am actually executing a cataloged procedure (proc) that has three steps, and only the third of those steps (//GO within the proc) executes the program intended to receive the PARM:

```
//STEP020  EXEC  PROC=COB2J,
//      PDS='CSCJGJ.CSC.COBOL',
//   MEMBER='PARMDEMO',
//   PARM.GO='401-999,OVERTIME REPORT'
```

In this code, PDS and MEMBER are supplying values for symbolic parameters &PDS and &MEMBER in the COB2J proc itself. PARM.GO follows the pattern *PARM.procstepname.*

7.11 Sending PARM Data Into the Compiler

As a final example of JCL related to PARMs, I want to show you how to code JCL to execute a compile proc supplying a new PARM to set its options. When you do this, you have to supply a complete replacement PARM.

Figure 7.5a shows you a versatile way to execute a VS COBOL compile/link/go proc such as IBM's standard COBUCLG. The several lines of coding starting with PARM.COB supply a complete replacement PARM string to the compiler at the //COB step. I like this continued-line coding style because I can document each line and can turn a given compiler parm option off just by commenting it out. VS COBOL II uses different PARM values than does VS COBOL. Figure 7.5b shows you JCL in continued-line format suited to the VS COBOL II compiler and IBM's COB2UCLG proc. (Both of these figures are from another of my books, *VS COBOL II: Highlights and Techniques,* published by John Wiley & Sons in 1992.)

```
EDIT --- CSCJGJ.CSC.CNTL(A1OLD) - 01.01 -------------------- COLUMNS 001 072
COMMAND ===>                                                  SCROLL ===> PAGE
***** **************************** TOP OF DATA ******************************
000001 //CSCJGJA   JOB 1,'BIN 7 JANOSSY',MSGCLASS=X,MSGLEVEL=(1,1),
000002 // NOTIFY=CSCJGJ
000003 //*
000004 //*    THIS JCL = CSCJGJ.CSC.CNTL(A1OLD)
000005 //*
000006 //STEPA    EXEC PROC=COBUCLG,
000007 // PARM.COB=('SIZE=1024K',
000008 //           'STATE',
000009 //           'FLOW=30',
000010 //           'SXR',
000011 //           'LIB',
000012 //           'DYN',
000013 //           'DMAP',
000014 //           'APOST',
000015 //           'MIGR'),
000016 //        PDS='CSCJGJ.CSC.COBOL',
000017 //    MEMBER='A1OLD'
```

COBUCLG is the standard IBM proc to process VS COBOL programs. When you override the compiler PARM this way you have to replace the entire PARM.

(a)

```
EDIT ---- A1092JJ.LIB.JCL(A1NEW) - 01.02 -------------------- COLUMNS 001 072
COMMAND ===>                                                  SCROLL ===> PAGE
***** **************************** TOP OF DATA ******************************
000001 //A1092JJA   JOB (1092,COB2),'JANOSSY',CLASS=A,MSGCLASS=X,
000002 // NOTIFY=A1092JJ
000003 //*
000004 //* THIS JCL = A1092JJ.LIB.JCL(A1NEW)
000005 //*
000006 //STEPA    EXEC COB2UCLG,
000007 // PARM.COB2=('NOADV',
000008 //            'NOCMPR2',
000009 //            'DATA(31)',
000010 //            'DYN',
000011 //            'FASTSRT',
000012 //            'LANGUAGE(UE)',
000013 //            'NUMPROC(PFD)',
000014 //            'NOMAP')
000015 //COB2.SYSIN  DD  DSN=A1092JJ.LIB.COBOL(A1NEW),DISP=SHR
000016 //GO.TICKDATA DD  DSN=A1092JJ.LIB.JCL(TICKDATA),DISP=SHR
000017 //GO.TICKLIST DD  SYSOUT=*
000018 //GO.SYSOUT   DD  SYSOUT=*
000019 //
```

COB2UCLG is the standard IBM proc for VS COBOL II. You can override the compiler PARM or use the PROCESS statement to change compiler parameters.

(b)

Figure 7.5 Sending PARMs into VS COBOL and VS COBOL II Compilers

(a) You can supply a new PARM to set the options of the VS COBOL compiler by providing a replacement PARM when you invoke proc COBUCLG. (b) IBM's VS COBOL II compiler uses different PARM values from VS COBOL. (Reprinted by permission of the publisher from James Janossy, *VS COBOL II: Highlights and Techniques*, John Wiley & Sons, 1992.)

7.12 Background of the COND Parameter

Probably no single thing within all of MVS/JCL has as notorious a reputation as the COND parameter of EXEC. The purpose of COND is actually quite simple. Once you understand this purpose, using COND becomes for you, if not completely straightforward, at least workable. COND exists for only two reasons:

1. To let you define conditions under which you want a step of a normally executing job to be *shut off*. You code this in the form COND= (4,LT,COB) or COND=(4,LT).
2. To let you tell MVS to process a step even if a previous step in the job has already abended, or only if a previous step abended. Ordinarily, MVS would throw out the whole job when a step abends and ignore all steps that follow. You code this in the form COND=EVEN or COND=ONLY.

This is all that was in the minds of the designers of JCL, and therefore this is all you can do with COND. JCL is not a language capable of much decision making. You can't, for example, use COND to define conditions under which a step *will* execute. You can't define a loop in JCL to make a step execute more than once, and you can't branch forward or backward. All you can do is shut steps off.

Before even the limited capabilities of COND make much sense, though, you have to understand how any program has the ability to communicate to other programs using the COND CODE, which some languages also call the **return code.**

7.13 Why a Program Sets Its COND CODE

Any program that you execute has the ability to leave behind a number in the range 0 through 4095 when it finishes execution (the upper limit applies because the value is stored as a 12-bit number). MVS will preserve this number and make it visible in its system reporting. This is the value that appears after COND CODE for every step. Every step has its own COND CODE value. At its simplest, COND CODE can represent communication from the program to the outside world. Look at Appendix D and you'll see the meanings various IBM utility programs associate with their COND CODE values.

The number printed as COND CODE has no inherent meaning to MVS; that is, leaving behind a nonzero COND CODE does not automatically make

MVS treat subsequent steps any differently. But IBM software, such as compilers and utility programs, follows this convention with COND CODE values:

```
COND CODE 0000    Program execution was completely successful
COND CODE 0004    Execution was OK but caused warning messages
COND CODE 0008    Program execution was seriously flawed
COND CODE 0012    Program execution was very seriously flawed
COND CODE 0016    The program failed disastrously
```

For example, if you compile a program and the compiler detects no syntax errors at all, the compiler issues COND CODE 0000. If the compiler detects minor, unimportant syntax errors, it issues COND CODE 0004. But if the compiler detects one or more major errors that make it impossible to predict successful operation of the program being compiled, it leaves behind a COND CODE greater than 0004.

Why is this useful? Think about what you would like the linkage edit and the "go" step of a compile/link/go to do if the compiler indicates that the program is flawed. You would not want the link and //GO to be attempted. Any step following the compiler, such as the linkage edit or the //GO step, can test the compiler's COND CODE and shut itself off if the compiler says the program is flawed. EXEC's COND parameter is what you use to make this test.

Look at the COB2J JCL in Figure 7.2 and you'll see this coding to invoke the linkage editor (a program named IEWL):

```
//LKED    EXEC  PGM=IEWL,
//   COND=(4,LT,COB),
```

This COND is saying, "If 4 is less than the value of the COND CODE at the //COB2 step, shut off this EXEC." This will be true if the compiler set its COND CODE to 0005 or greater; IBM's convention will have it set it to 0008 or greater when the compiler detects serious source code errors.

Look at the //GO step of Figure 7.2. You'll see

```
//GO     EXEC  PGM=*.LKED.SYSLMOD,
//   COND=((4,LT,COB2),(4,LT,LKED))
```

This COND is saying, "If 4 is less than the value of COND CODE in any prior step, shut off this EXEC." So the linkage editor (the //LKED step) will not attempt to run if the compile is flawed, and we won't try and run //GO if either the compile or linkage edit failed. Very neat, very appropriate, and very easy once you know this much about COND!

Figure 7.6 graphically shows you how you can code COND on the second and subsequent steps of a job stream to shut off steps under different conditions.

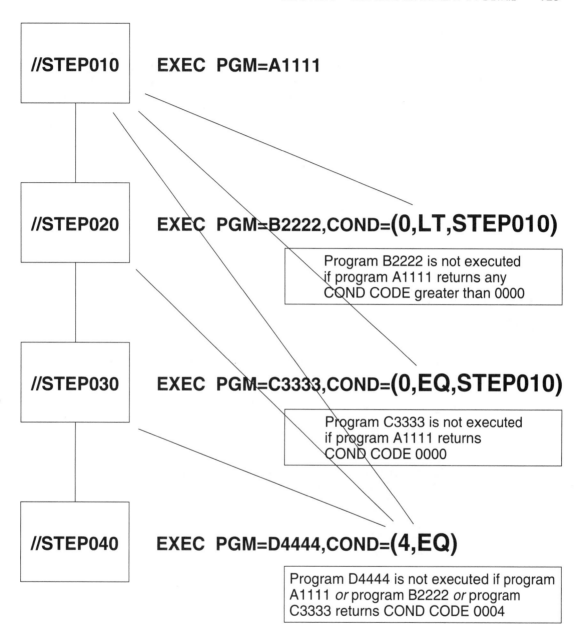

Figure 7.6   COND on EXEC Statements

You can code COND on the second and subsequent steps of a job stream. COND can define one or more conditions. If any condition in a COND is true, the step will not execute.

7.14 How a Program Sets Its COND CODE

Most programming languages used on IBM mainframes give you the capability to leave behind a desired COND CODE. But each language uses a different syntax to do this. Assembler makes the workings of the mechanism the clearest; you leave the COND CODE value you want (in the range 0 to 4095) in general purpose register 15 just before you end program execution. The first thing MVS does after receiving control from the program is to take the value in register 15 and move it to the COND CODE field.

Here is how you set a desired value (such as 0025) in COND CODE in other languages:

	Explanation	*An Example*
COBOL:	MOVE value TO RETURN-CODE.	MOVE 25 TO RETURN-CODE.
PL/I:	CALL PLIRETC(value);	CALL PLIRETC(25);
C:	EXIT(value);	exit(25);
FORTRAN:	STOP value	STOP 25

7.15 General Format of COND

This is the pattern you have to follow when you code the COND parameter:

```
COND=(value,operator,stepname)
```

For example,

```
//LKED  EXEC  PGM=IEWL,COND=(4,LT,COB)
```

If you want this test to be applied to each of the COND CODEs of *all* prior steps, just leave off the reference to a specific step. This says, "If 4 is less than the COND CODE of *any* prior step, shut off this step":

```
//GO  EXEC  PGM=NEWPROG,COND=(4,LT)
```

If you want to make a compound test (a test involving two to eight individual tests), you code COND this way:

```
COND=((value,operator,stepname),(value,operator,stepname))
```

For example:

```
//GO  EXEC  PGM=NEWPROG,COND=((4,LT,COB),(4,LT,LKED))
```

But keep in mind that all you can ever do is define conditions that, when satisfied, cause the step to be shut off. There is an implied OR in any compound COND test. Any one condition that is satisfied is sufficient to shut off the step. You can't code COND is such a way that all conditions have to be satisfied to shut off the step. And you can't code COND in such a way that the step runs *because* conditions have been satisfied.

7.16 COND Operators

Figure 7.7 shows you the full set of COND CODE operators. Here is what these two-character codes mean:

GT   ***greater than***
LT   ***less than***
EQ   ***equal to***
NE   ***not equal to***
GE   ***greater than or equal to***
LE   ***less than or equal to***

The number of operators can make you think that complex COND coding is commonplace or desirable. In fact, the only practical thing you can use COND for is to shut off a step when prior conditions indicate this is appropriate.

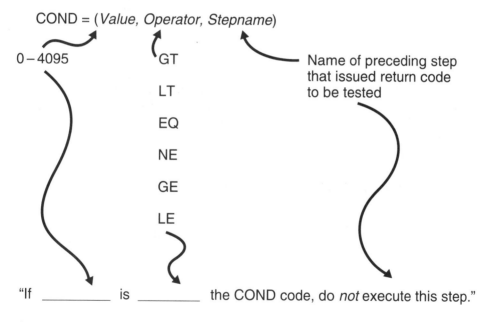

Figure 7.7   Format of COND Coding and Operators

You can use the operators shown here to form COND tests on the EXEC statement. If the test made by any COND coding is true, the step will not be executed.

7.17 What EVEN and ONLY Do

To understand what EVEN and ONLY do, you have to understand that MVS "sees" each job as progressing in one of two modes: *normal processing mode* and *abnormal termination mode*. All jobs start out in normal processing mode. But when a program abends (that is, "blows up," thereby getting a system completion code such as 0C7), MVS changes the job to abnormal termination mode. I've shown these two modes as columns in Figure 7.8. The rows of that figure show you how MVS processes a step depending on your COND coding for it.

In normal processing mode, MVS recognizes each step (each EXEC) and attempts to execute the program coded at it. If any COND conditions on an EXEC are true, MVS does not run that step but goes on to the next step.

A job gets into abnormal termination mode because a program has abended. When this happens, MVS simply wants to dump out the program that failed and "flush" out the remainder of the job with no further processing. Ordinarily, MVS will acknowledge the presence of the steps remaining after the step that failed but will not process them. *Here is where EVEN and ONLY come in.*

Both EVEN and ONLY stick a foot in front of MVS to trip it on its mad rush to the abend exit door. If you code COND=EVEN on an EXEC, MVS will still try to process a step *even* when the job was already put into abnormal termination mode by the failure of a previous step. Quite the opposite from EVEN, coding ONLY will gain MVS processing for a step only if the job is already in abnormal termination mode (such a step will be ignored in normal processing mode).

7.18 How and When to Code EVEN or ONLY

You can code either EVEN or ONLY on a step by itself to gain MVS's attention in abnormal termination mode, but you can't code both of them together.

```
//STEP040   EXEC   PGM=IEBGENER,COND=EVEN
```

or

```
//STEP040   EXEC   PGM=IEBGENER,COND=ONLY
```

Neither EVEN nor ONLY do any checking of COND CODE values. But you can also code EVEN or ONLY in combination with an ordinary COND CODE test. The following JCL, for example, gets processing attention for //STEP040 even if a previous step has abended, but the 4,LT,STEP010 test, if true, will still shut off this step:

```
//STEP040   EXEC   PGM=IEBGENER,COND=((4,LT,STEP010),EVEN)
```

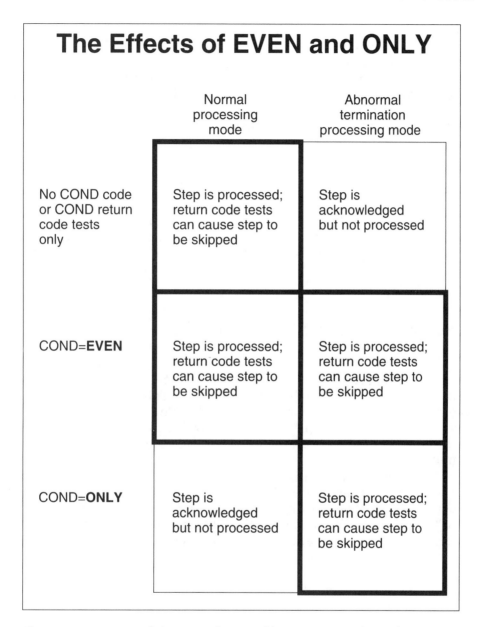

The Effects of EVEN and ONLY

	Normal processing mode	Abnormal termination processing mode
No COND code or COND return code tests only	Step is processed; return code tests can cause step to be skipped	Step is acknowledged but not processed
COND=**EVEN**	Step is processed; return code tests can cause step to be skipped	Step is processed; return code tests can cause step to be skipped
COND=**ONLY**	Step is acknowledged but not processed	Step is processed; return code tests can cause step to be skipped

Figure 7.8 EVEN and ONLY and Normal/Termination Job Modes

MVS processes jobs in one of two modes. All jobs start in *normal processing mode* but switch to *abnormal termination mode* when a step abnormally ends (abends). In normal processing mode, any step (except one coded with ONLY) gets a chance to process and may be shut off by a COND CODE test that is true. In abnormal termination mode, only steps that have EVEN or ONLY will get a chance to execute, and a COND CODE test that is true can still shut off such a step.

MVS will try to process //STEP040 even if a previous step abended. If I had not coded EVEN, and a previous step abended, //STEP040 would have no chance of executing.

You'll find that ONLY is sometimes used for the final step of a job, where several newly created data sets are deleted if the step executes. This type of step is often used to clear away data sets created in the run if any program in the run abended, to make it possible to rerun the job:

```
//STEP999   EXEC  PGM=IEFBR14,COND=ONLY
//...
//...        (data set deletions)
//...
```

//STEP999 step will not execute unless some prior step has abended, so ordinarily the data set deletions will not occur. I'll show you how to code the DD statements for this type of data set deletion step in Chapters 10 and 12.

7.19 COND and EVEN and ONLY Examples

Figure 7.9 shows you the source code for several small programs. The first three of these programs just set a specific COND CODE and then stop. Each program name describes what COND CODE it sets: JSETZERO, JSET4, and JSET8. The last program, named EXPLODE, blows up when you try to run it; it gets a system completion code of 0C7 since it tries to add 1 to an uninitialized counter (this amounts to trying to do arithmetic with a non-numeric value).

I compiled and link edited each of the programs in Figure 7.9, and put the machine language for each into a load module library. This way, I can execute each without having to compile and link it when I want to run it. (You'll see //JOBLIB coded after the JOB statement in the JCL that follows, to tell MVS about this load module library. I explain more about //JOBLIB in Chapter 16.)

In Figure 7.10 you see a job stream named E2COND that executes the JSETZERO, JSET4, JSET8, and EXPLODE programs. I have annotated the MVS output of this job stream to recap how COND CODE testing and EVEN and ONLY work.

```
EDIT --- CSCJGJ.CSC.COBOL(JSETZERC) - 01.00 ---------------- COLUMNS 007 078
COMMAND ===>                                                 SCROLL ===> PAGE
****** **************************** TOP OF DATA ****************************
000100   IDENTIFICATION DIVISION.
000200   PROGRAM-ID.     JSETZERO.
000300   ENVIRONMENT DIVISION.
000400   DATA DIVISION.
000500   PROCEDURE DIVISION.
000600   0000-MAINLINE.
000700       MOVE 0 TO RETURN-CODE.
000800       STOP RUN.
```

```
EDIT --- CSCJGJ.CSC.COBOL(JSET4) - 01.00 ------------------ COLUMNS 007 078
COMMAND ===>                                                 SCROLL ===> PAGE
****** **************************** TOP OF DATA ****************************
000100   IDENTIFICATION DIVISION.
000200   PROGRAM-ID.     JSET4.
000300   ENVIRONMENT DIVISION.
000400   DATA DIVISION.
000500   PROCEDURE DIVISION.
000600   0000-MAINLINE.
000700       MOVE 4 TO RETURN-CODE.
000800       STOP RUN.
```

```
EDIT --- CSCJGJ.CSC.COBOL(JSET8) - 01.00 ------------------ COLUMNS 007 078
COMMAND ===>                                                 SCROLL ===> PAGE
****** **************************** TOP OF DATA ****************************
000100   IDENTIFICATION DIVISION.
000200   PROGRAM-ID.     JSET8.
000300   ENVIRONMENT DIVISION.
000400   DATA DIVISION.
000500   PROCEDURE DIVISION.
000600   0000-MAINLINE.
000700       MOVE 8 TO RETURN-CODE.
000800       STOP RUN.
```

```
EDIT --- CSCJGJ.CSC.COBOL(EXPLODE) - 01.00 ---------------- COLUMNS 007 078
COMMAND ===>                                                 SCROLL ===> PAGE
****** **************************** TOP OF DATA ****************************
000100   IDENTIFICATION DIVISION.
000200   PROGRAM-ID.     EXPLODE.
000300   ENVIRONMENT DIVISION.
000400   DATA DIVISION.
000500   WORKING-STORAGE SECTION.
000600   01  WS-COUNT              PIC 9(5).
000700   PROCEDURE DIVISION.
000800   0000-MAINLINE.
000900       ADD 1 TO WS-COUNT.
001000       STOP RUN.
```

Figure 7.9 Programs That Set COND CODE

These small programs are for experimentation only. Each of the first three set a COND CODE resembling their names (JSETZERO sets 0, JSET4 sets 4, and JSET8 sets 8). The last program, EXPLODE, abends with a system completion code of 0C7.

```
                    J E S 2   J O B   L O G  --  S Y S T E M   I B M 1  --  N O D E   N 1
15.19.49 JOB04356  IRR010I  USERID CSCJGJ   IS ASSIGNED TO THIS JOB.
15.19.49 JOB04356  ICH70001I CSCJGJ   LAST ACCESS AT 15:14:00 ON SATURDAY, NOVEMBER 14, 1992
15.19.50 JOB04356  $HASP373 CSCJGJA STARTED - INIT 3 - CLASS A - SYS IBM1
15.19.58 JOB04356  IEF450I CSCJGJA STEP060 - ABEND=S0C7 U0000 REASON=00000007
15.20.04 JOB04356  IEF450I CSCJGJA STEP100 - ABEND=S0C7 U0000 REASON=00000007
15.20.04 JOB04356  $HASP395 CSCJGJA ENDED
```

```
------ JES2 JOB STATISTICS ------
   14 NOV 92 JOB EXECUTION DATE
          19 CARDS READ
         190 SYSOUT PRINT RECORDS
           0 SYSOUT PUNCH RECORDS
          12 SYSOUT SPOOL KBYTES
        0.23 MINUTES EXECUTION TIME
```

A job can abend ("blow up") twice! The **COND** specifications **EVEN** and **ONLY** can secure MVS attention for a job step even if a prior step has abended, as this demonstration run illustrates.

```
  1 //CSCJGJA   JOB  1,'BIN 7 JANOSSY',CLASS=A,MSGCLASS=X,MSGLEVEL=(1,1),   JOB04356
    // NOTIFY=CSCJGJ                                                        00020000
  2 //JOBLIB    DD   DSN=CSCJGJ.CSC.LOADLIB,DISP=SHR                        00030000
  3 //          DD   DSN=SYS1.COB2LIB,DISP=SHR                              00040002
    //*                                                                     00050000
    //*     THIS JCL IS STORED AT CSCJGJ.CSC.CNTL(E1COND)                   00060000
    //*                                                                     00070000
  4 //STEP010   EXEC PGM=JSETZERO                                           00080001
  5 //STEP020   EXEC PGM=JSET4                                              00090000
  6 //STEP030   EXEC PGM=JSET8,COND=(4,EQ,STEP020)                          00100000
  7 //STEP040   EXEC PGM=JSET4,COND=EVEN                                    00110000
  8 //STEP050   EXEC PGM=JSET8,COND=ONLY                                    00120000
    //*------------------------------------------------------------        00130000
  9 //STEP060   EXEC PGM=EXPLODE                                            00140000
    //*------------------------------------------------------------        00150000
 10 //STEP070   EXEC PGM=JSET4                                             00160000
 11 //STEP080   EXEC PGM=JSET8,COND=EVEN                                    00170000
 12 //STEP090   EXEC PGM=JSET8,COND=ONLY                                    00180000
 13 //STEP100   EXEC PGM=EXPLODE,COND=(EVEN)                                00190003
```

```
IEF142I CSCJGJA STEP010 - STEP WAS EXECUTED - COND CODE 0000
      -
IEF142I CSCJGJA STEP020 - STEP WAS EXECUTED - COND CODE 0004       COND = (4,EQ,STEP020) true!
      -
IEF202I CSCJGJA STEP030 - STEP WAS NOT RUN BECAUSE OF CONDITION CODES
IEF272I CSCJGJA STEP030 - STEP WAS NOT EXECUTED.
      -
IEF142I CSCJGJA STEP040 - STEP WAS EXECUTED - COND CODE 0004       Execution blocked by ONLY
      -
IEF202I CSCJGJA STEP050 - STEP WAS NOT RUN BECAUSE OF COND = ONLY
IEF272I CSCJGJA STEP050 - STEP WAS NOT EXECUTED.
      -
IEF472I CSCJGJA STEP060 - COMPLETION CODE - SYSTEM=0C7 USER=0000 REASON=00000007    Abend
      -
IEF272I CSCJGJA STEP070 - STEP WAS NOT EXECUTED.   Execution blocked by abend
      -
IEF142I CSCJGJA STEP080 - STEP WAS EXECUTED - COND CODE 0008
      -                                                            EVEN and ONLY
IEF142I CSCJGJA STEP090 - STEP WAS EXECUTED - COND CODE 0008
      -
IEF472I CSCJGJA STEP100 - COMPLETION CODE - SYSTEM=0C7 USER=0000 REASON=00000007    Abend
```

```
IEF375I  JOB /CSCJGJA / START 92319.1519
IEF376I  JOB /CSCJGJA / STOP  92319.1520 CPU    0MIN 00.77SEC SRB    0MIN 00.12SEC
```

Figure 7.10 MVS System Output Showing COND CODE and Effects

Chapter 7 Review

Mini-Glossary

Load module library A partitioned data set that houses the machine language instructions of a program

Normal processing mode The mode in which MVS begins processing all job streams; every step is given attention.

Abnormal termination mode The mode MVS switches to when a step has abended; the step is dumped and subsequent steps are not processed unless you code EVEN or ONLY on them.

Review Questions

1. Explain what happens when you don't code either PGM= or PROC= on an EXEC statement but instead code EXEC *name.*
2. What happens if you code TIME=(3,0) on the JOB statement for a job stream and TIME=(3,5) on an EXEC within the job?
3. A programmer coded REGION=2M on an EXEC in a multistep job stream, but the job abended with a system completion code of 80A. What two things could cause this failure?
4. Explain what PARM does and briefly describe how it does it.
5. Give an overview description of what COND does, covering the operation of both successful and abending jobs.

Exercises

A. Copy the JSET4 program from Figure 7.9 and use your local COBOL compile/link/go proc to process the program. Circle each COND CODE in the MVS system output. Then change line 000700 to MOVE 1234 TO RETURN-CODE and process the program again, noting the COND CODES. Finally, change the word PROCEDURE in line 000500 to PORKCHOP. Process the program a third time and note the COND CODEs.

B. Copy the EXPLODE program from Figure 7.9 and include in it the statement MOVE 25 TO RETURN-CODE immediately after line 000800. Use your local COBOL compile/link/go proc to process the program and find the system completion code 0C7 in your MVS system reporting for the job. Does COND CODE 0025 appear as a result of this MOVE statement or not? Comment out original line 000900 (the ADD statement), process the program again, and compare your result to the previous run.

Chapter Eight

DD STATEMENTS FOR READING DATA SETS

Each DD statement you code "hooks up" one program input or output to a physical data set. And each DD statement falls into one of these three categories:

- reading a data set
- sending information to the printer via the spool
- writing (creating) a new data set

DD statements of the first two categories are the easiest to code. In this chapter I'll show you what you need to know to code DD statements for reading data sets. I'll also show you some of the extra support MVS provides to give you convenience and flexibility in data set reading.

8.1 The Simplest DD Statement for Reading

You code the simplest (and most common) DD statement for reading a data set like this:

```
//SYSUT1   DD   DSN=CSCJGJ.CSC.CNTL(WORKERS),
//  DISP=SHR
```

You're already familiar with the role of the DDname, which in this case is //SYSUT1. You have to code this name in your JCL to match the symbolic name for the data set (usually hardcoded) in the program you are executing. DDname can be up to eight characters long. The first character must be a letter, and the remaining characters can be letters or numbers or @, #, or $. As a programmer you usually have to code DDname following an installation naming convention.

DSN, which you can also code as DSNAME, is a keyword parameter. As you might suspect, DSN stands for "data set name." It makes sense that you need to state in your JCL the name of the data set that you are trying to read! The name I've shown above—CSCJGJ.CSC.CNTL(WORKERS)—consists of a partitioned data set name followed by a member name within parentheses. To read a sequential or VSAM data set, you code DSN even more simply (even though a VSAM data set is internally much more complex than a sequential data set, this reading DD statement for it is simple):

```
//SYSUT1  DD  DSN=CSCJGJ.CSC.MASTFILE,
//  DISP=SHR
```

The only thing you need to state on a DD statement for reading a data set, in addition to DSN, is DISP. DISP is a keyword parameter that stands for "disposition." DISP is actually a much more complicated parameter than you see in this statement. It has three positional subparameters as I'll explain in Chapter 11. When you code DISP=SHR you're really just specifying the first of DISP's three subparameters. When you're reading a data set, you can specify either DISP=SHR or DISP=OLD. You *must* code one of these!

8.2 What DISP=SHR Means

When you code DISP=SHR, you are telling MVS that you do not need exclusive access to the data set you're reading. That is, you don't care if someone else is using the data set while you are. Coding DISP=SHR also means that if someone else is already reading the data set when you want to use it, you can accept shared use of it.

DISP=SHR is by far the most common way you'll see DISP coded for reading a disk data set. Up to 127 jobs can access a disk data set at the same time. I'd suggest that you always code DISP=SHR for reading unless you really do need entirely exclusive use of the data set.

8.3 DISP=OLD: Exclusive Use!

The opposite of coding DISP=SHR is coding DISP=OLD. If you code DISP=OLD on a DD statement for reading a data set, you are telling MVS that you must have exclusive use of the data set. Exclusive use means that you must have the data set all to yourself. This may just sound selfish and harmful to others, but it can hurt you too! Here's why:

- DISP=OLD will deny access to the data set to any other job so long as you are using it. This delays *them*.
- DISP=OLD will delay your job from running until whoever is already using the data set you want to read stops using it. This delays *you*!

In Figure 8.1a you see some JCL you're already familiar with; it's the JCL to execute IEBGENER to copy data to the printer. But there's one difference between this JCL and the JCL you saw in earlier chapters. Previously I coded DISP=SHR for the data set I am trying to read. Now I have coded DISP=OLD.

Figure 8.1b shows you the result when I submit this version of a "print" job. Notice that the MVS job log now contains some strange messages. These messages tell me that my job (named CSCJGJA) can't have access to data set CSCJGJ.CSC.CNTL; the job is "waiting for data sets." My job has been delayed. My coding of DISP=OLD asked for exclusive use of the data set, but someone else has exclusive use of it. Who? Me!

Notice that the data I am trying to read is a member of data set CSCJGJ.CSC.CNTL, my JCL library. When I was in the TSO edit mode submitting the JCL, TSO held the data set for exclusive updating use. TSO didn't care if another job wanted to read the data set, which is what DISP= SHR implies. But DISP=OLD is incompatible with TSO's use of the data set; it implies that my IEBGENER job also wants to update the data set! So my IEBGENER job waited until I left the edit function, when TSO relinquished its use of the data set. You see? Coding DISP=OLD when it's not necessary is like trying to dance with your shoe strings tied together. Always use DISP=SHR to read a data set!

8.4 Problem: Omitting DISP When Reading a Data Set

The first subparameter of DISP can be one of four values: SHR, OLD, NEW, or MOD. I'll explain the meaning of these to you in detail in Chapter 11, because the last two really apply to creating a new data set. I mention this now only because of what happens if you don't code DISP at all. If you don't code DISP, it defaults to NEW, and MVS thinks you are trying to create a new data set. Because of the error messages MVS uses, this is a particularly confusing problem.

Figure 8.2 shows you my IEBGENER job with no DISP on the //SYSUT1 DD statement, where I'm trying to read a data set. Notice that MVS complains in two ways but doesn't tell me the real problem here: my failure to code DISP!

In Figure 8.2 the first indication of a problem is the "waiting for data sets" message in the job log. You have already seen that you get this when you are trying to get exclusive use of the data set and it's already in use. The default DISP=NEW that MVS uses when you don't code DISP is another request for exclusive use of a data set.

The second error message in Figure 8.2 is very confusing: "UNIT FIELD SPECIFIES INCORRECT DEVICE NAME." I have not coded any "unit" field, so what is this message talking about?

```
EDIT ---- CSCJGJ.CSC.CNTL(F1OLD) - 01.00 ------------------- COLUMNS 001 072
COMMAND ===> sub                                            SCROLL ===> PAGE
****** ************************** TOP OF DATA ******************************
000100 //CSCJGJA   JOB 1,'BIN 7 JANOSSY',CLASS=A,MSGCLASS=X,MSGLEVEL=(1,1),
000200 //  NOTIFY=CSCJGJ
000300 //*
000400 //*    THIS JCL IS STORED AT CSCJGJ.CSC.CNTL(F1OLD)
000500 //*
000600 //*****************************************************************
000700 //*                                                               *
000800 //*    LIST THE WORKER DATA WITHOUT FORMATTING IT FOR PRINT       *
000900 //*                                                               *
001000 //*****************************************************************
001100 //STEP010   EXEC  PGM=IEBGENER
001200 //SYSUT1    DD  DSN=CSCJGJ.CSC.CNTL(WORKERS),        <=== INPUT
001300 // DISP=OLD
001400 //SYSUT2    DD  SYSOUT=*                             <=== OUTPUT
001500 //SYSPR     DD  DUMMY
001600 //SYSIN     DD  DSN=NULLFILE,DISP=SHR
001700 //

JOB CSCJGJA(JOB     ) SUBMITTED
***
```
OLD not SHR?

DSN = NULLFILE acts like DUMMY but has relevance for work with procedures; it's incidental to this figure

(a)

```
                J E S 2   J O B   L O G  --  S Y S T E M   I B M 1  --  N O D E   N 1

17.43.59 JOB04907  IRR010I USERID CSCJGJ   IS ASSIGNED TO THIS JOB.
17.44.00 JOB04907  ICH70001I CSCJGJ    LAST ACCESS AT 17:42:29 ON SATURDAY, NOVEMBER 14, 1992
17.44.00 JOB04907  $HASP373 CSCJGJA  STARTED - INIT  3 - CLASS A - SYS IBM1
17.44.00 JOB04907  IEF861I FOLLOWING RESERVED DATA SET NAMES UNAVAILABLE TO CSCJGJA
17.44.00 JOB04907  IEF863I DSN = CSCJGJ.CSC.CNTL CSCJGJA
17.44.00 JOB04907 *IEF099I JOB CSCJGJA  WAITING FOR DATA SETS
17.44.26 JOB04907  $HASP395 CSCJGJA  ENDED

------ JES2 JOB STATISTICS ------
   14 NOV 92 JOB EXECUTION DATE
       16 CARDS READ
       62 SYSOUT PRINT RECORDS
        0 SYSOUT PUNCH RECORDS
        4 SYSOUT SPOOL KBYTES
     0.42 MINUTES EXECUTION TIME
        -
        -
        -
```

(b)

OLD asks for exclusive use of a data set. In this case the data set I am trying to print from is already being held exclusively by TSO since I am editing it (that's where this JCL is!). The system messages indicate that the job is waiting for the data set to become available on an exclusive basis. **SHR** doesn't have this problem!

Figure 8.1 Coding DISP=OLD Requests Exclusive Data Set Access

(a) You need to code DISP=SHR or DISP=OLD on a DD statement that reads a data set. DISP=SHR requests shared access while DISP=OLD requests exclusive access. Shared access is most common. (b) Coding DISP=OLD may needlessly delay your job.

```
            J E S 2   J O B   L O G  --  S Y S T E M   I B M 1  --  N O D E   N 1

17.48.18 JOB04918  IRR010I  USERID CSCJGJ   IS ASSIGNED TO THIS JOB.
17.48.19 JOB04918  ICH70001I CSCJGJ   LAST ACCESS AT 17:44:00 ON SATURDAY, NOVEMBER 14, 1992
17.48.19 JOB04918  $HASP373 CSCJGJA  STARTED - INIT  1 - CLASS A - SYS IBM1
17.48.19 JOB04918  IEF861I FOLLOWING RESERVED DATA SET NAMES UNAVAILABLE TO CSCJGJA
17.48.19 JOB04918  IEF863I DSN = CSCJGJ.CSC.CNTL CSCJGJA
17.48.19 JOB04918 *IEF099I JOB CSCJGJA  WAITING FOR DATA SETS
17.48.27 JOB04918  IEF453I CSCJGJA - JOB FAILED - JCL ERROR
17.48.27 JOB04918  $HASP395 CSCJGJA  ENDED

------ JES2 JOB STATISTICS ------
   14 NOV 92 JOB EXECUTION DATE
          15 CARDS READ
          39 SYSOUT PRINT RECORDS
           0 SYSOUT PUNCH RECORDS
           3 SYSOUT SPOOL KBYTES
        0.13 MINUTES EXECUTION TIME
```

Lack of DISP implies DISP=(NEW,KEEP,KEEP) which requires that you specify UNIT as well as SPACE. By leaving off DISP, you make MVS think that you want to *create* the data set!

```
   1 //CSCJGJA   JOB 1,'BIN 7 JANOSSY',CLASS=A,MSGCLASS=X,MSGLEVEL=(1,1),   JOB04918
     //  NOTIFY=CSCJGJ                                                       00020000
     //*                                                                     00030000
     //*    THIS JCL IS STORED AT CSCJGJ.CSC.CNTL(F2NODISP)                  00040000
     //*                                                                     00050000
     //**********************************************************            00060000
     //*                                                                 *   00070000
     //*    LIST THE WORKER DATA WITHOUT FORMATTING IT FOR PRINT         *   00080000
     //*                                                                 *   00090000
     //**********************************************************            00100000
   2 //STEP010  EXEC  PGM=IEBGENER                                           00110000
   3 //SYSUT1    DD   DSN=CSCJGJ.CSC.CNTL(WORKERS)          INPUT            00120000
   4 //SYSUT2    DD   SYSOUT=*                         <=== OUTPUT           00130000
   5 //SYSPRINT  DD   DUMMY                                                  00140000
   6 //SYSIN     DD   DSN=NULLFILE,DISP=SHR                                  00150000

ICH70001I CSCJGJ   LAST ACCESS AT 17:44:00 ON SATURDAY, NOVEMBER 14, 1992

IEF210I CSCJGJA STEP010 SYSUT1 - UNIT FIELD SPECIFIES INCORRECT DEVICE NAME
IEF272I CSCJGJA STEP010 - STEP WAS NOT EXECUTED.
IEF373I STEP /STEP010 / START 92319.1748
IEF374I STEP /STEP010 / STOP  92319.1748 CPU    0MIN 00.00SEC SRB    0MIN 00.00SEC
IEF375I JOB /CSCJGJA / START 92319.1748
IEF376I JOB /CSCJGJA / STOP  92319.1748 CPU    0MIN 00.00SEC SRB    0MIN 00.00SEC
```

Figure 8.2 UNIT Error Message Results from Omitting DISP

Omitting DISP on the //SYSUT1 DD statement makes MVS use a default DISP= NEW for it. But to create a data set you also need to specify UNIT as well as other things. MVS interprets your JCL by converting it to a special "internal" format. The error message referring to the "unit" field is talking about the MVS internal form of the JCL. But unfortunately, MVS reporting does not show you that internal format, so the error message makes you think it's complaining about *your* (nonexistent!) coding of UNIT!

8.5 An Insight Into How MVS Executes JCL

The first thing that MVS does to your submitted JCL is to pick apart its somewhat free format and build an interpreted "internal" version of it. During this process it quickly detects syntax errors in your JCL, such as missing commas or misspelled statement types. MVS also forms "control blocks" from the interpreted JCL to communicate characteristics of data sets to its different software modules. One of the things MVS needs to know about a data set is what type of "unit" it resides on, such as tape or disk.

DISP is one of many DD statement parameters. UNIT is actually another; I'll describe it to you in Chapter 12. When you create a data set, you have to specify UNIT. But when you read a data set, MVS can ordinarily find out what kind of unit the data set uses by looking in the system catalog. Because coding either DISP=SHR or DISP=OLD implies that the data set exists, MVS itself fills in the "type of unit" field in its interpreted JCL when you read a cataloged data set.

Some parameters have default values, values that MVS will use when you don't code the parameter in a DD statement. DISP has a default, but UNIT has no default. When you omit DISP on a DD statement, MVS puts "NEW" into the DISP field in its interpreted JCL. So MVS has assumed a disposition of NEW for the data set at //SYSUT1, CSCJGJ.CSC.CNTL, in my JCL in Figure 8.2.

The error message you see at the bottom of Figure 8.2 is generated by an MVS module that checks the MVS-interpreted JCL. That module is telling MVS that UNIT in the interpreted JCL is incorrect. A serious shortcoming in MVS reporting is that it doesn't show you the interpreted JCL, which is really what the "incorrect device type" error message is referring to. All the MVS reporting shows you is your own JCL, and for this, the error message is misleading and potentially confusing!

8.6 DUMMY and NULLFILE

Take a second look at Figure 8.1 and you'll see another difference between it and the JCL you saw earlier. It was my intention to "dummy out" the //SYSIN DD statement, at which IEBGENER seeks control statement input. I don't have any control statements for it (I want a "straight" copy of all the records in their original format). But instead of coding this:

```
//SYSIN  DD   DUMMY
```

as I did earlier, I have now coded this at line 1600:

```
//SYSIN  DD   DSN=NULLFILE,DISP=SHR
```

You can code DD DUMMY on any input DD statement to simulate an empty file. The program reading at such a dummied out DD statement immediately gets an end-of-file notification when it first attempts to read.

For data set reading, NULLFILE coding does exactly the same thing as DD DUMMY. NULLFILE is a special dummy data set name to MVS. If you use NULLFILE, you still have to code DISP, and you may also code other parameters on the DD statement. Whatever parameters you code here are checked for syntax purposes but are otherwise ignored.

I wanted to show you NULLFILE not because you need to use it right now but because it does relate to data set reading. NULLFILE coding has relevance to your use of cataloged procedures, which I'll explain in Chapter 18. When you execute a proc, you have the ability to override existing data set names in it. Overriding a real data set name with NULLFILE is a way to dummy out an input that is hardcoded within a proc.

8.7 Instream Data

As a convenience in reading a small quantity of program statements or control information, MVS lets you include these non-JCL items right in the middle of your JCL. To do this you use a feature called *instream data.* It's very simple. In Figures 8.3a and 8.3b I compare filed-stored and instream data. Here I am using the IDCAMS utility program to "dump" to paper the contents of a member of my CSCJGJ.CSC.CNTL library named THUMPER. Figure 8.3a shows you how I can house these control statements for IDCAMS as instream data:

```
PRINT         INFILE (DD1)—      DD1 is DDname of file to dump
              COUNT(15)—         Number of records to dump
              DUMP               Dump records in character and hex
```

Below the dark line, you see the same JCL but with the control statements removed and placed into a member named CONTROL1. Now the //SYSIN DD statement refers to this data set and member as DSN= CSCJGJ.CSC.CNTL(CONTROL1) and (of course) also includes the phrase DISP=SHR.

The output at Figure 8.4 was produced from the instream version of my dump job. Notice that whatever you read in as instream data *does not* appear in the MVS-produced listing of your JCL. If this data is entering a program that is kind enough to echo it back to you, as IDCAMS does, you may see it later in the output.

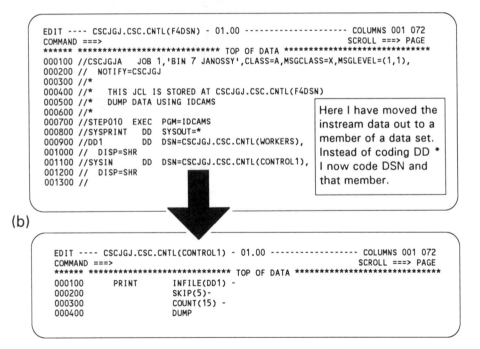

```
EDIT ---- CSCJGJ.CSC.CNTL(F3INSTRE) - 01.02 ----------------- COLUMNS 001 072
COMMAND ===>                                              SCROLL ===> PAGE
****** **************************** TOP OF DATA ******************************
000100 //CSCJGJA   JOB 1,'BIN 7 JANOSSY',CLASS=A,MSGCLASS=X,MSGLEVEL=(1,1),
000200 //  NOTIFY=CSCJGJ
000300 //*
000400 //*   THIS JCL IS STORED AT CSCJGJ.CSC.CNTL(F3INSTRE)
000500 //*    DUMP DATA USING IDCAMS
000600 //*
000700 //STEP010  EXEC  PGM=IDCAMS
000800 //SYSPRINT   DD  SYSOUT=*
000900 //DD1        DD  DSN=CSCJGJ.CSC.CNTL(WORKERS),
001000 //  DISP=SHR
001100 //SYSIN     DD  *
001200     PRINT        INFILE(DD1) -
001300                  SKIP(5)-
001400                  COUNT(15) -
001500                  DUMP
001600 /*
001700 //
```
DD * begins "instream" data. There are no slashes at the start of these lines because they are not JCL.

(a)

```
EDIT ---- CSCJGJ.CSC.CNTL(F4DSN) - 01.00 -------------------- COLUMNS 001 072
COMMAND ===>                                              SCROLL ===> PAGE
****** **************************** TOP OF DATA ******************************
000100 //CSCJGJA   JOB 1,'BIN 7 JANOSSY',CLASS=A,MSGCLASS=X,MSGLEVEL=(1,1),
000200 //  NOTIFY=CSCJGJ
000300 //*
000400 //*   THIS JCL IS STORED AT CSCJGJ.CSC.CNTL(F4DSN)
000500 //*    DUMP DATA USING IDCAMS
000600 //*
000700 //STEP010  EXEC  PGM=IDCAMS
000800 //SYSPRINT   DD  SYSOUT=*
000900 //DD1        DD  DSN=CSCJGJ.CSC.CNTL(WORKERS),
001000 //  DISP=SHR
001100 //SYSIN      DD  DSN=CSCJGJ.CSC.CNTL(CONTROL1),
001200 //  DISP=SHR
001300 //
```
Here I have moved the instream data out to a member of a data set. Instead of coding DD * I now code DSN and that member.

(b)

```
EDIT ---- CSCJGJ.CSC.CNTL(CONTROL1) - 01.00 ----------------- COLUMNS 001 072
COMMAND ===>                                              SCROLL ===> PAGE
****** **************************** TOP OF DATA ******************************
000100     PRINT        INFILE(DD1) -
000200                  SKIP(5)-
000300                  COUNT(15) -
000400                  DUMP
```

Figure 8.3   Comparing Instream and File-Stored Control Statements

(a) I first used instream data to house the control statements to tell the IDCAMS utility to dump a data set. (b) I took the control statements out of the JCL and put them into member CONTROL1 of my library CSCJGJ.CSC.CNTL; //SYSIN then has to refer to this data set.

```
                    J E S 2   J O B   L O G   --   S Y S T E M   I B M 1   --   N O D E   N 1

23.34.45 JOB05315  IRR010I USERID CSCJGJ  IS ASSIGNED TO THIS JOB.
23.34.46 JOB05315  ICH70001I CSCJGJ  LAST ACCESS AT 23:31:54 ON SATURDAY, NOVEMBER 14, 1992
23.34.46 JOB05315  $HASP373 CSCJGJA  STARTED - INIT 1 - CLASS A - SYS IBM1
23.34.46 JOB05315  $HASP395 CSCJGJA  ENDED

------ JES2 JOB STATISTICS ------
  14 NOV 92 JOB EXECUTION DATE
      16 CARDS READ
     109 SYSOUT PRINT RECORDS
       0 SYSOUT PUNCH RECORDS
       8 SYSOUT SPOOL KBYTES
    0.01 MINUTES EXECUTION TIME

   1 //CSCJGJA  JOB 1,'BIN 7 JANOSSY',CLASS=A,MSGCLASS=X,MSGLEVEL=(1,1),       JOB05315
     // NOTIFY=CSCJGJ                                                          00020000
     //*                                                                       00030000
     //*      THIS JCL IS STORED AT CSCJGJ.CSC.CNTL(F3INSTRE)                   00040000
     //*      DUMP DATA USING IDCAMS

   2 //STEP010   EXEC  PGM=IDCAMS
   3 //SYSPRINT  DD    SYSOUT=*
   4 //DD1       DD    DSN=CSCJGJ.CSC.CNTL(WORKERS),
     //                DISP=SHR
   5 //SYSIN     DD    *

ICH70001I CSCJGJ  LAST ACCESS AT 23:31:54 ON SATURDAY, NOVEMBER 14, 1992

IEF236I ALLOC. FOR CSCJGJA STEP010
IEF237I JES2 ALLOCATED TO SYSPRINT
IEF237I 111 ALLOCATED TO DD1
IEF237I JES2 ALLOCATED TO SYSIN
IEF142I CSCJGJA STEP010 - STEP WAS EXECUTED - COND CODE 0004
IEF285I   CSCJGJ.CSCJGJA.JOB05315.D00000102.?        SYSOUT
IEF285I   CSCJGJ.CSC.CNTL                            KEPT
IEF285I   VOL SER NOS= USER00.
IEF285I   CSCJGJ.CSCJGJA.JOB05315.D00000101.?        SYSIN
IEF373I STEP /STEP010 / START 92319.2334
IEF374I STEP /STEP010 / STOP  92319.2334 CPU    0MIN 00.22SEC SRB  0MIN 00.00SEC VIRT  188K SYS  240K EXT  4K SYS
IEF375I JOB /CSCJGJA / START 92319.2334
IEF376I JOB /CSCJGJA / STOP  92319.2334 CPU    0MIN 00.22SEC SRB  0MIN 00.00SEC

IDCAMS  SYSTEM SERVICES                                            TIME: 23:34:46           11/14/92     PAGE      1

   PRINT     INFILE(DD1) -                          00120000
             SKIP(5)-                                00130002
             COUNT(15)-                              00131002
             DUMP                                    00140000
```

MVS does not list your instream data (control statements in this case) with the JCL

IDCAMS issues COND CODE 0004 because there are fewer records to print than I asked for. I said "skip the first 5" and then print (count) 15. But there are only 16 records in the whole item!

IDCAMS lists the control statements I supplied to it at SYSIN DD *

TIME: 23:34:46

LISTING OF DATA SET -CSCJGJ.CSC.CNTL

Same byte; hex is at left, character print at right

```
RECORD SEQUENCE NUMBER - 6
000000 F2F1F5F7 F440C1C8 40404040 40404040 40C7C5D6 D9C7C540 40404040 F0F0D7C8   *21574 AH        GEORGE    400PH*
000020 D6E3D640 C4C5D7C1 D9E3D4C5 D5E34040 40404040 40404040 40404040 40404040   *OTO DEPARTMENT            *
000040 40404040 40404040                                                          *        *

RECORD SEQUENCE NUMBER - 7
000000 F2F1F6F6 F840E9D6 D6D9C940 40404040 40D4D6C5 40404040 40404040 F1F7F9D7D3  *21668 ZOORI     MOE       179PL*
000020 E4D4C2C9 D5C740E2 E4D7D7D3 C9C5E240 40404040 40404040 40404040 40404040   *UMBING SUPPLIES           *
000040 40404040 40404040                                                          *        *

RECORD SEQUENCE NUMBER - 8
000000 F2F5F1F1 F240C3C1 C2D6D6E2 C5404040 40D3E4C3 C5404040 40404040 F0F5C6E4   *25112 CABOOSE    LUCE     305FU*
000020 D9D5C9E3 E4D9C540 40404040 40404040 40404040 40404040 40404040 40404040   *RNITURE           *
000040 40404040 40404040                                                          *        *
```

Starting byte position in this line in hexadecimal (hex 20 = decimal 32, hex 40 = decimal 64)

```
RECORD SEQUENCE NUMBER - 12
000000 F3F3F3F7 F740E6C8 C9E94040 40404040 40C74840 40404040 40404040 F5F7D7C5   *33377 WHIZ      G.        357PE*
000020 D9E2D6D5 C1D34CC3 D6D4D7E4 E3C5D9E2 40404040 40404040 40404040 40404040   *RSONAL COMPUTERS          *
000040 40404040 40404040                                                          *        *

RECORD SEQUENCE NUMBER - 13
000000 F3F3F4F8 F040E3D6 E4D94040 40404040 40C44B40 40404040 40404040 F6F0E6D6   *33480 TOUR      D.        160WO*
000020 D4C5D5E2 40C3D3D6 E3C8C9D5 C7404040 40404040 40404040 40404040 40404040   *MENS CLOTHING             *
000040 40404040 40404040                                                          *        *

RECORD SEQUENCE NUMBER - 14
000000 F3F3F4F8 F340C9D5 C1404040 40404040 40C3C1D9 D6D34040 40404040 F5F3D9C5   *33483 INA       CAROL     530RE*
000020 D4D6C4C5 D3C9D5C7 40E2E4D7 D7D3C9C5 E2404040 40404040 40404040 40404040   *MODELING SUPPLIES         *
000040 40404040 40404040                                                          *        *

RECORD SEQUENCE NUMBER - 15
000000 F3F9F3F2 F140C1C2 C1D4C140 40404040 40C1D340 40404040 40404040 F4F2F0E6D6  *39321 ABAMA     AL        420WO*
000020 D4C5D5E2 40C3D3D6 E3C8C9D5 C7404040 40404040 40404040 40404040 40404040   *MENS CLOTHING             *
000040 40404040 40404040                                                          *        *

RECORD SEQUENCE NUMBER - 16
000000 F3F9F3F2 F240E3E4 C3D2E840 40404040 40D2C5D5 40404040 40404040 F5F0C8C1   *39322 TUCKY     KEN       350HA*
000020 D9C4E6C1 D9C54040 40404040 40404040 40404040 40404040 40404040 40404040   *RDWARE            *
000040 40404040 40404040                                                          *        *
```

IDC11462I REQUESTED RANGE END BEYOND END OF DATA SET.

This IDCAMS message says essentially that I requested more records to be printed than exist to print. This causes the "warning" COND CODE 0004.

```
IDC0005I NUMBER OF RECORDS PROCESSED WAS 11
IDC0001I FUNCTION COMPLETED, HIGHEST CONDITION CODE WAS 4
IDC0002I IDCAMS PROCESSING COMPLETE. MAXIMUM CONDITION CODE WAS 4
```

Figure 8.4 IDCAMS Dump Using Instream Control Statements

8.8 Instream Data Variations

The most common way of coding instream data is to start it with DD * and end it with /*:

```
//SYSIN  DD  *
  --data--
  --data--
  --data--
/*
```

The line starting with /* is optional here because MVS can detect when your execution JCL resumes; your JCL resumes with the first line starting with //. But you can also code instream data in this way:

```
//SYSIN  DD  DATA
  --data--
  --data--
  --data--
/*
```

When you use DD DATA, you *must* use the /* delimiter to tell MVS when the data ends and your execution JCL begins.

Finally, you could also define your own delimiter as follows, if the data you are processing contain JCL (with // or /* in it):

```
//SYSIN  DD  DLM=$$          Make $$ any two characters
  --data--
  --data--
  --data--
$$
```

You will most often see instream data used with //SYSIN, the standard IBM name for utility program control statement or source code input. *But you can use instream data at any DD statement where you want to read 80-byte "punch card image" records, including ordinary data input to programs.*

8.9 A Nasty Problem with Unintentional Instream Data

MVS does you a "favor" in connection with //SYSIN DD *. You will probably not appreciate it if you experience it. If you leave a blank line in your JCL (no slashes) or make a mistake and key in something other than // to start a line, MVS thinks you have included instream data. It automatically generates a //SYSIN DD * statement and inserts it in your JCL at that point. But because instream data is not listed with your JCL, you won't see the offending line you actually coded. (Surely some misguided software engineer back in 1964 thought this would be a great feature!) Figure 8.5 illustrates this problem for you.

```
EDIT ---- CSCJGJ.CSC.CNTL(F5MVSGEN) - 01.00 ----------------- COLUMNS 001 072
COMMAND ===>                                              SCROLL ===> PAGE
****** *************************** TOP OF DATA *********************************
000100 //CSCJGJA   JOB 1,'BIN 7 JANOSSY',CLASS=A,MSGCLASS=X,MSGLEVEL=(1,1),
000200 // NOTIFY=CSCJGJ
000300 //*
000400 //*   THIS JCL IS STORED AT CSCJGJ.CSC.CNTL(F5MVSGEN)
000500 //*
000600 //STEP010  EXEC  PGM=IEBGENER
000700 //SYSUT1     DD  DSN=CSCJGJ.CSC.CNTL(WORKERS),
000800 // DISP=SHR
000900 //SYSUT2     DD  SYSOUT=*
001000 HEY THERE!
001100 //SYSPRINT   DD  SYSOUT=*
001200 //SYSIN      DD  DUMMY
001300 //
```

This line is totally bogus! It's garbage, but MVS will create a SYSIN DD * statement before it as if it was intended to be control statement input. (a)

```
                          J E S 2   J O B   L O G  --  S Y S T E M   I B M 1  --  N O D E   N 1
01.26.10 JOB05433  IRRO10I USERID CSCJGJ   IS ASSIGNED TO THIS JOB.
01.26.11 JOB05433  ICH70001I CSCJGJ   LAST ACCESS AT 01:23:11 ON SUNDAY, NOVEMBER 15, 1992
01.26.11 JOB05433  $HASP373 CSCJGJA  STARTED - INIT 1 - CLASS A - SYS IBM1
01.26.11 JOB05433  $HASP395 CSCJGJA  ENDED
------ JES2 JOB STATISTICS ------
    15 NOV 92 JOB EXECUTION DATE
         12 CARDS READ
         45 SYSOUT PRINT RECORDS
          0 SYSOUT PUNCH RECORDS
          3 SYSOUT SPOOL KBYTES
       0.00 MINUTES EXECUTION TIME

     1 //CSCJGJA   JOB 1,'BIN 7 JANOSSY',CLASS=A,MSGCLASS=X,MSGLEVEL=(1,1),      JOB05433
       // NOTIFY=CSCJGJ                                                          00020000
       //*                                                                       00030000
       //*                                                                       00040000
       //*   THIS JCL IS STORED AT CSCJGJ.CSC.CNTL(F5MVSGEN)                      00050000
     2 //STEP010  EXEC  PGM=IEBGENER                                             00060000
     3 //SYSUT1     DD  DSN=CSCJGJ.CSC.CNTL(WORKERS),                            00070000
       // DISP=SHR                                                               00080000
                                                                                 00090000
     4 //SYSUT2     DD  SYSOUT=*            GENERATED STATEMENT
     5 //SYSIN      DD  *
     6 //SYSPRINT   DD  SYSOUT=*                                                  00110000
     7 //SYSIN      DD  DUMMY                                                     00120000
ICH70001I CSCJGJ   LAST ACCESS AT 01:23:11 ON SUNDAY, NOVEMBER 15, 1992
IEF236I ALLOC. FOR CSCJGJA STEP010
IEF237I 111  ALLOCATED TO SYSUT1
IEF237I JES2 ALLOCATED TO SYSUT2
IEF237I JES2 ALLOCATED TO SYSIN
IEF237I JES2 ALLOCATED TO SYSPRINT
IEF237I DMY  ALLOCATED TO SYSIN
IEF142I CSCJGJA STEP010 - STEP WAS EXECUTED - COND CODE 0012
IEF285I     CSCJGJ.CSC.CNTL
IEF285I     VOL SER NOS= USER00.
IEF285I     CSCJGJ.CSCJGJA.JOB05433.D0000102.?        SYSOUT
IEF285I     CSCJGJ.CSCJGJA.JOB05433.D0000101.?        SYSIN
IEF285I     CSCJGJ.CSCJGJA.JOB05433.D0000103.?        SYSOUT
IEF373I STEP /STEP010 / START 92320.0126
IEF374I STEP /STEP010 / STOP  92320.0126 CPU    0MIN 00.07SEC SRB    0MIN 00.00SEC
IEF375I JOB /CSCJGJA / START 92320.0126
IEF376I JOB /CSCJGJA / STOP  92320.0126 CPU    0MIN 00.07SEC SRB    0MIN 00.00SEC
DATA SET UTILITY - GENERATE
HEY THERE!                                                                       00100000
IEB336I      INVALID COMMAND IN COL. 05
```

(b)

Figure 8.5 MVS Solves a Coding Error by Making Problems!

(a) I coded a "totally bogus" HEY THERE! at line 001000 in this JCL, but MVS does not catch it. (b) MVS thinks I intended line 001000 to be instream data to a // SYSIN statement, and it generates the //SYSIN DD * statement for me. Thanks a lot for the "favor," MVS! This job fails because the MVS-generated //SYSIN comes first and takes precedence over my actual //SYSIN coding, so IEBGENER gets the bogus "data" and complains about it.

8.10 Concatenating Data (Sequential Files)

MVS provides a powerful feature for data set reading in the form of data set concatenation. Simply put, this lets you string input data sets together for reading by listing their names at a DD statement. The data sets can be sequential files or members of partitioned data sets.

Figure 8.6 shows you three highly nutritional members of my CSCJGJ.CSC.CNTL library, named FRUITS, VEGE, and GRAINS. I put a few records into each of these members in alphabetical order and identified each one with its food group (the member name). Figure 8.7 shows you how I concatenated all three of these members into the //SORTIN input of the sort utility:

```
//SORTIN   DD   DSN=CSCJGJ.CSC.CNTL(FRUITS),DISP=SHR    No commas
//         DD   DSN=CSCJGJ.CSC.CNTL(VEGE),DISP=SHR          here!
//         DD   DSN=CSCJGJ.CSC.CNTL(GRAINS),DISP=SHR
```

Notice that these are not "continued" JCL statements; there are no commas after the SHR in the first two lines. These are just DD statements that have all been stacked under the same DD name. You can also see that I have used instream data at //SYSIN to give the sort utility its control statement, which asks for an ascending sort on the first ten characters of the input records, in which the food name is stored. I directed //SORTOUT to SYSOUT=* to send the sorted output to print. You can see the combined contents of all three concatenated inputs at the bottom of this run.

8.11 Rules for Concatenating Sequential Data Sets

Suppose I had stored my food data (Figure 8.6) in separate data sets rather than as members of the same library. I could still concatenate them. I would code this the same way in all releases (versions) of MVS, but the rules governing the permitted characteristics of the data sets vary between releases. Here is how the coding would look in all versions:

```
//SORTIN   DD   DSN=CSCJGJ.CSC.FRUITS,DISP=SHR
//         DD   DSN=CSCJGJ.CSC.VEGE,DISP=SHR
//         DD   DSN=CSCJGJ.CSC.GRAINS,DISP=SHR
```

You can even intermix sequential data sets and members of partitioned data sets when concatenating them:

```
//SORTIN   DD   DSN=CSCJGJ.CSC.FRUITS,DISP=SHR        Sequential data set
//         DD   DSN=CSCJGJ.CSC.CNTL(VEGE),DISP=SHR    PDS member
//         DD   DSN=CSCJGJ.CSC.GRAINS,DISP=SHR        Sequential data set
```

```
EDIT --- CSCJGJ.CSC.CNTL(FRUITS) - 01.01 -------------------- COLUMNS 001 072
COMMAND ===>                                              SCROLL ===> PAGE
****** **************************** TOP OF DATA *****************************
000001 APPLES     RED     692  FRUIT
000002 APRICOT    ORANGE  835  FRUIT
000003 BANANAS    YELLOW  840  FRUIT
000004 KIWI       GREEN   274  FRUIT
000005 MANGO      YELLOW  926  FRUIT
000006 ORANGES    ORANGE  110  FRUIT
000007 PEACHES    ORANGE  462  FRUIT
```

```
    EDIT --- CSCJGJ.CSC.CNTL(VEGE) - 01.01 -------------------- COLUMNS 001 072
    COMMAND ===>                                              SCROLL ===> PAGE
    ****** **************************** TOP OF DATA *****************************
    000001 ASPARGUS   GREEN   484  VEGETABLE
    000002 BROCOLLI   GREEN   191  VEGETABLE
    000003 CARROTS    ORANGE  233  VEGETABLE
    000004 CORN       YELLOW  867  VEGETABLE
    000005 PEAS       GREEN   958  VEGETABLE
```

```
        EDIT --- CSCJGJ.CSC.CNTL(GRAINS) - 01.01 -------------------- COLUMNS 001 072
        COMMAND ===>                                              SCROLL ===> PAGE
        ****** **************************** TOP OF DATA *****************************
        000001 BARLEY     WHITE   221  GRAIN
        000002 BRAN       BROWN   172  GRAIN
        000003 RICE       BROWN   300  GRAIN
        000004 WHEAT      BROWN   635  GRAIN
```

Figure 8.6   Three Separate Members That I Will Concatenate

These three separate members of my CSCJGJ.CSC.CNTL library all contain 80-byte records. I concatenate them as input to a sort in the JCL shown in Figure 8.7.

These rules apply to concatenated data sets before release 4 of MVS/ESA:

1. If you concatenate simple sequential data sets containing fixed length records, the records in all data sets have to be of the same length.
2. The data set with the biggest block size has to be listed first (I'll tell you about block size in Chapters 10 and 13; for now, just realize that all members of the same partitioned data set have the same block

```
EDIT --- CSCJGJ.CSC.CNTL(F6CONCAT) - 01.01 ----------------- COLUMNS 001 072
COMMAND ===>                                              SCROLL ===> PAGE
****** ************************** TOP OF DATA ******************************
000100 //CSCJGJA   JOB 1,'BIN 7 JANOSSY',CLASS=A,MSGCLASS=X,MSGLEVEL=(1,1),
000200 //   NOTIFY=CSCJGJ
000300 //*
000400 //*    THIS JCL IS STORED AT CSCJGJ.CSC.CNTL(F6CONCAT)
000500 //*
000600 //**********************************************************************
000700 //*                                                                  *
000800 //*    CONCATENATE FRUITS, VEGETABLES, GRAINS INTO A SORT BY NAME    *
000900 //*                                                                  *
001000 //**********************************************************************
001100 //STEP010   EXEC  PGM=SORT
001200 //SYSOUT     DD   SYSOUT=*
001300 //SORTWK01   DD   UNIT=SYSDA,SPACE=(CYL,1)
001400 //SORTWK02   DD   UNIT=SYSDA,SPACE=(CYL,1)
001500 //SORTIN     DD   DSN=CSCJGJ.CSC.CNTL(FRUITS),DISP=SHR
001600 //           DD   DSN=CSCJGJ.CSC.CNTL(VEGE),DISP=SHR
001700 //           DD   DSN=CSCJGJ.CSC.CNTL(GRAINS),DISP=SHR
001800 //SORTOUT    DD   SYSOUT=*
001900 //SYSIN      DD   *
002000        SORT FIELDS=(1,10,CH,A)
002100 //
```

Concatenated inputs (PDS members)

(a)

(b)

```
APPLES     RED      692   FRUIT
APRICOT    ORANGE   835   FRUIT
ASPARGUS   GREEN    484   VEGETABLE
BANANAS    YELLOW   840   FRUIT
BARLEY     WHITE    221   GRAIN
BRAN       BROWN    172   GRAIN
BROCOLLI   GREEN    191   VEGETABLE
CARROTS    ORANGE   233   VEGETABLE
CORN       YELLOW   867   VEGETABLE
KIWI       GREEN    274   FRUIT
MANGO      YELLOW   926   FRUIT
ORANGES    ORANGE   110   FRUIT
PEACHES    ORANGE   462   FRUIT
PEAS       GREEN    958   VEGETABLE
RICE       BROWN    300   GRAIN
WHEAT      BROWN    635   GRAIN
```

Figure 8.7   Concatenating Data Into a Sort

(a) I have concatenated members named FRUITS, VEGE, and GRAINS at the //SORTIN DD statement in lines 1500 through 1700. Data set concatenation is a great convenience provided by MVS. The program reading the data is unaware of the details of the concatenation and doesn't even know that concatenation is occurring. (b) The sort produces this output.

size, but different PDSs and sequential data sets can have different block sizes).

3. All of the data sets have to be on the same type of device; that is, all have to be on tape or all on disk.

Release 4 of MVS/ESA relaxes requirements 2 and 3. If your installation is running MVS/ESA Release 4 or beyond, you can concatenate data sets in any sequence regardless of their block size and intermix disk and tape data sets.

You can concatenate up to 255 sequential data sets. Individual members of partitioned data sets count as sequential data sets.

8.12 Rules for Concatenating Libraries (PDS)

In certain cases an input to a program such as the compiler consists of an entire partitioned data set. For example, in your COBOL programs you can code COPY statements that each refer to a member of a partitioned data set. COPY is typically used to bring in installation-standard record layouts and other source code at compile time. Your compile/link/go proc identifies the partitioned data set (library) from which COPY members will be brought in. A compiler typically expects to find this library at a //SYSLIB DD name:

```
//SYSLIB  DD  DSN=CSCJGJ.CSC.COBOL,DISP=SHR
```

You can concatenate whole libraries at these types of DD statements. Your concatenation follows the same rules of syntax and sequence that apply in your installation to simple concatenations:

```
//SYSLIB  DD  DSN=CSCJGJ.CSC.COBOL,DISP=SHR        No comma
//       DD  DSN=CSCXXX.CSC.COPYLIB,DISP=SHR        here!
```

In this case, the compiler will seek each COPY item first from my library, CSCJGJ.CSC.COBOL, by looking at its directory. If it can't find the item there, it then goes down the concatenation list and looks in the directory of the next library, and so forth. Some extra rules apply when you concatenate whole partitioned data sets:

- You can't mix concatenations of whole partitioned data sets and sequential data sets.
- You can concatenate libraries only as input to programs (such as compilers and some utilities) that are "smart" enough themselves to seek individual members.
- You can concatenate up to 16 whole partitioned data sets.

I'll show you more about concatenated source code libraries at //SYSLIB and concatenated load modules libraries at //STEPLIB in Chapter 16.

8.13 When You Need to Code UNIT and VOL on a "Reading" DD

It's sometimes necessary for you to code more than DSN and DISP on a DD statement for reading a data set. These minimal items are sufficient when the data set is cataloged. The catalog can tell MVS other things it needs to know about the data set to read it, such as where (physically) the data is located and what kind of device this media requires. If the data set is not known to the catalog, you have to code UNIT and VOL=SER to tell this to MVS:

```
//SYSUT1   DD   DSN=CSCJGJ.CSC.WORKERS,
//   DISP=SHR,
//   UNIT=SYSDA,
//   VOL=SER=ACSCAC
```

In Figure 8.8a I show you the TSO 3.2 screen I used to uncatalog my data set CSCJGJ.CSC.WORKERS. I now have to code the //SYSUT1 DD statement with UNIT and VOL=SER to read it. SYSDA is the name on most IBM MVS mainframes that is associated with a list of all disk devices. VOL=SER stands for Volume Serial number and identifies a particular disk volume. SYSDA and VOL=SER are the two things that MVS would have gotten from the system catalog if it could have found the name CSCJGJ.CSC.WORKERS there. (I only knew that the data set was on disk volume ACSCAC because I recorded this fact when I created it.)

I explain more to you about UNIT coding and VOL=SER coding in Chapters 12 and 15. At this point I just wanted to show you that on rare occasions you may see a few additional things coded on a "reading" DD statement.

8.14 Problems in Coding Too Much on a "Reading" DD

MVS is fussy about what you *do* code on a DD statement for reading. If you code more than you have to, you may inadvertently instruct MVS not to check the system catalog. For example, if I coded this in my job in Figure 8.8, the job would again fail with a "data set not found" error:

```
//SYSUT1   DD   DSN=CSCJGJ.CSC.WORKERS,
//   DISP=SHR,
//   VOL=SER=ACSCAC
```

The problem here is that MVS assumes, because I told it one thing it would have found out from the catalog (VOL=SER), that I don't want it to check the catalog at all. *If you code either UNIT or VOL=SER you are telling MVS not to check the catalog for data set information.* Just as with good negotiation technique, you shouldn't say more than you have to on your DD statements.

```
------------------------- DATA SET UTILITY ------------------------------
OPTION  ===> U

   A - Allocate new data set          C - Catalog data set
   R - Rename entire data set         U - Uncatalog data set
   D - Delete entire data set
   blank - Display data set information

ISPF LIBRARY:
   PROJECT ===> CSCJGJ
   LIBRARY ===> CSC
   TYPE    ===> COBOL

OTHER PARTITIONED OR SEQUENTIAL DATA SET:
   DATA SET NAME ===> CSC.WORKERS
   VOLUME SERIAL ===>               (If not cata

DATA SET PASSWORD ===>          (If password protected)
```

The name you put here overrides the ISPF LIBRARY fields. TSO automatically puts your TSO user id in front of this name unless you surround it with apostrophes.

(a)

(b)

```
EDIT --- CSCJGJ.CSC.CNTL(F7FIND) - 01.01 ------------------ COLUMNS 001 072
COMMAND ===> sub                                          SCROLL ===> PAGE
****** *************************** TOP OF DATA ******************************
000100 //CSCJGJA   JOB 1,'BIN 7 JANOSSY',CLASS=A,MSGCLASS=X,MSGLEVEL=(1,1),
000200 //  NOTIFY=CSCJGJ
000300 //*
000400 //*   THIS JCL IS STORED AT CSCJGJ.CSC.CNTL(F7FIND)
000500 //*
000600 //*********************************************************************
000700 //*                                                                  *
000800 //*    LIST THE WORKER DATA WITHOUT FORMATTING IT FOR PRINT          *
000900 //*                                                                  *
001000 //*********************************************************************
001100 //STEP010   EXEC  PGM=IEBGENER
001200 //SYSUT1     DD   DSN=CSCJGJ.CSC.WORKERS,
001300 //  DISP=SHR,
001400 //  UNIT=SYSDA,           Reading an uncataloged data set
001500 //  VOL=SER=ACSCAC
001600 //SYSUT2     DD   SYSOUT=*
001700 //SYSPRINT   DD   DUMMY

JOB CSCJGJA(JOB03641) SUBMITTED

15.36.39 JOB 3641 $HASP165 CSCJGJA  ENDED AT N1 CN(00)
15.36.39 JOB 3641 $HASP165 IEF097I CSCJGJA  - USER CSCJGJ   ASSIGNED CN(00)
***
```

Figure 8.8 Reading an Uncataloged Data Set

(a) I used TSO's 3.2 function to uncatalog CSCJGJ.CSC.WORKERS after creating it. It is dangerous to uncatalog a data set because you then have to keep track of the disk or tape volume on which it is stored. (b) To read an uncataloged data set you have to code UNIT and VOL=SER. SYSDA is a name for a list of disk devices, as I explain in Chapter 12, and VOL=SER is the volume serial number of a disk or tape, as I explain in Chapter 15.

Chapter 8 Review
Mini-Glossary

DISP DISPosition, a parameter you must code as either DISP=SHR or DISP=OLD on a DD statement to read a data set

OLD DISP coding to gain data set access on an exclusive basis

SHR DISP coding to gain data set access on a shared basis

NULLFILE A "dummy" data set name that acts like DD DUMMY

Instream data Data within JCL, following //DDname DD *

Concatenated data Two or more data sets read as one data set

Review Questions

1. Explain the impact of coding DISP=OLD instead of DISP=SHR on a DD statement at which a program is reading a data set.
2. Describe what MVS does if you completely omit the DISP parameter on a DD statement in which a data set is being read.
3. Describe three ways to code the beginning of instream data and the corresponding mechanisms for marking its end.
4. Identify four of the rules for concatenated sequential and partitioned data sets, indicating which of these are relaxed in newer releases of MVS/ESA.

Exercises

A. Using TSO/ISPF, create a member in your CNTL library named BIGLITTL. Enter all of the letters of the alphabet in capital letters on one line, all of the letters in lowercase letters on the next line (use the CAPS OFF option of TSO/ISPF!), the numbers 0 through 9 on the third line, and some punctuation symbols and spaces on the fourth line. Then, using Figure 8.3a and the JOB statement from your earlier exercises, code a one-step job that uses IDCAMS to dump the contents of this member. Code the control statements as instream data. Compare your output to Figure 8.4.
B. Using Exercise A or a previous exercise, put a blank line in your JCL. Submit it and confirm that MVS generates a //SYSIN DD * statement as you see in Figure 8.5.

Chapter Nine

DD STATEMENTS FOR PRINTING: SYSOUT

SYSOUT is the generalized print-handling mechanism of MVS. You hand over material destined to be printed to SYSOUT, one line of print (record) at a time. SYSOUT stores the lines in a large disk file called the *spool* and arranges to send them to the one or more print output devices attached to the computer. Printlines residing in the spool awaiting print have been "queued for print." As Figure 9.1 illustrates, you can view them by using TSO/ISPF before they print. In this chapter I'll show you several "convenience" parameters that apply only to SYSOUT and print and how to use them.

9.1 Mainframe Versus Microcomputer Printing

Microcomputers generate lines of print as records in "text file" format. These records contain special symbols for horizontal tabs, carriage return, and line feed. These control characters direct a printer's actions as the printlines are sent to it. You can display text file data on a terminal screen just as easily as printing it because the control characters are handled in the same way on both types of output devices and cause the same text-formatting effects.

IBM mainframe print output is not in text file format. It's much like punch cards, except that printlines carry 132 or more bytes of data, not just 80. Just as with the punch card, blanks are present for each unprinted position, and there is no such thing as a tab character. The first position of each printline is treated as a vertical tab, or carriage control byte. This byte *does not* cause the appropriate vertical tabbing on mainframe video terminals. When you view print output using TSO, it will all appear single spaced. To see the print formatting, you actually have to print the output.

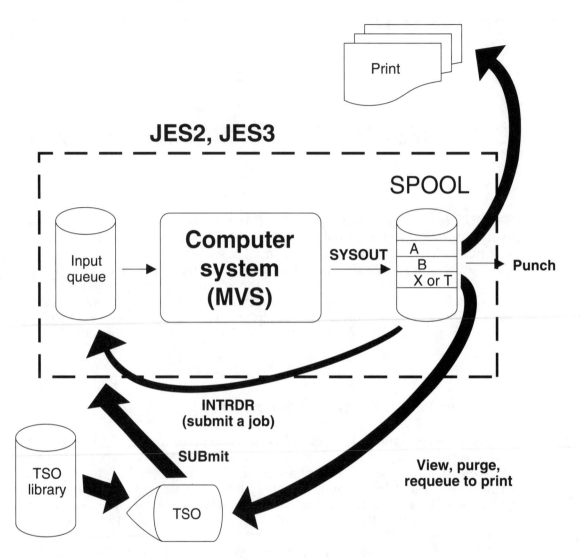

Figure 9.1 Output Queue, or Spool

The print output of all programs—and MVS output itself—is handled by a large disk file called the "spool." You send lines of print into the spool by coding SYSOUT=y, where "y" is a print class defined by your installation. Print class is coded as MSGCLASS=y on the JOB statement. Print class A has traditionally been the "print it as soon as possible" print class, and B has been the print class for material to be punched on cards. Print class X or T usually functions as the "held" class, which allows you to view output before printing; Q may be used in some shops.

These are the most common values used in the carriage control byte to cause vertical tabbing:

+	No advance; overstrike last line printed
space	Advance one line; single space
0	Advance two lines; double space
-	Advance three lines; triple space
1	Advance to top of next page

You'll occasionally see these symbols at the beginning of print output that you view in the spool using TSO/ISPF. "Top of page" was formerly defined on mainframe impact printers using a paper tape (the carriage control tape) that traveled around a sprocket in synchronization with the pin-fed paper being printed. Top of page is now defined electronically, but the same first-byte control codes shown above still apply.

9.2 Common Coding for Print

Using SYSOUT to handle print allows your program to produce one report or many reports at a time. You simply code the DD statement for each print output with SYSOUT=*. For example, here is how I send the two print outputs from IEBGENER to the SYSOUT print spool:

```
//STEP010    EXEC   PGM=IEBGENER
//SYSIN      DD     DUMMY
//SYSUT1     DD     DSN=CSCJGJ.CSC.CNTL(WORKERS),DISP=SHR
//SYSUT2     DD     SYSOUT=*
//SYSPRINT   DD     SYSOUT=*
```

SYSOUT=* tells MVS to substitute at the asterisk the print destination coded at MSGCLASS on the JOB statement. You could alternatively code one or all SYSOUTs literally as a print class:

```
//STEP010    EXEC   PGM=IEBGENER
//SYSIN      DD     DUMMY
//SYSUT1     DD     DSN=CSCJGJ.CSC.CNTL(WORKERS),DISP=SHR
//SYSUT2     DD     SYSOUT=A
//SYSPRINT   DD     SYSOUT=A
```

9.3 Print Classes

Print class and MSGCLASS are single-position codes that are established locally. These print class codes are traditional:

A	Print to be produced on default system printer without viewing via TSO/ISPF
B	Spooled output destined to be punched on cards (obsolete in most installations)
X or T or Q	"Held" output; remains on the print spool for you to view with TSO/ISPF

Your installation can (and probably does) create other single-character print class codes. The print class is really a subdivision of the print spool. By having print segregated into different classes, it's possible to treat different types of print differently.

9.4 How Output Leaves the Print Spool

Lines of print remain on the spool until directed to a printer. The software that picks material from the spool and prints it is called an *output writer.* Output writers run at the direction of the computer operator and are not visible to applications programming personnel or end users. Several output writers may be running at once.

An output writer is directed by the console operator to pick certain print classes from the spool and print them. However, at a given time it's possible that no output writer may be picking off and printing some print classes. If you make a mistake in coding a SYSOUT and specify a little-used or nonexistent print class, your output might sit on the spool indefinitely. It can be "requeued" by the console operator to a different print class so that it can be printed.

SYSOUT can accept lines longer than a printer can handle. Impact printers are generally limited to 132 printable positions, whereas laser printers have an upper limit as high as 200 or more printable positions per line. Mainframe printers generally drop the excess positions of printlines sent to them and do not "wrap around" lines of print like mini- and microcomputer printers.

9.5 OUTLIM: Limiting the Quantity of Print

One of the most useful optional parameters you can code with SYSOUT is OUTLIM:

```
//REPORT1  DD  SYSOUT=*,OUTLIM=1000
```

The number that you code at OUTLIM puts a limit on the number of lines (records) that SYSOUT will accept into the spool from this DDname. You can use this to prevent accidents in situations where a program logic loop involving a WRITE statement might generate enormous amounts of print output very quickly. The danger in such an occurrence is more than just the possibility of your wasting money, time, and paper. A program being tested that runs wild can generate enough printline output to seriously degrade spool operation or to fill the spool data set completely. If the spool fills up, the entire computer system has to be stopped.

OUTLIM takes the form OUTLIM=n, where the value of "n" can range from 1 to 16777215 coded without commas. If the output limit is reached, MVS cancels the job with a system completion code of 722. The lines already output to the spool remain there and can be printed.

OUTLIM is a limit of logical records written to the spool, not of lines taken from the spool and printed. If you coded COPIES on the same DD statement, multiple copies of the partial output can be generated. You can still consume large quantities of paper even with a relatively low OUTLIM limit if many of the lines you're writing have a page eject carriage control character of "1" in the first byte.

9.6 Using Print Class for Print Routing

In some installations, different print classes are established to send print material to different locations. DePaul University, for example, has computer labs at four locations, all tied to our IBM ES/9000 training mainframe. If you code SYSOUT=A, your print is routed to the downtown Administrative Center; if you code SYSOUT=L, your print goes to the Lincoln Park campus. Coding SYSOUT=N sends output to the Northwest Center, and your print is sent to Oakbrook if you code SYSOUT=O.

But there are other ways to accomplish print routing, and different print classes may instead be set up to control the way printing occurs. Installations that use mainframe laser printers often set the default printing mode to be two-sided to economize on paper costs. One-sided print can then be assigned a special print class such as S. This lets an appropriately tailored output writer handle the majority of print in two-sided manner, while allowing outputs intended for one-side printing to be handled by a different output writer.

9.7 DEST for Print Routing

Sometimes an installation configuration is too complex to allow the use of print classes as routing codes. You can also use the DEST parameter of SYSOUT to route print if you know the identifier of remote printers. Remote job entry and printing stations each have an identifying number from 1 to 1000; the printer local to the computer itself is remote 0. You can code DEST with SYSOUT to send each of several print outputs to different destinations:

```
//BT3766U1    DD    SYSOUT=A,DEST=R0
//BT3766U2    DD    SYSOUT=A,DEST=R5
//BT3766U3    DD    SYSOUT=A,DEST=R14
```

This would send one print to the printer local to the computer system, a second output to remote printer R5, and a third report to remote printer 14. I specified print class A because of all print classes it is the most likely to have an active output writer.

9.8 /*ROUTE for Print Routing (JES2 Only)

Although it's not a part of your SYSOUT specification itself, you can also use a "job parm" statement named /*ROUTE to route all SYSOUT outputs that lack an explicit DEST parameter. For example, you can code this form of statement immediately after your JOB statement:

```
/*ROUTE PRINT R15
```

This statement looks like a strange perversion of the instream delimiter statement, which starts with /*. But Job Entry System 2 (if your installation uses it) will act on it. This would send all output coded with SYSOUT and without DEST to remote printer 15. You can view output routed with /*ROUTE and placed into the print class X or T hold queue using TSO-/ISPF, as usual. The routing applies when and if you release the output for printing.

9.9 //*FORMAT for Print Routing (JES3 Only)

Although, it's not a part of your SYSOUT specification itself, you can also use a "job parm" statement named //*FORMAT to route any output of your job to a desired destination. For example, you can code this form of statement immediately after your JOB statement:

```
//*FORMAT PR,
//*DDNAME=STEP010.REPT1,
//*DEST=BREWSTER
```

This looks like a series of comments, but if your installation is using Job Entry Subsystem 3 (JES3), it will route the output at DDname //REPT1 in

//STEP010 to the node on your computer network named BREWSTER. Only very large installations use JES3 instead of JES2.

9.10 COPIES: Printing Multiple Copies

The default mode of operation for the SYSOUT print mechanism is to print one copy of a given print output from the spool and then delete the item from the spool. Using the COPIES parameter, you can have SYSOUT print from 1 to 255 copies of the printlines for an item before deleting it. You can code COPIES with or without other parameters:

```
//BT3766U1  DD   SYSOUT=A,COPIES=3
//BT3766U2  DD   SYSOUT=A,DEST=R5,COPIES=6
```

Each copy of the output receives its own MVS-generated job separator pages. If the output consists of only a page or two, using COPIES will often result in more separator pages being generated than actual desired output!

9.11 /*JOBPARM for Multiple Copies (JES2 Only)

You can code /*JOBPARM COPIES=nnn immediately after your JOB statement to cause a given number of copies of all print items from the job, including the system allocation/deallocation reports, to be produced. You can make the "nnn" any number from 1 to 255. If you use a /*ROUTE PRINT statement with /*JOBPARM COPIES=nnn, then nnn copies of all job print output will be sent to the specified remote printer.

There's a potential snag in using /*JOBPARM COPIES=nnn. If you use it but direct print to the held print class, /*JOBPARM is ignored, and only one copy will ultimately be printed.

9.12 //*FORMAT for Multiple Copies (JES3 Only)

If you are working in a JES3 environment, you can obtain multiple copies of a given print output using the //*FORMAT PR control statement. This amounts to just one additional item on this statement:

```
//*FORMAT PR,
//*DDNAME=STEP010.REPT1,
//*DEST=BREWSTER,
//*COPIES=3
```

9.13 OUTPUT JCL: Sending Print to Multiple Destinations

You can use a special feature of JCL called the OUTPUT statement to create printing specifications that any SYSOUT parameter can refer to. An OUTPUT statement looks like this:

```
//OAKBR   OUTPUT   CLASS=O,COPIES=3
```

You can code one or more OUTPUT statements immediately after your JOB statement. Any number of SYSOUT parameters (on different DD statements) can refer to the same OUTPUT statement by using its name, such as OAKBR in this example. And a given SYSOUT parameter can refer to more than one OUTPUT statement to ask JES (Job Entry Subsystem) to print the lines you have put into the spool multiple times, in multiple places.

OUTPUT statements are interesting and powerful. They let you communicate directly with JES2 or JES3. As opposed to /* or //* JES control statements, OUTPUT statements are not particular to the version of JES that your installation uses.

Figure 9.2a shows you how I used OUTPUT statements to send the same print output to multiple places, with different numbers of copies at different locations. Figures 9.2b and 9.2c show you the type of outputs that are produced when I run this JCL. Use these illustrations and their legends as a guide to experimenting with OUTPUT statements. OUTPUT has been supported in MVS JCL for several years. But its use—involving the need to code a null SYSOUT=(,) along with references to an OUTPUT statement—was so poorly documented that even some experienced programmers don't know about it!

9.14 Sequence of Multiple Print Outputs at a Step

There's no limit, within practicality, to the number of print outputs you can produce in one program. Whether a program generates one print output or a dozen, you can handle them all by using SYSOUT. Each print output emerges at a different DDname, and you just code SYSOUT for each.

Under JES2, if one of your programs produces more than one print output, the order in which the reports are printed is the order in which you code the DD statements for the step. You can have whatever print output you want appear first just by arranging the DD statements for the outputs in that order in your JCL. Under JES3, you can't control the sequence that your print outputs will be printed in this way.

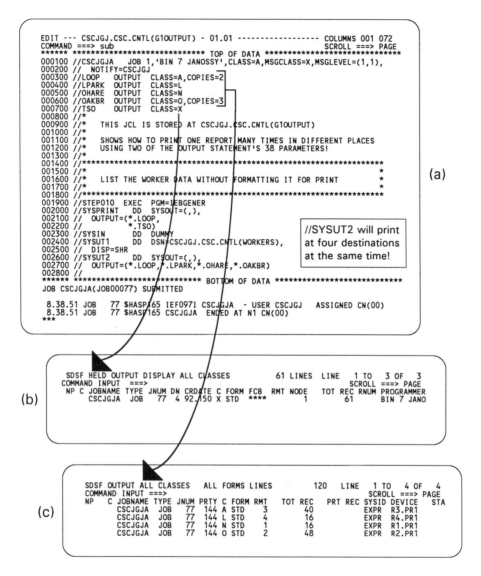

```
EDIT --- CSCJGJ.CSC.CNTL(G1OUTPUT) - 01.01 ----------------- COLUMNS 001 072
COMMAND ===> sub                                            SCROLL ===> PAGE
****** ************************** TOP OF DATA ********************************
000100 //CSCJGJA   JOB 1,'BIN 7 JANOSSY',CLASS=A,MSGCLASS=X,MSGLEVEL=(1,1),
000200 //   NOTIFY=CSCJGJ
000300 //LOOP    OUTPUT   CLASS=A,COPIES=2
000400 //LPARK   OUTPUT   CLASS=L
000500 //OHARE   OUTPUT   CLASS=N
000600 //OAKBR   OUTPUT   CLASS=O,COPIES=3
000700 //TSO     OUTPUT   CLASS=X
000800 //*
000900 //*    THIS JCL IS STORED AT CSCJGJ.CSC.CNTL(G1OUTPUT)
001000 //*
001100 //*    SHOWS HOW TO PRINT ONE REPORT MANY TIMES IN DIFFERENT PLACES
001200 //*    USING TWO OF THE OUTPUT STATEMENT'S 38 PARAMETERS!
001300 //*
001400 //******************************************************************
001500 //*                                                                *
001600 //*    LIST THE WORKER DATA WITHOUT FORMATTING IT FOR PRINT        *
001700 //*                                                                *
001800 //******************************************************************
001900 //STEP010  EXEC  PGM=IEBGENER
002000 //SYSPRINT  DD  SYSOUT=(,),
002100 //   OUTPUT=(*.LOOP,
002200 //           *.TSO)
002300 //SYSIN     DD  DUMMY
002400 //SYSUT1    DD  DSN=CSCJGJ.CSC.CNTL(WORKERS),
002500 //   DISP=SHR
002600 //SYSUT2    DD  SYSOUT=(,),
002700 //   OUTPUT=(*.LOOP,*.LPARK,*.OHARE,*.OAKBR)
002800 //
****** ********************** BOTTOM OF DATA *********************************
JOB CSCJGJA(JOB00077) SUBMITTED

  8.38.51 JOB   77 $HASP165 IEF097I CSCJGJA - USER CSCJGJ   ASSIGNED CN(00)
  8.38.51 JOB   77 $HASP165 CSCJGJA  ENDED AT N1 CN(00)
***
```

(a)

//SYSUT2 will print at four destinations at the same time!

```
SDSF HELD OUTPUT DISPLAY ALL CLASSES         61 LINES  LINE   1 TO   3 OF  3
COMMAND INPUT   ===>                                       SCROLL ===> PAGE
NP C JOBNAME TYPE JNUM DN CRDATE C FORM FCB  RMT NODE   TOT REC RNUM PROGRAMMER
     CSCJGJA  JOB   77 4 92.150 X STD ****        1          61      BIN 7 JANO
```

(b)

```
SDSF OUTPUT ALL CLASSES   ALL FORMS LINES        120  LINE   1 TO  4 OF  4
COMMAND INPUT ===>                                         SCROLL ===> PAGE
NP   C JOBNAME TYPE JNUM PRTY C FORM RMT   TOT REC  PRT REC SYSID DEVICE   STA
       CSCJGJA  JOB   77  144 A STD    3        40           EXPR  R3.PR1
       CSCJGJA  JOB   77  144 L STD    4        16           EXPR  R4.PR1
       CSCJGJA  JOB   77  144 N STD    1        16           EXPR  R1.PR1
       CSCJGJA  JOB   77  144 O STD    2        48           EXPR  R2.PR1
```

(c)

Figure 9.2   Using OUTPUT JCL to Replicate Printing

(a) You can code OUTPUT statements immediately after your JOB statement. Then you can refer to any of these in SYSOUT parameters. This gives you the capability to tell the output processor (JES2 or JES3) that you want the same spool-stored printlines to be printed at several different places or in several different ways. Here I want two copies of the //SYSPRINT output to be printed at CLASS=A, and a copy to remain in the held (TSO) queue for viewing. (b) The //TSO OUTPUT statement sends //SYSPRINT to the held queue. (c) the //LOOP, //LPARK, //OHARE, and //OAKBR OUTPUT statements send output to the output queue for immediate simultaneous printing.

9.15 SYSOUT Parameter "Long Form"

Your common SYSOUT=A coding of the SYSOUT parameter is actually the "short form" of this parameter. The "long form" of SYSOUT reveals that it really has three positional subparameters:

SYSOUT = (*print-class*, writer-name, form-id/code-id)

You already know about print class. You might also be interested in the other two specifications.

9.16 SYSOUT Writer-Name Subparameter and INTRDR

SYSOUT = (print-class, *writer-name*, form-id/code-id)

Writer-name is the name of a program similar to an output writer, but one that is external to the SYSOUT mechanism. When you specify writer-name, the writer-name must represent a member within SYS1.LINKLIB or another default load module library on the system. The program you name is loaded by the system and used to process the output, rather than assigning the output to one of the customary output writers.

One special output writer provided by MVS is called INTRDR, or the *internal reader.* If you direct output this way:

```
//JCLOUT   DD  SYSOUT=(A,INTRDR)
```

the program INTRDR is given control to remove the material from the spool and send it into the input queue. (The input queue is also part of the system spooling mechanism.)

INTRDR is an interesting feature because it allows you to copy or form JCL statements in a job step and feed them into the system to submit another job. The output you process in this way has to be 80-byte records, starting with a JOB statement. MVS accepts it as if it were being SUBmitted using TSO/ISPF. This is a useful capability in the production environment. It's sometimes necessary to let a user initiate a job by running a job that just uses IEBGENER to copy the "real" JCL into the input queue. This prevents the user from having any access to the real JCL.

Figures 9.3 and 9.4 give you a complete example of how to use INTRDR. This feature of MVS JCL is specialized and related to control and security in the production environment. You should be aware of INTRDR because it makes it possible to minimize certain types of vulnerabilities created by complete access to JCL.

```
EDIT --- CSCJGJ.CSC.CNTL(G2RUNIT) - 01.01 ------------------ COLUMNS 001 072
COMMAND ===> sub                                            SCROLL ===> PAGE
****** *************************** TOP OF DATA *********************************
000100 //CSCJGJA    JOB 1,'BIN 7 JANOSSY',CLASS=A,MSGCLASS=X,MSGLEVEL=(1,1),
000200 //  NOTIFY=CSCJGJ
000300 //*
000400 //*    THIS JCL IS STORED AT CSCJGJ.CSC.CNTL(G2RUNIT)
000500 //*
000600 //*    THIS IS AN IEBGENER THAT COPIES OTHER JCL TO THE INTERNAL READER
000700 //*    USING THE SYSOUT INTRDR FEATURE.  YOU COULD GIVE THIS JCL TO AN
000800 //*    END USER SO HE/SHE COULD RUN A JOB WITHOUT TOUCHING THE REAL JCL.
000900 //*    NOTICE THAT THE REAL JCL IS HIDDEN IN A LIBRARY NAMED DIFFERENTLY
001000 //*    THAN WHERE THIS JCL IS.  SECURITY SOFTWARE COULD PREVENT A USER
001100 //*    FROM HAVING DIRECT ACCESS TO A LIBRARY SUCH AS CSCJGJ.CSC.XCNTL.
001200 //*                                                  ----------------
001300 //STEP010  EXEC  PGM=IEBGENER
001400 //SYSPRINT   DD   SYSOUT=*                                "REAL"
001500 //SYSIN      DD   DUMMY                                   JCL IS
001600 //SYSUT1     DD   DSN=CSCJGJ.CSC.XCNTL(G3HIDDEN),DISP=SHR  <=== HIDDEN
001700 //SYSUT2     DD   SYSOUT=(A,INTRDR)
001800 //
****** *************************** BOTTOM OF DATA ******************************
JOB CSCJGJA(JOB00073) SUBMITTED

 8.35.24 JOB   73 $HASP165 CSCJGJA  ENDED AT N1 CN(00)
 8.35.24 JOB   73 $HASP165 IEF097I CSCJGJA  - USER CSCJGJ   ASSIGNED CN(00)
 8.35.29 JOB   74 $HASP165 CSCJGJA  ENDED AT N1 CN(00)
 8.35.29 JOB   74 $HASP165 IEF097I CSCJGJA  - USER CSCJGJ   ASSIGNED CN(00)
***
```

```
  SDSF HELD OUTPUT DISPLAY ALL CLASSES        174 LINES  COMMAND ISSUED
  COMMAND INPUT  ===>                                     SCROLL ===> PAGE
  NP C JOBNAME TYPE JNUM DN CRDATE  C FORM FCB  RMT NODE  TOT REC RNUM PROGRAMMER
       CSCJGJA  JOB   73  4 92.150  X STD  ****      1        51      BIN 7 JANO
       CSCJGJA  JOB   74  5 92.150  X STD  ****      1       123      BIN 7 JANO
```

Two job outputs exist: job 73 is the job submitted above,
and job 74 is the job run by the JCL put into the internal
reader using (A,INTRDR)

Figure 9.3   Using INTRDR to Submit a JOB

This JCL simply uses IEBGENER to copy safeguarded JCL into the internal reader (input queue) to submit it, by using SYSOUT=(A,INTRDR). By running this JCL, I will just cause another job to be submitted. The messages at the bottom of the screen show that my G2RUNIT job received job number 73, whereas the job it copied into the internal reader got job number 74. Both jobs ran very quickly and have already finished. JCL like this is handy if you have to let a novice end user submit work, but can't, for security reasons, allow the "real" JCL that runs the job to be handled by the user, or perhaps even seen by him or her.

```
EDIT --- CSCJGJ.CSC.XCNTL(G3HIDDEN) - 01.00 ---------------- COLUMNS 001 072
COMMAND ===>                                                 SCROLL ===> PAGE
****** *************************** TOP OF DATA ********************************
000100 //CSCJGJA   JOB 1,'BIN 7 JANOSSY',CLASS=A,MSGCLASS=X,MSGLEVEL=(1,1),
000200 //    NOTIFY=CSCJGJ
000300 //*
000400 //*     THIS JCL IS STORED AT CSCJGJ.CSC.XCNTL(G3HIDDEN)
000500 //*
000600 //*     THIS JOB IS JUST A DEMONSTRATION OF JCL THAT COULD BE KEPT
000700 //*     OUT OF THE REACH OF SOMEONE WHO MUST SUBMIT IT.  I WILL SUBMIT
000800 //*     THIS BY RUNNING AN IEBGENER JOB THAT COPIES THIS JCL TO THE
000900 //*     INPUT QUEUE USING INTRDR.  THE JCL HERE COULD DO ANYTHING AND
001000 //*     IT COULD HAVE AS MANY STEPS AS YOU LIKE.
001100 //*
001200 //**********************************************************************
001300 //*                                                                   *
001400 //*     SORT WORKER DATA DESCENDING BY NUMBER OF HOURS WORKED          *
001500 //*                                                                   *
001600 //**********************************************************************
001700 //STEP010  EXEC  PGM=SORT
001800 //SYSOUT     DD  SYSOUT=*
001900 //SORTWK01   DD  UNIT=SYSDA,SPACE=(CYL,1)
002000 //SORTWK02   DD  UNIT=SYSDA,SPACE=(CYL,1)
002100 //SORTIN     DD  DSN=CSCJGJ.CSC.CNTL(WORKERS),DISP=SHR
002200 //SORTOUT    DD  DSN=&&WORKERS,
002300 //    UNIT=SYSDA,
002400 //    DISP=(NEW,PASS,DELETE),
002500 //    DCB=(RECFM=FB,LRECL=80,BLKSIZE=3840),
002600 //    SPACE=(TRK,1)
002700 //SYSIN      DD  *                                   SORTING
002800        SORT FIELDS=(28,3,ZD,D)               <=== INSTRUCTIONS
002900 /*
003000 //*
003100 //**********************************************************************
003200 //*                                                                   *
003300 //*     LIST SORTED WORKER DATA                                        *
003400 //*     FIELDS ARE SPACED FOR EASIER READING USING INSTRUCTIONS        *
003500 //*     TO THE "IEBGENER" PROGRAM AT ITS //SYSIN DD STATEMENT          *
003600 //*                                                                   *
003700 //**********************************************************************
003800 //STEP020  EXEC  PGM=IEBGENER
003900 //SYSPRINT   DD  DUMMY
004000 //SYSUT1     DD  DSN=&&WORKERS,
004100 //  DISP=(OLD,DELETE)
004200 //SYSUT2     DD  SYSOUT=*
004300 //SYSIN      DD  *
004400    GENERATE  MAXFLDS=99,MAXLITS=80
004500        RECORD  FIELD=(5,1,,1),
004600                FIELD=(2,' ',,6),
004700                FIELD=(11,7,,8),
004800                FIELD=(2,' ',,17),
004900                FIELD=(10,18,,21),
005000                FIELD=(2,' ',,31),
005100                FIELD=(2,28,,33),
005200                FIELD=(1,' ',,35),
005300                FIELD=(1,30,,36),
005400                FIELD=(2,' ',,37),
005500                FIELD=(20,31,,39)
005600 /*
005700 //
```

Figure 9.4   Hidden JCL Submitted by My INTRDR JCL

This JCL is referred to in Figure 9.3 as G3HIDDEN. Notice that it is stored in a library named CSCJGJ.CSC.XCNTL, not in the same library as the JCL that copies it into the internal reader. This way, I could set system security to prevent the person who submits the job in Figure 9.3 from ever directly accessing and changing G3HIDDEN. G3HIDDEN could contain JCL to do anything; the JCL in Figure 9.3 will always be the same because it is simply a "copy to the card reader" job. All the end user ever sees is the JCL in Figure 9.3!

9.17 The SYSOUT Form-id/Code-id Subparameter

SYSOUT = (print-class, writer-name, *form-id/code id*)

You can specify form-id in the third positional subparameter slot. It's a name that may be from one to four characters in length. The value that you put here is provided to the computer console operator when the output is about to be printed so that the necessary preprinted or special-dimension form can be mounted on the printer. Certain laser printers that store form images electronically respond automatically to the form-id.

Code-id is a value that appears similar to form-id. However, it represents a code name for a JES2 /*OUTPUT statement that you have to include in your JCL immediately after the job statement.

9.18 FCB: Forms Control Buffer

Physical carriage control tapes have been replaced on some mainframe printers by an electronic forms control buffer. The image of a carriage control tape, stored as a member in a library called SYS1.IMAGELIB, is fed into the forms control buffer automatically to govern certain print characteristics. Names of members in SYS1.IMAGELIB may be up to eight bytes in length, but the fcb-name consists of only the last four characters. When this feature is available in an installation, you can send the appropriate electronic carriage control tape to the printer by coding:

FCB = (fcb-name, operator-action)

An example of coding is

```
//BT3722U2   DD   SYSOUT=A,FCB=(F12A,ALIGN)
```

Operator-action is an optional specification. If you code ALIGN here, the operator is sent a message asking that form alignment be checked prior to printing. If you code VERIFY here, MVS sends the operator a message to check the printer's chain or train-printing elements to confirm that the appropriate font is in place.

9.19 UCS: Character Set Specification

Certain printers can automatically respond to a JCL-coded specification to use a certain character set for a print job. Other printer models cannot automatically make use of a specially indicated character set but can at least check electronically to see what character print train is mounted and request the operator to mount the desired one if it is not on the printer. You code print character set specification using the UCS parameter:

UCS = (character-set, FOLD, VERIFY)

An example of such coding is

```
//BT3722U2   DD   SYSOUT=A,UCS=(SN,FOLD,VERIFY)
```

Local documentation indicates what the UCS codes are for your printers. UCS is not used much with impact printers because of the delays introduced by having to change the printing element. You can code UCS with FCB if you have to specify a character set and also load the printer with an electronically stored carriage control tape image.

The optional FOLD subparameter doesn't deal with paper processing. Instead, it causes printers that can respond to it to print lowercase letters in uppercase. The optional VERIFY subparameter requires the operator to confirm that a print sample indicates the correct print chain or train is in use.

Chapter 9 Review

Mini-Glossary

Carriage control byte   The first byte of a printline, which carries a code indicating vertical tabbing to the printer

SYSOUT   The MVS-provided print buffering mechanism

Print class   The one-byte value that you code as MSGCLASS or at any SYSOUT= parameter

Output writer   An MVS-operated program that copies lines of print from the spool to a printer

INTRDR   The "internal reader," to which you can copy a set of JCL to have one job submit another job

Review Questions

1. Describe how printlines output by a mainframe are different than those output by a mini- or microcomputer.
2. What is the print spool, and what does it do?
3. Explain what print classes are and why SYSOUT=X (or T or Q) is called the "held" print class.
4. A programmer coded SYSOUT=E on a DD statement at which print-lines are written by a program, but the output never printed. Why did this happen? How could she print it?
5. Can you send the print output of a single DD statement to several different destinations *simultaneously*? Explain why or why not and, if it is possible, how this can be done.

Exercise

A. Using your local system documentation, find out what print classes are used on your computer system. Code a set of JCL named PRINT-FUN that uses IEBGENER to copy a member of your CNTL library to SYSOUT. Code MSGCLASS on your JOB statement to send the MVS system reporting to the held queue and IEBGENER's //SYSUT2 output to a print class that is not held. Run the job and confirm how it works.

Chapter Ten

DD STATEMENTS TO CREATE (WRITE) DATA SETS

DD statements to read a data set or to send an output to the printer are the easiest DD statements to code. By contrast, the hardest DD statement for you to develop is the type that services a program output destined for retention in machine-readable form. To handle records emerging from a program that are to be stored in a disk or tape file, you have to code a DD statement with several potentially complex parameters.

My goal for this chapter is to help you become familiar enough with "writing" DD statements to be able to code them fairly efficiently for new disk data sets. With the background knowledge and familiarity you'll gain here, you'll have the foundation you need to explore each of the "writing" DD statement parameters in greater depth in Chapters 11 through 14. In Chapter 15 I'll give you the extra information you need to be able to code DD statements to write tape data sets.

10.1 Allocating a Disk Data Set Using TSO/ISPF

There is no inherent connection between job control language and TSO/ISPF. But you can create a new disk data set using TSO, a process that TSO/ISPF calls **allocating** a data set. (Watch out! TSO command lists use the word *allocate* differently; there, you allocate a data set to associate it with your interactive session.) I'm going to show you how to allocate a data set using TSO/ISPF because the parallels between doing that and creating a data set with JCL are very obvious. By seeing how you do this using TSO/ISPF, you'll quickly understand why you have to code several things in your "writing" DD statements.

You allocate a data set by using TSO/ISPF function 3.2. Figure 10.1a shows you the 3.2 data set utility screen. When you select option A and enter a data set name, such as CSCJGJ.CSC.JUMBLE in this example, you receive the screen shown in Figure 10.1b. The name of the data set you want to create carries over to this screen, and you have to enter several fields of information:

```
VOLUME SERIAL   ===>              Leave blank
GENERIC UNIT    ===>              Leave blank
SPACE UNITS     ===> TRKS         Requests space in disk tracks
```

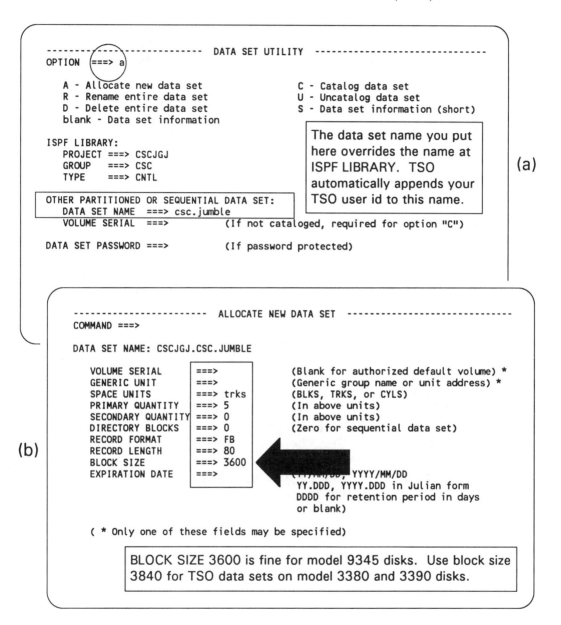

Figure 10.1   Allocating a Disk Data Set Using TSO/ISPF 3.2

(a) I allocate a new data set named CSCJGJ.CSC.JUMBLE starting with this screen (TSO/ISPF function 3.2). I name the data set at the OTHER PARTITIONED OR SEQUENTIAL DATA SET field, which overrides the ISPF LIBRARY fields. At this field, TSO automatically prefaces anything you enter with your TSO user-id (enclose the name in apostrophes if you want to enter the whole name). (b) To allocate a disk data set, you need to specify all of the characteristics here (see Section 10.2).

```
PRIMARY QUAN        ===> 5         Size of initial piece of space
SECONDARY QUAN      ===> 0         Size of up to 15 extra pieces
DIRECTORY BLOCKS    ===> 0         Greater than zero means a PDS
RECORD FORMAT       ===> FB        Fixed length records, "blocked"
RECORD LENGTH       ===> 80        Size of each record
BLOCK SIZE          ===> 3840      48 x 80 in this case
```

To fully understand all of these specifications for data set characteristics, you'll have to read Chapters 11 through 14. Right now I want to give you a high-level summary to give you some perspective and let you begin experimenting.

10.2 Data Set Characteristics

You can become familiar with the major characteristics of a data set by studying Figure 10.1b. Here is what each of the entries on the TSO data set allocation screen refers to and how you enter each:

VOLUME SERIAL   or GENERIC UNIT identifies one or a group of disks. Leave this blank; MVS will pick out a suitable disk for the data set.

SPACE UNITS   can be tracks, cylinders, or blocks. A track is the smallest unit of space you can specify and houses about 50,000 bytes or so, depending on the disk model your installation uses. A cylinder is a collection of 15 tracks. (To understand blocks, you'll have to read Chapters 13 and 14. We'll use tracks for now.)

PRIMARY QUAN   answers the question, "How many space units do you want?" Putting 5 here and putting TRKS at SPACE UNITS means that I want five tracks of space.

SECONDARY QUAN   makes it possible to get more space after the primary allocation if the data set grows as you use it. I stated zero because I don't plan on adding records to the data set once I have created it.

RECORD FORMAT, RECORD LENGTH, and **BLOCK SIZE**   describe the characteristics of the records to be housed in the new data set. The simplest format of record is fixed length, which means that every record in the data set is the same size. Grouping records in blocks serves the same purpose as packaging eggs in cartons. We group several records together so that they can be stored more compactly and read back with fewer physical input/output actions. I want to group together 48 80-byte records to form blocks 3840 bytes long. (I'll explain the rules for choosing a block size in Chapter 14.) For now, just realize that blocks of roughly 4,000 bytes in size are efficient for interactive software such as TSO to access.

Figure 10.2a shows you how TSO/ISPF confirms that my data set allocation actions for CSCJGJ.CSC.JUMBLE were successful. Figure 10.2b is

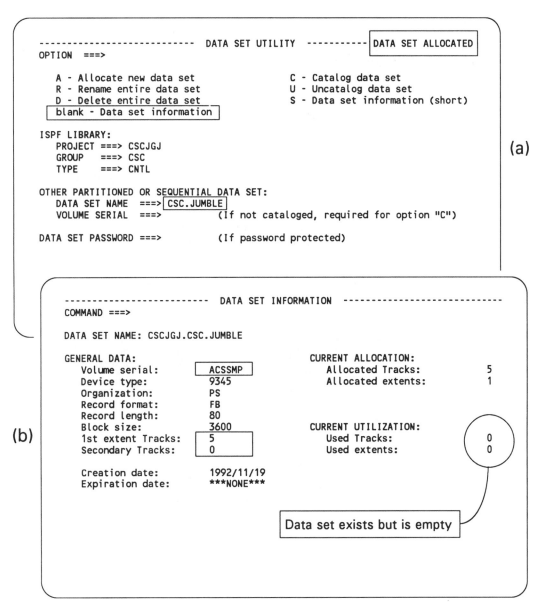

```
-------------------------- DATA SET UTILITY ----------|DATA SET ALLOCATED|
OPTION ===>

    A - Allocate new data set          C - Catalog data set
    R - Rename entire data set         U - Uncatalog data set
    D - Delete entire data set         S - Data set information (short)
    | blank - Data set information |

ISPF LIBRARY:
    PROJECT ===> CSCJGJ
    GROUP   ===> CSC
    TYPE    ===> CNTL

OTHER PARTITIONED OR SEQUENTIAL DATA SET:
    DATA SET NAME  ===>| CSC.JUMBLE |
    VOLUME SERIAL  ===>           (If not cataloged, required for option "C")

DATA SET PASSWORD ===>          (If password protected)
```

(a)

```
-------------------------- DATA SET INFORMATION --------------------------
    COMMAND ===>

    DATA SET NAME: CSCJGJ.CSC.JUMBLE

    GENERAL DATA:                      CURRENT ALLOCATION:
       Volume serial:    | ACSSMP |       Allocated Tracks:    5
       Device type:        9345           Allocated extents:   1
       Organization:       PS
       Record format:      FB
       Record length:      80
       Block size:         3600        CURRENT UTILIZATION:
       1st extent Tracks:  | 5 |          Used Tracks:         0
       Secondary Tracks:   | 0 |          Used extents:        0

       Creation date:      1992/11/19
       Expiration date:    ***NONE***

                              | Data set exists but is empty |
```

(b)

Figure 10.2   Confirmation of Data Set Allocation

(a) You arrive back at the TSO/ISPF 3.2 screen when you successfully allocate a data set. The top-of-screen message confirms that the data set you wanted to allocate has been created. (b) If you press **<Enter>**, you will "read back" information from the system catalog and disk volume table of contents.

a data set information screen; it shows me that TSO/ISPF has had MVS create the data set with the characteristics I intended. The data set exists, but it has no records in it; it is empty.

10.3 You Can't Allocate Two Data Sets with the Same Name

I tried to allocate CSCJGJ.CSC.JUMBLE a second time, and Figure 10.3 shows you the result. Because the MVS system catalog can't store information about two data sets with the same name, TSO/ISPF won't let you allocate the same data set twice. In Figure 10.3 I also used the "tso listcat" command to query the catalog about all the data set names in it that begin with my TSO user-id, CSCJGJ. You see the list of these names at the bottom of the screen, including CSCJGJ.CSC.JUMBLE.

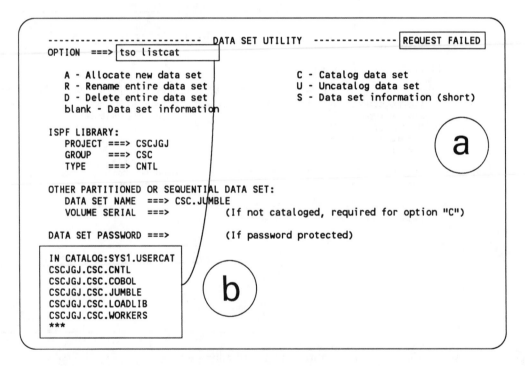

Figure 10.3 Trying to Allocate a Second Time Fails

This screen shows you two actions. (a) I tried to allocate the same data set a second time. (b) I used the "tso listcat" command to see what data sets already exist with names beginning with my TSO user-id.

10.4 Allocating a Data Set Using JCL

You can allocate a data set using JCL. When you do this, you have to tell MVS the same things about data set characteristics that you do with the TSO/ISPF 3.2 allocate screen. Figure 10.4a shows you JCL that I coded to allocate CSCJGJ.CSC.JUMBLE.

The JCL in Figure 10.4 has two steps. The first step uses the capabilities of DISP=(MOD,DELETE) to have MVS delete a data set if it exists or be permissive of not finding a data set of the name specified to be deleted. You will often see this type of "housekeeping" delete as the first step in any job that creates a new data set. Unlike TSO/ISPF, MVS *will* let you create duplicate-name data sets, but the second and subsequent data sets cannot be cataloged. Duplicate-name data sets are potentially dangerous because they are hard to locate after they are created. Consistent use of housekeeping delete steps avoids duplicate data set name problems.

I will explain the details of the DISP, UNIT, DCB, and SPACE parameters, which you see at lines 2300 through 2700 in Figure 10.4a, in Chapters 11 through 14. These chapters will explain why the coding you see in Figure 10.4a is present to create the new data set. Figure 10.4b is part of the output produced when I ran the allocate job stream. You can see that MVS tells you what it did with the data sets involved, albeit in a confusing way. The words like UNCATALOGED, DELETED, and KEPT are so far to the right that it's a bit hard to see which data set name lines up with which message.

10.5 Allocating a Data Set and Writing to It

My allocation job stream in Figure 10.4a accomplished nothing more than creating an empty data set. But the JCL in Figure 10.5a actually allocates and writes to the new data set all at once. In this JCL, I have arranged an IEFBR14 step to delete the existing copy of CSCJGJ.CSC.JUMBLE, as before. But //STEP020 now executes IEBGENER to copy data from CSCJGJ.CSC.CNTL(WORKERS) to a new CSCJGJ.CSC.JUMBLE.

To allocate and write to the new data set, all I have to do is code the same DD statement at IEBGENER's //SYSUT2 as I previously did in //STEP020 with IEFBR14. You see this at lines 2600 through 3000 in Figure 10.5a. The MVS system messages in Figure 10.5b indicate that //STEP010 uncataloged and deleted the existing CSCJGJ.CSC.JUMBLE. //STEP020 creates and catalogs a new data set of the same name.

```
EDIT ---- CSCJGJ.CSC.CNTL(H1ALLOC) - 01.00 ------------------ COLUMNS 001 072
COMMAND ===>                                                   SCROLL ===> PAGE
****** ************************** TOP OF DATA ******************************
000100 //CSCJGJA    JOB 1,'BIN 7 JANOSSY',CLASS=A,MSGCLASS=X,MSGLEVEL=(1,1),
000200 //  NOTIFY=CSCJGJ
000300 //*
000400 //*   THIS JCL IS STORED AT CSCJGJ.CSC.CNTL(H1ALLOC)
000500 //*
000600 //*****************************************************************
000700 //*                                                               *
000800 //*   HOUSEKEEPING DELETE BEFORE ALLOCATE (FOR SAFETY)            *
000900 //*                                                               *
001000 //*****************************************************************
001100 //STEP010  EXEC  PGM=IEFBR14
001200 //DELETE1     DD  DSN=CSCJGJ.CSC.JUMBLE,
001300 //  DISP=(MOD,DELETE),
001400 //  UNIT=SYSDA,           Deletes a data set even if it doesn't exist!
001500 //  SPACE=(TRK,0)
001600 //*
001700 //*****************************************************************
001800 //*                                                               *
001900 //*   ALLOCATE A NEW DATA SET OF THE SAME NAME AS JUST DELETED     *
002000 //*                                                               *
002100 //*****************************************************************
002200 //STEP020  EXEC  PGM=IEFBR14
002300 //ALLOC1      DD  DSN=CSCJGJ.CSC.JUMBLE,
002400 //  DISP=(NEW,CATLG,DELETE),
002500 //  UNIT=SYSDA,
002600 //  DCB=(RECFM=FB,LRECL=80,BLKSIZE=3840),
002700 //  SPACE=(TRK,5)
002800 //
```

(a)

```
                    J E S 2   J O B   L O G  --  S Y S T E M   I B M 1  --  N O D E   N 1

09.50.58 JOB05762  IRR010I USERID CSCJGJ   IS ASSIGNED TO THIS JOB.
09.50.58 JOB05762  ICH70001I CSCJGJ   LAST ACCESS AT 09:42:13 ON THURSDAY, NOVEMBER 19, 1992
09.50.58 JOB05762  $HASP373 CSCJGJA STARTED - INIT 1 - CLASS A - SYS IBM1
09.51.00 JOB05762  $HASP395 CSCJGJA ENDED

------ JES2 JOB STATISTICS ------
    19 NOV 92 JOB EXECUTION DATE
        28 CARDS READ
        60 SYSOUT PRINT RECORDS
         0 SYSOUT PUNCH RECORDS
         4 SYSOUT SPOOL KBYTES
      0.02 MINUTES EXECUTION TIME
            -
            -
            -

IEF236I ALLOC. FOR CSCJGJA STEP010
IEF237I 113 ALLOCATED TO DELETE1
IEF142I CSCJGJA STEP010 - STEP WAS EXECUTED - COND CODE 0000
IEF285I    CSCJGJ.CSC.JUMBLE                          UNCATALOGED
IEF285I    VOL SER NOS= ACSSMP.
IEF285I    CSCJGJ.CSC.JUMBLE                          DELETED
IEF285I    VOL SER NOS= ACSSMP.
IEF373I STEP /STEP010 / START 92324.0950
IEF374I STEP /STEP010 / STOP  92324.0950 CPU    0MIN 00.02SEC SRB    0MIN 00.00SEC

IEF236I ALLOC. FOR CSCJGJA STEP020
IEF237I 113 ALLOCATED TO ALLOC1
IEF142I CSCJGJA STEP020 - STEP WAS EXECUTED - COND CODE 0000
IEF285I    CSCJGJ.CSC.JUMBLE                          CATALOGED
IEF285I    VOL SER NOS= ACSSMP.
IEF373I STEP /STEP020 / START 92324.0950
IEF374I STEP /STEP020 / STOP  92324.0951 CPU    0MIN 00.02SEC SRB    0MIN 00.00SEC
IEF375I JOB /CSCJGJA / START 92324.0950
IEF376I JOB /CSCJGJA / STOP  92324.0951 CPU    0MIN 00.04SEC SRB    0MIN 00.00SEC
```

(b)

Figure 10.4 Allocating a Data Set Using JCL

(a) You can do the same disk data set allocation using JCL instead of TSO.
//STEP010 is for safety, to delete any existing cataloged data set named
CSCJGJ.CSC.JUMBLE. //STEP020 allocates the new data set using the DISP
parameter, UNIT, DCB, and SPACE. (b) The system messages indicate that the
existing data set CSCJGJ.CSC.JUMBLE was uncataloged and then deleted and that a
new (empty) data set CSCJGJ.CSC.JUMBLE was created.

```
EDIT ---- CSCJGJ.CSC.CNTL(H2WRITE) - 01.00 ------------------ COLUMNS 001 072
COMMAND ===>                                               SCROLL ===> PAGE
****** *************************** TOP OF DATA ******************************
000100 //CSCJGJA   JOB 1,'BIN 7 JANOSSY',CLASS=A,MSGCLASS=X,MSGLEVEL=(1,1),
000200 //  NOTIFY=CSCJGJ
000300 //*
000400 //*   THIS JCL IS STORED AT CSCJGJ.CSC.CNTL(H2WRITE)
000500 //*
000600 //****************************************************************
000700 //*                                                             *
000800 //*    HOUSEKEEPING DELETE BEFORE ALLOCATE (FOR SAFETY)         *
000900 //*                                                             *
001000 //****************************************************************
001100 //STEP010  EXEC  PGM=IEFBR14
001200 //DELETE1    DD  DSN=CSCJGJ.CSC.JUMBLE,
001300 //  DISP=(MOD,DELETE),
001400 //  UNIT=SYSDA,
001500 //  SPACE=(TRK,0)
001600 //*
001700 //****************************************************************
001800 //*                                                             *
001900 //*   CREATE A NEW DATA SET AS YOU PUT RECORDS IN IT            *
002000 //*                                                             *
002100 //****************************************************************
002200 //STEP020  EXEC  PGM=IEBGENER
002300 //SYSPRINT   DD  SYSOUT=*
002400 //SYSIN      DD  DUMMY
002500 //SYSUT1     DD  DSN=CSCJGJ.CSC.CNTL(WORKERS),DISP=SHR
002600 //SYSUT2     DD  DSN=CSCJGJ.CSC.JUMBLE,
002700 //  DISP=(NEW,CATLG,DELETE),
002800 //  UNIT=SYSDA,
002900 //  DCB=(RECFM=FB,LRECL=80,BLKSIZE=3840),
003000 //  SPACE=(TRK,5)
003100 //
```

(a)

Send output emerging at //SYSUT2 into a data set allocated right now

(b)
```
IEF236I ALLOC. FOR CSCJGJA STEP010
IEF237I 113  ALLOCATED TO DELETE1
IEF142I CSCJGJA STEP010 - STEP WAS EXECUTED - COND CODE 0000
IEF285I    CSCJGJ.CSC.JUMBLE                        UNCATALOGED
IEF285I    VOL SER NOS= ACSSMP.
IEF285I    CSCJGJ.CSC.JUMBLE                        DELETED
IEF285I    VOL SER NOS= ACSSMP.
IEF373I STEP /STEP010 / START 92324.0957
IEF374I STEP /STEP010 / STOP  92324.0957 CPU   0MIN 00.03SEC SRB   0MIN 00.00SEC

IEF236I ALLOC. FOR CSCJGJA STEP020
IEF237I JES2 ALLOCATED TO SYSPRINT
IEF237I DMY  ALLOCATED TO SYSIN
IEF237I 111  ALLOCATED TO SYSUT1
IEF237I 113  ALLOCATED TO SYSUT2
IEF142I CSCJGJA STEP020 - STEP WAS EXECUTED - COND CODE 0000
IEF285I    CSCJGJ.CSCJGJA.JOB05771.D0000101.?       SYSOUT
IEF285I    CSCJGJ.CSC.CNTL                          KEPT
IEF285I    VOL SER NOS= USER00.
IEF285I    CSCJGJ.CSC.JUMBLE                        CATALOGED
IEF285I    VOL SER NOS= ACSSMP.
IEF373I STEP /STEP020 / START 92324.0957
IEF374I STEP /STEP020 / STOP  92324.0957 CPU   0MIN 00.16SEC SRB   0MIN 00.01SEC
IEF375I JOB /CSCJGJA / START 92324.0957
IEF376I JOB /CSCJGJA / STOP  92324.0957 CPU   0MIN 00.19SEC SRB   0MIN 00.01SEC

DATA SET UTILITY - GENERATE
PROCESSING ENDED AT EOD
```

New data set created and cataloged

Figure 10.5   Creating a New Data Set as Program Output

(a) This JCL is almost the same as the JCL in Figure 10.4, except that data set allocation and also placement of records in the data set occur in one action. //STEP020 now executes IEBGENER to copy my WORKERS data to a new CSCJGJ.CSC.JUMBLE. (b) The MVS system messages indicate that the existing data set was uncataloged and then deleted and a new CSCJGJ.CSC.JUMBLE created.

10.6 Are TSO-Created and JCL-Created Data Sets Different?

It makes no difference to MVS whether you allocate a data set using TSO/ISPF or create it using JCL—the result is the same. Even though it was now created using JCL instead of TSO/ISPF, the TSO/ISPF 3.2 data set information screen would now reveal the characteristics shown in Figure 10.2b. If I access the JCL-created data set using TSO Edit function 2, as in Figure 10.6a, I can see and edit the contents of it, as shown in Figure 10.6b.

10.7 The Need to Capture Printlines for Report Reprinting

The data set that I created with the JCL in Figure 10.5a contains 80-byte records. You have seen quite a few data sets with records of that length. But on an MVS mainframe, records can be any length up to 32,760 bytes. I want to show you another different example in this overview of "writing" DD statements.

The JCL in Figure 10.7 executes PARMDEMO, a reporting program you already saw in Chapter 7. In this job stream my intention is to capture in a data set the printlines PARMDEMO produces for a report. By doing this, I can print the report but also reprint it if necessary without rerunning the program. Admittedly, PARMDEMO doesn't do much processing, and rerunning it wouldn't impose much of a burden. But this example of capturing printlines for possible reprinting later applies to all types of processes. Some updating programs would be very burdensome to rerun if you had to reprint the reports they produce!

10.8 How You Create a Printline Data Set

To capture and store records that represent printlines, you need to create a data set to hold them. Here is how the JCL in Figure 10.7 does it.

//STEP010 is a housekeeping delete for CSCJGJ.CSC.OVERTIME.REPORT, the data set in which I will capture printlines. Every time I run this JCL, any existing copy of the printlines will first be deleted.

At //STEP020, I coded a "writing" DD statement at //GO.WORKREPT, where program PARMDEMO produces its report. You can see that this DD statement follows a familiar pattern but that the logical record length LRECL is now 133. Printlines are usually coded as one carriage control byte followed by 132 printing positions.

In //STEP030, I use IEBGENER to copy the printlines stored in CSCJGJ.CSC.OVERTIME.REPORT to the printer. I could run just this step again later to reprint the report.

```
-------------------------- EDIT - ENTRY PANEL ------------------------------
COMMAND ===>

ISPF LIBRARY:
   PROJECT ===> CSCJGJ
   GROUP   ===> CSC         ===>           ===>           ===>
   TYPE    ===> CNTL
   MEMBER  ===>                 (Blank or pattern for member selection list)

OTHER PARTITIONED OR SEQUENTIAL DATA SET:
   DATA SET NAME  ===> csc.jumble
   VOLUME SERIAL  ===>              (If not cataloged)

DATA SET PASSWORD ===>             (If password protected)

PROFILE NAME      ===>             (Blank defaults to data set type)

INITIAL MACRO     ===>       LMF LOCK  ===> YES    (YES, NO or NEVER)

FORMAT NAME       ===>       MIXED MODE ===> NO     (YES or NO)
```

(a)

```
EDIT ---- CSCJGJ.CSC.JUMBLE --------------------------------- COLUMNS 001 072
COMMAND ===>                                                  SCROLL ===> PAGE
****** ***************************** TOP OF DATA *****************************
000001 21256 NILLY      WILLY      402CASHIERS OFFICE
000002 21257 IPPI       MRS.       378PHOTO DEPARTMENT
000003 21260 MALLOW     MARSHA     390KITCHEN APPLIANCES
000004 21307 WARE       DELLA      246FURNITURE
000005 21310 SHAW       ARKAN      300HARDWARE
000006 21574 AH         GEORGE     400PHOTO DEPARTMENT
000007 21668 ZOORI      MOE        179PLUMBING SUPPLIES
000008 25112 CABOOSE    LUCE       305FURNITURE
000009 25189 HOW        IDA        005SUITCASES AND BAGS
000010 33102 IFORNIA    CAL        200TRAVEL DEPARTMENT
000011 33261 CANNON     LUCE       316TOYS
000012 33377 WHIZ       G.         357PERSONAL COMPUTERS
000013 33480 TOUR       D.         160WOMENS CLOTHING
000014 33483 INA        CAROL      530REMODELING SUPPLIES
000015 39321 ABAMA      AL         420WOMENS CLOTHING
000016 39322 TUCKY      KEN        350HARDWARE
****** ***************************** BOTTOM OF DATA **************************
```

(b)

You can use TSO to edit a data set created by a JCL job stream

Figure 10.6   Viewing the New Data Set Using TSO Function 2 Edit

(a) You can begin an edit of one of your sequential data sets by putting the last parts of its name at the OTHER PARTITIONED OR SEQUENTIAL DATA SET area on the Edit-Entry (TSO 2) screen. (b) Here you see what is in CSCJGJ.CSC.JUMBLE as a result of running the JCL in Figure 10.5. The data in CSCJGJ.CSC.JUMBLE was copied from CSCJGJ.CSC.CNTL(WORKERS).

```
EDIT ---- CSCJGJ.CSC.CNTL(H3PLINES) - 01.00 ----------------- COLUMNS 001 072
COMMAND ===>                                                  SCROLL ===> PAGE
****** *************************** TOP OF DATA ******************************
000100 //CSCJGJA   JOB 1,'BIN 7 JANOSSY',CLASS=A,MSGCLASS=X,MSGLEVEL=(1,1),
000200 // NOTIFY=CSCJGJ
000300 //*
000400 //*   THIS JCL IS STORED AT CSCJGJ.CSC.CNTL(H3PLINES)
000500 //*
000600 //*   DEMONSTRATE HOW TO CREATE A DATA SET TO HOUSE PRINTLINES
000700 //*   CREATED BY A PROGRAM IN A DATA SET, THEN PRINT (OR REPRINT)
000800 //*
000900 //****************************************************************
001000 //*                                                              *
001100 //*   HOUSEKEEPING DELETE BEFORE ALLOCATE (FOR SAFETY)           *
001200 //*                                                              *
001300 //****************************************************************
001400 //STEP010  EXEC  PGM=IEFBR14
001500 //DELETE1    DD   DSN=CSCJGJ.CSC.OVERTIME.REPORT,
001600 //  DISP=(MOD,DELETE),
001700 //  UNIT=SYSDA,
001800 //  SPACE=(TRK,0)
001900 //*
002000 //****************************************************************
002100 //*                                                              *
002200 //*   COMPILE, LINK, AND RUN PARMDEMO LISTING PROGRAM            *
002300 //*                                                              *
002400 //****************************************************************
002500 //STEP020 EXEC  PROC=COB2J,
002600 //       PDS='CSCJGJ.CSC.COBOL',
002700 //    MEMBER='PARMDEMO',
002800 //    PARM.GO='401-999,OVERTIME REPORT'
002900 //GO.WORKERS   DD   DSN=CSCJGJ.CSC.CNTL(WORKERS),DISP=SHR
003000 //GO.WORKREPT  DD   DSN=CSCJGJ.CSC.OVERTIME.REPORT,
003100 //  DISP=(NEW,CATLG,DELETE),
003200 //  UNIT=SYSDA,
003300 //  DCB=(RECFM=FB,LRECL=133,BLKSIZE=6118),
003400 //  SPACE=(TRK,5,RLSE)
003500 //*
003600 //****************************************************************
003700 //*                                                              *
003800 //*   COPY THE STORED PRINTLINES TO PRINTER                      *
003900 //*                                                              *
004000 //****************************************************************
004100 //STEP030   EXEC   PGM=IEBGENER
004200 //SYSPRINT   DD   DUMMY
004300 //SYSIN      DD   DUMMY
004400 //SYSUT1     DD   DSN=CSCJGJ.CSC.OVERTIME.REPORT,DISP=SHR
004500 //SYSUT2     DD   SYSOUT=*
004600 //
```

Figure 10.7 Putting Printlines in a Newly Created Data Set

Storing printlines in data sets for possible report reprint is a common technique of production data processing. Reports sometimes get lost, and the jobs that create them do too much complex processing to rerun them from scratch. The "housekeeping delete" at //STEP010 makes sure that no cataloged data set named CSCJGJ.CSC.OVERTIME.REPORT exists on the system before I try to create a data set of this name. At the //GO.WORKREPT DD statement, the LRECL (logical record length) is 133 bytes, and the BLKSIZE (block size) is the biggest multiple of 133 that fits into 6,233 bytes, a common optimum block size value for disk data sets. RLSE on the SPACE parameter releases any unused tracks from my disk space allocation. IEBGENER in //STEP030 copies the printlines to SYSOUT. I can run //STEP030 alone to reprint the report later by coding either a separate job with just this step or by adding the parameter RESTART=STEP030 to the JOB statement.

10.9 Block Size for Printline Data Sets

In //STEP020 of the JCL in Figure 10.7 I coded a block size of 6118 for data set CSCJGJ.CSC.OVERTIME.REPORT. Without belaboring this point, here are the factors related to your choice of block size:

1. If your printline data set is going to be housed on disk and your installation uses a mixture of disk devices, you can use a block size of 6118 bytes (46 133-byte records per block), which is adequately efficient on all models of disk.
2. If your printline data set is going to be housed on disk and your installation uses only 3380 model disks, you can use 23408 as a block size (176 133-byte records per block) for slightly greater efficiency.
3. If your printline data set is going to be housed on disk and your installation uses only 3390 model disks, you can use 27930 bytes as a block size (210 133-byte records per block) for greater efficiency.
4. If your printline data set is going to be housed on tape, you can use a block size of 32718 bytes (246 133-byte records per block).
5. And if your installation uses MVS/ESA, you can let the system itself choose the best block size by simply *not coding* BLKSIZE in your JCL!

I'll tell you more about optimal block sizes, which vary according to the release of MVS that your installation uses, in Chapters 13 and 14 as well as in Appendix A.

10.10 Viewing a Printline Data Set

I can view or edit the data set that I created in //STEP020 of the JCL in Figure 10.7, CSCJGJ.CSC.OVERTIME.REPORT. Figure 10.8a shows how I entered its name at OTHER PARTITIONED OR SEQUENTIAL DATA SET on the TSO/ISPF Function 2 Edit-Entry screen. Figure 10.8b shows you what the edit screen looks like when I actually view the data set. The carriage control characters—which you would not see in a print of this data—are readily apparent in the first position of each record.

```
-------------------------- EDIT - ENTRY PANEL ----------------------------
COMMAND ===>

ISPF LIBRARY:
   PROJECT ===> CSCJGJ
   GROUP   ===> CSC        ===>           ===>           ===>
   TYPE    ===> CNTL
   MEMBER  ===>                  (Blank or pattern for member selection list)

OTHER PARTITIONED OR SEQUENTIAL DATA SET:
   DATA SET NAME   ===> csc.overtime.report
   VOLUME SERIAL   ===>           (If not cataloged)

DATA SET PASSWORD ===>           (If password protected)

PROFILE NAME      ===>           (Blank defaults to data set type)

INITIAL MACRO     ===>           LMF LOCK   ===> YES    (YES, NO or NEVER)

FORMAT NAME       ===>           MIXED MODE ===> NO     (YES or NO)
```

(a)

```
EDIT ---- CSCJGJ.CSC.OVERTIME.REPORT ----------------------- COLUMNS 001 072
COMMAND ===>                                                 SCROLL ===> PAGE
****** **************************** TOP OF DATA ****************************
000001 1*************************************************************
000002  OVERTIME REPORT              LO=40.1  HI=99.9     PAGE      1
000003  *************************************************************
000004 0
000005  21256   WILLY NILLY            40.2  CASHIERS OFFICE
000006  33483   CAROL INA              53.0  REMODELING SUPPLIES
000007  39321   AL ABAMA               42.0  WOMENS CLOTHING
000008 ORECORDS READ        16
000009  RECORDS LISTED       3
****** **************************** BOTTOM OF DATA ****************************
```

(b)

When you view printlines stored in a data set you can see the carriage control byte, which is the first byte in each record. The value here controls the vertical tabbing action of the printer. This byte does not print and you ordinarily don't see it.

Figure 10.8 Viewing a Printline Data Set

(a) Because I put the printlines for this report into a data set, I can use TSO/ISPF to view them. (b) The first byte of each record is dedicated to carriage control; "1" means advance to top of page, "0" means advance two lines, and space means advance one line. This leading character is not normally printed but controls vertical spacing (tabbing) of a printer. The carriage control byte has no effect on a terminal screen so you see these printlines as single-spaced lines.

10.11 Going Further . . .

If you understand what you've read so far in this book, you can now tackle jobs that require all three types of DD statements: those that read data sets, those that print things, and those that create new data sets. The examples of DD statements for writing data sets that I've shown you in this chapter are entirely sufficient for you to compose your own JCL for data set creation tasks. I've suggested some exercises in the review section of this chapter that will help you experiment with what you have learned.

Specialized areas of disk data set creation exist, and you will benefit from more detailed knowledge. The next four chapters home in on the practical aspects of the DISP, UNIT, DCB, and SPACE parameters for disk data set creation. I've grouped in Chapter 15 the information that you need about the LABEL and VOL parameters to be able to write data sets to magnetic tape.

Chapter 10 Review

Mini-Glossary

Allocate   To identify and set aside disk space for a data set

TSO LISTCAT   A command you can use on the TSO/ISPF command line to see the names of all of your cataloged data sets

Housekeeping delete   A data set deletion step usually placed at the beginning of a job stream to make sure that newly created data sets don't duplicate existing data set names

Review Questions

1. Are TSO-allocated and JCL data sets different? Discuss this in connection with the characteristics of the data sets themselves, not the process by which you create them.
2. When you allocate a data set using the TSO 3.2 screen, why should you usually leave the VOLUME SERIAL field blank?
3. When you allocate a data set using the TSO 3.2 screen, what does it contain?
4. Can you allocate a data set using JCL and write records into it immediately? If so, explain how.

Exercise

A. Use the TSO 3.2 function to allocate a data set named appropriately for your installation, with the last part of the name DATA45. Make the records 45 bytes in length, the block size 6210 bytes, with record format FB; allow 1 track of space with no secondary space and no directory blocks. After allocating this data set, use the TSO 2 edit function to put ten records into it, each containing the number and name of a chapter from the first half of this book. Then code and run a one-step job that executes IEBGENER to copy this data set to the printer, using as a guide //STEP030 of Figure 10.7.

Chapter Eleven

DISP: DATA SET DISPOSITION

In Chapter 10 I showed you the essentials of a DD statement that creates a new disk data set and puts records into it. That JCL involved the DD statement parameters DISP, UNIT, DCB, and SPACE. My explanations of these parameters in Chapter 10 were enough to get you started writing disk data sets but not sufficient for you to understand many of the details. I'll now cover DISP, UNIT, DCB, and SPACE in separate chapters and then discuss VOL and LABEL in a chapter devoted to tape data sets.

In its "short form" you code data set disposition as DISP=SHR or DISP= OLD. You've already seen the short form used to read a data set. But DISP is actually more complicated. It has three parts. The second two parts assume defaults that are appropriate when you code just DISP=SHR or DISP=OLD. In this chapter I explain to you how to code DISP in its full three-positional parameter form. I'll also tell you about the complicated set of default rules that make DISP an especially thorny aspect of MVS JCL. Finally, I'll show you how to use DISP to delete a data set that doesn't exist and why this is often a necessary task!

11.1 The Many Purposes of DISP

You use the DISP parameter to indicate all of these things to MVS about a data set:

- Whether or not the data set exists when a job step begins
- Whether the data set can be shared with other jobs during the step
- What is to be done with the data set after the job step ends normally
- What is to be done with the data set if the job step ends abnormally (abends)

Unless you create and delete a data set in the same step, you'll need to code DISP on a DD statement.

11.2 DISP General Format

Figure 11.1 shows you the general format of the complete DISP parameter for MVS and MVS/XA. Compare Figure 11.1 to the following JCL, which is possible with MVS/ESA. You'll see that although DISP does not change between these versions, other parts of a "writing" DD statement can differ. I'll explain those differences, which involve DCB, in Chapters 13 and 14.

```
//SYSUT2   DD   DSN=CSCJGJ.CSC.JUMBLE,
//    DISP=(NEW,CATLG,DELETE),
//    UNIT=SYSDA,
//    RECFM=FB,
//    LRECL=80,
//    AVGREC=U,
//    SPACE=(80,10000,RLSE)
```

You can see all of the potential values for each of the three parts of DISP coding in Figure 11.1. I have highlighted the default values that DISP will assume if you omit it: DISP=(NEW,DELETE,DELETE). Unlike other defaults, however, the assumed values for the second and third parts of DISP are not the same in all cases. The values they take on depend on the way you code the first part!

How do you interpret the meaning of DISP coding? Here is what DISP= (NEW,DELETE,DELETE)—the default when you don't code DISP at all— means:

- Start-status NEW says the data set does not exist before this step and will be created now
- End-status-normal DELETE says the data set will be deleted when this step finishes
- End-status-abend DELETE says the data set will be deleted if this step abends

This particular choice of DISP values may seem strange to you, but they are useful. You won't see DISP coded on work files (files used just as an extension of memory by programs such as the sort utility) because the default DISP=(NEW,DELETE,DELETE) is precisely what they require.

11.3 Start-Status Values

```
//    DISP=(NEW,CATLG,DELETE),
```

Start-status indicates the status of the data set at the start of the step (*not* at the start of your job!) and the desired manner of access you want for an existing data set. You can code OLD, SHR, NEW, or MOD here.

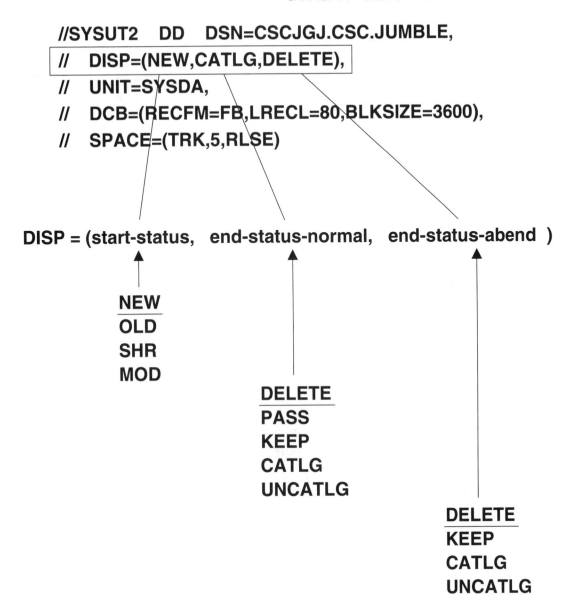

Figure 11.1   Overview of the DISP Parameter

OLD tells MVS that the data set exists and must exist or an error will result. OLD also specifies exclusive use of the data set and doesn't permit sharing the data set among jobs running at the same time. A job that carries a DISP of OLD for a data set will await execution until all other jobs already using the data set complete execution. Coding a DD statement with DISP start-status OLD for a data set excludes any other program from using that data set.

SHR says that the data set exists but lets up to 126 other jobs read it at the same time. A step with a DDname carrying a DISP=SHR will not be forced to wait for disk data set access if other jobs are already accessing the data set with DISP=SHR. But DISP=(SHR,DELETE) is contradictory and is treated as (OLD,DELETE) by MVS. You can't expect to gain concurrent access to a data set with other jobs reading it and then whisk the rug out from under them with DELETE!

NEW means that the data set does not presently exist and will be created during this step. It implies that either the program or your JCL will supply data set characteristics that are needed by the system to create the data set, such as record format, record length, and (perhaps) block size, an appropriate UNIT, and SPACE.

MOD means that the data set can be a new one or can already exist; MOD is the only start-status for which you don't have to know whether or not the data set already exists. Like OLD, it dictates exclusive use of a data set. If the data set does not already exist, MOD creates it if you have also met these conditions in the DD statement:

- You supplied the data set characteristics either in the program or with a DCB parameter
- You coded an appropriate UNIT parameter
- You coded the SPACE parameter (disk data sets)
- You did not code a specific VOL=SER volume serial number

MOD also lets you append more records to the end of an existing data set, as I'll explain in Section 11.19.

11.4 End-Status-Normal Values

```
//  DISP=(NEW,CATLG,DELETE),
```

The end-status-normal specification for the DISP parameter tells MVS what is to be done with the data set when the job step ends, assuming that the step ends without a problem. Here you can code DELETE, PASS, CATLG, KEEP, or UNCATLG.

DELETE indicates that the data set is to be deleted when the step ends. For example, DISP=(OLD,DELETE) will allow a program to read a data set but will have MVS uncatalog it and delete it when the program finishes with it. But don't code this to delete a member of a partitioned data set (library)! For example, if you code this you will not delete the member named MYSTUFF, you will delete the *entire library*:

```
//***********************************************************
//*                                                         *
//*    INVALID EXAMPLE! DO NOT TRY THIS TO DELETE A MEMBER!  *
//*                                                         *
//***********************************************************
//STEP010   EXEC  PGM=IEFBR14
//DEL1         DD  DSN=CSCJGJ.CSC.CNTL(MYSTUFF),
//  DISP=(OLD,DELETE)
```

PASS tells MVS that one or more steps following will access the data set. MVS retains a passed data set in a mounted condition, speeding subsequent access to it. You can pass a permanent sequential or partitioned data set, but not a VSAM data set. It's much more common to code DISP= (NEW,PASS) when you create a temporary data set as shown in Figure 11.2.

CATLG retains a data set that you have created and asks MVS to put its name, volume identifier of its location, unit type, and (if it's on tape) relative file number in the system catalog. You can access a cataloged data set simply by data set name. You can catalog a previously uncataloged data set by using the DISP=(OLD,CATLG) on a DD statement that accesses it (see Section 11.20).

KEEP coded as the end-status when a data set is created retains it but does not catalog it; MVS won't remember where it is. Most new data sets are created using CATLG instead of KEEP because of the advantage of having information about the data set recorded in the system catalog. You

```
//SORTOUT   DD   DSN = &&TRANSORT,
//   DISP=(NEW,PASS,DELETE),
//   UNIT=SYSDA,
//   DCB=(RECFM=FB,LRECL=80,BLKSIZE=6160),
//   SPACE=(TRK,5,RLSE)
```

Figure 11.2   Typical DISP Coding for a Temporary Data Set

can't code an end-status of KEEP or CATLG with a temporary data set name because this is inconsistent.

UNCATLG requests that MVS remove a data set name from the catalog but retain the data set itself. In any future reference to the data set you will have to specify the volume (VOL=SER=) on which it resides and the UNIT (or code a volume referback as illustrated in Section 11.18).

11.5 End-Status-Abend Values

```
// DISP=(NEW,CATLG,DELETE),
```

The third DISP subparameter indicates what you want to do with the data set if the job step abends. This specification is also known as the **conditional disposition.** If you don't code this, it defaults to the same value as the end-status-normal. If you omit both end-status-normal and end-status-abend, they both default to DELETE for NEW or PASSed data sets and KEEP for all others.

You can't expect the end-status-abend value to get rid of data sets if a job stream abends. End-status-abend only works within the step that abends. Once a step finishes successfully, the permanent data sets created by it remain. If a later step fails and terminates the job, these data sets are not affected. This is why you have to take special actions using COND with ONLY to clean up after a failed run.

Once you understand the values for end-status-normal, you already understand the values for end-status-abend. All of the same values are possible except PASS. You can't code PASS as an end-status-abend because PASSed data sets are automatically eliminated by MVS at job end.

There's no simple rule for how to code end-status-abend. What you code depends on how you plan to handle the rerunning or restarting of a failed job. It's most common to delete data sets being created at a step if the step fails by coding DISP=(NEW,CATLG,DELETE) so that incomplete data sets don't litter the system. Notice that you don't get this if you simply code DISP=(NEW,CATLG). By not coding the end-status-abend in this case, you get DISP=(NEW,CATLG,CATLG).

11.6 Summary of DISP Default Values

MVS follows this set of rules if you omit DISP on a DD statement, or you code only part of it:

1. If you don't code start-status, it defaults to NEW
2. If you don't code end-status-normal, it defaults to preserve the status quo

3. If you don't code end-status-abend, it defaults to the same thing as end-status-normal

This is a lot of rules to remember, and just knowing the rules doesn't really show you actual examples of DISP coding. Figure 11.3 gives you a summary of the most common DISP codings and the effect of these rules on DISP interpretation by MVS.

Common DISP Coding ...	Is used for ...
DISP=(NEW,CATLG,DELETE)	Creating a new permanent data set
DISP=SHR	Reading an existing permanent data set
DISP=(NEW,PASS,DELETE)	Creating a new passed data set
DISP=(OLD,PASS)	Reading and passing on a passed data set
DISP=(OLD,DELETE)	Reading and deleting a passed data set

(a) Most Common DISP Coding

DISP coded as ...	Defaults to ...
(no DISP)	DISP=(NEW,DELETE,DELETE)
DISP=SHR	DISP=(SHR,KEEP,KEEP)
DISP=OLD	DISP=(OLD,KEEP,KEEP)
DISP=(NEW,PASS)	DISP=(NEW,PASS,PASS)
DISP=(,CATLG)	DISP=(NEW,CATLG,CATLG)
DISP=(,PASS)	DISP=(NEW,PASS,PASS)

(b) Summary of DISP Defaults

Figure 11.3   Summary of Common DISP Codings and Defaults

11.7 Partitioned Data Sets, DISP, and the MVS Catalog

When you write a new member to an existing partitioned data set, DISP refers to the data set as a whole, not to the member. When, for example, you write a new member to an existing partitioned data set, you code DISP= OLD or DISP=SHR, not DISP=(NEW, ...). Here is how I write a new member named STUFF to a library using IEBGENER, copying data from a sequential data set named CSCJGJ.CSC.JUMBLE:

```
//*************************************************************
//*                                                           *
//*      WRITE A NEW MEMBER TO A PARTITIONED DATA SET          *
//*                                                           *
//*************************************************************
//STEP010    EXEC  PGM=IEBGENER
//SYSPRINT   DD    SYSOUT=*
//SYSIN      DD    DUMMY
//SYSUT1     DD    DSN=CSCJGJ.CSC.JUMBLE,         <=== INPUT
//  DISP=SHR
//SYSUT2     DD    DSN=CSCJGJ.CSC.CNTL(STUFF),    <=== OUTPUT
//  DISP=SHR
//
```

STUFF is just a new member, and the partitioned data set's directory is updated to know about it. The partitioned data set as a whole already exists, and you can't code NEW for it.

11.8 //STEPLIB and Its DISP

The DDname //STEPLIB serves a special purpose at any job step. It indicates the partitioned data set in which MVS is to look for the program load module named at EXEC PGM=. You need to code //STEPLIB if the program you are trying to execute is not in the normal production library on your system:

```
//*************************************************************
//*                                                           *
//*  HOW TO CODE //STEPLIB FOR PRIVATE LOAD MODULE LIBRARY     *
//*                                                           *
//*************************************************************
//STEP010   EXEC  PGM=COPYIT
//STEPLIB    DD    DSN=CSCJGJ.CSC.LOADLIB,
//  DISP=SHR
//...
//...
```

The name following PGM is the member name of the program load module in the library named at //STEPLIB. //STEPLIB is treated as a normal DD statement, and the DISP coded at it will be processed by MVS as usual. You therefore have to be very careful to code DISP=SHR for it. You could inadvertently delete an entire load module library by specifying DISP= (OLD,DELETE) at //STEPLIB! Even coding DISP=OLD for //STEPLIB can cause major problems because as long as your step is active, other jobs won't be able to use programs in the load module library.

11.9 DISP and VSAM Data Sets

It's appropriate for you to code only OLD or SHR on a DD statement that accesses a VSAM data set. VSAM provides its own safeguards against concurrent access, beyond the DISP parameter, in the form of the SHAREOP-TIONS attribute. You set this attribute when you define the data set using the IDCAMS utility.

VSAM data set design and IDCAMS utility program usage are more complicated and involved than JCL. I'd suggest you see another of my books, *Practical VSAM For Today's Programmers*, (John Wiley & Sons, Inc., 1988), for detailed coverage of SHAREOPTIONS and its coding.

11.10 Data Set Housekeeping with DISP=(MOD,DELETE)

Any job stream that creates a new data set has to first make sure that no data set of the same name is present on the system. The easiest way to do this is for the job stream to delete any existing data set of the same name. You can accomplish this with a "housekeeping" first step, coding it with the appropriate DISP and using DELETE as the end-status-normal:

```
//****************************************************************
//*                                                              *
//*                HOUSEKEEPING DATA SET DELETE                  *
//*                                                              *
//****************************************************************
//STEP010   EXEC  PGM=IEFBR14
//DEL1          DD  DSN=CSCJGJ.CSC.JUMBLE,
//   DISP=(MOD,DELETE),
//   UNIT=SYSDA,
//   SPACE=(TRK,0)
```

Data set housekeeping is interesting because it involves the use of a program named IEFBR14. IEFBR14 is called the "null" program because it does nothing. The only instruction in this program is the assembler instruction BR 14, which is the equivalent of "stop." Executing IEFBR14 is simply an excuse for interacting with MVS. You can code DD statements at an IEFBR14 step to have MVS act on their DISP parameters.

IEFBR14 contains no logic to deal with data sets. So how did we determine that //DEL1 was a legitimate DDname for IEFBR14? In fact, the DDname //DEL1 means nothing. Although you can't omit a DD statement required by a program, it's perfectly acceptable to MVS to see "extra" DD statements associated with a step ("extra" means "more than the program requires"). MVS always processes all the DD statements and acts on their DISP parameters, if the step is executed at all. This is true even if a program doesn't do anything with a given DD statement.

11.11 Why and How MOD Works

At a data set housekeeping step, we must face the fact that the data set we wish to eliminate may not always be present. Our goal is to create robust JCL that will always run. This means that the same JCL should work the very first time we run the job stream (with no data set to delete) and every time thereafter (when there usually will be a data set to delete). We can't simply code DISP=(OLD,DELETE) for the data set disposition because OLD as a start-status disposition means that the data set must exist. If the data set doesn't exist and you use OLD on a DD statement referring to it, your job stream fails.

MOD's greatest utility as the start-status in a housekeeping delete step is that it is permissive of finding or not finding a given data set. To deliver this capability, MOD operates in a flexible way. If the data set in the DD statement is on the system, MOD finds it and prepares to let you append records to it. If the data set is not on the system, MOD allocates it and then prepares to let you append records to it. Either way, there is a data set present to be deleted when it comes time for MVS to process the end-status-normal.

For MOD to be able to create a data set when necessary, you have to code UNIT and SPACE when you use it. MVS ignores these parameters at the DD statement if the data set already exists but uses them if directed by MOD to create a data set. The most general way to code UNIT for a disk data set is UNIT=SYSDA. It ordinarily makes no sense to code SPACE=(TRK,0) for a disk data set because this means "provide zero tracks of disk space." But MOD is satisfied with it because all MOD really does to "create" a data set is put its name into the volume table of contents of a disk volume. And when it "deletes" the data set, it really just deletes that name from the disk's VTOC.

11.12 Housekeeping Deletion for Tape Data Sets

The data set I gave housekeeping treatment to in Section 11.10 is a disk
data set. If it were a tape data set, I would have to code the DD statement
for it slightly differently in a deletion step:

```
//**************************************************************
//*                                                            *
//*       DELETE A CATALOGED TAPE DATA SET USING IEFBR14       *
//*                                                            *
//**************************************************************
//STEP010  EXEC  PGM=IEFBR14
//DEL1        DD  DSN=CSCJGJ.CSC.TAPEDATA,
//   UNIT=(TAPE,,DEFER),
//   DISP=(MOD,DELETE)
//
```

This involves no SPACE parameter because SPACE is associated only with
disk data sets. The DEFER in the UNIT parameter is particularly important
in this case because it tells MVS that the mounting of the tape can be
deferred until the program opens the data set. Because IEFBR14 never opens
any data sets, the DEFER means that an operator will not be asked to mount
a tape. If you omit DEFER and code UNIT=TAPE, a tape that will not be
used will have to be mounted. This is a manual action, and therefore omitting DEFER slows down your job. (Omitting DEFER will also irritate operations personnel because this wastes their time!) See Section 12.14 for
more information about DEFER.

11.13 Deleting Multiple Data Sets

You can delete any number of disk or tape (mixed is fine) data sets at a
single IEFBR14 step. If you have to delete more than one tape data set,
using a DD statement for each, it's highly desirable to minimize the number
of tape drives assigned to the step. The more tape drives MVS thinks you
need, the harder MVS will find it to schedule your job. You can minimize
the number of tape drives that you need by using the affinity specification,
AFF, on the second and subsequent tape data sets, pointing to the first tape
DDname:

```
//**************************************************************
//*                                                            *
//*    DELETE MULTIPLE TAPE DATA SETS ALLOCATING ONE DRIVE     *
//*                                                            *
//**************************************************************
//DELSTEP   EXEC  PGM=IEFBR14
//DEL1         DD  DSN=FS62.A31.ACCTSLOG,
//   UNIT=(TAPE,,DEFER),
//   DISP=(MOD,DELETE)
//*
//DEL2         DD  DSN=FS62.A31.JOURNLOG,
//   UNIT=AFF=DEL1,                       <=== AFF USES SAME UNIT
//   DISP=(MOD,DELETE)
//*
//DEL3         DD  DSN=FS62.A31.VOUCHLOG,
//   UNIT=AFF=DEL1,                       <=== AFF USES SAME UNIT
//   DISP=(MOD,DELETE)
```

The DEFER subparameter of UNIT delays mounting of a tape until called for by the program. But there is no way to escape the assignment of a tape drive to the step above, and one tape drive will be assigned to it (but not used) when it executes. See Section 12.15 for more information about AFF.

11.14 How PASS Actually Works

When you code PASS for end-status-normal, MVS keeps information about the data set (such as its unit and volume) in a special list called the "pass list." MVS uses this list in a behind-the-scenes "first in, first out" manner. If passed data sets are created under the same name by successive steps in the same job (as will happen when you execute the same cataloged procedure more than once in a job stream), each PASS will generate an entry of the same name on the pass list. You can encounter problems because of this if you are sloppy in your disposition of passed data sets.

When a job step accesses the pass list with a disposition such as (OLD,PASS), the OLD removes the oldest entry of the given data set name on the pass list. The PASS end-status-normal disposition causes another entry for the name to be placed at the bottom of the list. When (OLD,DELETE) or (OLD,KEEP) is coded for a data set passed from a prior step, no new entry is made in the pass list for the data set name.

11.15 Avoiding PASS Problems

A given step receiving a passed data set, where many passed data sets have been created under the same name, is not necessarily going to get the data set you might expect. The step will get the data set referenced by the then-oldest entry in the pass list for that given data set name. The actual data set pointed to by this list entry will depend on prior accesses by other job steps. You can avoid pass list problems by

- Using a different name for each temporary data set that you pass within a job stream or proc
- Coding DISP=(OLD,DELETE) instead of DISP=(OLD,PASS) for a passed temporary data set at the last step that accesses it

When a job invokes more than one instream or cataloged procedure or invokes the same procedure more than once, "end of job" is not synonomous with "end of procedure." Following the rules above lets you create job streams (and ultimately, procs) that avoid problems with pass list operation.

11.16 PASSing Permanent Cataloged Data Sets

A permanent data set is one that carries an ordinary name such as CSCJGJ.CSC.WORKERS. There's no guarantee of its permanency; it can be deleted. But unlike its opposite, a temporary data set, a permanent data set has the *potential* to remain on the system. A temporary data set with a name like &&TRANSORT has no potential of remaining on the system. You often use DISP=(NEW,PASS) with temporary data sets. But you can also use PASS with permanent data sets; passed data sets are more efficient to access than cataloged data sets.

You can use PASS and still have a newly created data set cataloged because MVS acts on the end-status-abend value for a passed data set even after the step in which it is created. Suppose you want to create a permanent data set and catalog it but also want to access it in subsequent steps. You can create it using DISP=(NEW,PASS,CATLG). Subsequent steps that need to access this data set can each receive it and pass it on with DISP=(OLD,PASS,CATLG). The final step receiving it can use DISP=(OLD,CATLG,CATLG) to retain and catalog it. The purpose of the end-status-abend disposition of CATLG on the creating and intermediate receiving DD statements is to have the data set cataloged if a job step abends.

11.17 Coding a Data Set "Finder" Step

The IEFBR14 null program has other uses related to the DISP parameter. Under MVS it's truly amazing what you can accomplish with a program that has nothing in it!

In some job streams it's important to find out early if a certain data set is present and accessible for exclusive use. You can do this in the first step of the job stream even if the data set will not actually be used until a later step. Just code an IEFBR14 step with a DD statement for the data set and use a DISP that does not alter the current status of the data set:

```
//**************************************************************
//*                                                            *
//*             "FINDER" STEP FOR A DATA SET                    *
//*                                                            *
//**************************************************************
//STEP010   EXEC  PGM=IEFBR14
//FIND1       DD   DSN=CSCJGJ.CSC.WHATSIT,
//  DISP=OLD
```

If this step does not find the data set or can't obtain exclusive access to it, the step will fail and the job will terminate.

11.18 Using a Finder Step and VOL Referback

A finder step like the one shown above can do more than just confirm that a certain data set is present. You can access some of the information about the data set that MVS acquires in the finder step and use it in a subsequent step. For example, one of the things that MVS finds out by executing a finder step is the volume serial number of the disk or tape on which the data set resides. You can code a volume referback in a subsequent step to write a new data set to the same volume without having to know what that volume is:

```
//**************************************************************
//*                                                            *
//*             "FINDER" STEP FOR A DATA SET                    *
//*                                                            *
//**************************************************************
//STEP010   EXEC  PGM=IEFBR14
//FIND1       DD   DSN=CSCJGJ.CSC.WHATSIT,
//  DISP=SHR
//*
```

```
//*****************************************************************
//*                                                               *
//*      WRITE A NEW DATA SET FORCING IT TO THE SAME VOLUME       *
//*                                                               *
//*****************************************************************
//STEP020     EXEC  PGM=IEBGENER
//SYSPRINT      DD  SYSOUT=*
//SYSIN         DD  DUMMY
//SYSUT1        DD  DSN=CSCJGJ.CSC.JUMBLE,              <=== INPUT
//  DISP=SHR
//SYSUT2        DD  DSN=CSCJGJ.CSC.JUNK,                <=== OUTPUT
//  DISP=(NEW,CATLG,DELETE),
//  UNIT=SYSDA,
//  DCB=(RECFM=FB,LRECL=80,BLKSIZE=6160),
//  SPACE=(TRK,1),
//  VOL=REF=*.STEP010.FIND1                  <=== PUT ON SAME VOL AS
//                                                CSCJGJ.CSC.WHATSIT
```

11.19 Writing Data Sets Using OLD or MOD

You usually think of coding OLD for start-status when you are reading a data set and want exclusive use of it. But you can code OLD when you want to write to an existing data set. When you do this, any existing contents of the data set are obliterated. The records you write begin at the start of the data set.

Coding MOD for start-status when you write to an existing data set produces different results. MOD dictates exclusive control of a data set, just as OLD does. But MOD makes the records you write to the data set begin at the end of the existing data; the new records are *appended* to the existing records in the data set. This was the original purpose of MOD and the reason for its name, MODify.

You could, for example, allocate a disk data set using IEFBR14; the data set will have no contents. A subsequent job step, or a different job running later, can access the data set using a start-status of MOD and write records in it. In fact, you could run several such jobs, one at a time, each appending data to the data set. But "extending" a data set in this way carries some risk of corrupting it. If a job step MODding onto a data set abends, the data set could be left in an unusable condition. A better approach to accumulating data is to use a generation data group, as I show you in Chapter 17.

In a COBOL program, opening a data set for OUTPUT and coding start-status MOD in your JCL produces the appending effect. But you can also append data to an existing data set by coding start-status OLD in your JCL and opening the data set for EXTEND in a COBOL program, because what a program says overrides what your JCL says.

11.20 Cataloging and Uncataloging Data Sets

You can use IEFBR14 to catalog an existing uncataloged data set. To do this you have to specify the UNIT and VOL parameters to tell MVS how to find the data set and obtain its other characteristics from its data set label:

```
//**********************************************************
//*                                                        *
//*            CATALOG AN UNCATALOGED DATA SET             *
//*                                                        *
//**********************************************************
//STEP010   EXEC  PGM=IEFBR14
//CAT1         DD  DSN=CSCJGJ.CSC.HOOPLE,
//   DISP=(OLD,CATLG),
//   UNIT=SYSDA,
//   VOL=SER=ACSCAA
```

The DDname you use (CAT1 here) is arbitrary. If the data set is already cataloged, this action causes its entry in the catalog to be updated. If a cataloged data set of the same name already exists on a different disk or tape, you'll get a NOT CATLG 2 warning error in the MVS system output and the catalog will not be changed. You can uncatalog a data set with similar coding:

```
//STEP010   EXEC  PGM=IEFBR14
//CAT1         DD  DSN=CSCJGJ.CSC.HOOPLE,
//   DISP=(OLD,UNCATLG)
```

Chapter Twelve

UNIT: HOW YOU DESIGNATE
AN I/O DEVICE

You store information in electronic form by encoding it in bits that form characters and numeric values. Your programs place information into this form and manipulate it in machine memory. But memory is not suitable for permanent information storage. How do you tell MVS what kind of external device you want to use to store or retrieve electronically coded bits of information?

Any device capable of recording on/off bits can be used to store digital information. Media such as punched paper tape, magnetic wire, magnetic cards, and soft plastic surfaces in which a laser can burn dimples have been used for this purpose. But the most popular devices for external information storage in the IBM mainframe environment use magnetic disk and magnetic tape.

In this chapter I'll explain how you use the UNIT parameter to specify the device to be used to access a data set. I'll also point out when you don't have to code UNIT on your DD statements.

12.1 Format of the UNIT Parameter

Figure 12.1 is an annotated map of the UNIT parameter. You use the UNIT parameter of the DD statement to tell MVS about the device a data set requires. You can also use UNIT to specify *how many* devices you will need for the data set and to ask MVS to delay mounting of a tape until the data set on it is opened by a program.

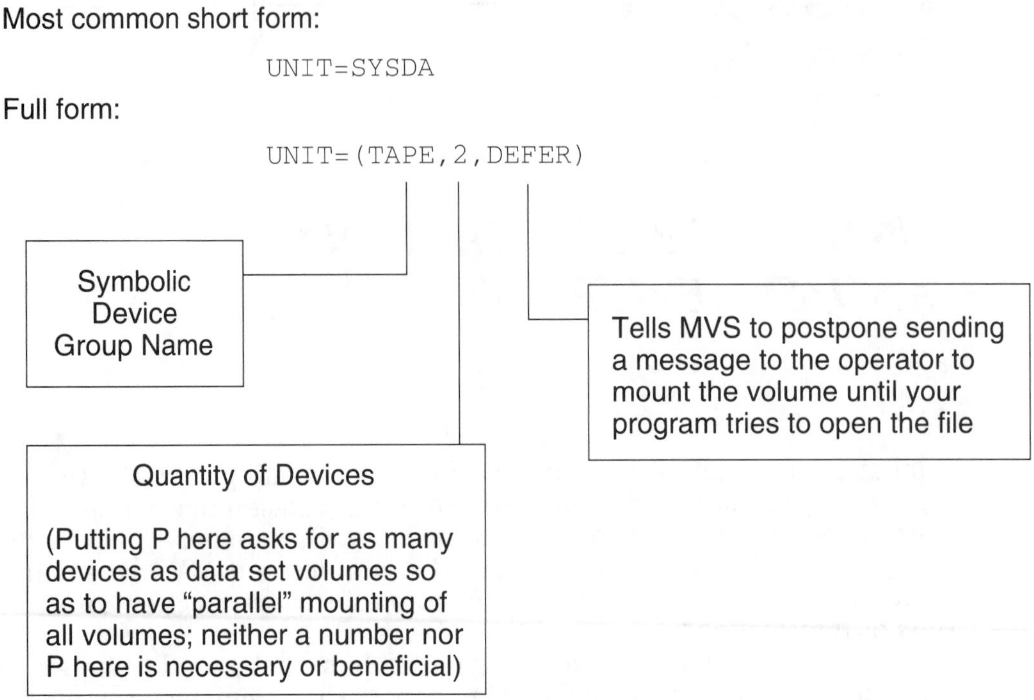

Most common short form:

```
UNIT=SYSDA
```

Full form:

```
UNIT=(TAPE,2,DEFER)
```

Symbolic Device Group Name

Quantity of Devices

(Putting P here asks for as many devices as data set volumes so as to have "parallel" mounting of all volumes; neither a number nor P here is necessary or beneficial)

Tells MVS to postpone sending a message to the operator to mount the volume until your program tries to open the file

Figure 12.1   Format of the UNIT Parameter

12.2 Context of UNIT and Its Common Coding

You'll very often have the need to code UNIT in this way at a DD statement where you create a data set:

```
//SYSUT2       DD   DSN=CSCJGJ.CSC.NEWSTUFF,
//   DISP=(NEW,CATLG,DELETE),
//   UNIT=SYSDA,
//   DCB=(RECFM=FB,LRECL=80,BLKSIZE=6160),
//   SPACE=(TRK,1)
```

Two forms of UNIT coding will be the most common in your JCL:

```
//   UNIT=SYSDA                Common for writing disk data sets
//   UNIT=(TAPE,,DEFER)        Common for writing tape data sets
```

You'll often be instructed by your installation to code names other than DISK or TAPE with UNIT, because systems programmers in every installation create these names. I'll explain these names, called **symbolic device group names,** in Section 12.8.

12.3 When You Have to Code UNIT

There are certain instances when you definitely have to code UNIT on a
DD statement:

- Specify UNIT if you are creating a data set. How else will MVS know
  what kind of device you want the data set to go to?
- Specify UNIT if you are reading a data set that is not cataloged because, for uncataloged data sets, the system has no way of figuring
  out what type of device the data set needs.
- Specify UNIT if you are reading a foreign tape (a tape not created in
  your installation) because the data set you are reading is entirely
  unknown to your system and catalog. I'll explain more about this type
  of action in Chapter 15.
- Specify UNIT as UNIT=(,,DEFER) when you are reading a cataloged
  tape data set to defer mounting until the program opens the data set;
  see Section 12.14.

12.4 When Not to Code UNIT

You omit coding UNIT on a DD statement under several circumstances:

- Don't code UNIT when you are reading a cataloged disk data set. The
  MVS system catalog knows what kind of device the data set is on.
  This is true no matter whether the data set is on disk or tape and no
  matter what its organization is, including VSAM. But for tape, you
  may want UNIT=(,,DEFER) to defer tape mounting until a program
  actually needs it, if there is some possibility that the program may
  not use the tape.
- Don't code UNIT when you receive the data set at a DD statement as
  a result of a PASS from a prior step. The system retains information
  about PASSed data sets, including device type, until the end of your
  job.
- Don't code UNIT when you write printlines to SYSOUT. When you
  send printlines to SYSOUT, they do wind up on disk in the system
  spool data set, but the SYSOUT mechanism automatically handles
  the designation of the appropriate data set and unit.
- Don't code UNIT when you write records to a VSAM data set. You
  can't create VSAM data sets without the help of the IDCAMS utility
  or SMS (Storage Management Subsystem); either of these tells MVS
  about the unit.

12.5 Ways You Can Specify I/O Devices with UNIT

As Figure 12.2 shows you, MVS gives you three ways to indicate the device to be used to access a data set:

- By hardware address
- By device model number
- By symbolic device group name

Unless you are a systems programmer, you'll probably never use hardware address and may never have any reason to use device model number either. But you should be aware of these to understand how symbolic device group names are created by your installation and what they really are.

```
//SYSUT2   DD   DSN=CSCJGJ.CSC.JUMBLE,
//   DISP=(NEW,CATLG,DELETE),
//   UNIT=SYSDA,
//   DCB=(RECFM=FB,LRECL=80,BLKSIZE=6160),
//   SPACE=(TRK,5,RLSE)
```

Specifying UNIT:

* By hardware address:

```
// UNIT=A49
```

* By device type:

```
// UNIT=3390
```

* By symbolic device group list:

```
// UNIT=SYSDA
```

Figure 12.2 Variations in Coding the UNIT Parameter

12.6 UNIT Coding Using Hardware Address

Your installation may have anywhere from a few to a hundred or more disk drives and one to scores of tape drives. Each disk or tape drive has a unique *hardware address.* It's actually a bit more complicated than this, but think of this address as a uniquely labeled plug to which the device is attached. Device addresses take the form of three hexadecimal characters. For example, a given tape drive may be attached at hardware address A58, another may be attached at 959, and still another at D5A. Each disk unit is attached at a specific address, as is every printer or other I/O device. To access the first of these devices you could code UNIT as:

```
//  UNIT=A58              Coding device by machine address
```

But as a programmer you have no business trying to access a specific unit address to write data. You won't, in fact, even know at what hardware address a given device is located, and the locations are subject to change as your mainframe configuration evolves. As you can see in the IEF237I messages just above the COND CODE in your MVS system output for every step (as in Chapter 10, Figure 10.5), you do get to see hardware addresses regardless of how you code UNIT. (MVS always gets down to the level of address because that's actually how it communicates with the device):

```
            -
            -
            -
IEF236I ALLOC. FOR CSCJGJA STEP010
IEF237I 124 ALLOCATED TO DELETE1
IEF237I 121 ALLOCATED TO SYS06754
IEF142I CSCJGJA STEP010  STEP WAS EXECUTED   COND CODE 0000
            -
            -
            -
```

12.7 UNIT Coding Using I/O Device Model Numbers

Every item of equipment that IBM makes for attachment to a mainframe carries a model number. Disk units in a modern installation include the 3380 and 3390 units. Tape drives include the 3490 cartridge tape drive, the 3480 cartridge tape drive, and the older model 3430 reel-to-reel tape drive. Printers, video display station control units, video terminals, optical character readers, and other devices all have unique model numbers. Literally thousands of these devices can be attached to your mainframe at the same time.

MVS maintains lists of the hardware addresses where each model of device is located. The "name" of each list is the model number, such as 3390. Because of these lists, MVS knows where each device of each model is located. If you code UNIT with a device model number like this:

```
//  UNIT=3390                   Coding device by model number
```

you are asking to use any one device of the model that you stated. MVS will pick an available one for you from the list and assign it to the DD statement. Coding by device type lets MVS satisfy a unit need even when some devices of the type that you need are out of service ("varied off-line") or busy. The device assigned to the request is indicated by its hardware address in your MVS system output.

A UNIT request by model is broader than a request coded by hardware address. But for disk data sets a UNIT request by model is still needlessly constrained. Why do you care what model of disk a new data set goes on? If you code UNIT by device model number, you'll have to change your JCL when a new model of device replaces the one that you coded!

12.8 UNIT Coding by Symbolic Device Group Name

Your installation can build lists of the hardware addresses of devices and give a unique name to each such list. The same device hardware address can appear in many such lists. The most common device group list is provided by IBM and is named SYSDA. It specifies the addresses of all system direct access (disk) devices (subject to modification by your systems programmers). If you code UNIT=SYSDA for a data set that you are writing, MVS can select any available disk device to house the data set:

```
//  UNIT=SYSDA           Coding device by symbolic device group name
```

Even if your installation has not established any of its own symbolic device group address lists, you can code UNIT=SYSDA for disk. IBM literature sometimes calls the symbolic device group name an *esoteric device name.* But this implies that device group names are specialized or exotic. They're not! Symbolic device group names are meat-and-potatoes JCL coding.

Not all installations let end users and programmers code UNIT=SYSDA. Some installations create less comprehensive lists of disk hardware addresses (with names other than SYSDA) to force data sets onto specific pools of disk devices. Your local documentation tells you what locally created symbolic device group names you are authorized to use.

12.9 Local Symbolic Device Group Lists

An installation will typically maintain device address lists under at least two symbolic names such as DISK (or some variant) and TAPE. The list named DISK will contain the addresses of all of the installation's production-preferred disk devices, most likely its newest, highest-capacity, and fastest-access disk drives. You need to find out what symbolic device group name such as DISK exists in your shop, if any does exist in addition to SYSDA.

An installation will usually create a symbolic device group name list of the addresses of its production-preferred tape drives. In the modern environment these will most likely be the addresses of 3490 or 3430 tape drives, but not a combination of the two. Why not a combination? Because 3430 and 3490 drives are not compatible. The 3430 handles older style reel-to-reel tapes, whereas the 3490 is a tape cartridge drive. If these different types of devices were put into the same symbolic device list, tape reels would get directed to 3490s, and data sets on tape cartridges would be directed to reel-to-reel drives!

Your installation can create additional symbolic device names—in fact, many of them. For example, the name TEST might be used to identify a list of addresses where disk drives devoted to test data sets are located. If you coded UNIT=TEST, a new data set would automatically be directed to this select group of disks. UNIT=WORK might identify high-speed disks to be used for sort or compiler work files.

12.10 Why Coding by Symbolic Device Group Name Is Important

Installations strongly prefer you to code UNIT by symbolic device group name because this makes it easier to cope with the ongoing upgrade of peripheral equipment attached to the mainframe. As older disk devices are replaced by newer ones, an installation can attach new devices to the system and smoothly phase in their use by adding their addresses to the device group lists. Your JCL does not have to be changed at all. Had you coded UNIT by hardware address or model number, your JCL would have to be extracted from production libraries, modified, and replaced as the equipment configuration changes.

12.11 Virtual Input/Output (VIO) for UNIT

You can, for certain purposes, make use of a special type of UNIT coding. You can write a data set to virtual disk storage by coding UNIT=VIO. VIO (which stands for "virtual input/output") looks as if it represents just the name of a symbolic device group list. But it's really a form of storage that makes use of the same system memory that MVS itself uses for its virtual storage operations. VIO storage is handy for two types of data sets:

1. Work files, such as those used by the sort utility or a compiler
2. Temporary data sets that you use to "pipe" data from one program (step) to another

VIO is faster than ordinary disk. Think of it as "ram" disk. You can't permanently retain data sets that you write to VIO. These data sets last, at most, for the duration of your job execution.

12.12 Summary of "Long Form" UNIT Coding

The format of the complete UNIT parameter is

```
//   UNIT=( device-type, device-count, DEFER )
```

Device-type is actually one of three subparameters that you can code. When this is all you code, you omit the parentheses and commas of the long form coding. All of the parameters for UNIT are positional; MVS recognizes them based on their position following the word UNIT. You specify device-type by hardware address, model number, symbolic device group list, or VIO as I explained in Sections 12.6 through 12.11.

You should almost never specify device-count. If you put a number here, it must be from 1 (the default) through 59. This tells MVS how many devices you want allocated to the DD statement. Any number other than 1 "hogs" devices that would be better used by other jobs. Section 12.13 gives you details on device-count.

Code DEFER to tell MVS that it should defer sending a message to the computer operator to physically put the volume (disk or tape) onto a drive until the program tries to open the data set on it. To code UNIT with TAPE and DEFER but not device-count, just omit the device-count. Section 12.14 gives you details of DEFER operation:

```
//   UNIT=(TAPE,,DEFER)
```

12.13 Device-Count and Parallel Mounting

Device-count is a vestige of the past, and you should rarely, if ever, code it. When you omit it, it defaults to 1. In the early days we used to code device-count when a disk data set spanned more than one storage volume (disk pack) and it was necessary to have all volumes mounted at the same time "in parallel." This had some relevance to large indexed files on demountable disks. But due to the critical mechanical tolerances involved in dense information storage, modern mainframe hard disk drives don't have demountable disks. Disk packs are now permanently mounted.

You can only read or write tape data sets serially, so coding device-count has little relevance. With device-count as 1 (the default) for a multiple-volume tape data set, MVS automatically notifies the operator to demount a tape that has been completely processed (read or written) and mount the next tape cartridge or reel (volume). Thus, you can process a multiple-volume data set one volume at a time using as little as one tape drive.

At the opposite extreme of the default device count of 1 is a device count equal to the number of volumes housing the data set. Instead of indicating the number of devices needed to achieve concurrent (parallel) mounting of all volumes, you could code "P" instead of a number at device-count. This works only if MVS already knows how many volumes the data set spans. MVS will know this if the data set is cataloged or if you state all of its volume serial numbers using the VOL parameter.

You might get the impression that parallel mounting of the several tapes storing a large data set is an appealing option. After all, all of the tapes would be mounted at the start of the step, and processing would not be interrupted for tape changes, right? But you could actually experience significant delay in running your job. The fewer resources such as tape drives that your job uses, the easier MVS is able to supply resources and start the job. Jobs that require more than a few tape drives will usually take a lot longer to start.

12.14 DEFER to Defer the Operator's Tape Mount Message

DEFER lets you speed your jobs by eliminating unnecessary tape mounts. MVS will ordinarily send a message to the computer operator to mount a tape when a step accessing it becomes active. If you code DEFER, MVS postpones sending this mount message until the program being run at that step actually tries to open the data set.

The advantage of coding DEFER for tape data sets is that if a given job step never opens the tape data set at the DD statement, MVS never tells the computer operator to mount the tape. Think about any housekeeping delete IEFBR14 step in which you are trying to delete, allocate, or simply "find" a data set. IEFBR14 never opens any files at all. But if you forget to code DEFER on a DD statement for a tape here, MVS will still tell the operator to mount it and, almost immediately afterwards, to remove it!

DEFER has relevance for programs other than IEFBR14. Many programs do not open all data sets at beginning of job; instead, they do so only as needed. Although DEFER now has no meaning for disk data sets, you can totally generalize a UNIT specification for an existing cataloged data set with this coding:

```
//   UNIT=(,,DEFER)
```

Because this coding omits both device-type and device-count, MVS still uses the catalog to figure out the appropriate device and uses the default 1 as the device-count.

DEFER has no effect on device allocation, which is the MVS process that assigns system resources to a job. Whether or not you code DEFER for tapes, it will still appear to MVS that you need at least one tape drive for every DD statement in a step that deals with a tape file. The AFF specification *does* give you the capability to minimize the number of device allocations.

12.15 AFF for Unit Affinity Specification

You can code a form of referback from one DD statement to another to force MVS to use the same device for a data set that it used earlier. This can minimize the number of tape drives that your job requires. However, you can only refer back to a DD statement in the same step. And of course, this works only if the data sets at these DD statements don't need to use the same device at the same time!

Suppose you are executing a program named TABUPDAT that reads data from tape at DDname //TABLEIN, loads it to a table in memory, and closes the input file. During its execution, the program updates the table. At its end of job, the program writes the table to another tape (a "scratch" tape) at DDname //TABLEOUT. You can code this JCL to run the program using only one tape drive:

```
//*******************************************************************
//*                                                                 *
//*         READ TABLE DATA FROM TAPE, WRITE TO NEW TAPE            *
//*                                                                 *
//*******************************************************************
//STEP012    EXEC   PGM=TABUPDAT
//TABLEIN      DD   DSN=XYZ123.TRAINING.TABLE1,
//   DISP=OLD,
//   UNIT=(,,DEFER),
//TABLEOUT     DD   DSN=XYZ123.TRAINING.TABLE2,
//   DISP=(NEW,CATLG,DELETE),
//   UNIT=AFF=TABLEIN,                          <=== USE SAME TAPE DRIVE
//   DCB=(RECFM=FB,LRECL=80,BLKSIZE=32720),
//   LABEL=RETPD=30
     -
     -
```

An opposite-sounding SEP parameter for "channel separation" formerly existed within the syntax of UNIT. SEP is not supported under MVS, MVS/XA, or MVS/ESA.

12.16 Using AFF to Sort a Tape with One Tape Drive

Many business data processing tasks require you to sort data. If the data to be sorted is stored on tape and the sorted data set is to be stored on another tape, you may think that two tape drives are required. But in fact you need only one tape drive because of the way sort utilities such as IBM's DFSORT, Computer Associate's CA-SORT, and SYNCSORT work. They read all the data to be sorted into memory and disk first, do their work, and then copy the sorted data to the output data set. Here is how you can code AFF to use just one tape drive when you do a sort from and to tape:

```
//**************************************************************
//*                                                            *
//*    SORT DATA FROM TAPE TO TAPE USING ONLY ONE TAPE DRIVE   *
//*                                                            *
//**************************************************************
//STEP012    EXEC  PGM=SORT
//SORTIN        DD  DSN=AK00.C99.TRANSIN,
//  DISP=(OLD,KEEP)
//SORTOUT       DD  DSN=AK00.C99.TRANSORT,
//  DISP=(NEW,CATLG,DELETE),
//  UNIT=AFF=SORTIN,
//  DCB=(RECFM=FB,LRECL=80,BLKSIZE=32720),
//  LABEL=RETPD=12
//SORTWK01      DD  UNIT=DISK,SPACE=(CYL,2,,CONTIG)
//SORTWK02      DD  UNIT=DISK,SPACE=(CYL,2,,CONTIG)
//SORTWK03      DD  UNIT=DISK,SPACE=(CYL,2,,CONTIG)
//SYSOUT        DD  SYSOUT=*
//SYSIN         DD  *
    SORT FIELDS=(1,4,CH,A)
/*
//
```

You can also use AFF to minimize tape drive allocation in IEFBR14 housekeeping steps. Arrange for any second and subsequent tape data sets to be assigned to the same tape drive as the first tape data set.

12.17 Common Problems with UNIT

If you forget to code DISP at a data set that you are reading (an easy mistake for newcomers to make), like so:

```
//SYSUT1  DD  DSN=XYZ123.TRAINING.DATA1          DISP is missing!
```

you will get an error message stating INCORRECT DEVICE TYPE SPECI-FIED. This can really be confusing, because you didn't even code UNIT!

The problem here is that DISP defaults to DISP= (NEW,DELETE,DELETE) if you omit it. In the //SYSUT1 DD statement coding shown above, MVS thinks you are trying to create a new data set rather than read an existing data set. To create a data set, you need UNIT, and that is missing too. Cure the problem above by coding the DISP=SHR that you forgot, not UNIT!

You can encounter a related problem if you are accessing a cataloged data set and you code UNIT. If the UNIT you indicate is not consistent with the catalog, the job will fail with a message referring to incorrect device type.

Chapter Thirteen

DCB: DATA CONTROL BLOCK

The DCB parameter can be more complicated than any other aspect of a "writing" DD statement. Why you should need the DCB parameter at all may be a little hard to understand too, especially if your background is in micro- or minicomputers. The DCB essentially lets you tell MVS about the characteristics of the data set that it needs to know to work with it. The program you are running can tell MVS these things, such as record length, record format (fixed length or variable length), and block size. But it's easier to change JCL than to change a program, and the DCB makes manipulation of data sets easier.

In this chapter I'll show you what the DCB is all about. To help you understand how to use it, I'll show you how it affects the way MVS works in what is known as the ***dcb merge.*** And I'll show you in detail the different blocked and unblocked record storage formats supported by MVS.

13.1 How MVS Itself Is Modularized

MVS—the operating system software itself—consists of over 10,000,000 lines of code. That's a huge amount of logic, much more than anyone could manage in a single program. MVS consists of thousands of software modules, each of which performs specific tasks. These modules communicate with one another by sharing information in memory.

When one MVS module wants to call upon another to provide a service it first locates an available chunk of memory. It gains authority to use this memory as a "mailbox." It puts into this mailbox the information that the module it is calling needs to do its work. The "caller" then gives the address of the memory mailbox to the "called" program and passes control to that module. The called module retrieves its marching orders from the mailbox. Figure 13.1 shows you how MVS calls its Input/Output Control Subsystem (IOCS) to accomplish data set reading and writing.

13.2 What MVS Control Blocks Are

Scores of different electronic mailbox formats exist as interfaces between various MVS modules. MVS refers to these communication memory formats as **control blocks.** Control block fields and formats are documented in *System/360 Control Blocks*, IBM publication GC28–6628.

Control blocks are given names that describe what they do. Data set labels are a type of control block. The records in a disk volume table of contents (VTOC) are called Data Set Control Block or DSCB records; these are the data set labels for disk data set. Data sets on tape have labels too, and they are also called control blocks. These consist of two 80-byte records placed immediately before each data set on tape, as I illustrate in Chapter 15.

Understanding what MVS control blocks are is the key to understanding what the DCB parameter is. The MVS **data control block** is the electronic mailbox that MVS uses to tell its input/output subsystem about the characteristics of the records you want it to read or write. And the DCB parameter is what you code in a DD statement to put information into an MVS data control block.

As Figure 13.1 shows you, the information that MVS puts into the data control block can come from three different sources: the program being executed, your JCL for the step, or the data set label that was recorded with the data set when it was created.

13.3 The DCB Merge

The data control block—not the DCB parameter of JCL but the actual area of MVS electronic mailbox memory—is formed by MVS from three sources. MVS follows this sequence, called the **dcb merge,** in seeking information to put into the data control block for a data set:

1. The program being executed
2. Your DCB parameter in the DD statement for the data set
3. The label of the data set

In preparing to deal with a data set, MVS first creates a data control block. It initializes its fields to default values, such as block size 0. Then MVS begins the dcb merge.

MVS first looks in the program that you are executing for information about the record size, block size, and organization of the data set. It puts this into the data control block, replacing default values. A COBOL or other higher-level language program will typically convey the record length and data set organization. An Assembler program has the ability to provide much more information for the data control block (and often does.)

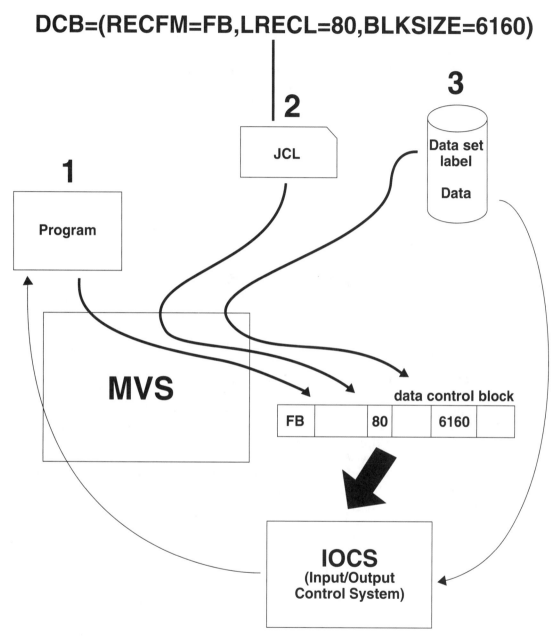

Figure 13.1 How the DCB Merge Works

The information that MVS puts into the data control block can come from three different sources: the program being executed, your JCL for the step, or the data set label recorded with the data set when it was created. MVS follows the sequence "program, JCL, data set label" in seeking information to put into the data control block. This is called the *dcb merge.*

After drawing on the program for as much information about the data set as it can find, MVS next looks in your JCL at the DCB you coded at the DD statement. It seeks only the information that it still needs about the data set to complete the data control block. The JCL is the second source of data control block information. If it states things, such as the record length, that MVS has already found in the program, the coding in the JCL has no effect. You can't override in JCL what a program says about the characteristics of a data set.

It's possible for information to be lacking in the data control block even after MVS looks in the program and in your JCL DCB coding. If this is the case, MVS then seeks the necessary information in the label of the data set as a last resort. Because the data set label is consulted last, whatever it says about characteristics of the data set is ignored except for those things that both the program and your JCL declined to state.

13.4 Effect of the DCB Merge on "Reading" DD Statements

Based on the "program, JCL, data set label" sequence of the dcb merge, you can now see why we specify only DSN and DISP when reading a cataloged data set. We want MVS to form the dcb for data set access from the data set label.

In reading a data set, we arrange for the program to state only minimal information about the characteristics of the data set being read; MVS doesn't get much from it to complete the dcb. We don't specify data set characteristics in the JCL with a DCB parameter, so MVS can't get any information about the data set there. Finally, MVS seeks dcb information from the data set's label. Because MVS itself composed the data set label when the data set was created, it reads back correct information about the nature of the data set and uses this to complete the dcb.

If you code a DCB in your JCL (on the DD statement) for a data set you're reading, MVS will use that information for the dcb instead of looking farther for the information in the data set label. We say that your JCL "overrides" the data set label. In a few instances you might find this useful, but ordinarily it's dangerous to code a DCB in cases like this where you don't need it. If there is no data set label (as with an unlabeled "foreign" tape, as described in Chapter 15), all of the information for the dcb has to come from the program or your JCL, and you *do* have to code a DCB.

By the same token, if the program being executed at a step "says too much" about data set characteristics, it overrides whatever you have coded in your JCL or whatever the data set label says. We typically do not want block size to be specified in a program for a data set it is reading, and we don't want to specify block size in JCL using DCB either. We want block size to come from the data set label, where it is known to be true and accurate.

13.5 Blocks, Logical Records, and Physical Records

The terminology used in the IBM mainframe environment in connection with data sets is potentially confusing because some of the same words are used to mean different things. "Block" is one of those words. "Record" is another. I will explain these multiple meanings to you.

In the previous sections, I've told you about MVS control blocks in general and the data control block in particular. When we talk about control blocks, "block" means an area of memory dedicated to intermodule communication. Groups of records are also known as blocks of records. When we talk of a block of records, it means a group of records processed as a single, contiguous stream of bytes.

Records are groups of fields, made up of bytes. A record is the unit of information storage that is read and written by most programs. But when we talk about actual storage of records on disk or tape, we have to distinguish between *logical records* and *physical records.* The type of record you normally think about in programming terms is a logical record. *Physical record is actually another name for a block of records.*

Information is recorded on disk or tape in streams of bits. The bits making up the end of one record are separated from the bits where the next record starts by markers called *interrecord gaps.* These gaps do not contain data. They are made up of signals recognizable by tape or disk drive.

If you store information *unblocked*, you place one logical record between interrecord gaps, as shown in Figure 13.2a. In this case, the terms "logical record," "physical record," and "block" all mean the same thing.

You can store logical records in groups to make input/output and storage more efficient. This is called *blocking* the records. If you do this, the group of records appears to tape and disk hardware as a physical record, as shown in Figure 13.2b. In this case, a logical record is smaller than a physical record. MVS blocks and deblocks the logical records for you as you write and read the data set. It would be more correct here to call the gap between recorded information an *interblock gap*, but that's not commonly done.

You can also house records in a "spanned" organization. This applies only to very long records. If a record is more than 32,760 bytes long, it will have to be housed across more than one physical record. Here the record is larger than the block. This is rarely necessary because it's usually possible to design data sets to avoid having such huge records.

13.6 Why Do We Block Records?

We block records for the same reason that eggs are sold in cartons of 12; it's more efficient to store and move them around in groups that way. If you had to drive to the store to buy each of 12 eggs separately, it would take a long time, and you would waste a lot of motion. If you buy 12 eggs at a time, you only have to go to the store one twelfth as many times (at least for eggs).

Figure 13.3 shows you a simple graph of input/output efficiency and a tape drive. "Going to the store" in regard to tape or disk-stored data means executing over 5,000 machine language instructions to set up the electronic pathway for the data transfer. Without record blocking, you have to do this once for each record. The more records you group into a block, the fewer times you have to do physical input/output. You do pay for this by having to use more memory to hold the block of records, but these days memory is cheap and available. MVS automatically gives you one record at a time as you read a blocked data set, and MVS manages the buffer when you write a data set. When you read a data set, you don't even know how it has been blocked.

Record blocking not only economizes on processing, it makes better use of tape and disk capacity. On tape, for example, the interrecord gap is a fixed .3 inch. This may not sound like much, but .3 inch can store .3 × 6,250 = 1,875 bytes, even on older open reel tapes. Processing speed and both tape and disk storage capacity benefit greatly from an appropriate level of record blocking. Later in this chapter I explain to you how you can code your programs and JCL for optimal data set blocking.

13.7 DCB Merge for New Data Sets

Figure 13.1 should make it plain to you why your JCL for a new data set usually has to contain a DCB (or, under MVS/ESA, at least some of the elements of DCB coding). All of the information MVS needs for the data set's dcb has to come from either the program or your JCL; there is no data set label yet!

Because it's easier to change JCL than to change, compile, and linkage edit a program, we try to arrange for programs to say as little as possible about data set characteristics. For new data sets, whatever data set characteristics the program declines to state have to be stated in your JCL. You ordinarily have to arrange for programs to pass up their opportunity to state block size because we want flexibility in controlling it. Either your JCL or MVS itself should specify block size, not the program.

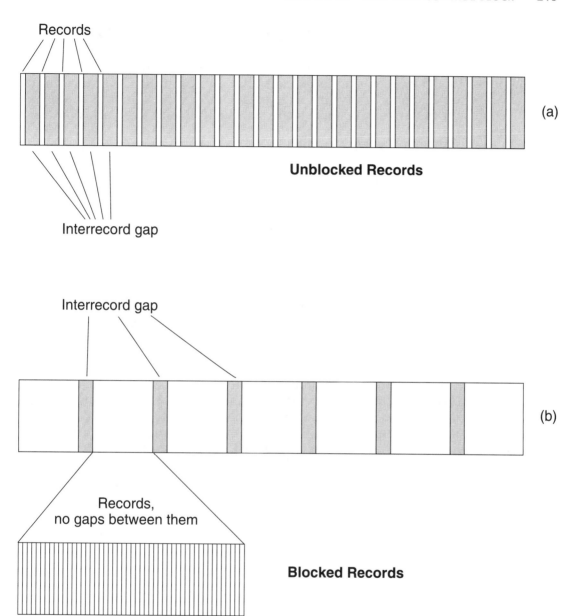

Figure 13.2   Unblocked and Blocked Records

(a) If you store information unblocked, you place one logical record between interrecord gaps. This is inefficient for input/output and wastes tape and disk capacity. (b) You can store logical records in groups to make input/output and storage more efficient. This is called ***blocking*** the records.

13.8 Programs Can Pass Up the Opportunity to State Block Size

Programs get the first opportunity to supply information to the data control block. To allow block size to be controlled by JCL or MVS, a program has to pass up its opportunity to specify block size. How you code a program to cause it to pass up its opportunity to specify block size varies between languages.

In VS COBOL and VS COBOL II programs, you code BLOCK CONTAINS 0 RECORDS in the file definition (FD) for a data set to pass up the opportunity to supply block size. When you do this, the compiler supplies 0 as the block size, which is the MVS default for block size in the dcb. MVS does not see the program supplying a value for the block size and consequently continues dcb merge actions for it. If you just omit BLOCK CONTAINS 0 RECORDS in your FD, the COBOL compiler assumes a block size equal to the record length. In this case, MVS *does* see your program supplying a value for block size and does not continue the dcb merge for that item. Leaving out BLOCK CONTAINS for a data set that you are reading usually produces an abend with system completion code 001–4 because almost all data sets are blocked for efficiency. Writing a data set without BLOCK CONTAINS 0 RECORDS creates a very inefficient unblocked data set.

Arranging for a program to pass up the opportunity to specify block size is easier in PL/I. In a PL/I program, you omit BLKSIZE from the ENVIRONMENT option to do this. And in C and FORTRAN programs it's even easier; you have no way to specify block size!

For an Assembler program to pass up the opportunity to specify a block size and allow this to be done in your JCL, you omit BLKSIZE in the DCB instruction in the program. But IBM utility programs such as the sort utility and compilers (written in Assembler) control the block size for their own work files themselves. This is why you don't code DCB on the DD statements for these work files. If you do code DCB information on the DD statement for these data sets, it's ignored by MVS anyway, due to the sequence of the dcb merge.

13.9 Coding DCB for New Data Sets (MVS and MVS/XA)

Let's look now at a DD statement in which a data set is being created by a locally written program. For this example, I'm going to use the JCL you have already seen in Chapter 10 as Figure 10.7, specifically lines 3000 through 3400. This is the DD statement named WORKREPT, where I am creating a data set named CSCJGJ.CSC.OVERTIME.REPORT to house the 133-byte printline records written as a report by program PARMDEMO:

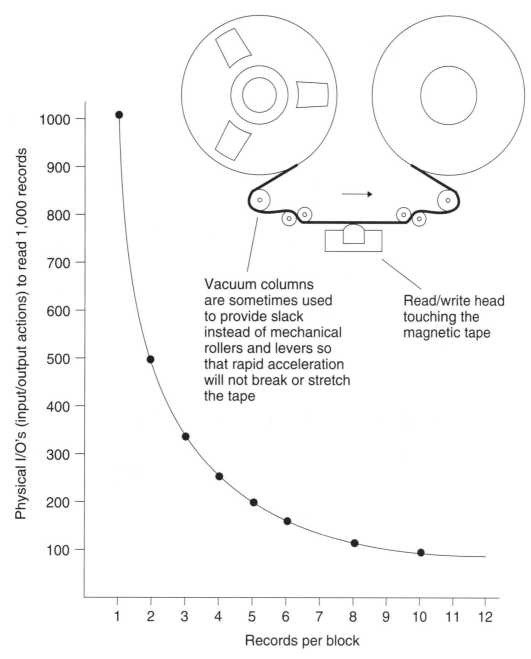

Figure 13.3   Decrease in Input/Output Actions with Blocking

With unblocked records, you have to do a physical input action every time you
read a record. The more records you group into a block, the fewer times you have
to do physical input/output for a given number of records.

```
//GO.WORKREPT  DD  DSN=CSCJGJ.CSC.OVERTIME.REPORT,
//   DISP=(NEW,CATLG,DELETE),
//   UNIT=SYSDA,
//   DCB=(RECFM=FB,LRECL=133,BLKSIZE=6118),
//   SPACE=(TRK,5,RLSE)
```

This DCB is present in its "traditional" form. But if you look at the source code for PARMDEMO (see Chapter 7, Figure 7.4) you'll see that some of the DCB coding is superfluous. The program itself tells MVS that the records are 133 bytes in length, and therefore LRECL (logical record length) in the JCL is going to be ignored. The program also tells MVS that the records are fixed length, but it doesn't say what the block size is, so MVS doesn't know from the program if record blocking is intended. RECFM (record format) in the JCL DCB tells MVS that fixed length records (F) are involved but also that blocking (B) is intended. BLKSIZE in this JCL tells MVS we intend blocks to be 6,118 bytes long.

Coded as shown, the slightly redundant DCB is quite adequate. While LRECL could really be omitted, having it in the DCB documents why I chose the BLKSIZE that I used. Under MVS and MVS/XA, you have to specify the block size you want. For fixed length records this will be a multiple of LRECL. Later in this chapter I show you more about block size for variable length records.

13.10 Simplified DCB Coding for New Data Sets Under MVS/ESA

MVS/ESA is the newest version of MVS. It's intended for the ES/9000 family of machines and the System/390. If your installation is using MVS/ESA, you can optionally code the information for the data control block in a simpler way. Here is what the DD statement I've shown in the previous section could look like under MVS/ESA:

```
//GO.WORKREPT  DD  DSN=CSCJGJ.CSC.OVERTIME.REPORT,
//   DISP=(NEW,CATLG,DELETE),
//   UNIT=SYSDA,
//   RECFM=FB,
//   LRECL=133,
//   SPACE=(TRK,5,RLSE)
```

MVS/ESA simplifies DCB coding by promoting each of the keyword sub-parameters of the old DCB parameter to be parameters of their own. You don't have to code DCB=(...) anymore; the DCB keywords themselves can stand alone. Unless you know the background of the DCB, however, the new style obscures what's really happening. The freestanding keywords are still your pipeline to the fields of the MVS data control block!

You'll notice that I completely omitted BLKSIZE in the MVS/ESA coding. That's not a mistake. Optimal block size depends on the type of unit the data set will be written to and is different for various models of disk and tape. You have traditionally had to worry about those factors in coding your DCB parameters under MVS and MVS/XA. If you don't code block size in your program or JCL, MVS/ESA computes it for you, using tables it maintains about the optimal block sizes for all the devices on your system. This is one of the nicest improvements in JCL in about 25 years!

Under MVS/ESA, the actual DD statement you code for a new data set such as CSCJGJ.CSC.OVERTIME.REPORT will probably differ even more from the old MVS and MVS/XA version. It might be affected by an additional (new) parameter, AVGREC, if your installation uses Storage Management Subsystem (SMS):

```
//GO.WORKREPT  DD  DSN=CSCJGJ.CSC.OVERTIME.REPORT,
//   DISP=(NEW,CATLG,DELETE),
//   UNIT=SYSDA,
//   RECFM=FB,
//   LRECL=133,
//   AVGREC=U,
//   SPACE=(133,10000,RLSE)
```

AVGREC is in MVS/ESA only with storage management subsystem

With AVGREC=U the 133 is the average record length and =U means that the 10000 is a "unit" estimate of the quantity of records to be written (10000 times 1)

Because AVGREC deals with a simplified way to specify disk space, I'll explain it to you in detail in Chapter 14. Storage Management Subsystem makes even more drastic simpifications possible as I explain in Appendix A. It standardizes the things originally specified in the DCB and houses them under names that your installation creates locally.

13.11 DCB "Short Form" Coding with a Single Keyword

All DCB subparameters are keywords. The order in which you code them in a traditional DCB parameter makes no difference. When you need to code only one keyword subparameter, you can code DCB in a short form with parentheses omitted:

```
//   DCB=keyword=xxxx
```

One example of short form DCB coding is DCB=RECFM=FBA, and another is DCB=BLKSIZE=80.

You may see the short form DCB coded in older JCL, especially where DUMMY is coded at a data set being created (to discard it). Block size is needed by MVS I/O routines to allocate the memory buffer where output is directed. In earlier versions of MVS, it was necessary to code DUMMY in this way to provide a buffer of at least one record length:

```
//REPORT2   DD   DUMMY,DCB=BLKSIZE=133
```

You may still see MVS tag on this short form of DCB coding to your specification of instream data as it interprets your JCL:

```
//SYSIN     DD   *                     As you coded it
//SYSIN     DD   *,DCB=BLKSIZE=80       As MVS reports it
```

13.12 DCB Subparameters

The data control block fields used by different input/output devices differ because devices such as tapes, disks, magnetic stripe scanners, and diskette readers have different characteristics and data formatting requirements. Several DCB subparameters besides RECFM, LRECL, and BLKSIZE exist. About 40 exist now, and IBM creates new keyword subparameters as new devices (and control block fields) are developed. The following sections show you the DCB subparameters you're likely to see in existing JCL and perhaps have occasion to use.

13.13 BLKSIZE

BLKSIZE specifies the maximum length of the block, which can range between 18 and 32760. The lower limit is dictated by tape drive circuitry that can't distinguish electrical "noise" from data in bursts shorter than 18 bytes. The upper limit is imposed by MVS channel program instructions (EXCPs in MVS system reporting) that actually handle input and output operations. For data sets coded in ASCII (not EBCDIC) on magnetic tape with ASCII standard labels, the block size limit is only 2,048 bytes per block.

For fixed length unblocked (RECFM=F) records, the block size and the record length are the same. For fixed length blocked (RECFM=FB) records, block size must be a multiple of record length, and the block size must be no larger than 32,760 bytes. All 32,760 bytes represent data accessible to you.

For variable length unblocked (RECFM=V) and variable length blocked (RECFM=VB) records, block size must be 4 bytes more than LRECL but no larger than 32,760 bytes. Because there is no way to predict the specific length of any block (don't forget, variable length records vary in length!), you usually code block size as disk half-track capacity or 32,760 bytes for tape. (As I discuss in Section 13.19, MVS automatically prepends 4 bytes of record length information called the **record descriptor word** to the front of each variable length record and prepends 4 more bytes of block length information called the **block descriptor word** to the front of each block. Unblocked variable length records are handled as a subset of blocked records and receive the same treatment.)

For undefined format (RECFM=U) records, the block size is best specified as the capacity of half a track of disk space. If you don't know what type of disk your installation uses, code block size for these data sets as BLKSIZE=6233 under MVS and MVS/XA or omit it under MVS/ESA to allow MVS to determine it.

13.14 BUFL

The length of each data buffer defaults to the size of the block. You can code BUFL to specify a value from as low as the block size to as high as 32,760. An example is BUFL=13000. For disk data sets you can gain efficiency by having the buffer size larger than the default, allowing more blocks from the same track or cylinder to be brought into program-accessible memory with a given revolution of the disk. But BUFL is not relevant to VSAM data sets, in which the AMP subparameter BUFFERSPACE serves this purpose.

13.15 BUFNO

You can code this value from 1 to 255; each buffer is one block length of memory or the size set by the BUFL subparameter. The default is two buffers; this way, MVS refills one buffer while your program processes the other. The default is usually sufficient, but you can make it larger to speed processing of large sequential data sets. An example of the syntax is BUFNO=6. You can specify both BUFNO and BUFL together to control the size and number of data buffers. You can't use BUFNO with VSAM data sets; you code the AMP subparameters BUFND and BUFNI to govern the number of buffers for VSAM data and index components.

13.16 DEN

Values from 0 to 4 are valid and signify open-reel tape (not disk) recording density in bits per inch:

0	200 bpi
1	556 bpi
2	800 bpi
3	1,600 bpi
4	6,250 bpi

The default for DEN is defined by your installation. In a contemporary mainframe installation, densities under 1600 bpi are obsolete. Recording densities of 200 bpi and 556 bpi applied only to seven-track tape drives, which became obsolete in 1964. An installation may now have one or more 800-bpi drives only to be able to read low-density nine-track tapes created by older minicomputer key-to-disk data entry equipment. IBM's newest tape drives are the 18-track, cartridge-loading 3480s and 3490s. These record at a density of 38,800 bpi. They do not respond to the DEN subparameter.

13.17 DSORG

DSORG specifies the basic nature of a data set. The following DSORG codes exist:

PS Physical sequential (default)
PO Partitioned organization; partitioned data set
IS ISAM (now obsolete)
DA Direct access non-ISAM
VS VSAM; Virtual Storage Access Method

If you append a U to PS, PO, IS, and DA data set organization codes, it means that a data set is unmovable. This indicates that the data set contains device-dependent information such as relative track addresses. Unmovable data sets are rarely used because they hamper disk space management.

13.18 EROPT

You can code EROPT to set it to one of the three values described below, or allow it to default to the first of these values, EROPT=ABE:

EROPT=ABE ABE stands for "abend." MVS is to initiate an abend with a system completion code and (possibly) a memory dump if an I/O error occurs for a non-VSAM data set.

EROPT=SKP   SKP stands for "skip." MVS is to simply skip over and ignore a bad block of records if an I/O error occurs. Most often you can't live with this, but it might be useful as a last resort to salvage at least some data from a bad tape.

EROPT=ACC   ACC means "accept." MVS is to accept any block of records on which an I/O error occurred. This is not usually satisfactory because data that you receive this way may be garbled or incomplete. But if an Assembler program (which has more capabilities than higher-level language programs) is to deal with low-level I/O errors itself, you should code EROPT=ACC so that MVS will not abend at these errors.

EROPT can be confusing because some MVS error messages tell you that "EROPT=ABE" and give the impression that this is inappropriate. ABE is the default, and it's very appropriate!

13.19 LRECL

You express LRECL in bytes. This represents the actual length of fixed length records and the size of the largest record plus 4 for variable length records. LRECL is ordinarily smaller than block size (BLKSIZE), but it can exceed block size when the record format is variable spanned (RECFM= VS or RECFM=VBS). For common fixed (RECFM=F), fixed-blocked (RECFM=FB), variable (RECFM=V), and variable-blocked (RECFM=VB) record formats, LRECL typically ranges from under 100 bytes to several thousand bytes.

For fixed length records, LRECL can be as low as 1 to as high as 32,760 bytes. All 32,760 bytes are accessible to you. For variable length unblocked (RECFM=V) and variable length blocked (RECFM=VB) records, LRECL includes an extra 4 bytes of MVS-applied length information (the record descriptor word) and so is 4 bytes more than the longest record in the data set. For variable length records, LRECL can be as high as 32,760, but a maximum of only 32,752 bytes are accessible to you. Even a maximum-sized block with one maximum-sized record in it will have a 4-byte record descriptor word and a 4-byte length field (the block descriptor word) prepended to the front of it.

For undefined format (RECFM=U) records, you code LRECL as 0. RECFM=U tells MVS to omit any record-deblocking actions for each burst of information between interrecord gaps on the storage media. Program load modules are of this format; they are continuous streams of program storage areas and machine language instructions, and the concept of records does not apply to them. Some types of key-entry data on unlabeled tapes can be read with RECFM=U.

13.20 OPTCD

You can specify a total of 35 different optional input/output services by using single letter codes. Some letter codes have a different meaning for different data set organizations, and not all optional services are relevant for each data set organization. You can specify some letter codes in combination, but many OPTCD values are now obsolete. The most common modern use of OPTCD is in reading "foreign" tapes, which are tapes created on minicomputers and other non-IBM equipment:

```
//SYSUT1   DD DSN=CSCJGJ.VENDOR.TAPEIN,
//   DISP=(OLD,KEEP),
//   UNIT=(TAPE8,,DEFER),
//   DCB=(RECFM=FB,LRECL=64,BLKSIZE=1280,OPTCD=QB),
//   VOL=SER=(DON891,SUE452),
//   LABEL=(1,NL)
```

Optional I/O service codes

I'll tell you about volume serial number and data set label in Chapter 15

In this JCL I am reading two separate tapes conveying keypunched data from a minicomputer to the mainframe. I have to code the complete DCB to tell MVS about the nature of the records it is to read. OPTCD tells MVS that both tapes are to be processed as one data set and that the data is to be converted from ASCII to EBCDIC as it is read:

B   The MVS logic that handles end-of-volume tasks ordinarily regards the end-of-file (EOF) trailer label on a data set as the end of the data set. But sometimes it's useful to treat such an end-of-file indication as if it were simply the end of one volume (reel) of a multivolume data set. Coding OPTCD=B lets this happen. This is useful when data from several sources or covering several data entry cycles is conveyed on separate tapes.

Q   This requests that the data from a tape being read be converted from ASCII to EBCDIC as it is input. For a tape being output, this requests that the EBCDIC encoding of the IBM mainframe be converted to ASCII as the data is written.

13.21 RECFM

RECFM indicates the nature of the records stored in a data set. MVS supports four basic types of records:

F   Fixed length records
V   Variable length records
U   Undefined length records
D   Variable length ANSI records

You can modify some of these codes by putting B after them. For example, F, V, and D records can be blocked as follows:

FB Fixed length blocked records
VB Variable length blocked records
DB Variable length ANSI records, blocked

Even more codes can be appended to specify variations in record content, format, and treatment:

A   The records contain a carriage control character in the first byte to control the printer. For example, printlines stored as blocked records in a data set have the format FBA. The A tells the printer to use the first-byte character for vertical tabbing rather than print it.
M   The records contain machine-specific device control characters other than carriage control in the first byte. You can code either A or M but not both.
S   The records are not to be written with a short final block (fixed length record formats), or the records span blocks (logical record size exceeds block size in variable length records).
T   Records can be bigger than the track capacity on disk.

The valid combinations of these format specifications are:

Fixed length records			Variable length records		
FB	FBA	FBM	VB	VBA	VBM
FS	FSA	FSM	VS	VSA	VSM
FT	FTA	FTM	VT	VTA	VTM
FBS	FBSA	FBSM	VBS	VBSA	VBSM
FBT	FBTA	FBTM	VBT	VBTA	VBTM
FBST	FBSTA	FBSTM	VBST	VBSTA	VBSTM

For undefined format records, which are data written or read without MVS blocking/deblocking services, only U, UA, UM, UT, UTA, and UTM code combinations are valid.

13.22 What Variable Length Records Are

Machine-readable records were first stored on punch cards. Every punch card is the same (fixed) length: 80 bytes. When we group "punch card image" records into blocks, the block size must be a multiple of the record length. There is no such thing as a variable length punch card.

Records on magnetic tape and disk can be organized in such a way that not all records in a data set are the same length. Variable length records are widely used in production applications in which large amounts of data are handled to conserve storage space on disk and tape. They are almost always blocked and have RECFM=VB. You can house variable length records in sequential, partitioned, or VSAM data sets. But DCB coding applies only to their non-VSAM storage.

13.23 How MVS Handles Variable Length Records

MVS treats variable length records differently than fixed length records. As you can see in Figure 13.4, MVS prepends a four-byte field to the front of each variable length record. This is the "record descriptor word," or RDW. Each record you write is four bytes longer than its data length because of the RDW. MVS records the length of the record (including the extra four bytes) in binary in the first two bytes of the RDW, labeled the "ll" part. MVS doesn't actually use the two-byte "bb" part of the RDW.

Each block in a blocked variable length record data set is four bytes longer than the sum of the record lengths, because MVS prepends a "block descriptor word," or BDW, at its front. MVS puts the length of the block (including the extra four bytes for the BDW) in binary in the two-byte "LL" part of the BDW. MVS doesn't use the two-byte "BB" part of the BDW.

You can also create unblocked variable length record data sets (RECFM=V), but these are rarely used. This organization is really a subset of blocked variable length records. MVS treats the data set as if it were a blocked variable length record data set by prepending both a record descriptor word and a block descriptor word to the record.

MVS writes and reads the record and block descriptor words automatically, and you ordinarily do not even know that they exist. You won't see them when you read or dump the data set.

13.24 A Simple Type of Variable Length Record Data Set

The simplest type of variable length record data set houses records of a few different types and lengths. A COBOL file description (FD) coded as

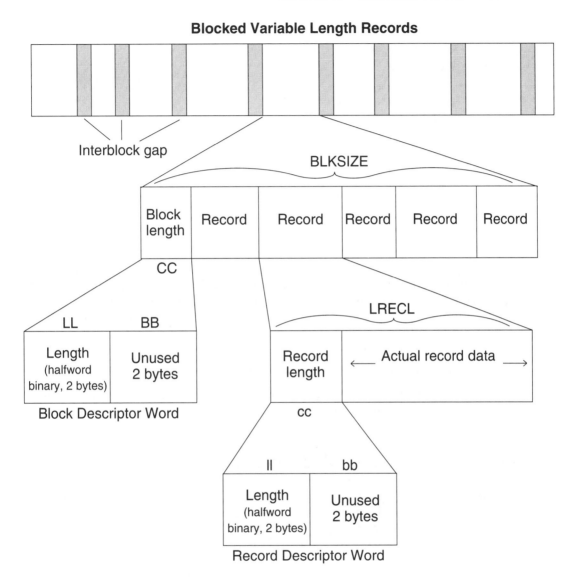

Figure 13.4 How Variable Length Blocked Records Are Stored

RECFM=VB means variable length blocked records. MVS prepends a four-byte field to the front of each variable length record. This field is called the "record descriptor word," or RDW. Each record you write is four bytes longer than its data length because of the RDW. Each block in a blocked variable length record data set is four bytes longer than the sum of the record lengths because MVS prepends a "block descriptor word," or BDW, at its front. MVS writes and reads the record and block descriptor words automatically, and you do not see them.

below defines a data set housing variable length records. Here three different record types of different lengths are housed in the data set:

```
FD   DATA-FILE
     RECORDING MODE IS V
     BLOCK CONTAINS 0 RECORDS
     RECORD CONTAINS 20 TO 100 CHARACTERS.
01   DR-FORMAT-1              PIC X(20).
01   DR-FORMAT-2              PIC X(80).
01   DR-FORMAT-3              PIC X(100).
```

When you use a file description like this, the program tells MVS the length of the record that you are writing based on the record name that you use with the WRITE action. For example, when you WRITE DR-FORMAT-1, you write a 20-byte record, but when you WRITE DR-FORMAT-2, you write an 80-byte record.

The record descriptor word that MVS automatically prepends to the front of every record takes four bytes. This makes LRECL=104 in this case. LRECL doesn't just take into account the data part of the record; LRECL becomes four bytes larger than your longest record. You could code the DCB for this data set as:

```
//   DCB=(RECFM=VB,LRECL=104,BLKSIZE=6233)
```

The value stored by MVS in the record descriptor word is 104 because the length value includes its own four-byte length.

13.25 More Complex Variable Length Records

Some variable length record data sets contain records of widely varying lengths. A COBOL file description like that shown below defines a data set that houses such records. In this case each record has the same 13-byte root segment and from 1 to 20 occurrences of a 15-byte variable (repeating) segment.

When you use a file description like this, the program tells MVS the length of the record that you are writing based on the value you put into the OCCURS DEPENDING ON field before you WRITE the record. For example, when you WRITE DATA-REC with DR-ORDER-COUNT as 1, you write a 4 + 13 + 15 = 32-byte record. MVS computes the length of data written (28 bytes) plus the 4-byte length of the record descriptor word and arrives at the value 32. It formats this value as a record descriptor word and prepends it to the front of the record. If you write this record with DR-

ORDER-COUNT having the value 10, you write a 4 + 13 + 10 (15) = 167-byte record.

```
FD   DATA-FILE
     RECORDING MODE IS V
     BLOCK CONTAINS 0 RECORDS
     RECORD VARYING 28 TO 313 CHARACTERS.
01   DATA-REC.
     05 DR-ROOT.
        10   DR-CUST-ID        PIC X(10).
        10   DR-ORDER-COUNT    PIC 9(3).
     05 DR-ORDERS          OCCURS 1 TO 20 TIMES
                           DEPENDING ON DR-ORDER-COUNT.
        10   DR-ORDER-DATE     PIC X(6).
        10   DR-ORDER-AMOUNT   PIC 9(7)V99.
```

The maximum data content of a record in this data set is 13 + 20 (15) = 313 bytes. This becomes 4 bytes larger due to the record descriptor word prepended by MVS. You would code the DCB for this data set as:

```
//   DCB=(RECFM=VB,LRECL=317,BLKSIZE=6233)
```

The block size in a variable length record data set is not a multiple of record length. You follow the rules I describe below to determine it or (under MVS/ESA) allow MVS to determine it.

13.26 Computing BLKSIZE for Variable Length Records

You cannot predict ahead of time how long a block of variable length records will be. MVS builds each block of this type of data set by filling a buffer with records as you write them. When the addition of the next record to the buffer would make it exceed the block size, MVS writes the block and starts a new one. For variable length record data sets, you simply code BLKSIZE as the largest appropriate value for the device that will house the data set.

You can code variable length record data set block size as either disk half-track capacity for disk data sets or 32,760 for tapes. If you do not know the disk track capacity or on what model of disk the data set will be recorded, you can code 6233 for disk. Under MVS/ESA, you can omit coding BLKSIZE and let MVS determine it.

13.27 Undefined Format Data Sets

A different type of variable length record data set also exists, named "un-defined" format. Records in such a data set are just a series of bytes, as I've illustrated in Figure 13.5. They have no prepended record or block descriptor words and can be any size up to 32,760 bytes. Records in an undefined format data set begin after an interrecord gap and end when the next gap starts. The concept of a logical record within a block does not apply to undefined format data sets.

Undefined format data sets are used primarily for machine language load modules. You might also use them for the type of "burst" data provided by point-of-sale or other remote data equipment. When you deal with undefined format records, you code RECFM=U. This simply tells MVS not to attempt any record deblocking actions.

If you are reading an uncataloged, undefined format data set, you code LRECL=0 and BLKSIZE=nnnn, where "nnnn" is the maximum length of data between interrecord gaps. In doing this, it does not matter if you guess high. If you are allocating or writing an undefined format data set, you make block size equal to 6233 or a more efficient, larger value specific to the device, up to the MVS block size limit of 32,760:

```
//  DCB=(RECFM=U,LRECL=0,BLKSIZE=6233)
```

You can house undefined format records in sequential or partitioned data sets, but you can't house them in VSAM data sets. Program machine language load modules can only be housed in a "real" partitioned data set, not in the new partitioned data set extended (PDSE) provided by MVS/ESA.

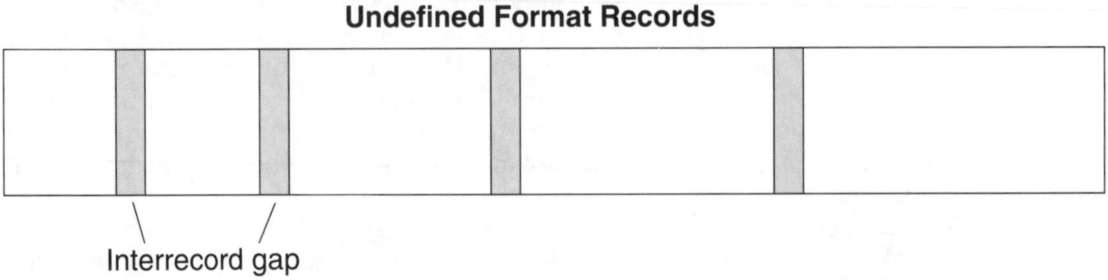

Undefined Format Records

Interrecord gap

Figure 13.5 How Undefined Format (RECFM=U) Data Is Stored

Records in an undefined format data set are just a variable length series of bytes. They have no prepended record or block descriptor words as do RECFM=V and RECFM=VB records, and they can be any size up to 32,760 bytes. The concept of a logical record within a block does not apply to undefined format data sets. When you code RECFM=U for a data set you are reading, you simply tell MVS not to attempt any record deblocking actions.

Chapter Fourteen

SPACE: DISK SPACE ALLOCATION

The SPACE parameter exists for one reason alone. You use it to tell MVS how much disk space to allow for a data set that you are creating. As opposed to mini- or microcomputers, MVS doesn't give disk space to data sets on an "open-ended" basis as needed. MVS requires you to plan your disk space usage and tell it, in advance, how much disk space a data set will use. In this chapter I show you how to think about your disk space requests and how to code the many positional subparameters of SPACE.

Figure 14.1 shows you how a general-purpose SPACE parameter looks and what its parts mean. Look over this example of SPACE coding in the context of a DD statement at which a disk data set is created so that the following sections make more sense to you. Later in this chapter I will show you how full-blown SPACE parameter coding can be even more complicated, in specialized instances, than this example!

14.1 The Physics of Mainframe Hard Disks

Disk is often called "dazz-dee" in the mainframe environment because IBM literature has traditionally called a disk unit a "direct access storage device," abbreviated as DASD. The most common direct access storage device is the movable-head hard disk, shown in simplified form in Figure 14.2. This drawing shows you how hard disks are made up of platters (discs) with surfaces coated with a magnetic material and arranged on a common rotating shaft.

Hard disks use magnetic recording techniques similar to those used by floppy disk, audio- and videocassette, and computer tape. As with tape, information is stored by coding the bits of each byte onto the magnetic surface as tiny magnetized spots. The pattern of the magnetized spots carries the on/off pattern of digital bits. Each such spot is created by passing an electrical current through the electrically conductive traces of the read/write head as the magnetic surface passes under it. When you read data back from the disk, each spot (bit) is detected by the electrical change it causes in the read/write head.

But hard disks are different from other magnetic media. A hard disk read/write head does not contact the magnetic surface. The surfaces are arranged as platters of very accurately machined flat aluminum. The platters are joined at a central hub and rotate 60 or more revolutions per second (this is 10 times as fast as a floppy!), dragging a film of air along the surface. The read/write heads are positioned over the disk surfaces on winglike arms that can position the heads across the surface. Each head flies a few millionths of an inch above a disk surface in the air layer it drags along as it rotates.

Hard disk read/write heads actually fly like airplanes. The air passing under the arm carrying the head moves at about 175 miles per hour, roughly the same speed that a jet reaches as it takes off. A head cannot fly when the disk and air film stop rotating; suddenly stopping a hard disk lets the read/write heads descend and damage both themselves and the magnetic surface. Normal shutdown of a hard disk involves allowing the heads to retract to a position away from the data-recording area of the surface before descending.

14.2 Hard Disk Tracks and Cylinders

Modern IBM hard disks use eight magnetic platters on a shaft, sometimes called a **spindle.** Both sides of the platters carry magnetic coating. Of the 16 surfaces, one is formatted with special signals and is used to control the positioning of the whole read/write head assembly. This leaves 15 surfaces to store data. The read/write head assembly, called an **actuator,** carries a separate read/write head for each surface.

Hard disk surfaces are electronically divided into tracks of recording space. Each incremental position of the head assembly between the outer circumference of the disk's recording area and its inner edge is a track. The IBM Model 3350 disk provides 555 tracks per disk surface, the IBM 3380 provides up to 2,655 tracks, the IBM 3390 provides up to 3,339 tracks, and the 9345 provides up to 2,156 tracks per disk surface.

All of the tracks at a given distance from the hub are electronically accessible at the same time. Such a group of tracks is called a **cylinder** because the tracks form this geometric shape. As a programmer or end user, you don't need to be concerned with specific tracks or cylinders. All tracks and cylinders on a disk are alike for data storage, and all tracks have the same byte storage capacity. (MVS system programmers *do* occasionally have to worry about specific tracks for operating system software. I don't cover that type of access here.)

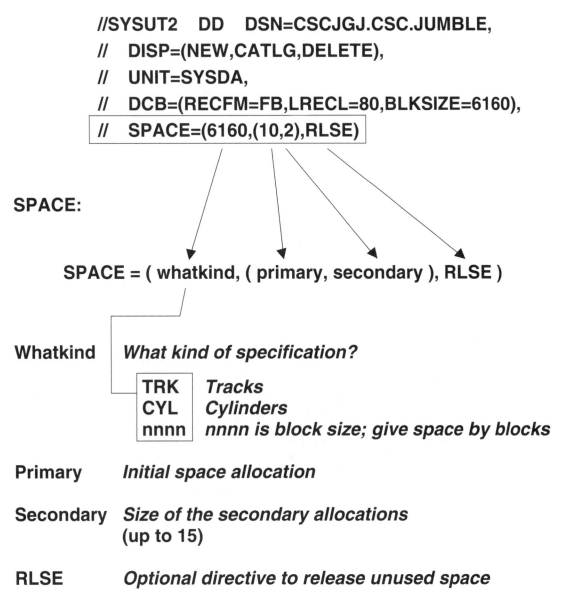

Figure 14.1 Typical Context and Coding of the SPACE Parameter

14.3 Comparing IBM Hard Disk Models

Different models of IBM mainframe hard disks have different track capacities, numbers of cylinders, and device capacity (Gb means gigabytes, or billions of bytes; 1 Gb equals 1,000 megabytes):

Disk model	Bytes per track	Tracks per cylinder	Bytes per cylinder	Total cylinders	Total bytes
3330–11	13,030	19	247,570	808	.200 Gb
3350	19,069	30	572,070	555	.317 Gb
3380–D	47,476	15	712,140	885	.630 Gb
3380–E	47,476	15	712,140	1,770	1.260 Gb
3380–K	47,476	15	712,140	2,655	1.890 Gb
3390–1	56,664	15	849,960	1,113	.946 Gb
3390–2	56,664	15	849,960	2,226	1.892 Gb
3390–3	56,664	15	849,960	3,339	2.838 Gb
9345–1	46,456	15	696,840	1,440	1.003 Gb
9345–2	46,456	15	696,840	2,156	1.502 Gb

For your convenience I've compiled a concise reference to the data storage characteristics of many modern IBM disk units in Appendix B. The 3330 and 3350 are obsolete. Modern System/3090 installations use the 3380 and 3390 disks. The 9345 DASD family is used with the IBM ES/9000 and is one of IBM's RAID disk unit models. RAID stands for "redundant array of inexpensive disks." A RAID disk unit is made up of a group of 5¼" hard disks and represents a new trend in mainframe disk storage.

Track capacity has a significant effect on your choice of physical record (block) size, as I show you later in this chapter. The single most burdensome task connected with disk space is determining the optimal block size for a given data set and the amount of disk space required by this block size. Under MVS and MVS/XA it's your job to know the types of disk units your installation uses and to do some arithmetic before coding SPACE. Under MVS/ESA your job is much easier; you can let MVS determine the block size and simply talk about how many records you want to store.

14.4 MVS Disk Data Storage Architecture and "Extents"

Disk devices in the MVS environment use a hard disk architecture known as "count, key, data" or CKD. This is different from the sectored organization of mini- and microcomputers, in which tracks are divided into 512-byte sectors. CKD formatting creates tracks on the magnetic surface but does not carve up the tracks into sectors. As a result, *the smallest unit of*

**16 Read/write heads
(15 for data,
1 for device control)**

**A typical
track**

Spindle

Actuator

Cylinder (all tracks
the same distance
from spindle)

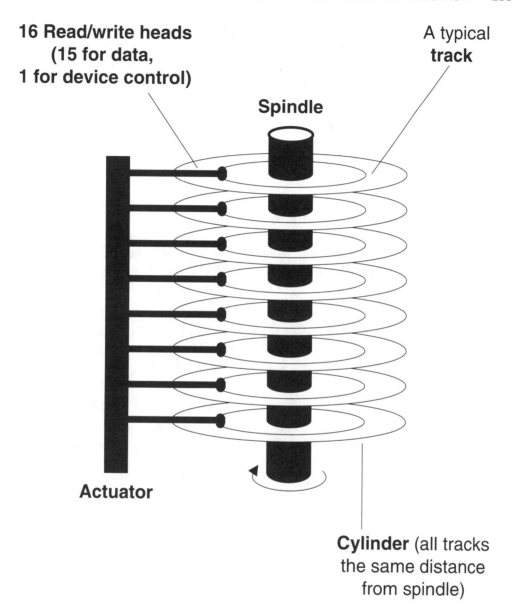

Figure 14.2   Internal Arrangement of a Mainframe Hard Disk

space on MVS *hard disks is one whole track.* This is one reason that partitioned data sets were invented; PDSs let you store more than one item (member) on each track. (IBM's DOS/VSE and VM operating systems use disks on which tracks *are* divided into sectors. That form of disk storage is called **fixed block architecture** and is not used by MVS.)

One or more contiguous tracks or cylinders allocated to a data set are called an **extent.** Don't be misled into thinking that extent is a shortened form of the word "extension"; it's not! Extent is just a synonym for "piece of disk space." Your primary space allocation is an extent.

14.5 Primary Space Allocation

You specify space at the time you create a data set by giving a figure for the **primary space allocation.** This is the amount of space that you think the data set will require. You can specify this in terms of tracks, cylinders, or data blocks, as shown in Figure 14.1. If you estimate too low for the primary space allocation and you don't provide for secondary allocations, your job will fail when the data set is completely filled and you try to write more to it. You'll receive a system completion code of D37, as documented in Appendix E. Here is an example of space allocation with only primary space:

    `// SPACE=(TRK,10)`   ***You get 10 tracks, period***

MVS ordinarily gives you your primary space allocation in one extent (that is, in one piece). But if available space on your mainframe disks is highly fragmented, it's possible that MVS will have to use multiple extents to meet your primary space allocation. MVS is ordinarily allowed to use up to five extents to fulfill your primary space allocation.

14.6 Secondary Space Allocation

When you create a disk data set, you can optionally give a value (tracks, cylinders, or blocks) for secondary allocation. If you permit them, secondary allocations can serve as a safety factor in case your estimate of the primary space allocation was too low. You will receive up to 15 secondary allocations. The real limit is the number of extents that the data set uses for its primary allocation. Here is an example of space allocation with secondary allocations allowed after the primary allocation:

    `// SPACE=(TRK,(10,2))`   ***You can get 10 + (15 x 2) = 30 tracks***

You can use 20% of the primary allocation value for the secondary allocation value as a common rule of thumb. A sequential or partitioned data set can have up to 16 extents (pieces of space) on a given disk unit. The limit of 16 extents per data set per disk unit is imposed by the way that the disk volume table of contents (VTOC) works.

Even though you code the SPACE parameter with your request for secondary allocation only when you create a data set, a data set that is allowed secondary allocations will receive them if it is later updated and expands. The ability to receive secondary allocations is a characteristic of the data set. The permitted size of secondary allocations is retained in the disk volume table of contents as part of the data set's label. For example, a TSO/ISPF library that you allocate with secondary space will receive secondary extents as necessary as you use it.

If you use more than one disk volume for a sequential data set, it can spread to 16 secondary allocations on each volume. Partitioned data sets can't span disk volumes. The limitation of 16 extents per data set per volume doesn't apply to modern VSAM data sets, which can exist with up to 123 extents.

14.7 Complete SPACE Parameter Syntax

SPACE can be a complex parameter to understand and to code. You have already seen it coded as simply as SPACE=(TRK,5) or SPACE= (TRK,5,RLSE). But in its full glory SPACE could look like this:

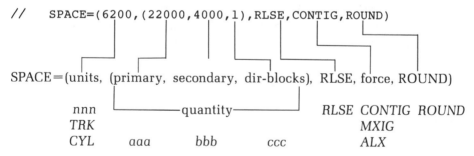

where:
> *nnn* is a number representing block size
> *TRK* and *CYL* are literals
> *quantity* is one positional subparameter
> *aaa* is number of units for the primary allocation
> *bbb* is number of units for each secondary allocation
> *ccc* is number of directory blocks for a PDS
> *RLSE, CONTIG, MXIG, ALX,* and *ROUND* are literals

All of the SPACE subparameters are positional; if you omit any of them, you have to code the commas that delimit their locations. The entire "(primary,secondary,dir-blocks)" is one positional subparameter, and both "secondary" and "dir-blocks" are optional within it.

You can see that the shortened form of SPACE omits all but the units and primary specification and as a result looks simple. This coding just requests 10 tracks of space in a primary allocation, with no secondary allocation:

    // SPACE=(TRK,10)   ***You get 10 tracks, period***

Things start getting more complicated when you want to request a secondary allocation. Here is how you request 10 tracks to start with, with the possibility of 15 x 2 = 30 more tracks in secondary allocations:

    // SPACE=(TRK,(10,2))   ***You can get 10 + (15 x 2) = 30 tracks***

If you are creating a partitioned data set, you have to state the number of directory blocks as a third part of the second subparameter:

    // SPACE=(TRK,(10,2,12))   ***... and create 12 directory blocks***

If you are creating a partitioned data set but don't want any secondary space allocation, you have to code the comma that identifies the third positional subparameter:

    // SPACE=(TRK,(10,,12))   ***... PDS with no secondary space***

And finally, if the data set you are creating is not intended to contain more space than presently needed, you can code RLSE to release unused tracks when the data set is closed by the program writing it:

    // SPACE=   ***For a partitioned data set***
(TRK,(10,2,12),RLSE)
    // SPACE=(TRK,(10,2),RLSE)   ***For a sequential data set***

14.8 Allocating Space by Tracks or Cylinders

Tracks on different disk units have different byte storage capacities. When you allocate space by tracks or cylinders, you therefore get a different amount of space based on the disk units in local use:

`//   SPACE=(TRK,10)`	*Requests 10 x 47,476 = 474,760 bytes on a 3380, and 10 x 56,664 = 566,640 bytes on a 3390!*
`//   SPACE=(CYL,10)`	*Requests 10 x 712,140 = 7.12 Mb on a 3380, and 10 × 849,960 = 8.49 Mb on a 3390!*

You can potentially be assigned to any model of disk in your mainframe equipment configuration when you use UNIT=SYSDA or a similar symbolic device group list. Because TRK or CYL are rather crude space specifications you'll see these used for TSO/ISPF library or large data set allocation only.

14.9 How You Allocate Space by Data Blocks

You can allocate space by data blocks. To do this you specify the block size instead of TRK or CYL as the first SPACE parameter:

`//   SPACE=(3840,200)`	*Requests 200 blocks each holding 3840 bytes, or 768,000 bytes on any disk*

Coding a space request by data block makes sense only when you have knowledge of how many records you want to store. In the instance above, for example, I had about 9,600 80-byte records to store. If I group 48 of them together in each block, I need 200 blocks to store them. But how much actual disk space (in tracks) will MVS give me?

When you specify disk space by blocks, MVS computes the number of tracks needed to provide sufficient space after it has chosen the disk device that will receive the data set. MVS contains tables that tell it the track capacity of each model of disk. The calculation will usually give you a little more space than necessary for the following reasons:

- MVS cannot split tracks between data sets
- The calculation is not as simple as it may appear
- The size of the blocks dictates how many blocks can fit on a track

Let's assume I am using a 3390 disk. According to Appendix B, I can fit 12 blocks on one track with a block size of 3,840. If I need to store 200 blocks of this size, I will receive 200/12 = 16.67 tracks, which I'll round up to 17 tracks. This will really let me store 17 x 12 = 204 blocks, which is 204 x 48 = 9,792 records. On a different model of disk, MVS will compute a different quantity of tracks to meet my space request.

There are times when you won't know the block size of a data set to be written to disk, as in the case of sort work data sets. In these cases the program itself supplies the record length to MVS, not your DCB parameter. All you can do in such cases is to provide disk resources using TRK or CYL. If you do know the record length or average record length and you are using MVS/ESA, you can use the AVGREC parameter to simplify your work and your JCL.

14.10 Using the AVGREC Parameter (MVS/ESA Only, with SMS)

As I explained in Chapter 13, MVS/ESA makes it possible for you to get out of the business of figuring optimal block sizes for different models of disk. If you code your programs and your JCL without specifying BLKSIZE, MVS/ESA will figure it out for you when you write data sets. In this DD statement for a new data set you see that I did not code BLKSIZE:

```
//GO.WORKREPT  DD   DSN=CSCJGJ.CSC.OVERTIME.REPORT,
//   DISP=(NEW,CATLG,DELETE),
//   UNIT=SYSDA,
//   RECFM=FB,
//   LRECL=133,
//   AVGREC=U,
//   SPACE=(133,10000,RLSE)
```

AVGREC is in MVS/ESA only! Coding LRECL and RECFM as parameters is also possible only with MVS/ESA

With AVGREC=U, the 133 in space is the average record length and =U means that the 10000 is a "unit" estimate of the quantity of records to be written

By not coding BLKSIZE, MVS/ESA will determine it based on the model of disk it chooses for the data set. But without knowing what this block size is, how could I request space allocation by blocks? The new AVGREC parameter completes the picture by letting me specify record length and quantity of records in the SPACE parameter. When you code AVGREC, you change the way the SPACE parameter works!

```
//   AVGREC=U,
//   SPACE=(133,10000,RLSE)
```
133 is record length; 10000
means 10,000 records

```
//   AVGREC=U,
//   SPACE=(80,(150,30),RLSE)
```
80 is record length; 150 means
150 records primary allocation; 30
means 30 records in each secondary
allocation

AVGREC also supports coding record quantity by thousands (AVGREC=K) and by millions (AVGREC=M):

```
//   AVGREC=U,
//   SPACE=(133,10,RLSE)
```
133 is record length; 10 means
10 records (U means "units")

```
//   AVGREC=K,
//   SPACE=(133,10,RLSE)
```
133 is record length; 10 means
10,000 records (K means "kilo")

```
//   AVGREC=M,
//   SPACE=(133,10,RLSE)
```
133 is record length; 10 means
10,000,000 records (M means "mega")

14.11 RLSE

SPACE=(units, (primary, secondary, dir-blocks), **RLSE**, force, ROUND)

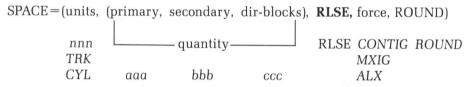

```
nnn                                          RLSE CONTIG ROUND
TRK                                               MXIG
CYL    aaa        bbb        ccc                   ALX
```

Requesting primary and secondary space allocations for a sequential data set is usually sufficient as far as SPACE parameter coding is concerned. However, you will often want to code one additional subparameter with SPACE to relinquish space that you requested but did not use. Suppose you had requested enough space to house 300 blocks of 6,200 bytes each:

```
//SYSUT2  DD  DSN=CSCJGJ.CSC.NEWSTUFF,
//   DISP=(NEW,CATLG,DELETE),
//   UNIT=SYSDA,
//   DCB=(RECFM=FB,LRECL=100,BLKSIZE=6200),
//   SPACE=(6200,300)
```

When your job executes, disk space for 300 blocks of size 6,200 bytes will be given to your data set. If you wrote only a few records to the data set, the remaining unused space would still be allocated to the data set and would not be usable by any other data set. You could cause all of the whole unused tracks to be returned to a free status by coding RLSE, the "release" subparameter:

```
//SYSUT2    DD   DSN=CSCJGJ.CSC.NEWSTUFF,
//   DISP=(NEW,CATLG,DELETE),
//   UNIT=SYSDA,
//   DCB=(RECFM=FB,LRECL=100,BLKSIZE=6200),
//   SPACE=(6200,300,RLSE)
```

If you had coded a secondary allocation, you would code RLSE this way:

```
//   SPACE=(6200,(300,60),RLSE)
```

When a data set "goes into secondaries" and you have coded RLSE, it releases unused tracks in the last active secondary.

Because MVS can't split tracks for use by different data sets, RLSE really means "release any unused tracks." You can't release unused space on the last track written upon. For example, if you write a single 80-byte record to a sequential data set at a DD statement like this, nothing is released:

```
//   DCB=(RECFM=F,LRECL=80,BLKSIZE=80),
//   SPACE=(80,1,RLSE)
```

14.12 When RLSE Works

RLSE is just one-time communication to MVS that may alter the last stages of its space allocation actions while creating data sets. In addition, RLSE only works when you access a data set via a DD statement carrying the RLSE on a SPACE parameter and close the data set normally. RLSE does not work if the step abends and the data set for which RLSE has been coded is not closed normally. RLSE also does not work when another job is sharing the data set or another job task (such as another DD statement in the same step) is opening, closing, or using the data set.

RLSE is not a retained characteristic of the data set. If you have requested secondary allocation and the data set is updated later using MOD to add records to it, no space release action occurs. If the data set is a partitioned data set library, keep in mind that RLSE works only when the data set is created. If you later edit members in the library and put more into them or you add members to the library, the library will gain whole secondary space allocations as it fills up existing allocated space. No space release action occurs at those times.

14.13 SPACE Coding for Partitioned Data Sets

You most commonly use partitioned data sets to house program source code and JCL. TSO/ISPF calls these data sets *ISPF libraries.* In addition to your own libraries, MVS "proc libs" for cataloged procedures such as

SYS1.PROCLIB also exist. But there is no inherent connection between PDSs and 80-character records. PDSs are also used to house program load modules (machine language). SYS1.LINKLIB is such a data set, housing the machine language of IBM utilities and compilers. (In Chapter 16 I show you how to create your own load module libraries.) The partitioned data set is a "creature" of BPAM, the MVS subsystem called Basic Partitioned Access Method. BPAM handles fixed, variable, and undefined format records of any valid length.

14.14 Partitioned Data Set Directory Block Allocation

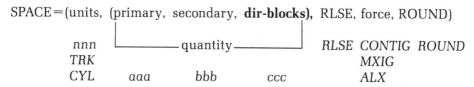

You'll recall from Figure 10.1 that you can allocate a new data set using TSO/ISPF function 3.2. When you do this, the only thing that distinguishes between a sequential or partitioned data set is how many *directory blocks* you want. ("Directory block" is yet a third meaning for the word "block." A directory block is not like a control block or a data block.) If you say that you want no directory blocks, you get a sequential data set. If you say you want one or more directory blocks, you get a partitioned data set.

The parallel between TSO/ISPF and JCL data set allocation is very close. You can establish a partitioned data set with a DD statement that names it and carries a disposition such as DISP=(NEW,CATLG,DELETE), UNIT, and perhaps DCB as well as a SPACE allocation. The only thing that makes allocating a PDS different from allocating a sequential data set is a number in your SPACE parameter that indicates how many directory blocks you want for the PDS:

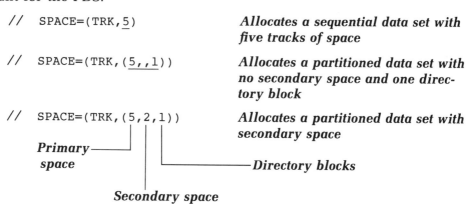

`// SPACE=(TRK,5)`	*Allocates a sequential data set with five tracks of space*
`// SPACE=(TRK,(5,,1))`	*Allocates a partitioned data set with no secondary space and one directory block*
`// SPACE=(TRK,(5,2,1))`	*Allocates a partitioned data set with secondary space*

Primary space — *Directory blocks*

Secondary space

14.15 How Many Directory Blocks Do You Need?

Calculating the number of directory blocks that you need for a partitioned data set depends on three factors:

1. Are you using a traditional partitioned data set or a partitioned data set extended (PDSE)? The PDSE is available only with MVS/ESA. Any PDSE can house hundreds of thousands of members without concern for directory size. If you are using a PDSE, code the new parameter DSNTYPE=LIBRARY and specify at least one directory block. Otherwise continue to factors 2 and 3.
2. How many members will you house in the PDS?
3. How much "statistics" information will you record about each member?

A traditional partitioned data set directory is composed of unblocked, 256-byte records hidden from your view and managed by MVS. The minimum directory block room you need for each member is only 12 bytes. This houses the 8-byte member name and a 4-byte binary-stored value called the **TTRC.** The TTRC indicates the relative track number and block where a member starts.

MVS allows applications such as TSO to store "user data" in PDS directory entries for each member via Assembler macros, and TSO makes use of this capability. If you retain statistics about each member, as TSO/ISPF normally does, each member takes 42 bytes of directory block space. You can normally store information about five TSO/ISPF library members in each directory block. Therefore, a rule of thumb in creating a PDS is to *estimate how many members you will want to house in the PDS and divide it by five* to calculate the number of directory blocks that you need.

14.16 Space for the PDS Directory

The amount of space that you carve out of the space allocated to a partitioned data set for its directory is determined when you create the data set. The whole directory is located at the start of the primary space allocation. The directory never extends into secondary allocations, even though the PDS data area might.

It's possible for a partitioned data set to have member storage space available but no ability to house more members due to its directory being filled. You'll get a system completion code of B14–0C in this case, as I have documented in Appendix E. In a pinch, you can use TSO function 3.5 to delete user statistics from the PDS, allowing the directory to house additional member entries. But a much better solution is to delete members no longer needed and/or to reorganize the partitioned data set.

You can't increase the size of a partitioned data set directory once it is allocated. But you can use the procedure that I discuss in Chapter 18, PDSREORG, to expand PDS directory size, space allocation, or block size and reorganize it as well. Or you can copy all members of a PDS with too small a directory to a new PDS that you allocate with a larger-sized directory.

14.17 The Importance of Block Size

It's natural to focus on the syntax of the SPACE parameter and its subparameters in considering JCL. But syntax is not the only issue. When it comes to disk space, the block size you choose is of overwhelming importance for efficient operation.

The logical records in data sets are grouped into blocks (physical records) to speed input/output. But on disk, unlike tape, you can't simply make blocks bigger and expect more storage space efficiency. Other factors also affect the block size decision:

- For disk, track utilization efficiency does not vary in a simple linear way; instead, it follows the sawtooth-shaped curve shown in Figure 14.3.
- Due to differing disk model characteristics, a different sawtooth efficency curve applies to each type of disk. An efficient block size on one model of disk is not necessarily efficient on another, but an installation will typically have a mixture of disk models configured in a system.
- Track capacity dictates the maximum efficient block size, and writing a block larger than track capacity is inefficient.
- Data sets accessed interactively should have block sizes under 4,096 bytes to conserve buffer space in teleprocessing software, whereas disk data sets used only for batch purposes can benefit from larger block sizes.
- Every member of a partitioned data set starts in a new block; a large block size for a PDS that houses small members can waste a lot of space even if a table tells you that the block size you have chosen is efficient for the disk.

These factors combine to create a complex situation. Examining Figure 14.3 you can see that efficiency can vary dramatically. By making a block one byte too large, you can drop from 98% disk efficiency to only 65%!

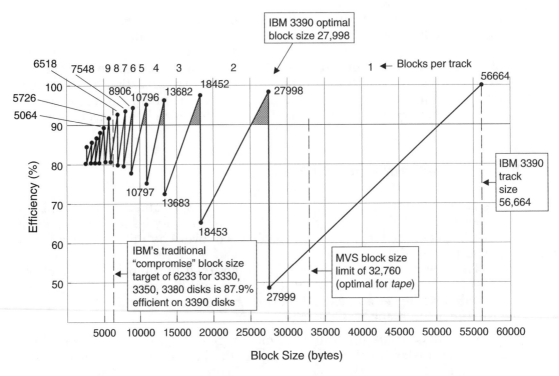

Figure 14.3   Disk Utilization Efficiency versus Block Size for IBM 3390 Disks

14.18 Compromise Block Sizes

Each of the models of disks commonly found in IBM mainframe installations have different characteristics concerning block size efficiency. But one block size, 6,233, is adequately efficient on 3350, 3380, and 3390 devices. If your installation runs MVS or MVS/XA and has a mixture of 3350, 3380, and 3390 disk devices under one symbolic device group name, IBM recommends that you aim for 6,233 as a block size. For the newer RAID technology 9345 disk drives, you can aim for 3,672 for TSO library block size or 22,928 for nonlibrary block sizes.

To use 6,233 as the target block size for a fixed length record data set, first divide 6,233 by the record size to be housed in the data set. For a record length of 133 (the length of an ordinary printline), this division gives you a value of 46.865. Drop the fractional part to arrive at an integer value, which is the number of whole records that will fit in 6,233: it is 46 in this case. Multiply the record length by this integer value to find the block size nearest to but not exceeding the target value of 6,233. In this case, 133 × 46 = 6,118. For printline records, a block size of 6,118 will provide adequate efficiency on 3350, 3380, and 3390 models of disk. For example, it provides efficiencies of 96.25% on an IBM 3350, 90.2% on an IBM 3380, and 86.4% on an IBM 3390.

Aim for a block size of 22,928 for a printline data set on 9345 model disks. This gives you 22,928/133 ≈ 172 records per block, and a block size of 133 × 172 = 22,876.

14.19 Automatic Block Size Computation Under MVS/ESA

If your installation uses MVS/ESA, you can achieve optimal blocking for disk and tape data sets by simply omitting BLKSIZE from your JCL or by coding it as BLKSIZE=0. This passes up the opportunity to specify block size in JCL. If the program creating the data set also passes up its opportunity to specify block size, MVS will compute it.

To compute block size for a new data set, MVS takes into account the device that it chooses for the data set. You receive block sizes approaching track or half-track capacity on the model of disk used or approaching 32,760 on tape. This is the recommended way to handle block size under MVS/ESA, except for TSO libraries (partitioned data sets).

14.20 Optimal Block Size for TSO Libraries

TSO libraries are partitioned data sets. They are no different than other types of data sets as far as disk space allocation and storage is concerned. But when you allocate a TSO library, you should think about not only the type of disk on which the library will reside but also the nature of the members to be stored in it.

In a partitioned data set, members are located by relative track and by block number within track. This means that every member of the PDS starts in a new data block. Extra space in the last data block holding a member is unusable. If a PDS has a large data block size but houses small members, you can waste a lot of space in each block even though the block size seems efficient for the disk.

A good compromise for the block size of a general purpose source code or JCL library is 3,840 bytes. Here are the reasons why I recommend it:

- It is adequately efficient on 3350, 3380, and 3390 disks.
- It stores 48 lines of source code or JCL per block. If you make blocks any bigger than this, especially for a library housing JCL, think of how many blocks will end up housing a member with only a few lines of JCL!
- It keeps input/output for interactive access to a reasonable size.

- It is in keeping with the default input buffer sizes of most compilers and the linkage editor.

If you are allocating TSO libraries using 6,160-byte blocks or even larger blocks such as half track-size blocks, think about what you are doing! A data block size of 6,160 stores 77 lines of source code or JCL in a data block. A member with less than 77 lines wastes a lot of data block space! A half track-sized 27,290-byte block on a 3390 disk holds 349 lines of code or JCL. This can seem efficient but be extremely wasteful for your program and JCL libraries.

On 9345 model disks, use 3600 as the block size for your TSO libraries. This is 85% efficient but a good compromise considering the likely size of many library members.

14.21 CONTIG, MXIG, ALX, and ROUND

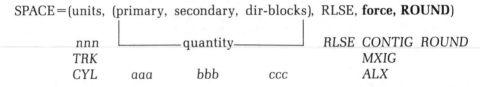

SPACE=(units, (primary, secondary, dir-blocks), RLSE, **force, ROUND**)

nnn	└──────quantity──────┘			RLSE CONTIG ROUND
TRK				MXIG
CYL	aaa	bbb	ccc	ALX

The subparameters of force and ROUND serve as one-time communication to MVS concerning allocation options available only at the time you create a data set.

CONTIG forces the primary allocation to be contiguous, in one extent only. Normally you get your primary allocation in such a condition. But if available space on a disk is fragmented into parts that are all smaller than what you requested for the primary allocation, MVS will make the primary allocation using up to five noncontiguous disk extents. If you code CONTIG, you tell MVS that it's not permitted to do that. With CONTIG, if enough contiguous space to satisfy your primary allocation is not available, your job fails. Code CONTIG only if there is some real performance necessity to have your primary allocation in one chunk—so much a necessity that your job should be prevented from running if the condition could not be met. Work files for large amounts of data being sorted fall into this category. (But some installations frown upon using CONTIG, and it's gradually slipping into obscurity as disk cache memory becomes more common.)

MXIG is a dangerous "force" specification. Its name is an abbreviation for "maximum extent contiguous." Through it, you tell MVS, "I'll settle for my requested primary allocation as a minimum, but if you have more in a contiguous chunk, I'll take the biggest such piece." Using MXIG can result in your obtaining all the space you requested or, conceivably, an entire disk. *Do not use MXIG unless you have explicit need and authorization!*

To understand **ALX,** you first need to understand MXIG. ALX is MXIG five times over! It stands for "all largest extents." ALX requests that MVS inventory the available contiguous space on disk and identify the five largest such pieces of disk space. Then of these five, any that are as large or larger than the amount of primary space requested are to be allocated to the data set. ALX is useful only when a very large data set is being allocated and you must reserve space immediately to ensure that subsequent access to it will be as efficient as present disk conditions allow. *Do not use ALX unless you have explicit authorization.*

ROUND is useful when you request space by data blocks—not tracks or cylinders—and for performance reasons you want to obtain whole cylinders of disk. ROUND requests MVS to calculate the amount of tracks needed to house the specified number of data blocks, round up to the next integer number of cylinders necessary to provide this many tracks, and then allocate that number of complete cylinders:

```
//  SPACE=(6200,22000,,,ROUND)
```

ROUND by itself can still allocate noncontiguous cylinders for the primary allocation. You can also use CONTIG to require that the primary allocation consist of complete cylinders adjacent to one another:

```
//  SPACE=(6200,22000,,CONTIG,ROUND)
```

And of course, it's possible that you will write fewer blocks than the amount of space you requested. You can code RLSE to release unused space when the data set is closed. If you code RLSE with ROUND, any unused cylinders are released, but unused tracks on the last cylinder that you used are not released:

```
//  SPACE=(6200,22000,RLSE,CONTIG,ROUND)
```

CONTIG applies only to your primary space allocation. There is no guarantee that additional extents for secondary allocations will be contiguous with the primary space allocation.

Under MVS/ESA with SMS, you can gain the convenience of coding space by quantity of records and still allocate whole cylinders by using AVGREC, CONTIG, and ROUND:

```
//  AVGREC=K,
//  SPACE=(133,100,,CONTIG,ROUND)
```
Makes 133 a record size; asks for space for 100,000 records but rounds up to the next whole cylinder needed

Chapter Fifteen

JCL FOR TAPE DATA SETS

When you process tape data sets, you have to code slightly different JCL than when you process disk data sets. To write a large tape data set you often have to code the VOL parameter. When you write any tape data set, you usually have to code LABEL. When you read a "foreign" tape (one produced at a different installation or on a different type of computer), you have to code VOL and LABEL. In this chapter I'll demonstrate how to do these things.

15.1 Magnetic Tape Equipment

You are probably familiar with magnetic tape in the form of audiocassette recording tape. Tape used in the mainframe environment is similar but wider than audio tape. It's ½ inch wide, like the tape in VHS videocassettes, and it is thicker for durability. Tape is well suited to storing sequential data sets representing on-line data sets for backup, data archival, and for batch processing.

Until 1985, the most common packaging for computer tape was 10½-inch plastic reels; these "open reels" are still sometimes used. The standard 10½-inch reel, which costs about $15, holds 2,400 feet (701 meters) of tape. Information storage capacity varies with the amount of data blocking, but a modern 10½-inch open-reel tape stores about 160 megabytes of information. This is about the same as 2.1 million punch cards, 444 IBM PC (360 K) diskettes, 200 Macintosh (800 K) diskettes, or more than 1,100 Apple II diskettes.

The IBM 3480 tape cartridge began replacing open-reel mainframe tape drives in 1985. Cartridges offer higher information storage capacity and greater read/write speed than open-reel tapes. The cartridge measures only 4 by 5 inches and houses 505 feet (154 meters) of half-inch-wide tape. A cartridge stores about 200 megabytes of information, which is equivalent to about 2.5 million punch cards, 555 IBM PC (360 K) diskettes, 250 Macintosh (800 K) diskettes, or almost 1,400 Apple II diskettes.

Model 3480/3490 cartridge tape drives are now very popular with mainframe installations because they (and their tapes) require much less space than the open-reel drives they have replaced. Although a cartridge packs much more information into a given unit of tape, its error detection and correction capabilities make it more reliable than older open-reel magnetic tape. IBM's cartridge tape drives contain memory to buffer data between the computer's channel and the read/write mechanism so they keep tape in more constant motion, increasing processing speed. Most installations keep one or a few open-reel drives in place to handle data exchanges with minicomputers and other installations using non-IBM mainframes.

15.2 The Physics of Magnetic Tape

No single tape drive handles both open-reel tapes and cartridges; these are separate pieces of equipment. Open-reel tapes are recorded with 9 longitudinal tracks, whereas the 3480 tape cartridge records data in 18 tracks. On both open-reel and cartridge tapes, a group of 8 tracks carries the bits of one byte, and a ninth track carries a parity bit for the byte for error detection. Error detection circuitry exists out of your sight in the tape drive itself.

Tape recording density is measured in **bpi**, which stands for "bits per inch." When referring to a group of nine tape tracks in cross section, you can take bpi to mean "bytes per inch." Various models of the open-reel IBM 3420/3430 tape drive can read and write at 800, 1,600, or 6,250 bpi. Unlike videocassette tape (which records using analog, rather than digital, techniques), there is no fidelity advantage to the lower densities; 800 and 1,600 bpi just take more tape and transfer data more slowly. Because lower-density equipment is generally less expensive, many minicomputers use 1,600-bpi equipment. You use the DCB subparameter DEN to indicate recording density when you process a tape from such a minicomputer. DEN= 2 indicates 800 bpi, DEN=3 indicates 1,600 bpi, and DEN=4 indicates 6,250 bpi for open-reel tapes only. DEN does not apply to 3480 cartridges, which record only at 38,800 bpi.

Prior to 1964, mainframes used only six bits, rather than eight, to represent each byte. Back then, magnetic tapes carried only seven tracks. Recording density and "tape recording technique" were significant JCL issues at the time of conversion to the System/360 (the ancestor of the System/390 and ES/9000) because different seven-track parity and information-encoding schemes were in use on older IBM and non-IBM computers. Parity and recording technique issues are now irrelevant unless an installation still receives tapes from "dinosaur" tape drives. Modern open-reel and cartridge tapes use standard parity and recording mechanisms.

15.3 Tape Handling by MVS

Regardless of how your JCL specifies the unit to be used for a tape data set, MVS ultimately issues console messages to the person who will mount the tape reels or cartridges that your job calls for. MVS tells that person what tape (what volume serial number) to mount and also tells him or her specifically what tape drive to use. A tape drive at hardware address 54C, for example, is named by MVS as "54C." A small sign with the device hardware address is usually attached to each tape drive.

Tape drives are manually loaded devices. The person handling tapes and mounting them on tape drives is a computer operator, not a programmer. Programmers usually don't handle tapes in the mainframe environment, and the drives are located in secure equipment areas. When instructed to mount a tape on a drive, an operator must first locate the tape on the shelves or racks of a "tape library," physically place it on the assigned drive, and may also have to perform threading tasks. Mounting a tape takes effort and time. As I explained in Chapter 12, you can *avoid* unnecessary tape-mounting actions by using UNIT=(TAPE,,DEFER). In this chapter I show you how VOL=(,RETAIN) makes it possible to *keep tapes mounted* between job steps to further minimize manual tape handling.

15.4 What Volume Serial Numbers Are

In the mainframe environment, every unit of disk and tape storage carries a unique identifier and is called a **volume.** The identifier for all forms of storage media is called the volume serial number. "Number" is a misnomer; the six-byte identifier can be and often is alphanumeric. For example, 103762, PUB493, STOR19, and ACSCAC are all valid volume serial numbers.

Volume serial numbers are applied to tapes and disks using the IEH-INITT, IEHDASDI, or IEHDASDR utilities. This is a one-time task performed by operations personnel for each tape or disk. Once assigned, the volume serial number does not change, regardless of what data sets are written to the tape or disk.

15.5 Purpose and Format of the VOL Parameter

The DD statement VOL parameter gives you the way to specify the volume serial number of the disk or tape on which a given data set is to be written or read. You use its SER keyword to specify this. VOL has four positional parameters that you code before SER= or REF=*.:

```
//   VOL=(private,  retain,  vol-seq-no,  qty-vols,  SER=zzzzzz)
```

,	,	,	,	SER=zzzzzz
PRIVATE	RETAIN	xxx	yyy	REF=*.name

where: *private* is the literal word PRIVATE
retain is the literal word RETAIN
xxx is a number from 2 through 255
yyy is a number from 6 through 255 volumes
SER= and *REF=*. are mutually exclusive and *zzzzzz* is one or
more volume serial numbers, while *name* refers to a prior
DDname or step

as in this coded example:

```
//   VOL=(PRIVATE,RETAIN,2,3,SER=(038272,013267,020133))),
```

Here is what VOL's subparameters do:

- PRIVATE limits access to a volume to your job, shutting out access to it by any other job running concurrently
- RETAIN keeps the tape in a mounted condition on the tape drive after the step ends, so subsequent steps can access it quickly
- Vol-seq-no lets you begin access to a multivolume data set at other than the first volume
- Qty-vols lets you estimate and prescribe how many volumes (tapes) an output data set requires

15.6 Coding VOL in Its Common Short Form (VOL=SER)

The most common coding you will see is really a "short form" of VOL that ignores its first four (positional) parameters:

```
//   VOL=SER=xxxxxx
```

If the data set spans more than one tape or disk volume, you identify all of the volumes in the sequence in which data was recorded on them:

```
//   VOL=SER=(xxxxxx,yyyyyy,zzzzzz)
```

You can specify up to 255 volumes, so you may need to continue a VOL parameter to a second line (or even more), as in the case of an uncataloged multivolume data set:

```
//   VOL=SER=(038272,013267,020133,015364,001845,
//   013444,032883,012713)
```

15.7 Writing a Tape Data Set: Non-Specific Volume Request

In almost all cases you'll omit coding VOL on a "writing" DD statement. When you create a data set and don't specify a volume serial number using VOL, your request is called a **non-specific** volume request:

```
//*************************************************************
//*                                                           *
//*   CREATE A DATA SET ON A SCRATCH TAPE; NO VOL IS CODED!   *
//*                                                           *
//*************************************************************
//STEP010    EXEC  PGM=IEBGENER
//SYSPRINT   DD    SYSOUT=*
//SYSIN      DD    DUMMY
//SYSUT1     DD    DSN=CSCJGJ.CSC.CNTL(WORKERS),          Input
//  DISP=SHR
//SYSUT2     DD    DSN=CSCJGJ.CSC.COPYOUT.DATA,           Output
//  DISP=(NEW,CATLG,DELETE),
//  UNIT=(TAPE,,DEFER),                              No VOL coded!
//  DCB=(RECFM=FB,LRECL=80,BLKSIZE=32760),
//  LABEL=RETPD=30                       Make Retention Period 30 Days
```

For tape output, MVS tells the console operator to mount a scratch tape on a designated tape drive. Scratch tapes carry data sets whose labels indicate an expiration date that has already been reached; these are usually stockpiled near the tape drives. MVS reads the data set label on the scratch tape. If MVS confirms that the expiration date has been reached, it proceeds to write your data set (and labels for it) to the tape and records its volume serial number(s) in the catalog. If MVS detects that the expiration date has not been reached, it sends a message to the operator and won't readily allow writing to the tape. The operator can force MVS to write to an unexpired tape but usually isn't authorized to do this.

15.8 Writing a Tape Data Set: Specific Volume Request

You can code VOL and LABEL in their short forms to specify that you want a particular disk or tape to be used to house a new data set and to set the expiration date. But you specify the volume serial number only if you have a real need to house the data set on a specific volume. You may have a need to do this if someone has conveyed a tape to you and asked that you record certain data on it and return the tape to them:

```
//************************************************************
//*                                                          *
//*          CREATE A DATA SET ON A SPECIFIC TAPE VOLUME     *
//*                                                          *
//************************************************************
//STEP010    EXEC  PGM=IEBGENER
//SYSPRINT   DD    SYSOUT=*
//SYSIN      DD    DUMMY
//SYSUT1     DD    DSN=CSCJGJ.CSC.CNTL(WORKERS),              Input
//  DISP=SHR
//SYSUT2     DD    DSN=CSCJGJ.CSC.COPYOUT.DATA,               Output
//  DISP=(NEW,CATLG,DELETE),
//  UNIT=(TAPE,,DEFER),
//  DCB=(RECFM=FB,LRECL=80,BLKSIZE=32760),
//  VOL=SER=ABC123,                             Specific Volume
//  LABEL=RETPD=180                 Make Retention Period 180 Days
```

15.9 PRIVATE Is Obsolete!

$$// \quad VOL=(\textbf{private}, \quad retain, \quad vol\text{-}seq\text{-}no, \quad qty\text{-}vols, \quad SER=zzzzzz)$$

	,	,	,	,	SER = zzzzzz
	PRIVATE	RETAIN	xxx	yyy	REF = *.name

PRIVATE is an obsolete specification included in 1960s JCL to deal with demountable disks. Before 1977, you could physically remove the assembly of hard disk platters, called a **disk pack,** from a disk drive and mount another in its place. Because MVS allows up to 127 jobs to access a given disk at the same time, JCL had to provide a way to tell MVS that your disk pack was private and was not to be used by other jobs. PRIVATE is how you coded a DD statement to indicate this.

PRIVATE is ignored for today's permanently mounted disks and for tapes. You may still see it coded in old JCL. In newer JCL the only thing you need to know about PRIVATE is that you still have to code the comma that marks the end of its position if you want to code any of VOL's other positional parameters. In the following VOL coding examples I eliminate PRIVATE and show you how you code VOL without it.

15.10 RETAIN: Keeping a Tape Mounted with RETAIN

```
//   VOL=(private, retain, vol-seq-no, qty-vols, SER=zzzzzz)
```

```
             ,         ,         ,           ,      SER=zzzzzz
      PRIVATE  RETAIN    xxx       yyy      REF=*.name
```

In many job streams, a tape created by one step is to be read by a following step, removed from the tape drive, and then kept for future use. MVS normally rewinds tapes when the job step finishes execution and issues a message for the operator to remove it from the tape drive. If you code RETAIN on a DD statement where a tape is processed, it tells MVS to leave the tape mounted on the drive for use by one or more subsequent steps. MVS will rewind it and position it to its "load point," ready for access by another step. You get the same effect when you code DISP=(NEW,PASS) or DISP=(OLD,PASS). Here is a common way to code RETAIN:

```
//   VOL=(,RETAIN)
```

RETAIN is effective even when steps access different data sets (different data set sequence numbers) on the same tape volume. But for a data set spanning multiple volumes, RETAIN only retains in a mounted condition the last volume processed. It does not avoid the operator intervention needed to remount the first tape reel or cartridge when a subsequent step reads a multivolume data set.

15.11 Volume Sequence Number (Vol-Seq-No)

```
//   VOL=(private, retain, vol-seq-no, qty-vols, SER=zzzzzz)
```

```
             ,         ,         ,           ,      SER=zzzzzz
      PRIVATE  RETAIN    xxx       yyy      REF=*.name
```

VOL's third positional parameter is not often useful. You can code this number from 1 to the number of volumes occupied by the data set, a maximum of 255. It tells MVS at what volume of an existing multivolume data set you want to begin processing. For example, if a cataloged data set named AK00.C99.PAYMAST occupied eight tape volumes and you knew that the data you wanted to read began on the fourth tape, you could code the DD statement this way:

```
//SYSUT1   DD   DSN=AK00.C99.PAYMAST,
//   DISP=OLD,
//   VOL=(,,4)
```

Processing will start with the fourth volume and will proceed from there to the fifth, sixth, seventh, and eighth volumes.

The following VOL parameter begins processing at the third volume of the series (020133) because I coded 3 at the volume sequence number:

```
//  VOL=(,,3,,SER=(038272,013267,020133,015364,
//  001845,013444,032883,012713))
```

If this data set were cataloged, MVS would keep track of the list of volume serial numbers on which the data set is carried. I could start accessing it at the third volume just by coding this as part of the DD statement:

```
//  VOL=(,,3)
```

If you are extending (appending to) a data set using DISP = (MOD,CATLG), the volume sequence number that you code on VOL overrides MOD. MOD tells MVS that record appending starts after the last record in the data set. If you code volume sequence number, MOD processing begins at the volume that you indicated, destroying the data on it and the following volumes, if any. You have little reason to code a volume sequence number with MOD to extend a tape data set. Extension of tape data sets is not a common practice. It conflicts with installation policies that prohibit writing on unexpired tapes.

15.12 Scratch Volume Count (Qty-Vols)

```
//  VOL=(private,  retain,  vol-seq-no,  qty-vols,  SER=zzzzzz)
```

				SER=zzzzzz
PRIVATE	RETAIN	xxx	yyy	REF=*.name

You specify the number of scratch volumes that may be required to house an output data set by using the fourth positional subparameter of VOL. It's relevant only for data sets being created or extended and estimated to require more than five volumes:

```
//  VOL=(,,,8)
```

Because the actual number of tapes needed to house a large tape data set may vary according to data blocking and the length of tape volumes used, MVS treats your scratch volume count as an estimate in this algorithmically unusual way:

- If you omit the volume count or code it as 1 through 5, MVS provides up to 5 volumes

- If you code volume count as 6 to 20, MVS provides up to 20 volumes
- If you code volume count as a value greater than 20, MVS gives you the multiple of 15 volumes exceeding your estimate, plus 5, up to a maximum of 255 volumes. For example, if you code volume count as 24, MVS system allows a maximum of 2 x 15 + 5 = 35 volumes.

It's lost to history who invented this scheme and how long it took them to so muddle the issue. It would be interesting (but probably horrifying!) to know what else they contributed to the development of OS and MVS.

15.13 VOL and UNIT Parameter Interplay

You use VOL in combination with the UNIT parameter to govern serial mounting of multiple volumes on the same drive or parallel mounting of all volumes on several drives at the same time. For example, if you code

```
//    UNIT=(TAPE,,DEFER),
//    VOL=SER=(038272,013267,020133)
```

one tape drive is allocated for the data set (device-count defaults to 1). The three volumes of the data set will be called for mounting one after another on this single drive as you read the data set. The same holds true if the data set is cataloged; in that case you don't need to code the VOL parameter. Serial tape processing is most desirable because tapes can only be processed sequentially anyway. If you code the following, though, MVS will allocate three separate tape drives to the job and will issue messages to the operator to mount all three volumes at once "in parallel":

> **Number of tape drives requested**

```
//    UNIT=(TAPE,3),
//    VOL=SER=(038272,013267,020133),
```

Parallel mounting of tapes is a luxury and is nearly always unnecessary. It "hogs" devices and would delay the start of your job because MVS will usually have more trouble finding enough free tape drives for it.

For a data set being written, the combination of P in the UNIT device count and a number in the VOL volume count also causes multiple devices to be assigned to the step:

```
//    UNIT=(TAPE,P),
//    VOL=(,,,2),
```

The number of devices allocated is the higher of the volume count or the number of volume serial numbers coded in the VOL parameter, if any. If you have a large number of on-line data sets to copy to tape (for backups) in a limited off-hours "processing time window," you can speed up the process at the expense of other batch jobs by having multiple tape drives tied up in this way. (You could also "tune up" the VSAM data set outputting process by increasing the number of VSAM buffers using the AMP sub-parameters BUFND and BUFNI. See *Practical VSAM For Today's Programmer,* by James Janossy and Richard Guzik, John Wiley & Sons, Inc., 1988.)

15.14 VOL and Catalog Interplay

When you code volume serial number at a DD statement, MVS does not refer to the catalog. Its philosophy is that because your JCL has specified volume serial number, you apparently want to become responsible for specifying all volumes of the data set to be accessed. This philosophy has three important consequences:

1. You can access one or a few volumes of an existing cataloged multivolume data set by specifying just the volume serial numbers of the volumes that you want to access. But you can do this only for specific volumes; you can't jump into the series of tapes and expect to proceed onward through the whole data set this way. To do that, code vol-seq-no as shown in Section 15.11.

2. When you specify VOL for a VSAM data set to process it by DDname with IDCAMS control statements, MVS does not become aware that the data set is of VSAM *Access Method Organization.* Why? Because MVS stores this fact in the catalog, and the presence of VOL causes MVS to not check the catalog! You have to tell MVS explicitly that the data set is VSAM by including the AMP parameter on your DD statement (AMORG stands for "Access Method ORGanization"):

   ```
   //   AMP='AMORG'
   ```

3. When you extend an existing data set using a disposition of MOD, you need to specify DISP=(MOD,CATLG). CATLG causes the system catalog to be updated with the volume serial numbers of any additional volumes used to house the data set. If you code just DISP=MOD, which defaults to DISP=(MOD,KEEP), the catalog will not be updated, and it will know only about the volumes on which the data set originally existed!

15.15 Volume Referbacks (VOL=REF= * ...)

You can use the keyword REF instead of SER on the VOL parameter when you want to refer back to the volume serial number in an earlier DD statement. This lets you access an uncataloged data set created earlier in the job or put several data sets onto the same volume without knowing the specific volume serial number of that disk or tape.

You can code a volume referback to refer back to another data set by name within the same step, to another DDname within the same step, or to a DDname in a prior step:

`VOL=REF=data-set-name`	*Referback to data set in same step*
`VOL=REF=*.DDname`	*Referback to DDname in same step*
`VOL=REF=*.stepname.DDname`	*Referback to DDname in prior step*

You can also refer back to a DDname in a cataloged procedure invoked by a prior step in the job stream. For example, a job stream may, in one or more of its steps, invoke a cataloged procedure which itself, of course, contains steps. You can refer back to a step in the proc in this way:

```
//  VOL=REF=*.stepname.procstepname.DDname
```

In this case "stepname" is the name of the prior step in this JCL that invokes the cataloged procedure, "procstepname" is the name of the step within the cataloged procedure at which the DDname occurs, and "DDname" is the DDname in the procstep.

Finally, you can refer back to a DDname that occurs at a step within a cataloged procedure you are invoking at the current step:

```
//  VOL=REF=*.procstepname.DDname
```

where "procstepname" is the name of the step within the cataloged procedure at which the DDname occurs and "DDname" is the DDname in the proc. The only purpose of this type of volume referback is to allow specifying the same volume for an override of another DD statement within the proc or for a DD statement not contained within the proc but supplied by the execution JCL (an "added" DD statement, as I describe in Chapter 18).

15.16 Putting Several Backup Data Sets Onto the Same Tape

An on-line system is commonly supported by several VSAM data sets, all of which need to be copied to tape nightly in a backup job. You can stack your backups onto the same tape or tapes to economize on the number of reels or cartridges needed. This also makes sure that all backups made on

the same date are kept together. Here is how to do this efficiently using
VOL's RETAIN and referback features:

```
//STEP010   EXEC   PGM=IDCAMS
//DDOUT1     DD   DSN=AK00.C27.CUSTOMERS,
//  DISP=(NEW,CATLG,DELETE),
//  UNIT=(TAPE,,DEFER),
//  VOL=(,RETAIN),  ◄──────────────────────────────┐
//  DCB=(RECFM=FB,LRECL=628,BLKSIZE=32656),         │
//  LABEL=(1,SL,RETPD=180)                          │
        (additional DD and IDCAMS statements follow ...)
    -                                               │
    -                                               │
//STEP020   EXEC   PGM=IDCAMS                        │
//DDOUT2      DD   DSN=AK00.C27.ORDERS,              │
//  DISP=(NEW,CATLG,DELETE),                         │
//  UNIT=(TAPE,,DEFER),                              │
//  DCB=(RECFM=FB,LRECL=212,BLKSIZE=32648),          │
//  VOL=(,RETAIN,REF=*.STEP010.DDOUT1), ────────────►│
//  LABEL=(2,SL,RETPD=180)                           │
        (additional DD and IDCAMS statements follow ...)
    -                                               │
    -                                               │
//STEP030   EXEC   PGM=IDCAMS                        │
//DDOUT3      DD   DSN=AK00.C27.PRODUCTS,            │
//  DISP=(NEW,CATLG,DELETE),                         │
//  UNIT=(TAPE,,DEFER),                              │
//  DCB=(RECFM=FB,LRECL=332,BLKSIZE=32536),          │
//  VOL=(,RETAIN,REF=*.STEP010.DDOUT1), ────────────┘
//  LABEL=(3,SL,RETPD=180)
        (additional DD and IDCAMS statements follow ...)
    -
    -
```

In this JCL you code no VOL parameter at the first step, so your request
for a tape is "non-specific." MVS will issue a message to the operator to
mount a scratch tape on a drive to receive this data set. You code RETAIN
in the first step's VOL parameter so that MVS will not dismount the tape
at the end of the step but will leave it mounted for faster access by the
next step.

Your second step uses a volume referback to tell MVS that the same
volume mounted in the first step be used to receive the second data set, to
be written as the second file on the tape. You don't need to know the specific
volume serial number of that tape; it's enough to specify that it be the same

volume as used in //STEP010, which is what the volume referback at //DDOUT2 does. The "2" in the LABEL parameter tells MVS to put the new data set as the second file on the tape. All data sets on the same tape should have the same retention period, and each is cataloged separately by MVS.

Your third and subsequent steps repeat the pattern and put more backup data sets on the same tape volume. If the tape fills up, MVS will tell the computer operator to mount additional scratch tapes and will automatically use them. MVS records the location of each data set in the catalog, including its file number on tape. You can access any of the backup data sets by name as usual without having to know either the tape volume serial number it's on or its file number on that tape.

15.17 The Tape Volume Label

Figure 15.1a shows you how MVS formats a magnetic tape to label it in machine-readable form. MVS stores the volume serial number of a tape immediately after a short length of silver foil attached to the tape about ten feet away from its physical beginning. This position is called the **load point.** The volume label is a single 80-byte card image that contains the literals VOL1 in positions 1 through 4 and the tape volume serial number in positions 5 through 10. When a tape is mounted, MVS positions the drive to the load point, reads the VOL1 tape volume label, and thereby identifies the tape.

When new tapes are acquired by an installation, they must be initialized prior to use, using the IEHINITT utility. Initialization puts the VOL1 label on the tape and is performed by the operations group of your installation. An operator will also attach a gummed label carrying the volume serial number to the side of the tape reel or cartridge. This makes it possible to locate the tape among the thousands of others that may exist in the installation. The outside label on a tape is called the **external label** but is not what tape "labeling" means. A "labeled" tape has a VOL1 label recorded on it and also has machine-readable data set labels recorded before and after each data set on it.

The end of recorded information on a tape is indicated by two tape marks. A **tape mark** is just a series of unique electronic signals that can be detected by the tape drive. One tape mark separates different data sets on tape, and two tape marks indicate the logical end of the tape. Two tape marks follow the VOL1 label immediately on a tape after it has been initialized but no data has yet been stored on it. When actual information is recorded on the tape, it obliterates existing tape marks, and new tape marks are written.

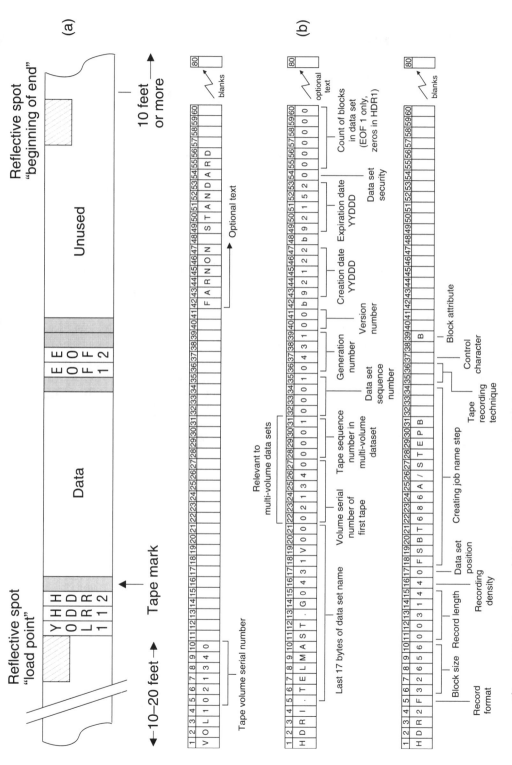

Figure 15.1 Layout of Magnetic Tapes and IBM Standard Tape Labels

(a) VOL1, HDR1, and HDR2 labels precede a data set recorded on tape; EOF1 and EOF2 labels follow the data set. (b) VOL1, HDR1, and HDR2 labels are simply 80-byte records with the field layout shown.

263

15.18 Tape Data Set Labels

Data sets written to tape are individually labeled when they are created. The labels are known as **IBM standard labels** and consist of two 80-byte card-image records that carry HDR1 and HDR2 in their respective first four bytes, as illustrated in Figure 15.1b. Positions 5 through 80 of these label records contain information about the data set such as its name, record length, block size, and other characteristics. The HDR1 and HDR2 records are commonly referred to as **header labels** because they are placed before the data set. Tape labels are categorized by MVS documentation as a form of control block.

The end of a data set on tape is denoted by one tape mark, followed by copies of the HDR1 and HDR2 records with the front literals now changed to EOF1 and EOF2. The EOF1 and EOF2 label records are identical to the HDR1 and HDR2 records except that the field within the EOF1 record carrying the number of blocks in the data set now contains a count. In the HDR1 record this field usually contains zeros. The EOF labels are commonly known as **trailer labels.**

Most often only one data set is recorded on a given tape. Figure 15.1a illustrates the VOL1 and HDR records in such a case as well as the data set and EOF records. For this one standard-labeled data set, three distinct items of information exist on the tape, separated from one another by tape marks: the VOL1/HDR1/HDR2 labels, the data set, and the EOF1/EOF2 trailer labels.

15.19 Multivolume Tape Data Sets

A data set can span more than one tape. In fact, a single data set can use up to 255 volumes. MVS automatically manages the tapes housing a multivolume data set. A program accessing a large data set can't tell when one tape volume ends and the next starts.

Figure 15.2 shows you the arrangement of data set labels when a data set spans more than one tape volume. The data set on the first tape is prefaced by the VOL1, HDR1, and HDR2 labels and a tape mark. At the end of the tape, the approach of the end is signalled by a reflective spot similar to the load point. (This marker is not at the actual end of the tape but warns that it is near.) The last part of the last data block follows the trailing reflective spot, followed by a tape mark and a copy of the HDR1 and HDR2 labels, with the first four characters changed to EOV1 and EOV2. EOV signifies "end of volume." The second tape carrying the data set begins with VOL1, HDR1, and HDR2 labels as usual, followed by a tape mark. The

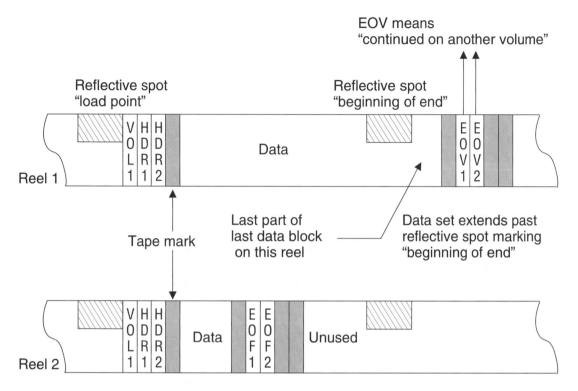

Figure 15.2 Multivolume Tape Data Set

A large data set can occupy up to 255 tape volumes. When a data set uses more than one tape volume, the end of each volume carries EOV1/EOV2 ("end-of-volume") labels rather than EOF1/EOF2 ("end-of-file") labels.

end of the data set on the last volume is indicated by a tape mark and EOF labels.

The separate tapes of a multivolume data set do not "point" to one another. Every volume in a multivolume data set does, however, point back to the first tape housing the data set in its HDR1 label. Each tape also indicates its own volume sequence number in the series of tapes housing the data set. Figure 15.3 is a dump of a tape label produced by an IBM tape analysis program named OS/DITTO (Program product 5798-ARD). If you compare the real tape data of Figure 15.3 with the HDR1 data set label layout shown in Figure 15.1, you'll see that this is a dump of the labels for tape volume 046742. It's the third tape of a multivolume data set that starts on volume 034857.

15.20 Multiple Data Sets on One Tape

You can record more than one data set on the same tape. Figure 15.4 shows you how the tape is organized when you do this. The tape begins with its VOL1 record, followed immediately by the HDR1 and HDR2 label records of the first data set. Then comes a tape mark, the actual contents of the first data set, a tape mark, and the EOF1 and EOF2 records for the first data set's trailer labels. Next comes one tape mark, the HDR1 and HDR2 label records for the second data set, a tape mark, the second data set, a tape mark, and the EOF1 and EOF2 records for the second data set. If the second data set is the last one on the tape, its EOF records are followed by two tape marks. If more data sets exist, the pattern repeats, finally ending in two tape marks.

To record one data set on tape, you do not need to worry about its data set sequence number because this defaults to 1. When you put more than one data set on a tape, you have to code the first positional subparameter of the LABEL parameter, data set sequence number.

15.21 Data Set Sequence Number

```
LABEL=(Data-set-seq-no, Label-type, PASSWORD, IN/OUT, RETPD/EXPDT)
       nnnn             SL          PASSWORD   IN       RETPD=
                        NL          NOPWREAD   OUT      EXPDT=
                        BLP
                        NSL
                        LTM
                        SUL
                        AL
                        AUL
```

The first positional LABEL subparameter lets you tell MVS a data set sequence number from 1 to 9999. If you do not code any other positional subparameters or RETPD/EXPDT, you can code LABEL in its "short form." This JCL reads an uncataloged fifth data set on a tape carrying volume serial number 023472:

```
//SYSUT1     DD   DSN=AK00.C18.HISTDATA,
//   DISP=OLD,
//   UNIT=(TAPE,,DEFER),
//   VOL=SER=023472,
//   LABEL=5
```

But the need for this coding is rare because we catalog data sets for easier access. When a data set is cataloged, MVS remembers everything necessary

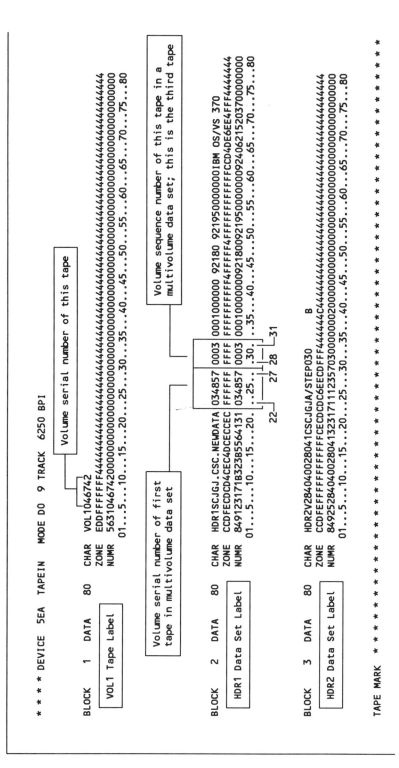

Figure 15.3 OS/DITTO Dump of Tape VOL1 and HDR1/HDR2 Labels

OS/DITTO is an IBM utility program that shows you the contents of magnetic tapes for analysis purposes. This dump illustrates how positions 22 through 27 of the HDR1 label tell you the first volume of a multivolume data set and how positions 28 through 31 reveal the tape sequence number (the number of this tape in the multiple volumes housing the data set).

267

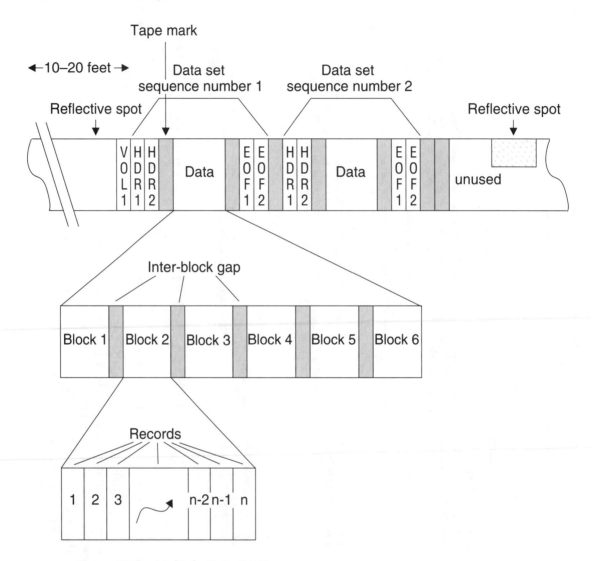

Figure 15.4 Multiple Data Set Tape

You can record more than one data set on the same tape. Each data set has its own HDR1/HDR2 and EOF1/EOF2 labels. You refer to a data set on a multiple data set tape by its data set sequence number, coded in the LABEL parameter: LABEL=2 or LABEL=(2,SL).

to access it, including its data set sequence number. (The data set, not the tape, is cataloged.) Every one of potentially many data sets on a tape can be cataloged, and each receives its own catalog entry.

When you create a data set, you have to specify the data set sequence number if it is other than 1. MVS does not provide any automatic way to determine the next available data set sequence number on a tape. This JCL outputs a new data set as the seventh one on standard labeled tape 034112 and sets its expiration date to 180 days in the future:

```
//SYSUT2    DD  DSN=AK00.C27.ARCVMASP,
//  DISP=(NEW,CATLG,DELETE),
//  UNIT=(TAPE,,DEFER),
//  DCB=(RECFM=FB,LRECL=173,BLKSIZE=32697),
//  VOL=SER=034112,
//  LABEL=(7,RETPD=180)
```

This would write a new data set as the seventh on tape 034112, overwriting whatever existed as the seventh data set on this tape if its expiration date had been reached. The expiration date of a data set is contained in its HDR1 and EOF1 data set labels. If there were not already six data sets on the tape, this coding would cause a job failure. If there was an existing seventh data set and its label did not carry an expiration date that had been reached, MVS would prompt the console operator for permission to overwrite this unexpired data set. (Most likely an operator would not allow this, and the job would then fail.)

You couldn't code a DD statement to put the seventh data set on a tape, as I've shown above, without having some control over the volume used, either with a VOL=SER or VOL=REF=*. If you did not control VOL, you would have no way of knowing how many data sets were present on the scratch tape that MVS gave you to house the data set.

15.22 LABEL Type Coding

LABEL=(Data-set-seq-no,	**Label-type**,	PASSWORD,	IN/OUT,	RETPD/EXPDT)
nnnn	SL	PASSWORD	IN	RETPD=
	NL	NOPWREAD	OUT	EXPDT=
	BLP			
	NSL			
	LTM			
	SUL			
	AL			
	AUL			

In the period immediately following the introduction of the System/360 in 1964, many installations faced the task of reading data from other computer systems. This made it necessary for OS/MVS to provide a means of handling the then-current variations in tape labeling on different lines of equipment. A total of eight different label codings are possible. The default is SL, for IBM "standard labels."

15.23 SL: IBM Standard Labels

HDR1 and HDR2 and corresponding end-of-data-set EOF1 and EOF2 labels are the IBM standard labels denoted by SL in LABEL's second positional subparameter. You might see SL coded in the second position even though it is redundant to the default. All of these mean the same thing:

```
//   LABEL=(1,SL,RETPD=180)
//   LABEL=(1,RETPD=180)
//   LABEL=RETPD=180
```

15.24 NL: No Labels

Nonlabeled tapes are written by MVS when you code NL in the label-type field for an output data set. If you create a tape this way, the existing VOL1 volume label of the tape is obliterated, and no HDR1 and HDR2 data set labels are written. The tape is created with the data set immediately following the reflective spot load point (no leading tape mark), and the data set is followed immediately by two tape marks. MVS refers to the tape in the job log by a system-concocted volume serial number consisting of an "L" and five digits.

Writing nonlabeled tapes on a mainframe serves no purpose. Because MVS does not record an expiration date for the data set, the tape becomes immediately available for use as a scratch tape by other jobs. Attempting to write tapes this way is more or less like an airline pilot choosing, just for fun, to take off with one of two engines out, low fuel, and no radio. (It can be done, but it's foolish.) Nonlabeled tapes require operator involvement for reinitialization when such a tape is to be used as a standard-labeled tape again.

Reading nonlabeled tapes on a mainframe is fairly common. Data entry tapes are typically created on minicomputers without VOL1, HDR1, and HDR2 labels. To read such a tape, you code NL as the label-type in the DD statement where the tape is accessed. You also code DCB and VOL:

```
//***********************************************************
//*                                                        *
//*         COPY A NON-LABELED DATA ENTRY TAPE TO DISK      *
//*                                                        *
//***********************************************************
//STEPA       EXEC  PGM=IEBGENER
//SYSPRINT    DD    SYSOUT=*
//SYSIN       DD    DUMMY
//SYSUT1      DD    DSN=AK00.C99.KEYTRANS,
//   DISP=(OLD,KEEP),
//   UNIT=TAPE,
//   DCB=(RECFM=FB,LRECL=122,BLKSIZE=1220,OPTCD=Q),
//   VOL=SER=LB0809,
//   LABEL=(1,NL)
//*
//SYSUT2      DD    DSN=AK00.C99.KTRNDISK,
//   DISP=(NEW,CATLG,DELETE),
//   UNIT=SYSDA,
//   DCB=(RECFM=FB,LRECL=122,BLKSIZE=6222),
//   SPACE=(6222,(100,20),RLSE),
//
```

Because the tape you are reading carries no data set label indicating the characteristics of the data set, you need to code the complete DCB for it. If the tape was keyed in the ASCII character set, you code OPTCD=Q to convert it to EBCDIC.

If your installation uses a tape and disk management software product, you might have to code EXPDT in an unusual way to read a nonlabeled tape:

```
//   LABEL=(1,NL,EXPDT=98000)
```

This is a common way that you tell supplemental tape management software that you are processing a foreign tape, a tape not created and managed locally.

You might wonder why VOL=SER and DSN are coded for the nonlabeled foreign tape in the above JCL since there is no VOL1 or HDR1 label on the tape to identify volume serial number or data set name. You code the JCL as shown for a very practical reason. Even though there are no machine readable labels on the tape for MVS to read, you need the VOL=SER in your JCL to make formation of a useful mount message to the computer operator possible. DSN is part of the mount messsage and further identifies the tape to the computer operator. To read a nonlabeled tape you code any descriptive data set name permitted by your security system.

If you specify NL to indicate that you are reading a nonlabeled tape, the data set must not have a VOL1 label as the first record. MVS checks for such a label record. The presence of this label record is taken as inconsistent with your NL indication. If a VOL1 label is present, your job will fail.

Although you can place more than one data set on an unlabeled tape, it becomes confusing for the party reading the tape to recognize what is being conveyed. Reading such a tape can be especially troublesome because the DCB for each of the separate data sets can be different and must be coded.

15.25 BLP: Bypass Label Processing

BLP is easy to confuse with NL as a means of reading an unlabeled or foreign tape. But BLP really isn't a label format at all. It just tells MVS to omit invoking the routines that it normally uses to check for the presence of VOL1 and HDR1/HDR2 labels when processing a tape. If you code BLP as the second positional subparameter of LABEL, MVS regards everything on the tape as data, including the volume and data set labels. Each of these becomes accessible to you by using the data set sequence number. But in this case the data set sequence number counts each set of labels and data sets between tape marks as a data set:

	BLP data set sequence number
VOL1/HDR1/HDR2 labels	1
first data set	2
first data set EOF1/EOF2 labels	3
second data set HDR1/HDR2 labels	4
second data set	5
second data set EOF1/EOF2 labels	6
third data set HDR1/HDR2 labels	7
third data set	8
third data set EOF1/EOF2 labels	9
	(and so forth)

BLP is not a production method to read data sets but a tool for use in analyzing tape contents. BLP is made inactive in many installations because it allows data set security based on data set name to be circumvented. If BLP is inactive, it's usually treated as NL and fails if you try to read a labeled tape data set using it.

15.26 Miscellaneous Label Types and ASCII Labels

Five label-type designations are little used in the majority of mainframe installations:

AL means ANSI standard labels, in a form defined by the ANSI "Version 1" or "Version 3" standard. This is used by some minicomputers.

AUL indicates that the tape carries AL labels and, in addition, that data set header records beyond HDR1, HDR2, and HDR3 are also present. User labels are extra labeling records that a given installation might write with locally developed operating system enhancements.

NSL indicates that a tape and its data sets carry nonstandard labels. This tells MVS not to do any standard label processing and to hand label processing over to custom written, locally developed and maintained routines.

LTM stands for "leading tape mark" and indicates that a tape mark follows immediately after the load point and before the VOL1 label. The IBM DOS/VSE operating system creates tapes using LTM. Aside from ignoring the tape mark, MVS processes LTM as it does BLP.

SUL means "standard user labels" and is the same as SL for standard labels, except that additional, custom user labels may follow the HDR1/HDR2 label records. User labels are a carryover from earlier days when various installations developed customized routines to label tapes and disks. Most installations no longer find it desirable or productive to do this.

15.27 PASSWORD

```
LABEL=(Data-set-seq-no, Label-type, PASSWORD,  IN/OUT,  RETPD/EXPDT)
        nnnn              SL         PASSWORD   IN       RETPD=
                          NL         NOPWREAD   OUT      EXPDT=
                          BLP
                          NSL
                          LTM
                          SUL
                          AL
                          AUL
```

The third LABEL positional subparameter is part of a primitive data set security scheme that has been superceded by IBM's Resource Acquisition Control Facility (RACF) and by other products such as Computer Associates' ACF2 and Top Secret. PASSWORD is usually disabled when other security systems are used.

Position 54 of the HDR1 data set label contains a one-byte "security" flag. Ordinarily this is set to 0. If you code the PASSWORD subparameter when you create a data set, you set this flag to 1, indicating that the computer operator must supply a password when the data set is accessed. If you code NOPWREAD (NO PassWord READ), the security flag is set to 3 to indicate that the operator does not have to enter a password when the data set is read but has to do this when the data set is written to or deleted. You don't actually put a password here in this subparameter. MVS generates the passwords. Authorized personnel manipulate passwords using the IEHPROGM utility.

15.28 IN and OUT

```
LABEL=(Data-set-seq-no, Label-type, PASSWORD, IN/OUT, RETPD/EXPDT)
         nnnn               SL       PASSWORD  IN       RETPD=
                            NL       NOPWREAD  OUT      EXPDT=
                            BLP
                            NSL
                            LTM
                            SUL
                            AL
                            AUL
```

The fourth positional subparameter of LABEL is rarely used except with FORTRAN programs. FORTRAN programs open data sets for both input and output automatically. IN/OUT limits the way a program can actually open a data set and reduces the amount of computer operator intervention required to process a data set. Coding IN states that the data set will only be read and prevents a data set from being opened for output. Coding OUT states that the data set will only be written and prevents it from being opened for input.

15.29 EXPDT and RETPD: Data Set Expiration Date

```
LABEL=(Data-set-seq-no, Label-type, PASSWORD, IN/OUT, RETPD/EXPDT)
         nnnn               SL       PASSWORD  IN       RETPD=
                            NL       NOPWREAD  OUT      EXPDT=
                            BLP
                            NSL
                            LTM
                            SUL
                            AL
                            AUL
```

Positions 49 through 53 of the HDR1 data set label store a Julian date (a date in the form YYDDD such as 95365, for example, for the last day of 1995). This is called the *expiration date.* Until this date is reached, MVS will regard the data set as unexpired and will not readily allow you to overwrite it. Only the date is carried, not a time of day.

You can code RETPD to set the expiration date relative to the present date as a number from 1 to 9999. MVS uses this number and the current date to compute a date in the future that it then stores as the expiration date. The computation is a simple one that ignores leap years and assumes 365 days for every year. Both of these mean the same thing:

```
//   LABEL=(1,RETPD=180)
//   LABEL=RETPD=180
```

You can code EXPDT to make the expiration date a specific value, but this means you have to change your JCL from day to day to get the same time duration of retention. This sets the expiration date to January 1, 1997:

```
//   LABEL=EXPDT=97001
```

If you don't code LABEL to set the expiration date, it defaults to either zero (the current date, meaning the tape data set has expired) or another installation-defined value. Some EXPDT values are recognized by non-IBM tape-and-disk management systems as indications of special processing requirements.

15.30 Disk Data Sets and the LABEL Parameter

You do not usually code the LABEL parameter when you create a disk data set. For disk data sets, the label exists as part of a disk volume table of contents (VTOC), which serves as the "directory" on each disk. The disk data set label is the VTOC's "format 1" data set control block, or "DSCB" record. There can be no such thing as an unlabeled disk data set.

Data set sequence number is irrelevant for disk, because a disk VTOC is designed to deal with multiple data sets in a much more sophisticated way than a sequence number. The IN/OUT and PASSWORD subparameters have as little utility in connection with contemporary disk data set usage as they do with modern tape data sets. RETPD/EXPDT are little used with disk data sets. Expiration dates on a disk data set are undesirable because unlike tape data sets, disk data sets must be freely copied, reorganized, and deleted in the course of disk space management.

Chapter 16

CREATING AND USING LOAD MODULE LIBRARIES

When you write programs in languages such as COBOL, C, PL/I, FORTRAN, and Assembler, you usually use JCL that executes a compile/ link/go procedure to test your programs. Figure 5.3 in Chapter 5 graphically illustrates the three steps involved in this process. But compile/link/go is not the norm in production data processing. Once you have tested a program and have established confidence in its operation, there is no need to re- compile it each time it will be run. Instead, you can save the machine language resulting from compiling and linkage editing and just run the "go" step when the program is to be executed.

Imagine the job-stream flow chart in Figure 5.3 with compile/link/go separated into two parts. Compile and linkage edit are the first part, with the //SYSLMOD (system load module) output of the linkage editor directed to storage as a member of a permanent partitioned data set. (The output of the linkage editor is called a "load module" and the PDS is usually called a load module library.) Imagine the "go" step in Figure 5.3 as a freestanding, one-step job stream in itself. In this chapter I show you how to use such a two-part "compile/link" and separate "go" mechanism. You will see how to create and use a load module library and how to process COBOL and Assembler programs to put load modules into it. I'll also show you how to reorganize ("compress") your load module library.

16.1 Allocating a Load Module Library

A load module library is nothing more than a partitioned data set that houses records of undefined format, RECFM=U, LRECL=0, and BLKSIZE=6233 (you can make the block size larger if you prefer, up to half-track size on 3380, 3390, and 9345 disks). A space allocation of a few tracks is sufficient for experimenting with load module libraries. Produc- tion-sized load module libraries will contain 100 or more cylinders and store hundreds or thousands of program load modules.

You can allocate (create) a load module library using the TSO/ISPF 3.2 function, as shown in Figure 16.1a. You can, alternatively, run a batch job

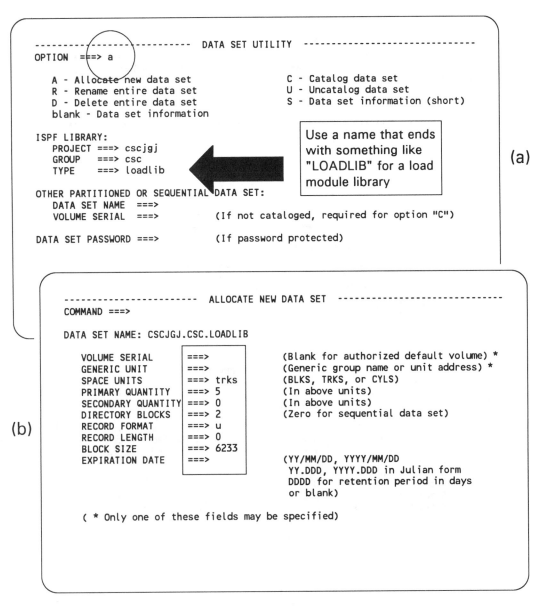

Figure 16.1 Allocating a Load Module Library

(a) You start at the TSO/ISPF 3.2 screen with option "a" when you want to allocate a load module library. (b) Enter the values shown at the second TSO 3.2 "allocate" screen to create a load module library. Five tracks is sufficient for a load module library for experimentation. Make sure you enter a nonzero value for DIRECTORY BLOCKS. Load modules must be housed as members of partitioned data sets (they cannot be freestanding like .EXE files).

```
EDIT ---- CSCJGJ.CSC.CNTL(J1ALLOC) - 01.00 ------------------ COLUMNS 001 072
COMMAND ===>                                              SCROLL ===> PAGE
****** ************************ TOP OF DATA ***************************
000100 //CSCJGJA   JOB 1,'BIN 7 JANOSSY',CLASS=A,MSGCLASS=X,MSGLEVEL=(1,1),
000200 // NOTIFY=CSCJGJ
000300 //*
000400 //*    THIS JCL IS STORED AT CSCJGJ.CSC.CNTL(J1ALLOC)
000500 //*    ALLOCATE A LOAD MODULE LIBRARY
000600 //*
000700 //****************************************************************
000800 //*                                                             *
000900 //*    HOUSEKEEPING DELETE BEFORE ALLOCATE (FOR SAFETY)         *
001000 //*                                                             *
001100 //****************************************************************
001200 //STEP010   EXEC  PGM=IEFBR14
001300 //DELETE1    DD   DSN=CSCJGJ.CSC.LOADLIB,
001400 //  DISP=(MOD,DELETE),
001500 //  UNIT=SYSDA,
001600 //  SPACE=(TRK,0)
001700 //*
001800 //****************************************************************
001900 //*                                                             *
002000 //*    ALLOCATE A NEW DATA SET OF THE SAME NAME AS JUST DELETED *
002100 //*                                                             *
002200 //****************************************************************
002300 //STEP020   EXEC  PGM=IEFBR14
002400 //ALLOC1     DD   DSN=*.STEP010.DELETE1,
002500 //  DISP=(NEW,CATLG,DELETE),
002600 //  UNIT=SYSDA,
002700 //  DCB=(RECFM=U,LRECL=0,BLKSIZE=6233),
002800 //  SPACE=(TRK,(5,,2))
002900 //
```

A DSN referback is convenient here

(a)

```
------------------------- DATA SET INFORMATION -----------------------
COMMAND ===>

DATA SET NAME: CSCJGJ.CSC.LOADLIB

GENERAL DATA:                          CURRENT ALLOCATION:
   Volume serial:      ACSCAT             Allocated tracks:      5
   Device type:        9345               Allocated extents:     1
   Organization:       PO                 Maximum dir. blocks:   2
   Record format:      U
   Record length:      0
   Block size:         6233            CURRENT UTILIZATION:
   1st extent tracks:  5                  Used tracks:           1
   Secondary tracks:   0                  Used extents:          1
                                          Used dir. blocks:      1
   Creation date:      1992/11/22         Number of members:     0
   Expiration date:    ***NONE***
```

(b)

The TSO/ISPF 3.2 function shows you the characteristics of a data set created via TSO or JCL. A load module library is of Partitioned Organization (PO) just as is any library,

16.2 (a) Allocating a Load Module Library Using JCL and (b) Viewing Data Set Information

to allocate a load module library, as shown in Figure 16.2. Both of these illustrations create the identical library named CSCJGJ.CSC.LOADLIB. After allocating a load module library using either TSO or JCL, you can view its characteristics using the "data set information option" of TSO function 3.2.

16.2 Compile/Link to Create a Load Module

Your installation provides cataloged procedures (procs) to compile and link programs written in a variety of programming languages. The IBM standard proc to compile and link a VS COBOL program is named COBUCL, whereas the proc for VS COBOL II is named COB2UCL. Figure 16.3a shows you how I used COB2CLJ (a locally customized version of COB2UCL at DePaul University) to compile and linkage edit COPYIT, a program I showed you in Chapter 5, Figure 5.2. Your execution of this or a similar proc may be a little different because your installation may have customized its procs too. Figure 16.3b shows you the actual COB2CLJ proc.

Figure 16.4 shows you some of the MVS system output, compiler output, and linkage editor output from my run of COB2CLJ to compile and link the COPYIT program. Notice that the output ends with a message that COPYIT "DID NOT PREVIOUSLY EXIST BUT WAS ADDED. . . ." This is not an error. It's a message from the linkage editor confirming that the load module for COPYIT has been created and stored as a member of the load module library.

16.3 What Does a Load Module Look Like?

You can actually see a load module by viewing it with the TSO/ISPF 1 browse function. Figure 16.5 shows you what the load module for COPYIT looks like. The periods stand for unprintable characters. Because a load module consists of machine language mixed with literal characters, most of it is unintelligible to people.

16.4 Executing a Load Module

Figure 16.6a shows you JCL to execute COPYIT from my load module library. There is only one step in this job, and I execute a program, not a proc. The name coded at EXEC PGM= is the member name COPYIT. At EXEC you code the name of a member of a load module library. I named my program COPYIT in its source code, I named the member storing it in my source library COPYIT, and I named the load module COPYIT. Naming source code and load modules the same is a common convention. But MVS

(text continues on page 284)

```
EDIT ---- CSCJGJ.CSC.CNTL(J2CLINK) - 01.00 ------------------ COLUMNS 001 072
COMMAND ===>                                                   SCROLL ===> PAGE
***** *************************** TOP OF DATA ***************************
000100 //CSCJGJA   JOB 1,'BIN 7 JANOSSY',CLASS=A,MSGCLASS=X,MSGLEVEL=(1,1),
000200 //  NOTIFY=CSCJGJ
000300 //*
000400 //*    THIS JCL IS STORED AT CSCJGJ.CSC.CNTL(J2CLINK)
000500 //*
000600 //***********************************************************************
000700 //* COMPILE AND LINK USING VS COBOL II                                  *
000800 //***********************************************************************
000900 //STEP010  EXEC  COB2CLJ,
001000 //     PDS='CSCJGJ.CSC.COBOL',        SOURCE CODE LIBRARY
001100 //     MEMBER='COPYIT',               MEMBER NAME HOUSING THE PROGRAM
001200 //     LOADLIB='CSCJGJ.CSC.LOADLIB'   NAME OF MACHINE LANGUAGE LIBRARY
001300 //
```

```
EDIT ---- CSC.PROCLIB(COB2CLJ) - 01.01 -------------------- COLUMNS 001 072
COMMAND ===>                                                   SCROLL ===> PAGE
***** *************************** TOP OF DATA ***************************
000100 //COB2CLJ  PROC PDS='***',       NAME OF SOURCE CODE LIBRARY
000200 //     MEMBER='***',             NAME OF PROGRAM MEMBER TO COMPILE
000300 //     PRINTAT='*',              PRINT DESTINATION
000400 //     LOADLIB='**'
000500 //***********************************************************************
000600 //*                                                                     *
000700 //*   DEPAUL UNIVERSITY  DEPT OF COMPUTER SCIENCE AND INFO SYSTEMS       *
000800 //*   COMPILE AND LINK USING VS COBOL II                                *
000900 //*                                      JIM JANOSSY 9/06/92            *
001000 //*                                                                     *
001100 //***********************************************************************
001200 //*
001300 //*   VS COBOL II COMPILE
001400 //*
001500 //COB2     EXEC PGM=IGYCRCTL,REGION=2048K,TIME=(,6), ****************
001600 //  PARM=('NOADV',             PGM RESERVES CC BYTE COL 1 **        **
001700 //       'NOCMPR2',            DON'T EMULATE RELEASE 2      **        **
001800 //       'NUMPROC(PFD)',       PREFERRED SIGN HANDLING      **        **
001900 //       'FLAG(I,E)',          ALL MSGS: IMBED ERROR MSGS   **        **
002000 //       'DYN',                USE DYNAMIC LOADING          **        **
002100 //       'LANGUAGE(UE)',       HEADING/MSGS UPPERCASE       **        **
002200 //       'APOST',              USE APOSTROPHE AS QUOTE      **        **
002300 //       'FDUMP',              GIVE FORMATTED ABEND DUMP    **        **
002400 //       'LIB',                COPY LIBRARY OK              **        **
002500 //       'NOMAP',              NO IMBEDDED CELL REFS        **        **
002600 //       'OBJ',                PRODUCE OBJECT CODE          **        **
002700 //       'RES',                MAKE CODE DYN RESIDENT       **        **
002800 //       'NOOPT',              GIVES LINE # ON ABEND        ** COMPILE **
002900 //       'XREF'),              PROVIDE IMBEDDED CROSS REF   **        **
003000 //STEPLIB  DD  DSN=SYS1.COB2COMP,DISP=SHR                   **        **
003100 //SYSIN    DD  DSN=&PDS(&MEMBER),DISP=SHR                   **        **
003200 //SYSLIB   DD  DSN=&PDS,DISP=SHR                            **        **
003300 //SYSPRINT DD  SYSOUT=&PRINTAT                              **        **
003400 //SYSLIN   DD  DSN=&&LOADSET,                               **        **
003500 //  DISP=(NEW,PASS),                                        **        **
003600 //  UNIT=VIO,                                               **        **
003700 //  SPACE=(TRK,(3,3),RLSE),                                 **        **
003800 //  DCB=(RECFM=FB,LRECL=80,BLKSIZE=3120)                    **        **
003900 //SYSUT1   DD  UNIT=VIO,SPACE=(CYL,(1,1))                   **        **
004000 //SYSUT2   DD  UNIT=VIO,SPACE=(CYL,(1,1))                   **        **
004100 //SYSUT3   DD  UNIT=VIO,SPACE=(CYL,(1,1))                   **        **
004200 //SYSUT4   DD  UNIT=VIO,SPACE=(CYL,(1,1))                   **        **
004300 //SYSUT5   DD  UNIT=VIO,SPACE=(CYL,(1,1))                   **        **
004400 //SYSUT6   DD  UNIT=VIO,SPACE=(CYL,(1,1))                   **        **
004500 //SYSUT7   DD  UNIT=VIO,SPACE=(CYL,(1,1)) ***************************
004600 //*
004700 //*   LINKAGE EDIT
004800 //*
004900 //LKED     EXEC  PGM=IEWL,                              ************
005000 //  PARM=('SIZE=2048K'),                                **        **
005100 //  TIME=(,6),                                          **        **
005200 //  COND=(4,LT,COB2)                                    **        **
005300 //SYSLIN   DD  DSN=&&LOADSET,DISP=(OLD,DELETE)           ** LINK   **
005400 //SYSLMOD  DD  DSN=&LOADLIB(&MEMBER),                    **        **
005500 //  DISP=SHR                                             **        **
005600 //SYSLIB   DD  DSN=SYS1.COB2LIB,DISP=SHR                 **        **
005700 //SYSUT1   DD  UNIT=VIO,SPACE=(CYL,(1,1))                **        **
005800 //SYSPRINT DD  SYSOUT=&PRINTAT ***************************
```

16.3 Executing the COB2CLJ Proc and the Proc Itself

```
                ┌──────────────────────────────────┐
                │  Jobname  Procstepname  DDname    │
                └──────────────────────────────────┘

IEF236I ALLOC. FOR CSCJGJA COB2 STEP010      ┌────────────────┐
IEF237I 110  ALLOCATED TO STEPLIB            │                │         ▲
IEF237I 111  ALLOCATED TO SYSIN              │    Compile     │        ███
IEF237I 111  ALLOCATED TO SYSLIB             │                │       █████
IEF237I JES2 ALLOCATED TO SYSPRINT           └────────────────┘      ███████
IEF237I VIO  ALLOCATED TO SYSLIN                                        ███
IEF237I VIO  ALLOCATED TO SYSUT1     MVS message about                  ███
IEF237I VIO  ALLOCATED TO SYSUT2     allocation of device prior         ███
IEF237I VIO  ALLOCATED TO SYSUT3     to execution of the step           ███
IEF237I VIO  ALLOCATED TO SYSUT4
IEF237I VIO  ALLOCATED TO SYSUT5
IEF237I VIO  ALLOCATED TO SYSUT6
IEF237I VIO  ALLOCATED TO SYSUT7
IEF142I CSCJGJA COB2 STEP010 - STEP WAS EXECUTED - COND CODE 0000 ─────────────
IEF285I    SYS1.COB2COMP                                 KEPT
IEF285I    VOL SER NOS= ACSRES.                                        ███
IEF285I    CSCJGJ.CSC.COBOL                              KEPT         █████    MVS messages
IEF285I    VOL SER NOS= USER00.                                     ███████   about device
IEF285I    CSCJGJ.CSC.COBOL                              KEPT         ███      deallocation
IEF285I    VOL SER NOS= USER00.                                      ▼███▼     after the step
IEF285I    CSCJGJ.CSCJGJA.JOB01462.D0000101.?           SYSOUT                 has executed
IEF285I    SYS92327.T105955.RA000.CSCJGJA.LOADSET       PASSED
IEF285I    SYS92327.T105955.RA000.CSCJGJA.R0177648      DELETED
IEF285I    SYS92327.T105955.RA000.CSCJGJA.R0177649      DELETED
IEF285I    SYS92327.T105955.RA000.CSCJGJA.R0177650      DELETED
IEF285I    SYS92327.T105955.RA000.CSCJGJA.R0177651      DELETED
IEF285I    SYS92327.T105955.RA000.CSCJGJA.R0177652      DELETED
IEF285I    SYS92327.T105955.RA000.CSCJGJA.R0177653      DELETED
IEF285I    SYS92327.T105955.RA000.CSCJGJA.R0177654      DELETED
IEF373I STEP /COB2   / START 92327.1059
IEF374I STEP /COB2   / STOP  92327.1059 CPU    0MIN 00.73SEC SRB    0MIN 00.01SEC

IEF236I ALLOC. FOR CSCJGJA LKED STEP010
IEF237I VIO  ALLOCATED TO SYSLIN             ┌────────────────────┐
IEF237I 112  ALLOCATED TO SYSLMOD            │                    │
IEF237I 110  ALLOCATED TO SYSLIB             │   Linkage edit     │
IEF237I VIO  ALLOCATED TO SYSUT1             │                    │
IEF237I JES2 ALLOCATED TO SYSPRINT           └────────────────────┘
IEF142I CSCJGJA LKED STEP010 - STEP WAS EXECUTED - COND CODE 0000
IEF285I    SYS92327.T105955.RA000.CSCJGJA.LOADSET       DELETED
IEF285I    CSCJGJ.CSC.LOADLIB                           KEPT
IEF285I    VOL SER NOS= ACSCAT.
IEF285I    SYS1.COB2LIB                                 KEPT
IEF285I    VOL SER NOS= ACSRES.
IEF285I    SYS92327.T105955.RA000.CSCJGJA.R0177655      DELETED
IEF285I    CSCJGJ.CSCJGJA.JOB01462.D0000102.?           SYSOUT
IEF373I STEP /LKED   / START 92327.1059
IEF374I STEP /LKED   / STOP  92327.1059 CPU    0MIN 00.26SEC SRB    0MIN 00.01SEC
IEF375I JOB  /CSCJGJA / START 92327.1059
IEF376I JOB  /CSCJGJA / STOP  92327.1059 CPU    0MIN 00.99SEC SRB    0MIN 00.02SEC
              -
              -
              -
PP 5668-958 IBM VS COBOL II RELEASE 3.2 09/05/90   DATE 11/22/92  TIME 10:59:56  PAGE   1

INVOCATION PARAMETERS:
NOADV,NOCMPR2,NUMPROC(PFD),FLAG(I,E),DYN,LANGUAGE(UE),APOST,FDUMP,LIB,NOMAP,OBJ,RES,NOOPT,XREF
OPTIONS IN EFFECT:
     NOADV
      APOST
     NOAWO          ┌─────────────────────────────────┐
       BUFSIZE(4096)│  Beginning of output from the   │
     NOCMPR2        │  VS COBOL II compiler            │
     NOCOMPILE(S)   │                                  │
       DATA(31)     └─────────────────────────────────┘
              -
              -
              -
MVS/DFP VERSION 3 RELEASE 3 LINKAGE EDITOR      10:59:57  SUN  NOV 22, 1992
JOB CSCJGJA    STEP STEP010    PROCEDURE LKED
INVOCATION PARAMETERS - SIZE=2048K
ACTUAL SIZE=(962560,86016)                    ┌─────────────────────┐
                                              │  Output from the    │
OUTPUT DATA SET CSCJGJ.CSC.LOADLIB IS ON VOLUME ACSCAT │ linkage editor │
** COPYIT   DID NOT PREVIOUSLY EXIST BUT WAS ADDED AND HAS AMODE ANY
** LOAD MODULE HAS RMODE 31                   └─────────────────────┘
** AUTHORIZATION CODE IS        0.
```

Figure 16.4   MVS System Output from Compile and Link

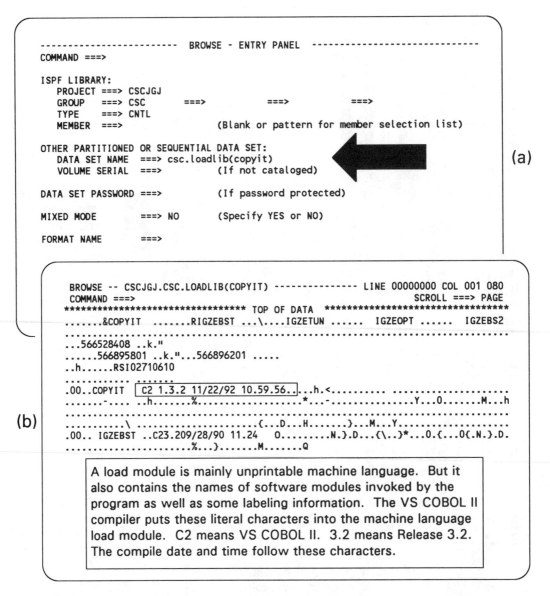

```
--------------------- BROWSE - ENTRY PANEL --------------------------
COMMAND ===>

ISPF LIBRARY:
   PROJECT ===> CSCJGJ
   GROUP   ===> CSC       ===>             ===>             ===>
   TYPE    ===> CNTL
   MEMBER  ===>                    (Blank or pattern for member selection list)

OTHER PARTITIONED OR SEQUENTIAL DATA SET:
   DATA SET NAME ===> csc.loadlib(copyit)
   VOLUME SERIAL ===>              (If not cataloged)

DATA SET PASSWORD ===>             (If password protected)

MIXED MODE       ===> NO      (Specify YES or NO)

FORMAT NAME      ===>
```

(a)

(b)

```
BROWSE -- CSCJGJ.CSC.LOADLIB(COPYIT) -------------- LINE 00000000 COL 001 080
COMMAND ===>                                        SCROLL ===> PAGE
***************************** TOP OF DATA *********************************
.......&COPYIT .......RIGZEBST ...\....IGZETUN ...... IGZEOPT ...... IGZEBS2
...............................................................................
...566528408 ..k."
......566895801 ..k."...566896201 .....
..h......RSI02710610
..............  ........
.00..COPYIT  C2 1.3.2 11/22/92 10.59.56.. ...h.<......... ....................
.......-.... ..h.....%.................*...-..............Y...0.......M...h
...............................................................................
...........\ ....................(...D...H.......}...M...Y..................
.00.. IGZEBST ..C23.209/28/90 11.24  0.........N.}.D...(\..)*...0.(...0(.N.}.D.
...................%...}.......M.......Q
```

> A load module is mainly unprintable machine language. But it
> also contains the names of software modules invoked by the
> program as well as some labeling information. The VS COBOL II
> compiler puts these literal characters into the machine language
> load module. C2 means VS COBOL II. 3.2 means Release 3.2.
> The compile date and time follow these characters.

Figure 16.5 Browsing a Load Module: What's in It?

This is what the COPYIT load module looks like if you view it using the TSO/ISPF
1 "browse" function. The dots are bytes containing unprintable bit patterns. You
can see the compile date imbedded by the VS COBOL II compiler in the load
module.

```
EDIT ---- CSCJGJ.CSC.CNTL(J3GO) - 01.00 --------------------- COLUMNS 001 072
COMMAND ===> sub                                          SCROLL ===> PAGE
****** *************************** TOP OF DATA ********************************
000100 //CSCJGJA   JOB 1,'BIN 7 JANOSSY',CLASS=A,MSGCLASS=X,MSGLEVEL=(1,1),
000200 // NOTIFY=CSCJGJ
000300 //*
000400 //*   THIS JCL IS STORED AT CSCJGJ.CSC.CNTL(J3GO)
000500 //*
000600 //********************************************************************
000700 //*    RUN THE COBOL-PRODUCED LOAD MODULE OF THE COPYIT PROGRAM     *
000800 //********************************************************************
000900 //STEP010   EXEC  PGM=COPYIT
001000 //STEPLIB    DD   DSN=CSCJGJ.CSC.LOADLIB,DISP=SHR
001100 //           DD   DSN=SYS1.COB2LIB,DISP=SHR
001200 //COPYIN     DD   DSN=CSCJGJ.CSC.CNTL(WORKERS),DISP=SHR
001300 //COPYOUT    DD   SYSOUT=*
001400 //SYSOUT     DD   SYSOUT=*
001500 //
****** *************************** BOTTOM OF DATA ****************************


JOB CSCJGJA(JOB01482) SUBMITTED
11.13.27 JOB01482 $HASP165 CSCJGJA  ENDED AT N1 CN(INTERNAL)
***
```

```
                     J E S 2   J O B   L O G  --  S Y S T E M   I B M 1  --  N O D E   N 1

11.13.24 JOB01482  IRR010I  USERID CSCJGJ   IS ASSIGNED TO THIS JOB.
11.13.25 JOB01482  ICH70001I CSCJGJ   LAST ACCESS AT 11:11:59 ON SUNDAY, NOVEMBER 22, 1992
11.13.25 JOB01482  $HASP373 CSCJGJA  STARTED - INIT 2 - CLASS A - SYS IBM1
11.13.27 JOB01482  $HASP395 CSCJGJA  ENDED

------ JES2 JOB STATISTICS ------
    22 NOV 92 JOB EXECUTION DATE
        14 CARDS READ
        65 SYSOUT PRINT RECORDS
         0 SYSOUT PUNCH RECORDS
         4 SYSOUT SPOOL KBYTES
      0.03 MINUTES EXECUTION TIME
            -
            -
ICH70001I CSCJGJ   LAST ACCESS AT 11:11:59 ON SUNDAY, NOVEMBER 22, 1992

IEF236I ALLOC. FOR CSCJGJA STEP010
IEF237I 112  ALLOCATED TO STEPLIB
IEF237I 110  ALLOCATED TO
IEF237I 111  ALLOCATED TO COPYIN
IEF237I JES2 ALLOCATED TO COPYOUT
IEF237I JES2 ALLOCATED TO SYSOUT
IEF142I CSCJGJA STEP010 - STEP WAS EXECUTED - COND CODE 0000
IEF285I   CSCJGJ.CSC.LOADLIB
IEF285I   VOL SER NOS= ACSCAT.
IEF285I   SYS1.COB2LIB                              KEPT
IEF285I   VOL SER NOS= ACSRES.                      KEPT
IEF285I   CSCJGJ.CSC.CNTL                           KEPT
IEF285I   VOL SER NOS= USER00.
IEF285I   CSCJGJ.CSCJGJA.JOB01482.D0000101.?        SYSOUT
IEF285I   CSCJGJ.CSCJGJA.JOB01482.D0000102.?        SYSOUT
IEF373I STEP /STEP010 / START 92327.1113
IEF374I STEP /STEP010 / STOP  92327.1113 CPU    0MIN 00.15SEC

IEF375I  JOB /CSCJGJA / START 92327.1113
IEF376I  JOB /CSCJGJA / STOP  92327.1113 CPU    0MIN 00.15SEC SRB    0MIN 00.02SEC

*** START OF COPYIT LISTING
21256 NILLY     WILLY      402CASHIERS OFFICE
21257 IPPI      MRS.       378PHOTO DEPARTMENT
        -
        -
```

> When I execute the load module for my COPYIT program I receive only one COND CODE, from the program itself. Since the load module is already in machine language form, no compile and linkage edit steps are involved.

Figure 16.6 Executing a Load Module

really doesn't care if you name them consistently; EXEC goes by load module member name.

You can see from Figure 16.6a that the COPYIT load module executed very quickly. Without having to be compiled and linkage edited, MVS has only to copy a load module to memory and give it control. The output from this run is also much more compact than from a compile/link/go, as shown in Figure 16.6b. All that MVS reports on is the program execution step. The COPYIT program outputs the same results from this run as in Figure 5.7. If I had coded COPYIT to receive a parm to control some aspect of its operation (as I did in program PARMDEMO in Chapter 7), I would execute it and pass it a parm in this way:

```
//STEP010   EXEC   PGM=COPYIT,PARM='xxxx'
```

16.5 //STEPLIB and //JOBLIB

MVS is aware of only a default load module library such as SYS1.LINKLIB. Because I want to have MVS execute a program from my own load module library, I have to tell it the name of that library using the //STEPLIB DD statement. //STEPLIB stands for "step library" and is not an ordinary DDname. It has nothing to do with data sets that a program reads or writes; //STEPLIB points to where the program itself is stored. In Figure 16.6a EXEC PGM=COPYIT refers to a member of CSCJGJ.CSC.LOADLIB. So I name this library at //STEPLIB:

```
//STEP010   EXEC   PGM=COPYIT
//STEPLIB   DD   DSN=CSCJGJ.CSC.LOADLIB,DISP=SHR
//          DD   DSN=SYS1.COB2LIB,DISP=SHR
```

Instead of coding //STEPLIB at each step, you can code one //JOBLIB statement after the JOB statement to serve for every step:

```
//CSCJGJA   JOB 1,'BIN 7 JANOSSY',MSGLEVEL=(1,1),MSGCLASS=X,
//   NOTIFY=CSCJGJ
//JOBLIB   DD   DSN=CSCJGJ.CSC.LOADLIB,DISP=SHR
```

Coding //JOBLIB is the same as coding //STEPLIB at each step. //STEPLIB overrides //JOBLIB at any step in which you code it.

You'll notice in the JCL above that I have concatenated data set SYS1.COB2LIB to my load module library at //STEPLIB. You occasionally have to do this when you execute load modules compiled by new versions of compilers, until the new compilers are fully installed.

16.6 DDNAME and Input to the Linkage Editor

You'll sometimes see these lines within a compile and linkage edit proc:

```
//SYSLIN   DD   DSN=&&LOADSET,DISP=(OLD,DELETE)
//         DD   DDNAME=SYSIN
```

At this point, the linkage editor reads the object file produced by the compiler (&&LOADSET), which consists of 80-byte punch card image records. The linkage editor can also accept card image control statements here to tell it to perform a variety of special services.

DDNAME concatenated here looks a bit strange. It concatenates another input to &&LOADSET by defining a new DDname, SYSIN. The linkage editor itself does not require a DD statement named SYSIN, but this is the common name used by IBM software products for control statement input. By concatenating DDNAME at //SYSLIN, it is possible for you to supply linkage editor control statements in your compile and link JCL this way:

```
//STEP010   EXEC   COB2UCLG,
//   PDS='CSCJGJ.CSC.COBOL',
//   MEMBER='COPYIT'
//   LOADLIB='CSCJGJ.CSC.LOADLIB'
//LKED.SYSIN   DD *
    NAME ABCD1234(R)
//
```

NAME is one of several control statements that the linkage editor accepts. NAME lets you code the intended name of the load module as a control statement if you don't want to code it as a member name within parentheses at its //SYSLMOD. The (R) means "replace" the module (if it already exists in the load module library).

One of the most common uses for linkage editor control statements in the old days was to list the names of subprograms called by a main program to statically link together ("hard link") the modules. This is now unnecessary and undesirable for batch programs if you use the compiler option DYN to allow called modules to be accessed dynamically at runtime. If you use the DYN feature, the linkage editor does exactly what is appropriate for single-program linkage edits without any control statement input.

It's perfectly acceptable not to supply control statement input to the linkage editor at the proc-defined new DDname //LKED.SYSIN. With no input here, you'll get the message in the MVS system output: "DDNAME REFERRED TO ON DDNAME KEYWORD IN PRIOR STEP WAS NOT RE-

SOLVED." You can ignore this informational message; it does not indicate an error.

If you need more information about linkage editor control statements, I'd suggest you see Chapter 18 in Gary Brown's book, *System 370/390 JCL* (third edition), also published by John Wiley & Sons, Inc.

16.7 Reorganizing (Compressing) a Load Module Library

You occasionally need to reorganize load module libraries, just as you have to perform this chore for your ordinary partitioned data set libraries. Every time you replace a program in a load module library, the replacement copy is written in new data space. The old load module member(s) of the same name remain, and the space they use is not available to house other load modules.

You can use the TSO/ISPF 3.1 "compress" function to reorganize a load module library to eliminate old copies of members. But I suggest that you use instead a batch proc for this purpose, such as the PDSREORG proc I show you in Chapter 18. PDSREORG lets you change the block size, directory size, and space allocation for a partitioned data set as a part of its reorganization. Figure 16.7 shows you how to execute the PDSREORG proc to reorganize a load module library.

16.8 Load Modules and the PDSE (MVS/ESA)

Under MVS/ESA you gain the convenience of the Partitioned Data Set Extended (PDSE) to house your source code libraries. You don't have to periodically reorganize a PDSE because it manages its internal space itself. But even under MVS you can't store load modules in a PDSE; load modules must still be stored in a real partitioned data set. You still face the task of reorganizing load module libraries under MVS/ESA.

```
EDIT ---- CSCJGJ.CSC.CNTL(J4REORG) - 01.01 ------------------ COLUMNS 001 072
COMMAND ===>                                                  SCROLL ===> PAGE
****** **************************** TOP OF DATA ******************************
000100 //CSCJGJA  JOB 1,'BIN 7 JANOSSY',CLASS=A,MSGCLASS=X,MSGLEVEL=(1,1),
000200 //  NOTIFY=CSCJGJ
000300 //*
000400 //*    THIS JCL IS STORED AT CSCJGJ.CSC.CNTL(J4REORG)
000500 //*
000600 //*******************************************************************
000700 //*                                                                 *
000800 //*     REORGANIZE A LOAD MODULE LIBRARY                            *
000900 //*                                                                 *
001000 //*******************************************************************
001100 //STEPA    EXEC  PDSREORG,
001200 //  PDS='CSCJGJ.CSC.LOADLIB',    DATA SET TO BE REORGANIZED
001300 //  ALLOC=TRK,                   ALLOCATION IS TO BE IN TRACKS
001400 //  QPRIM=10,                    PRIMARY SPACE IS TO BE 10 TRACKS
001500 //  QSEC=6,                      MAKE SECONDARY SPACE 6 TRACKS
001600 //  QDIRBLK=50,                  CREATE 50 DIRECTORY BLOCKS
001700 //  RECFORM=U,                   RECORD FORMAT UNDEFINED (LOAD MODULE)
001800 //  QREC=0,                      RECORD LENGTH IS 0
001900 //  QBLK=22928                   MAKE BLOCK SIZE BEST FOR 9345 DISK
002000 //
```

(a)

```
------------------------- DATA SET INFORMATION ----------------------------
COMMAND ===>

DATA SET NAME: CSCJGJ.CSC.LOADLIB

GENERAL DATA:                              CURRENT ALLOCATION:
    Volume serial:        ACSCAT             Allocated tracks:        10
    Device type:          9345               Allocated extents:        1
    Organization:         PO                 Maximum dir. blocks:     50
    Record format:        U
    Record length:        0
    Block size:           22928            CURRENT UTILIZATION:
    1st extent tracks:    10                 Used tracks:              2
    Secondary tracks:     6                  Used extents:             1
                                             Used dir. blocks:         1
    Creation date:        1992/11/22         Number of members:        1
    Expiration date:      ***NONE***
```

(b)

> I used the PDSREORG proc shown in Chapter 18 to reorganize
> my load module library and at the same time increase the size
> of its data space and directory, and change its block size to the
> most efficient for model 9345 disks. Use **23476** as block size
> for load module libraries on model 3380 disks, and **27998** as
> the block size for these libraries on 3390's.

Figure 16.7 JCL to Reorganize a Load Module Library with the PDSREORG Proc

PDSREORG is a proc for reorganizing partitioned data sets. I show you this proc in
Chapter 18. As you put new versions of the same programs into a load module
library, space in it depletes because the old versions of the program load modules
remain but are inaccessible. You can execute PDSREORG to reclaim unused space.

Chapter Seventeen

Generation Data Group Data Sets

"Production" programs form a regular part of everyday operation in an organization. A file maintenance routine such as a sequential update program is executed on a regular basis. Each time it's run, it draws in newly prepared transactions, applies them to an existing master file, and creates a new updated copy of the master file. The new master file (data set), the old master file, and master files from several previous runs are usually kept because they serve as ready-made data backups.

Every data set on the mainframe must have a unique name. With regular cyclical operation of the same programs, we want to be able to code JCL that doesn't have to be changed from run to run. How do we arrange for a unique data set name for every run of an update job stream? MVS provides the **generation data group,** or **GDG,** feature to support this cyclical processing. GDGs manage data set names automatically. In addition to sequential master files, backups of disk files are usually created as GDG generations. You can use generation data groups for sequential and partitioned data sets but not for VSAM data sets.

In this chapter I show you how to use the generation data group (GDG) feature of MVS. I'll show you, step by step, the actions you take to create a generation data group name, why you need to take them, and the special JCL coding you need when you create a "generation" of a GDG.

17.1 A Typical Generation Data Group Application

Figure 17.1 shows you a multistep job stream diagram in which I execute three programs in series. The first program is the sort utility, which sorts transaction records into ascending sequence. The sorted transaction records carry information about new records to be added to a master file, changes to existing records, and the identity of records to be deleted from the master file.

At the second step in Figure 17.1, I execute an "update" program named FSBT3708. This program applies sorted transaction records to the records from the old (present) master file and creates a new copy of the master file.

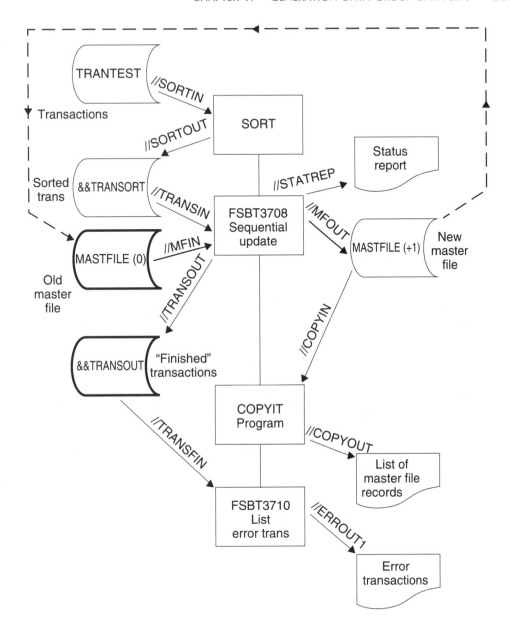

Figure 17.1 Generation Data Groups Support Cyclical Processing

The sequential update mapped out here will be run periodically. Making MASTFILE a generation data group (GDG) data set lets MVS manage its name so that we can refer to the old master file as (0) and the new master file as (+1). The (+1) generation becomes the (0) generation when the job stream ends. We don't have to change JCL to adjust data set names every time we run this job stream.

"Add" transactions have inserted new records into this file, and "change" transactions have altered the contents of some of the master file records. "Delete" transactions have prevented some records on the old master file from being copied to the new master file.

FSBT3708 also creates a data set containing "finished" transactions at //TRANSOUT. The records in this data set are slightly longer than the incoming transactions. They are formed by appending codes to each transaction, indicating if the transaction succeeded in its attempted update, and if not, why it failed. These finished transactions are read by a program named FSBT3710, which I execute at the third step. This program uses the finished transactions to produce a report that helps end users correct and resubmit flawed transactions.

17.2 A Generation Data Group Manages Data Set Names

I can create a generation data group to manage the master file in my update job stream. This way I can code the current (old) master file as the "zero" generation and the new master file as the "next" generation of the same data set name:

```
//MFIN        DD   DSN=CSCJGJ.CSC.MASTFILE(0),        Old master file
//   DISP=SHR
//MFOUT       DD   DSN=CSCJGJ.CSC.MASTFILE(+1),       New master file
//   DISP=(NEW,CATLG,DELETE),
//   UNIT=SYSDA,
//   DCB=(CSCJGJ.CSC.MODLDSCB,RECFM=FB,LRECL=80,BLKSIZE=6160),
//   SPACE=(6160,(3,2),RLSE)
```

(This DSN coding looks similar to that for partitioned data sets, but it has nothing to do with a PDS; CSCJGJ.CSC.MASTFILE is not a PDS.) At the end of the job (not at the end of the step) the (+1) generation becomes the "current" (0) generation, and the existing (0) generation becomes the (-1) generation. *But you can't just code a "writing" DD statement this way!* Before you can use a generation data group name for a new data set, you have to provide a model data set label (like CSCJGJ.CSC.MODLDSCB above), and you need to establish a GDG base for the generation data group.

17.3 What Are Generations?

Generation data groups are conceptually much like human generations. You create a new generation with each run of your JCL using the relative generation number (+1). You can access prior generations using (-1), (-2), and so forth:

Grandparent	(-2)
Parent	(-1)
Current generation	(-0) or (+0) or just (0)
Children	(+1)
Grandchildren	(+2)

You can code generations earlier than (-2) and later than (+2); this is just an example.

Names like CSCJGJ.CSC.MASTFILE(0) are called **_relative data set names_**. They exist only in your JCL. MVS uses information you put in the system catalog, in a "GDG base" for the data set, to manage the translation of relative data set name to absolute data set name.

17.4 Relative and Absolute Data Set Names

Every data set handled by MVS has to have a unique data set name. The data sets making up a generation data set group are no exception. In every respect, they are "normal" data sets; the GDG mechanism just provides a convenient way to manage their names and access them. Data set names can be up to 44 characters long:

Ordinary data set name:
```
XXXXXXXX.XXXXXXXX.XXXXXXXX.XXXXXXXX.XXXXXXXX
```

Relative generation name:
```
XXXXXXXX.XXXXXXXX.XXXXXXXX.XXXXXXXX(0)
```

Absolute data set name:
```
XXXXXXXX.XXXXXXXX.XXXXXXXX.XXXXXXXX.G0000V00
```

The real or **_absolute_** name of a data set in a generation data group consists of the name as we know it and a final name part made up of "GnnnnVzz," where "nnnn" is the **_generation number_** and "zz" is the **_version number_**. The final "GnnnnVzz" part of a name on GDG data sets, preceded by a period, takes 9 bytes. This means that the "name" part of a GDG name that we can code is limited to 44 − 9 = 35 characters.

When you create a new generation, MVS simply takes the (+1) relative data set name and adds the number that you coded in parentheses to the highest existing "Gnnnn" number for the data set name to form a new data set name. MVS always makes the "Vzz" a "V" followed by zeros. It keeps a correspondence table for itself in the system catalog (in the GDG base) equating absolute data set names to relative data set names and updates it when your job ends. Here are what the entries for several generations of my customer master file CSCJGJ.CSC.MASTFILE might look like in the catalog before an update run:

Relative data set name	Absolute data set name
CSCJGJ.CSC.MASTFILE(0)	CSCJGJ.CSC.MASTFILE.G0007V00
CSCJGJ.CSC.MASTFILE(-1)	CSCJGJ.CSC.MASTFILE.G0006V00
CSCJGJ.CSC.MASTFILE(-2)	CSCJGJ.CSC.MASTFILE.G0005V00
CSCJGJ.CSC.MASTFILE(-3)	CSCJGJ.CSC.MASTFILE.G0004V00

While my update job stream is executing, the entries in the catalog would look like this:

Relative data set name	Absolute data set name
CSCJGJ.CSC.MASTFILE(+1)	CSCJGJ.CSC.MASTFILE.G0008V00
CSCJGJ.CSC.MASTFILE(0)	CSCJGJ.CSC.MASTFILE.G0007V00
CSCJGJ.CSC.MASTFILE(-1)	CSCJGJ.CSC.MASTFILE.G0006V00
CSCJGJ.CSC.MASTFILE(-2)	CSCJGJ.CSC.MASTFILE.G0005V00
CSCJGJ.CSC.MASTFILE(-3)	CSCJGJ.CSC.MASTFILE.G0004V00

Immediately after the sequential update job stream ends, MVS adjusts the catalog entries to make them

Relative data set name	Absolute data set name
CSCJGJ.CSC.MASTFILE(0)	CSCJGJ.CSC.MASTFILE.G0008V00
CSCJGJ.CSC.MASTFILE(-1)	CSCJGJ.CSC.MASTFILE.G0007V00
CSCJGJ.CSC.MASTFILE(-2)	CSCJGJ.CSC.MASTFILE.G0006V00
CSCJGJ.CSC.MASTFILE(-3)	CSCJGJ.CSC.MASTFILE.G0005V00

The maximum number of generations that MVS can manage for a data set is 255, so a three-digit number is the largest that you can specify in a relative data set name. The highest generation number in an absolute data set name is 9999. Once the generation number becomes 9999 and you create another generation, the generation number rolls around to 0001 again.

All GDG data sets must be cataloged. You can manually create a "replacement" for a given "Gnnnn" generation by creating a cataloged data set with the same absolute name and the "Vzz" incremented upward by one, such as "V01." MVS uses the highest "Vzz" data set of a given "Gnnnn" for that generation.

17.5 Background of the Model Data Set Label (DSCB)

Generation data sets have always presented an air of mystery because of their connection with a *model data set label*, also called a model DSCB.

You need to understand a little background (and MVS lore) to feel comfortable with GDGs.

Every disk volume has a volume table of contents (VTOC). The records in the VTOC, called "data set control block" or DSCB records, keep track of the names, locations, and characteristics of data sets on the disk and the location of free space on the disk. Seven formats of VTOC records exist. The format 1 DSCB record carries information about data set name, DCB characteristics, and the location of the first of three disk data set extents; it is the data set label.

Models serve as a prototype to help create new things. A model data set label provides a pattern that MVS can use to create the label for a new data set. The idea of a model data set label for a generation data group stretches all the way back to the earliest days of System/360 OS. IBM's software engineers originally thought that you would create a separate model data set label for each generation data group name that you establish and put it on the same disk as the catalog. The data set attributes established in the label would apply to all data sets in the generation data group, making it unnecessary for you to code the DCB parameter in the DD statement at which a new data set is produced. Having a model label would let MVS create a new generation data group data set more quickly.

17.6 One Model DSCB Is All You Need

Few installations ever used the model data set label in the way IBM's software engineers envisioned. It's burdensome and unnecessary to create a separate model data set label for every generation data group. There is no requirement that all members of a GDG have the same DCB characteristics or even that they all reside on tape, or all reside on disk. Because DCB coding in your JCL overrides what's in a model data set label, you can use any existing data set to meet the requirement of referring to a data set label when you create a generation of a GDG.

Most installations create one model data set label and use it for all generation data groups. It's not necessary to bother with a unique, uncataloged model data set label for every different generation data group when you specify the model label name in the DCB for the new generation and code normal DCB parameters:

```
//MFOUT       DD  DSN=CSCJGJ.CSC.MASTFILE(+1),
//  DISP=(NEW,CATLG,DELETE),
//  UNIT=SYSDA,
//  DCB=(CSCJGJ.CSC.MODLDSCB,RECFM=FB,LRECL=80,BLKSIZE=6160),
//  SPACE=(6160,(3,2),RLSE)
```

We now use the model data set label not for its intended purpose but simply to meet the requirement of GDGs that we tie each new generation to a model. Because we override every relevant DCB characteristic, it really doesn't matter what's in the model.

Under MVS/ESA, the requirement for you to refer to a model when you create a generation is potentially lifted. But to make that possible, your installation must activate the Storage Management Subsystem. Most people will continue to see (and have to use) model data set labels for a long while yet. As you can see, the explanation lies in computer archaeology!

17.7 Creating a Model Data Set Label

You can best create a model data set label using JCL to execute IEFBR14 as I did in Figure 17.2a. You could also allocate a model data set using TSO function 3.2. The advantage of using JCL is that you can give the data set zero tracks; TSO will require you to waste at least one track for it.

My model data set label is named CSCJGJ.CSC.MODLDSCB. After creating it, I used TSO's 3.2 function to see its characteristics and allocation, shown in Figure 17.2b. Notice that it really uses no disk space. It is simply an entry in a disk VTOC.

17.8 Creating the GDG Base

You can create a GDG *base* with IDCAMS as shown in Figure 17.3. Here is what the parts of this coding mean:

NAME is the "base name" of the generation data set. You can make it up to 35 characters in length.

OWNER is optional descriptive information. This may be up to eight bytes in length and serves as only a comment.

FOR is the number of days for which the GDG base itself is to exist, not the retention period for individual generations of data sets. You can code FOR as a number of days from 0000 to 9999 or as a Julian date by coding TO and a date in the form YYDDD. Neither FOR or TO is necessary. Coding retention doesn't mean that MVS will delete the GDG at a specified date; it just makes deletion before that date a little harder. Even without a retention date, IDCAMS will not readily allow deletion of a GDG base as long as it has any generations associated with it.

LIMIT is the number of generations that the GDG will contain. You can make this value as little as 1 or as high as 255.

NOEMPTY and **EMPTY** are mutually exclusive. They establish what data sets in the GDG are affected when the generation LIMIT is reached.

```
EDIT ---- CSCJGJ.CSC.CNTL(K1MODL) - 01.02 ------------------- COLUMNS 001 072
COMMAND ===>                                                SCROLL ===> PAGE
****** *************************** TOP OF DATA *******************************
000100 //CSCJGJA   JOB 1,'BIN 7 JANOSSY',CLASS=A,MSGCLASS=X,MSGLEVEL=(1,1),
000200 // NOTIFY=CSCJGJ
000300 //*
000400 //*   THIS JCL IS STORED AT CSCJGJ.CSC.CNTL(K1MODL)
000500 //*
000600 //********************************************************************
000700 //*                                                                  *
000800 //*   CREATE A MODEL DSCB (MODEL DATA SET CONTROL BLOCK) FOR GDG     *
000900 //*   THE SINGLE MODEL CREATED HERE WILL SERVE FOR ALL GDG NAMES    *
001000 //*                                                                  *
001100 //********************************************************************
001200 //STEP010   EXEC  PGM=IEFBR14
001300 //MODL      DD   DSN=CSCJGJ.CSC.MODLDSCB,
001400 //   DISP=(MOD,CATLG,DELETE),
001500 //   UNIT=SYSDA,
001600 //   DCB=(RECFM=FB,LRECL=25,BLKSIZE=2500,DSORG=PS),
001700 //   SPACE=(TRK,0)
001800 //
```

(a)

Creates a VTOC entry but uses no disk data space

```
------------------------ DATA SET INFORMATION ------------------------------
COMMAND ===>

DATA SET NAME: CSCJGJ.CSC.MODLDSCB

GENERAL DATA:                           CURRENT ALLOCATION:
   Volume serial:      ACSCAT              Allocated Tracks:      0
   Device type:        9345                Allocated extents:     0
   Organization:       PS
   Record format:      FB
   Record length:      25
   Block size:         2500             CURRENT UTILIZATION:
   1st extent Tracks:  0                   Used Tracks:           0
   Secondary Tracks:   0                   Used extents:          0

   Creation date:      1992/11/24
   Expiration date:    ***NONE***
```

(b)

I will refer to data set CSCJGJ.CSC.MODLDSCB as my **model data set control block** in JCL to create new GDG generations. My JCL will *override* this model's characteristics. "DSCB" is the data set label, stored in a disk volume table of contents (VTOC).

Figure 17.2   JCL to Create a Model Data Set Label (DSCB)

(a) The edit screen shows you JCL to create a model data set label. (b) The data set information screen confirms that the model data set label consumes no data space at all.

NOEMPTY means that when the generation LIMIT has been reached and another generation is to be created, the SCRATCH specification is to be applied to the *oldest* existing generation. EMPTY indicates that when the generation LIMIT is reached and another generation is to be created, *all* existing generations are to be affected by the SCRATCH specification. NOEMPTY is the default.

SCRATCH and **NOSCRATCH** are mutually exclusive. SCRATCH indicates that affected data sets are to be uncataloged and deleted. NO-SCRATCH indicates that affected data sets are simply to be uncataloged. In either case, the affected data sets are removed from membership in the generation data set group, and you can no longer access them by relative data set name. You can still access them by absolute name if you know the volume on which they reside. NOSCRATCH is the default, but this is not usually desirable. SCRATCH can delete only disk data sets, not tape-stored data sets. The retention of a tape data set is governed by its expiration date.

17.9 Using a Generation Data Group

Figure 17.4 is JCL that implements the multistep job stream of Figure 17.1. If you look at lines 003600 and 004400, you'll see that (except for the very first run) the old master file is read as CSCJGJ.CSC.MASTFILE(0) and the new master file is written as CSCJGJ.CSC.MASTFILE(+1). But look also at line 006100, where the newly created master file is read by the COPYIT program to list it. I still refer to the new master file as the (+1) generation here; it will not undergo "reversion" to the (0) generation until the update job ends.

Figure 17.5a illustrates how you can edit a generation data group data set by specifying its relative name at the TSO function 2 Edit-Entry screen. Due to relative data set name reversion, when I wanted to edit the newly created master file generation after the update by using TSO/ISPF, I entered the zero generation. I entered CSC.MASTFILE(0) at the OTHER PARTITIONED OR SEQUENTIAL DATA SET field (TSO prefaced this with my TSO user id, so the data name MVS sees was actually CSCJGJ.CSC.MASTFILE (0)). Figure 17.5b is the edit screen itself. You can see that the data set name placed by TSO at the top of this screen is the absolute data set name.

Figure 17.6 shows you part of the MVS system reporting from my next run of the update job stream. The absolute name of the (old) master file is CSCJGJ.CSC.MASTFILE.G0002V00, and the name of the new master file is CSCJGJ.CSC.MASTFILE.G0003V00.

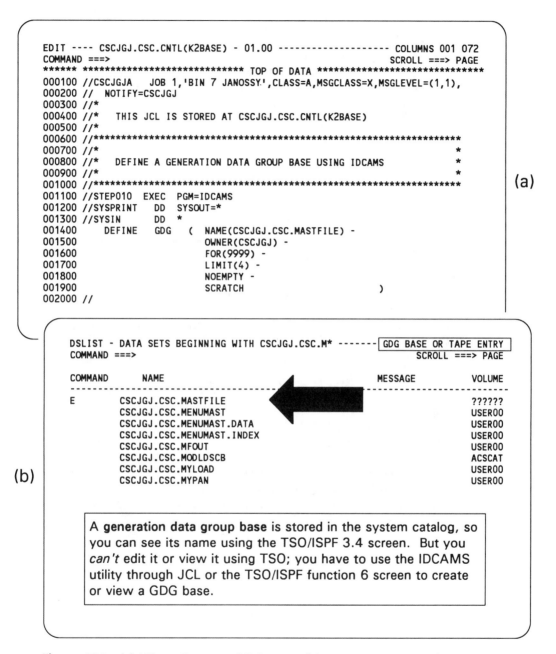

```
EDIT ---- CSCJGJ.CSC.CNTL(K2BASE) - 01.00 ------------------- COLUMNS 001 072
COMMAND ===>                                            SCROLL ===> PAGE
****** *********************** TOP OF DATA *****************************
000100 //CSCJGJA   JOB 1,'BIN 7 JANOSSY.',CLASS=A,MSGCLASS=X,MSGLEVEL=(1,1),
000200 //  NOTIFY=CSCJGJ
000300 //*
000400 //*   THIS JCL IS STORED AT CSCJGJ.CSC.CNTL(K2BASE)
000500 //*
000600 //**********************************************************************
000700 //*                                                                   *
000800 //*   DEFINE A GENERATION DATA GROUP BASE USING IDCAMS                 *
000900 //*                                                                   *
001000 //**********************************************************************
001100 //STEP010 EXEC  PGM=IDCAMS
001200 //SYSPRINT   DD  SYSOUT=*
001300 //SYSIN      DD  *
001400     DEFINE   GDG   (  NAME(CSCJGJ.CSC.MASTFILE) -
001500                       OWNER(CSCJGJ) -
001600                       FOR(9999) -
001700                       LIMIT(4) -
001800                       NOEMPTY -
001900                       SCRATCH                          )
002000 //
```

(a)

```
DSLIST - DATA SETS BEGINNING WITH CSCJGJ.CSC.M* ------| GDG BASE OR TAPE ENTRY |
COMMAND ===>                                          SCROLL ===> PAGE

COMMAND      NAME                              MESSAGE        VOLUME
-------------------------------------------------------------------------------
E        CSCJGJ.CSC.MASTFILE                                  ??????
         CSCJGJ.CSC.MENUMAST                                  USER00
         CSCJGJ.CSC.MENUMAST.DATA                             USER00
         CSCJGJ.CSC.MENUMAST.INDEX                            USER00
         CSCJGJ.CSC.MFOUT                                     USER00
         CSCJGJ.CSC.MODLDSCB                                  ACSCAT
         CSCJGJ.CSC.MYLOAD                                    USER00
         CSCJGJ.CSC.MYPAN                                     USER00
```

(b)

A **generation data group base** is stored in the system catalog, so you can see its name using the TSO/ISPF 3.4 screen. But you *can't* edit it or view it using TSO; you have to use the IDCAMS utility through JCL or the TSO/ISPF function 6 screen to create or view a GDG base.

Figure 17.3   (a) JCL to Create a GDG Base. (b) Trying to Use TSO/ISPF Function 3.4 (DSLIST) to See a Generation Data Group Base in the System Catalog.

```
EDIT ---- CSCJGJ.CSC.CNTL(K3GDG) - 01.01 -------------------- COLUMNS 001 072
COMMAND ===>                                                  SCROLL ===> PAGE
****** *************************** TOP OF DATA ****************************
000100 //CSCJGJA  JOB 1,'BIN 7--JANOSSY',CLASS=A,MSGCLASS=X,MSGLEVEL=(1,1),
000200 //          NOTIFY=CSCJGJ
000300 //*
000400 //*     THIS JCL IS STORED AT CSCJGJ.CSC.CNTL(K3GDG)
000500 //*
000600 //***************************************************************
000700 //*                                                             *
000800 //*     SORT THE TRANSACTIONS ON KEY AND TRAN TYPE CODE         *
000900 //*                                                             *
001000 //***************************************************************
001100 //STEP010  EXEC  PGM=SORT
001200 //SYSOUT    DD   SYSOUT=*
001300 //SORTIN    DD   DSN=CSCJGJ.CSC.TRANTEST,
001400 //          DISP=SHR
001500 //SORTOUT   DD   DSN=&&TRANSORT,
001600 //          DISP=(NEW,PASS,DELETE),
001700 //          UNIT=SYSDA,
001800 //          DCB=(RECFM=FB,LRECL=80,BLKSIZE=6160),
001900 //          SPACE=(6160,(3,2),RLSE)
002000 //SORTWK01  DD   UNIT=SYSDA,SPACE=(CYL,1)
002100 //SORTWK02  DD   UNIT=SYSDA,SPACE=(CYL,1)
002200 //SYSIN     DD   *
002300      SORT FIELDS=(1,8,CH,A)
002400 /*
002500 //*
002600 //***************************************************************
002700 //*                                                             *
002800 //*     RUN THE UPDATE PROGRAM                                  *
002900 //*                                                             *
003000 //***************************************************************
003100 //STEP020  EXEC  PGM=FSBT3708
003200 //STEPLIB   DD   DSN=CSCJGJ.CSC.LOADLIB,DISP=SHR
003300 //          DD   DSN=SYS1.COB2LIB,DISP=SHR
003400 //TRANSIN   DD   DSN=&&TRANSORT,
003500 //          DISP=(OLD,DELETE)
003600 //*FIN      DD   DSN=CSCJGJ.CSC.MASTFILE(0)
003700 //MFIN      DD   DSN=CSCJGJ.CSC.DATA(CMTEST),
003800 //          DISP=SHR
003900 //TRANSOUT  DD   DSN=&&TRANSOUT,
004000 //          DISP=(NEW,PASS,DELETE),
004100 //          UNIT=SYSDA,
004200 //          DCB=(RECFM=FB,LRECL=99,BLKSIZE=6138),
004300 //          SPACE=(6138,(3,2),RLSE)
004400 //MFOUT     DD   DSN=CSCJGJ.CSC.MASTFILE(+1),
004500 //          DISP=(NEW,CATLG,DELETE),
004600 //          UNIT=SYSDA,
004700 //          DCB=(CSCJGJ.CSC.MODLDSCB,RECFM=FB,LRECL=80,BLKSIZE=6160),
004800 //          SPACE=(6160,(3,2),RLSE)
004900 //STATREP   DD   SYSOUT=*
005000 //SYSOUT    DD   SYSOUT=*
005100 //SYSDBOUT  DD   SYSOUT=*
005200 //*
005300 //***************************************************************
005400 //*                                                             *
005500 //*     LIST THE RECORDS IN THE MASTER FILE                     *
005600 //*                                                             *
005700 //***************************************************************
005800 //STEP030  EXEC  PGM=COPYIT
005900 //STEPLIB   DD   DSN=CSCJGJ.CSC.LOADLIB,DISP=SHR
006000 //          DD   DSN=SYS1.COB2LIB,DISP=SHR
006100 //COPYIN    DD   DSN=CSCJGJ.CSC.MASTFILE(+1),
006200 //          DISP=SHR
006300 //COPYOUT   DD   SYSOUT=*
006400 //SYSOUT    DD   SYSOUT=*
006500 //SYSDBOUT  DD   SYSOUT=*
006600 //*
006700 //***************************************************************
006800 //*                                                             *
006900 //*     PRINT THE ERROR TRANSACTION REPORT                      *
007000 //*                                                             *
007100 //***************************************************************
007200 //STEP040  EXEC  PGM=FSBT3710
007300 //STEPLIB   DD   DSN=CSCJGJ.CSC.LOADLIB,DISP=SHR
007400 //          DD   DSN=SYS1.COB2LIB,DISP=SHR
007500 //TRANSFIN  DD   DSN=&&TRANSOUT,
007600 //          DISP=(OLD,DELETE)
007700 //ERROUT1   DD   SYSOUT=*
007800 //SYSOUT    DD   SYSOUT=*
007900 //SYSDBOUT  DD   SYSOUT=*
008000 //
```

Old master file for first run is a sequential data set. For all subsequent runs the old master file is the (0) generation.

Output is the (+1) generation

New master file remains the (+1) generation until job ends!

Figure 17.4 JCL for the Sequential Update

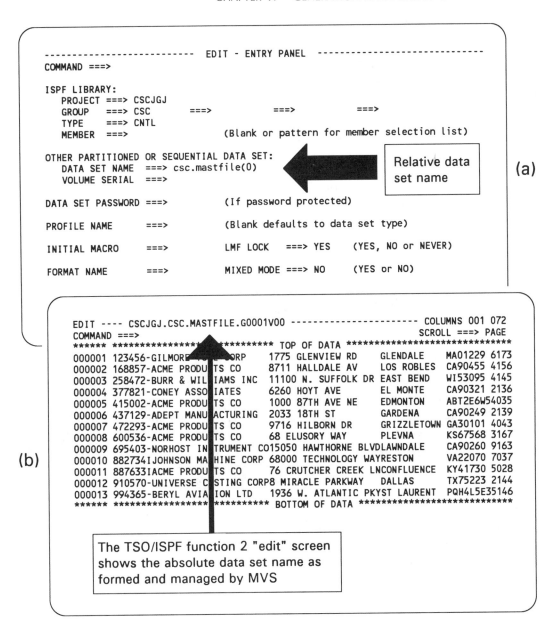

Figure 17.5   Editing a Generation Data Group Using TSO/ISPF

(a) The edit-entry screen shows you how to enter the relative data set name of a sequential data set. (b) The top of the edit screen itself shows you the absolute data set name.

```
                    J E S 2   J O B   L O G  --  S Y S T E M   I B M 1  --  N O D E   N 1

10.22.13 JOB05838  IRR010I USERID CSCJGJ   IS ASSIGNED TO THIS JOB.
10.22.14 JOB05838  ICH70001I CSCJGJ   LAST ACCESS AT 10:15:53 ON TUESDAY, NOVEMBER 24, 1992
10.22.14 JOB05838  $HASP373 CSCJGJA STARTED - INIT  1 - CLASS A - SYS IBM1
10.22.22 JOB05838  $HASP395 CSCJGJA ENDED

------ JES2 JOB STATISTICS ------
    24 NOV 92 JOB EXECUTION DATE
          79 CARDS READ
         282 SYSOUT PRINT RECORDS
           0 SYSOUT PUNCH RECORDS
          20 SYSOUT SPOOL KBYTES
        0.14 MINUTES EXECUTION TIME

     1 //CSCJGJA  JOB 1,'BIN 7--JANOSSY',CLASS=A,MSGCLASS=X,MSGLEVEL=(1,1),    JOB05838
       //   NOTIFY=CSCJGJ                                                      00020000
       //*                                                                     00030000
       //*    THIS JCL IS STORED AT CSCJGJ.CSC.CNTL(K3GDG)                     00040000
       //*                                                                     00050000
                       -
                       -
                       -
       //*******************************************************************   00260000
       //*                                                               *     00270000
       //*    RUN THE UPDATE PROGRAM                                     *     00280000
       //*                                                               *     00290000
       //*******************************************************************   00300000
     9 //STEP020   EXEC  PGM=FSBT3708                                          00310000
    10 //STEPLIB   DD    DSN=CSCJGJ.CSC.LOADLIB,DISP=SHR                       00320001
    11 //          DD    DSN=SYS1.COB2LIB,DISP=SHR                            00330001
    12 //TRANSIN   DD    DSN=&&TRANSORT,                                       00340000
       //   DISP=(OLD,DELETE)                                                  00350000
    13 //MFIN      DD    DSN=CSCJGJ.CSC.MASTFILE(0),    ┌─────────────────┐    00360002
       //   DISP=SHR                                     │ Old master file (0) │ 00380000
    14 //TRANSOUT  DD    DSN=&&TRANSOUT,                └─────────────────┘    00390000
       //   DISP=(NEW,PASS,DELETE),                                            00400000
       //   UNIT=SYSDA,                                                        00410000
       //   DCB=(RECFM=FB,LRECL=99,BLKSIZE=6138),                             00420000
       //   SPACE=(6138,(3,2),RLSE)                                            00430000
    15 //MFOUT     DD    DSN=CSCJGJ.CSC.MASTFILE(+1),  ┌──────────────────────┐00440000
       //   DISP=(NEW,CATLG,DELETE),                    │ New master file (+ 1) │00450000
       //   UNIT=SYSDA,                                 └──────────────────────┘00460000
       //   DCB=(CSCJGJ.CSC.MODLDSCB,RECFM=FB,LRECL=80,BLKSIZE=6160),          00470000
       //   SPACE=(6160,(3,2),RLSE)                                            00480000
                       -            ┌───────────────────────────────────┐
                       -            │ Note use of model DSCB in the DCB! │
                       -            └───────────────────────────────────┘

IEF142I CSCJGJA STEP020 - STEP WAS EXECUTED - COND CODE 0000
IEF285I    CSCJGJ.CSC.LOADLIB                       KEPT       ┌──────────────────┐
IEF285I    VOL SER NOS= ACSCAT.                                │ Old master file  │
IEF285I    SYS1.COB2LIB                             KEPT       │ read as input    │
IEF285I    VOL SER NOS= ACSRES.                                └──────────────────┘
IEF285I    SYS92329.T102214.RA000.CSCJGJA.TRANSORT  DELETED
IEF285I    VOL SER NOS= USER01.
IEF285I    CSCJGJ.CSC.MASTFILE.G0001V00             KEPT
IEF285I    VOL SER NOS= ACSSMP.
IEF285I    SYS92329.T102214.RA000.CSCJGJA.TRANSOUT  PASSED
IEF285I    VOL SER NOS= USER03.                                ┌──────────────────────┐
IEF285I    CSCJGJ.CSC.MASTFILE.G0002V00             CATALOGED  │ New master file is   │
IEF285I    VOL SER NOS= ACSCAT.                                │ the next generation  │
IEF285I    CSCJGJ.CSCJGJA.JOB05838.D0000103.?       SYSOUT     └──────────────────────┘
IEF285I    CSCJGJ.CSCJGJA.JOB05838.D0000104.?       SYSOUT
IEF285I    CSCJGJ.CSCJGJA.JOB05838.D0000105.?       SYSOUT
IEF373I STEP /STEP020 / START 92329.1022
IEF374I STEP /STEP020 / STOP  92329.1022 CPU    0MIN 00.32SEC SRB    0MIN 00.02SEC
                       -
                       -
```

Figure 17.6 MVS Systems Output Shows Absolute Data Set Name

17.10 Skipping Absolute Generation Numbers

Each time you create another generation of a GDG data set, MVS increases the Gnnnn number by the amount you specify in (+n). You can skip absolute generation numbers, either accidentally or on purpose, by creating a (+2) generation and no (+1) in the same job. This causes no error at creation or later but does leave a "hole" in the series of absolute data set names.

The absence of a generation number in the absolute name number series will not affect any reference to data sets by relative generation number. MVS doesn't care about specific "Gnnnn" numbers; it only uses them to make the names of generation data sets different from one another.

17.11 Using IDCAMS to List the Contents of a GDG Base

You can use the IDCAMS utility to list the catalog-stored contents of the GDG base at any time. The JCL and control statements to do this are in Figure 17.7a. Figure 17.7b shows you the base contents for CSCJGJ.CSC.MASTFILE after a few runs of my update job stream.

17.12 Mass Access to All Data Sets in a GDG

You can automatically concatenate all generations of a GDG and receive them as input to a program by simply coding the generation data group name without any relative generation number. I did this in the JCL shown in Figure 17.8. This is very handy when you use a GDG to "pool" raw data being conveyed via data entry tapes or transmissions and then process it all as one batch.

You can also delete all generations of a GDG with the same mass-access technique. Figure 17.9a shows you an IEFBR14 job that deletes all four generations of my CSCJGJ.CSC.MASTFILE. As you can see in the system output in Figure 17.9b, when you do a mass access to all generations of a GDG you get the most current (0) generation, then the next most current (-1) generation, then the next (-2) generation, and so forth. When you do delete all generations of a GDG, the base will remain but will have no data set "associations." Then if you create the next generation of the data set as the (+1) generation, its absolute data set name will end with .G0001V00.

(text continues on page 304)

```
EDIT ---- CSCJGJ.CSC.CNTL(K4LIST) - 01.00 ------------------- COLUMNS 001 072
COMMAND ===>                                              SCROLL ===> PAGE
***** **************************** TOP OF DATA *****************************
000100 //CSCJGJA   JOB 1,'BIN 7 JANOSSY',CLASS=A,MSGCLASS=X,MSGLEVEL=(1,1),
000200 // NOTIFY=CSCJGJ
000300 //*
000400 //*   THIS JCL IS STORED AT CSCJGJ.CSC.CNTL(K4LIST)
000500 //*
000600 //***********************************************************************
000700 //*                                                                   *
000800 //*   ASK IDCAMS TO LIST ENTRIES FOR A GENERATION DATA GROUP          *
000900 //*                                                                   *
001000 //***********************************************************************
001100 //STEP010  EXEC  PGM=IDCAMS
001200 //SYSPRINT   DD   SYSOUT=*
001300 //SYSIN      DD   *
001400    LISTCAT  GDG  ENTRIES('CSCJGJ.CSC.MASTFILE')  ALL
001500 /*
001600 //
```

(a)

```
IDCAMS  SYSTEM SERVICES              TIME: 10:30:03      11/24/92    PAGE   1

   LISTCAT  GDG  ENTRIES('CSCJGJ.CSC.MASTFILE')  ALL               00140000

GDG BASE ------ CSCJGJ.CSC.MASTFILE
      IN-CAT --- SYS1.USERCAT
      HISTORY
          DATASET-OWNER-----CSCJGJ      CREATION--------1992.329
          RELEASE---------------2       EXPIRATION------9999.999
      ATTRIBUTES
          LIMIT-----------------4       SCRATCH         NOEMPTY
      ASSOCIATIONS
        NONVSAM--CSCJGJ.CSC.MASTFILE.G0004V00
        NONVSAM--CSCJGJ.CSC.MASTFILE.G0005V00
        NONVSAM--CSCJGJ.CSC.MASTFILE.G0006V00
        NONVSAM--CSCJGJ.CSC.MASTFILE.G0007V00
```

(b)

(c)

```
------------------------ TSO COMMAND PROCESSOR ----------------------------
ENTER TSO COMMAND, CLIST, OR REXX EXEC BELOW:

===> listcat gdg entries('cscjgj.csc.mastfile') all



GDG BASE ------ CSCJGJ.CSC.MASTFILE
      IN-CAT --- SYS1.USERCAT
      HISTORY
          DATASET-OWNER-----CSCJGJ      CREATION--------1992.329
          RELEASE---------------2       EXPIRATION------9999.999
      ATTRIBUTES
          LIMIT-----------------4       SCRATCH         NOEMPTY
      ASSOCIATIONS
        NONVSAM--CSCJGJ.CSC.MASTFILE.G0004V00
        NONVSAM--CSCJGJ.CSC.MASTFILE.G0005V00
        NONVSAM--CSCJGJ.CSC.MASTFILE.G0006V00
        NONVSAM--CSCJGJ.CSC.MASTFILE.G0007V00
  ***
```

Figure 17.7   (a) JCL to List the Contents of a GDG Base. (b) Output Produced by This JCL. (c) TSO Command to Do the Same Thing.

```
EDIT ---- CSCJGJ.CSC.CNTL(K5MASS) - 01.00 ------------------- COLUMNS 001 072
COMMAND ===>                                              SCROLL ===> PAGE
****** *************************** TOP OF DATA *******************************
000100 //CSCJGJA   JOB 1,'BIN 7 JANOSSY',CLASS=A,MSGCLASS=X,MSGLEVEL=(1,1),
000200 // NOTIFY=CSCJGJ
000300 //*
000400 //*   THIS JCL IS STORED AT CSCJGJ.CSC.CNTL(K5MASS)
000500 //*
000600 //*****************************************************************
000700 //*                                                              *
000800 //*   HOUSEKEEPING DELETE FOR THE FILE TO BE CREATED             *
000900 //*                                                              *
001000 //*****************************************************************
001100 //STEP010   EXEC  PGM=IEFBR14
001200 //DEL1        DD  DSN=CSCJGJ.CSC.ONEHEAP,
001300 //  DISP=(MOD,DELETE),
001400 //  UNIT=SYSDA,
001500 //  SPACE=(TRK,0)
001600 //*
001700 //*****************************************************************
001800 //*                                                              *
001900 //*   MASS ACCESS ALL GENERATIONS OF GDG BY OMITTING GENERATION # *
002000 //*                                                              *
002100 //*****************************************************************
002200 //STEP020   EXEC  PGM=IEBGENER
002300 //SYSPRINT    DD  SYSOUT=*
002400 //SYSIN       DD  DUMMY
002500 //SYSUT1      DD  DSN=CSCJGJ.CSC.MASTFILE,
002600 // DISP=SHR
002700 //SYSUT2      DD  DSN=*.STEP010.DEL1,
002800 //  DISP=(NEW,CATLG,DELETE),
002900 //  UNIT=SYSDA,
003000 //  DCB=(RECFM=FB,LRECL=80,BLKSIZE=6160),
003100 //  SPACE=(6160,(3,2),RLSE)
003200 //
```

> This data set will house all generations, concatenated

(a)

> Not coding relative generation number causes MVS to process all generations, most recent to oldest

(b)

```
IEF142I CSCJGJA STEP020 - STEP WAS EXECUTED - COND CODE 0000
IEF285I   CSCJGJ.CSCJGJA.JOB05864.D0000101.?        SYSOUT
IEF285I   CSCJGJ.CSC.MASTFILE.G0007V00              KEPT
IEF285I   VOL SER NOS= ACSSMP.
IEF285I   CSCJGJ.CSC.MASTFILE.G0006V00
IEF285I   VOL SER NOS= ACSSMP.
IEF285I   CSCJGJ.CSC.MASTFILE.G0005V00
IEF285I   VOL SER NOS= ACSCAT.
IEF285I   CSCJGJ.CSC.MASTFILE.G0004V00              KEPT
IEF285I   VOL SER NOS= ACSSMP.
IEF285I   CSCJGJ.CSC.ONEHEAP                        CATALOGED
IEF285I   VOL SER NOS= ACSSMP.
IEF373I STEP /STEP020 / START 92329.1036
IEF374I STEP /STEP020 / STOP  92329.1036 CPU  0MIN 00.32SEC SRB   0MIN 00.01SEC
IEF375I JOB /CSCJGJA / START 92329.1036
IEF376I JOB /CSCJGJA / STOP  92329.1036 CPU  0MIN 00.36SEC SRB   0MIN 00.01SEC

DATA SET UTILITY - GENERATE
PROCESSING ENDED AT EOD
```

Figure 17.8 (a) JCL to Copy All Members of the GDG to a Single Data Set. (b) Output of This JCL.

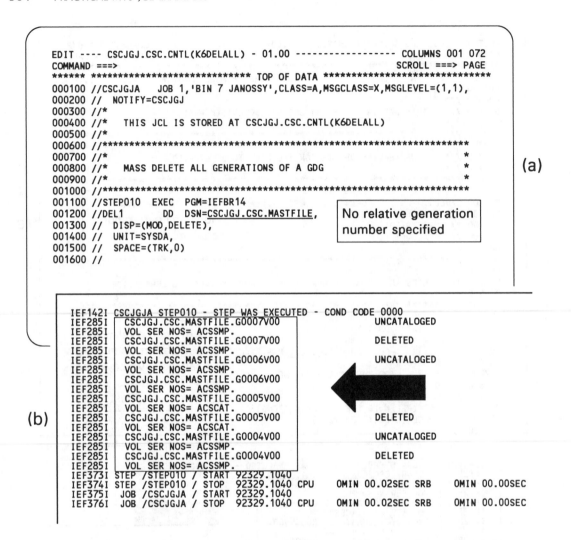

```
EDIT ---- CSCJGJ.CSC.CNTL(K6DELALL) - 01.00 ----------------- COLUMNS 001 072
COMMAND ===>                                          SCROLL ===> PAGE
****** ***************************** TOP OF DATA *****************************
000100 //CSCJGJA   JOB 1,'BIN 7 JANOSSY',CLASS=A,MSGCLASS=X,MSGLEVEL=(1,1),
000200 // NOTIFY=CSCJGJ
000300 //*
000400 //*   THIS JCL IS STORED AT CSCJGJ.CSC.CNTL(K6DELALL)
000500 //*
000600 //******************************************************************
000700 //*                                                              *
000800 //*   MASS DELETE ALL GENERATIONS OF A GDG                       *
000900 //*                                                              *
001000 //******************************************************************
001100 //STEP010   EXEC  PGM=IEFBR14
001200 //DEL1        DD  DSN=CSCJGJ.CSC.MASTFILE,
001300 // DISP=(MOD,DELETE),
001400 // UNIT=SYSDA,
001500 // SPACE=(TRK,0)
001600 //
```

(a)

No relative generation number specified

(b)

```
IEF142I CSCJGJA STEP010 - STEP WAS EXECUTED - COND CODE 0000
IEF285I   CSCJGJ.CSC.MASTFILE.G0007V00                    UNCATALOGED
IEF285I   VOL SER NOS= ACSSMP.
IEF285I   CSCJGJ.CSC.MASTFILE.G0007V00                    DELETED
IEF285I   VOL SER NOS= ACSSMP.
IEF285I   CSCJGJ.CSC.MASTFILE.G0006V00                    UNCATALOGED
IEF285I   VOL SER NOS= ACSSMP.
IEF285I   CSCJGJ.CSC.MASTFILE.G0006V00
IEF285I   VOL SER NOS= ACSSMP.
IEF285I   CSCJGJ.CSC.MASTFILE.G0005V00
IEF285I   VOL SER NOS= ACSCAT.
IEF285I   CSCJGJ.CSC.MASTFILE.G0005V00                    DELETED
IEF285I   VOL SER NOS= ACSCAT.
IEF285I   CSCJGJ.CSC.MASTFILE.G0004V00                    UNCATALOGED
IEF285I   VOL SER NOS= ACSSMP.
IEF285I   CSCJGJ.CSC.MASTFILE.G0004V00                    DELETED
IEF285I   VOL SER NOS= ACSSMP.
IEF373I STEP /STEP010 / START 92329.1040
IEF374I STEP /STEP010 / STOP  92329.1040 CPU   0MIN 00.02SEC SRB   0MIN 00.00SEC
IEF375I JOB /CSCJGJA / START 92329.1040
IEF376I JOB /CSCJGJA / STOP  92329.1040 CPU   0MIN 00.02SEC SRB   0MIN 00.00SEC
```

Figure 17.9 (a) JCL to Delete All Generations of a GDG. (b) MVS System Output Documenting the Deletions.

17.13 Deleting a GDG Base

You can use IDCAMS to delete a generation data group base with this IDCAMS control statement:

```
DELETE  CSCJGJ.CSC.MASTFILE  GDG
```

but this works only if the base had no expiration date or its expiration date has already been reached, and if no generations of the data set exist. When either of these conditions is violated, your GDG base deletion fails.

You can delete the GDG base even if its expiration has not been reached by coding the extra word PURGE, as shown in Figure 17.10. This deletion will fail if the base has any associations, that is, if there are data set generations still being managed by the base.

You can delete the GDG base even if generations still exist by coding the extra word FORCE:

```
DELETE   CSCJGJ.CSC.MASTFILE   GDG   PURGE   FORCE
```

DELETE with FORCE does not delete any generation data sets themselves. They still exist after the GDG base deletion, but you can only access them by their absolute names. Using DELETE with PURGE is common, but using it with FORCE is unusual.

17.14 Tape GDGs and Expiration Date

LIMIT in the GDG base controls how many generations of the data set the base will keep track of. When the limit is reached, you usually want the oldest then-existing generation to "drop off" the GDG.

When LIMIT is reached, you can have the GDG mechanism uncatalog and delete the oldest GDG data set if it is on disk and carries no expiration date or an expired date. (NOEMPTY and SCRATCH in the GDG base specify this.) For this and other reasons, you ordinarily do not put any expiration date on a disk data set. But tape data sets are not always mounted, and the expiration date for a tape data set is in its data set label (on the tape itself). The GDG mechanism can uncatalog a tape data set but can't actually "scratch" it.

The GDG mechanism manages data set names only. It has nothing to do with data set retention period. Retention of tape data sets is wholly dependent on their expiration date. *Just because a tape data set is carried in a GDG base as one of the generations doesn't protect the tape from being used as a scratch tape if its expiration date has been reached!*

For tape-stored GDG data sets, you need to code the DD statement LABEL parameter appropriately with a suitable expiration date or retention period. The value you specify for retention must be great enough to keep the data set alive until it "drops off" the GDG. You should specify a retention period for a tape GDG as conservatively long as possible. If an application becomes inactive, the tapes supporting it will disappear as they reach their expiration dates!

```
EDIT ---- CSCJGJ.CSC.CNTL(K7DELBAS) - 01.00 ----------------- COLUMNS 001 072
COMMAND ===>                                             SCROLL ===> PAGE
***** ***************************** TOP OF DATA ******************************
000100 //CSCJGJA   JOB 1,'BIN 7 JANOSSY',CLASS=A,MSGCLASS=X,MSGLEVEL=(1,1),
000200 //  NOTIFY=CSCJGJ
000300 //*
000400 //*    THIS JCL IS STORED AT CSCJGJ.CSC.CNTL(K7DELBAS)
000500 //*
000600 //*****************************************************************
000700 //*                                                              *
000800 //*    USE IDCAMS TO DELETE GDG BASE                             *
000900 //*                                                              *
001000 //*****************************************************************
001100 //STEP010  EXEC  PGM=IDCAMS
001200 //SYSPRINT    DD  SYSOUT=*
001300 //SYSIN       DD  *
001400     DELETE    CSCJGJ.CSC.MASTFILE  GDG  PURGE
001500 /*
001600 //

JOB CSCJGJA(JOB05896) SUBMITTED
10.54.13 JOB05896 $HASP395 CSCJGJA  ENDED AT N1 CN(INTERNAL)
***
```
(a)

```
                    J E S 2   J O B   L O G  --  S Y S T E M   I B M 1   --   N O D

10.54.12 JOB05896  IRR010I  USERID CSCJGJ   IS ASSIGNED TO THIS JOB.
10.54.13 JOB05896  ICH70001I CSCJGJ   LAST ACCESS AT 10:47:40 ON TUESDAY, NOVEMBER
10.54.13 JOB05896  $HASP373 CSCJGJA  STARTED - INIT 1 - CLASS A - SYS IBM1
10.54.13 JOB05896  $HASP395 CSCJGJA  ENDED

------ JES2 JOB STATISTICS ------
    24 NOV 92 JOB EXECUTION DATE
        15 CARDS READ
        44 SYSOUT PRINT RECORDS
         0 SYSOUT PUNCH RECORDS
         3 SYSOUT SPOOL KBYTES
      0.01 MINUTES EXECUTION TIME

     1 //CSCJGJA   JOB 1,'BIN 7 JANOSSY',CLASS=A,MSGCLASS=X,MSGLEVEL=(1,1),
       //  NOTIFY=CSCJGJ
       //*
       //*    THIS JCL IS STORED AT CSCJGJ.CSC.CNTL(K7DELBAS)
       //*
        -
        -

IEF142I CSCJGJA STEP010 - STEP WAS EXECUTED - COND CODE 0000
IEF285I    CSCJGJ.CSCJGJA.JOB05896.D0000102.?        SYSOUT
IEF285I    CSCJGJ.CSCJGJA.JOB05896.D0000101.?        SYSIN
IEF373I STEP /STEP010 / START 92329.1054
IEF374I STEP /STEP010 / STOP  92329.1054 CPU    0MIN 00.53SEC SRB    0MIN 00.00SEC
IEF375I  JOB /CSCJGJA / START 92329.1054
IEF376I  JOB /CSCJGJA / STOP  92329.1054 CPU    0MIN 00.53SEC SRB    0MIN 00.00SEC
```
(b)

```
IDCAMS  SYSTEM SERVICES              TIME: 10:54:13      11/24/92    PAGE   1

    DELETE   CSCJGJ.CSC.MASTFILE  GDG  PURGE                        00140000

IDC0550I ENTRY (B) CSCJGJ.CSC.MASTFILE DELETED
IDC0001I FUNCTION COMPLETED, HIGHEST CONDITION CODE WAS 0
```

```
IDC0002I IDCAMS PROCESSING COMPLETE. MAXIMUM CONDITION CODE WAS 0
```

Figure 17.10   JCL to Delete a GDG Base before Its Expiration Date Has Been Reached

Chapter Eighteen

INSTREAM AND CATALOGED PROCEDURES

Once you understand how to use JCL to write a job stream, you can take the next step and learn how to "package" the job stream for convenient, repeated execution. Packaging a job stream means housing it as a cataloged procedure. As a proc, the JCL is stored on the computer system hidden from view. You (or any other authorized person) can execute a proc with only a few lines of execution JCL.

Procs are widely used in business data processing. In this chapter I'll show you how to convert the JCL for a job stream into a proc.

18.1 A Simple Job Stream

The clearest way to understand how you package JCL as a proc is to see me do it with a very simple job stream. Figure 18.1 shows you a one-step job stream named L1DUMP that "dumps" the contents of a data set in character and hexadecimal. This JCL is "raw": it is not housed as a proc. It includes instream control statements to the IDCAMS utility, giving it instructions to dump up to 50 records.

I am going to convert this job stream to a proc so that I can simplify the task of submitting a dump and routing its print output.

18.2 How to Convert JCL to a Proc

You follow a checklist of nine actions to convert raw JCL into a proc. These actions are the same no matter how simple or complex your job stream is.

CHECKLIST
How to Convert JCL to a Procedure (Proc)

1. Test the job stream "raw." You should only convert already func-
   tioning JCL into a proc!
2. Separate the JOB statement from the JCL with a PROC statement
   giving the proc a name.
3. Separate the // null statement from the JCL with a PEND statement followed by an EXEC of the proc name.
4. Remove instream data and put it into a data set or member of a
   data set. Change the JCL to refer to that data and remove any
   vestige of instream data.
5. Replace whatever values in the JCL will change from run to run
   with **symbolic parameters,** which are place-holders for real
   values.
6. Code default values for the symbolic parameters on the PROC
   statement.
7. Test the proc "instream" (all in one piece).
8. Remove and give the tested proc to a person authorized to install
   it in a regular proc library such as SYS1.PROCLIB.
9. Compose execution JCL to confirm installation of the proc by
   using what remains of the instream proc: the JOB statement at
   the top and the EXEC PROC=procname at the bottom.

If this sounds like a lot of work, calm down. Most of these actions take just
a few seconds!

18.3 A First PROC Example: The Start

Figure 18.2 shows you how my L1DUMP proc looks after I've taken the first
few steps to convert it into a proc. I have inserted two lines of hyphens to
separate the JCL in the middle (which will eventually become the installed
proc) from the execution JCL at the top and bottom. I've installed a PROC
statement, naming it DUMPPROC, and applied a PEND statement followed
by an EXEC that executes the proc. And finally I've taken the control statements for IDCAMS out of the JCL (this was originally instream data at
//SYSIN DD *) and housed them separately as member CCDUMP (the CC
is an acronym for Control Card).

Lines 000700 through 001300 in Figure 18.2 make up a valid proc! I
could submit the JCL in Figure 18.2 to test the proc. But I've done only the
first four actions in the checklist.

```
 EDIT --- CSCJGJ.CSC.CNTL(L1DUMP) - 01.01 ------------------- COLUMNS 001 072
 COMMAND ===> sub                                           SCROLL ===> PAGE
 ****** ***************************** TOP OF DATA *******************************
 000100 //CSCJGJA   JOB 1,'BIN 7 JANOSSY',CLASS=A,MSGLEVEL=(1,1),MSGCLASS=X,
 000200 // NOTIFY=CSCJGJ
 000300 //*
 000400 //*    THIS JCL IS STORED AT CSCJGJ.CSC.CNTL(L1DUMP)
 000500 //*
 000600 //STEPA     EXEC  PGM=IDCAMS           ┌─────────────────────────┐
 000700 //SYSPRINT   DD   SYSOUT=*             │ Raw JCL contains a      │
 000800 //DD1        DD   DSN=CSCJGJ.CSC.CNTL(WORKERS), │ JOB statement,      │
 000900 // DISP=SHR                            │ EXECs and DDs, and      │
 001000 //SYSIN      DD   *                    │ an ending // null       │
 001100     PRINT        INFILE(DD1) -         │ statement               │
 001200                  COUNT(50) -           └─────────────────────────┘
 001300                  DUMP
 001400 //
 ****** ***************************** BOTTOM OF DATA ****************************

 JOB CSCJGJA(JOB08239) SUBMITTED
 ***
```

Figure 18.1   Raw JCL to Use IDCAMS to Dump a Data Set

This JCL executes the IDCAMS program and feeds it control statements housed as instream data to cause it to dump up to 50 records of a data set for analysis.

18.4 A First PROC Example: Continuing the Conversion

Every run of DUMPPROC shown in Figure 18.2 will dump the same data set. This isn't really very practical. In Figure 18.3 you see an additional change in the JCL. I have removed the data set name CSCJGJ.CSC.CNTL (WORKERS) at line 001000 and replaced it with a place-holder named &INPUT. A place-holder like this is called a *symbolic parameter.* You create symbolic parameters using a single ampersand & and up to seven characters. You can give symbolic parameters actual values through the JCL that executes the proc, and you can also define default values for them on the PROC statement. You can use the same symbolic parameter in many places in JCL to give the same execution-supplied or default value to several things automatically.

In Figure 18.3 you can see how I am giving the symbolic parameter &INPUT an actual value via the EXEC statement that invokes the proc

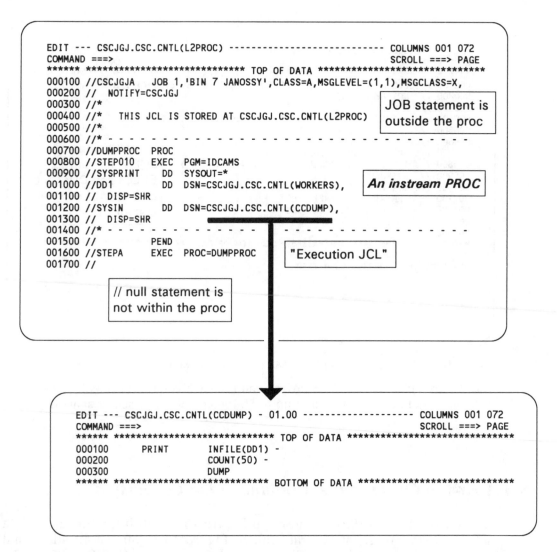

```
EDIT --- CSCJGJ.CSC.CNTL(L2PROC) -------------------------- COLUMNS 001 072
COMMAND ===>                                                SCROLL ===> PAGE
****** **************************** TOP OF DATA ******************************
000100 //CSCJGJA   JOB 1,'BIN 7 JANOSSY',CLASS=A,MSGLEVEL=(1,1),MSGCLASS=X,
000200 // NOTIFY=CSCJGJ
000300 //*                                            ┌─────────────────────┐
000400 //*    THIS JCL IS STORED AT CSCJGJ.CSC.CNTL(L2PROC)  JOB statement is │
000500 //*                                            │ outside the proc     │
000600 //* - - - - - - - - - - - - - - - - - - - - - -└─ - - - - - - - - - - ┘
000700 //DUMPPROC   PROC
000800 //STEP010   EXEC  PGM=IDCAMS
000900 //SYSPRINT    DD  SYSOUT=*                      ┌─────────────────────┐
001000 //DD1         DD  DSN=CSCJGJ.CSC.CNTL(WORKERS), │ An instream PROC     │
001100 // DISP=SHR                                     └─────────────────────┘
001200 //SYSIN       DD  DSN=CSCJGJ.CSC.CNTL(CCDUMP),
001300 // DISP=SHR
001400 //* - - - - - - - - - - - -   - - - - - - - - - - - -
001500 //          PEND                                ┌─────────────────────┐
001600 //STEPA     EXEC  PROC=DUMPPROC                 │ "Execution JCL"      │
001700 //                                              └─────────────────────┘
```

┌─────────────────────┐
│ // null statement is │
│ not within the proc │
└─────────────────────┘

```
EDIT --- CSCJGJ.CSC.CNTL(CCDUMP) - 01.00 ------------------- COLUMNS 001 072
COMMAND ===>                                                SCROLL ===> PAGE
****** **************************** TOP OF DATA ******************************
000100    PRINT        INFILE(DD1) -
000200                 COUNT(50) -
000300                 DUMP
****** **************************** BOTTOM OF DATA ***************************
```

Figure 18.2   The IDCAMS Dump as an "Inconvenient" Proc

This is a procedure ("proc") but it will always dump the same data set. It needs symbolic parameters to make it more convenient. I have removed the IDCAMS control statements and put them into a library as a member because procs can't contain instream data.

```
EDIT --- CSCJGJ.CSC.CNTL(L3SYMBOL) ------------------------ COLUMNS 001 072
COMMAND ===>                                                SCROLL ===> PAGE
****** *************************** TOP OF DATA ********************************
000100 //CSCJGJA    JOB 1,'BIN 7 JANOSSY',CLASS=A,MSGLEVEL=(1,1),MSGCLASS=X,
000200 // NOTIFY=CSCJGJ
000300 //*
000400 //*   THIS JCL IS STORED AT CSCJGJ.CSC.CNTL(L3SYMBOL)
000500 //*
000600 //* - - - - - - - - - - - - - - - - - - - - - - - - - -
000700 //DUMPPROC   PROC
000800 //STEP010    EXEC  PGM=IDCAMS
000900 //SYSPRINT    DD   SYSOUT=*
001000 //DD1         DD   DSN=&INPUT,
001100 // DISP=SHR
001200 //SYSIN       DD   DSN=CSCJGJ.CSC.CNTL(CCDUMP),
001300 // DISP=SHR
001400 //* - - - - - - - - - - - - - - - - - - - - - - - - - -
001500 //          PEND
001600 //STEPA     EXEC  PROC=DUMPPROC,INPUT='CSCJGJ.CSC.CNTL(WORKERS)'
001700 //
```

Figure 18.3   The Dump Proc with One Symbolic Parameter

I replaced the hardcoded name of a data set at //DD1 with the place holder &INPUT. This a *symbolic parameter*. It lets me specify a data set name to dump on the EXEC statement for the proc. I can specify a different data set to dump with each run.

(notice that you don't code the ampersand on the EXEC; you code it only in the proc):

```
//STEPA  EXEC  PROC=DUMPPROC,INPUT='CSCJGJ.CSC.CNTL(WORKERS)'
```

When you supply a value for a symbolic parameter in this way, you should understand what MVS actually does. It acts much like a word processor and simply substitutes the actual value for any occurrence of the symbolic parameter in the proc. You don't "frame" data set names with the IBM quote (the apostrophe) when you write JCL. But when you supply actual values for symbolic parameters, you do treat the values as character strings because that's how MVS handles symbolic parameter substitutions.

18.5 Running a Simple Proc Instream

Figure 18.4 shows you the system output produced when I submit the instream proc shown in Figure 18.3. Instream execution has MVS "read in" the instream proc, numbering all of it as one JCL statement. MVS stores it temporarily. Then, when MVS processes your EXEC PROC= ... statement, it "draws in" the proc as if it has been installed in a real proc library. As it does this drawing in, it edits the proc to substitute actual values for the symbolic parameters. Then (finally!) it interprets the JCL and executes it.

MVS changes the // on proc-supplied JCL to ++ when you invoke an instream proc. When you invoke an installed cataloged procedure (see Section 18.7), it changes the // to XX instead. You see the result of symbolic parameter substitutions differently in different versions of MVS. In Figure 18.4 you see the substitutions at the end of the JCL, as OS/MVS traditionally listed them. MVS/XA and MVS/ESA imbed this substitution information within the edited JCL, as shown in Figure 18.6.

18.6 Multiple Symbolic Parameters

I've enhanced my DUMPPROC in Figure 18.5 by adding a second symbolic parameter name &TO. I used this as a place-holder for the print class. By coding a default value for &TO on the PROC statement, it's possible to omit coding a value for TO on the EXEC and still have the proc function.

Once you have defined symbolic parameters, MVS **must** have a way to satisfy each of them. "Unresolved" symbolic parameters are those that receive no actual value either through the EXEC statement that invokes the proc or from a PROC statement default. MVS fails any job that contains unresolved symbolic parameters.

To code a default for a symbolic parameter you code its name (without &) on the PROC statement:

```
//DUMPPROC  PROC  TO='*'
```

In this case, //SYSUT2 output will be directed to SYSOUT=* by default unless I code a replacement value for TO on the EXEC statement. I didn't establish a default value for the &INPUT symbolic parameter because no default value seemed reasonable. It would be better to code the PROC statement as follows to make an invalid value the default for &INPUT and to document all symbolic parameters on the PROC statement with same-line comments:

```
//DUMPPROC  PROC  TO='*',     TO     IS OUTPUT PRINT CLASS
//  INPUT='***'               INPUT  IS DATA SET NAME TO DUMP
```

```
                     J E S 2   J O B   L O G   --   S Y S T E M   E X P R   --   N O D E   N 1

------- JOB 8268  IEF097I CSCJGJA  - USER CSCJGJ    ASSIGNED
17.18.45 JOB 8268  ICH70001I CSCJGJ   LAST ACCESS AT 17:16:35 ON SATURDAY, JUNE 27, 1992
17.18.45 JOB 8268  $HASP373 CSCJGJA  STARTED - INIT  2 - CLASS A - SYS EXPR
17.18.47 JOB 8268  $HASP395 CSCJGJA  ENDED

------ JES2 JOB STATISTICS ------
 27 JUN 92 JOB EXECUTION DATE
         16 CARDS READ
        154 SYSOUT PRINT RECORDS
          0 SYSOUT PUNCH RECORDS
         11 SYSOUT SPOOL KBYTES
       0.04 MINUTES EXECUTION TIME
```

```
      1    //CSCJGJA   JOB 1,'BIN 7 JANOSSY',CLASS=A,MSGLEVEL=(1,1),MSGCLASS=X,    JOB 8268
           //  NOTIFY=CSCJGJ                                                       00020000
           ***                                                                     00030000
           ***   THIS JCL IS STORED AT CSCJGJ.CSC.CNTL(L3SYMBOL)                    00040000
           ***                                                                     00050000
           *** - - - - - - - - - - - - - - - - - - - - - - - - - - - - - -         00060000
           //DUMPPROC  PROC                                                        00070000
           //STEP010   EXEC   PGM=IDCAMS                                           00080000
           //SYSPRINT  DD     SYSOUT=*                                              00090000
           //DD1       DD     DSN=&INPUT,                                           00100000
           //  DISP=SHR                                                            00110000
           //SYSIN     DD     DSN=CSCJGJ.CSC.CNTL(CCDUMP),                          00120000
           //  DISP=SHR                                                            00130000
           //* - - - - - - - - - - - - - - - - - - - - - - - - - - - - - -         00140000
           //          PEND                                                        00150000
      2    //STEPA     EXEC   PROC=DUMPPROC,INPUT='CSCJGJ.CSC.CNTL(WORKERS)'        00160000
      3    ++DUMPPROC  PROC                                                        00070000
      4    ++STEP010   EXEC   PGM=IDCAMS                                           00080000
      5    ++SYSPRINT  DD     SYSOUT=*                                              00090000
      6    ++DD1       DD     DSN=&INPUT.                                           00100000
           ++  DISP=SHR                                                            00110000
      7    ++SYSIN     DD     DSN=CSCJGJ.CSC.CNTL(CCDUMP),                          00120000
           ++  DISP=SHR                                                            00130000
           *** - - - - - - - - - - - - - - - - - - - - - - - - - - - - - -         00140000
```

a

b

```
STMT NO. MESSAGE

      6    IEF653I SUBSTITUTION JCL - DSN=CSCJGJ.CSC.CNTL(WORKERS),
```

c

Jobname	Stepname in proc	Stepname in execution JCL

```
IEF236I ALLOC. FOR CSCJGJA STEP010 STEPA
IEF237I JES2 ALLOCATED TO SYSPRINT
IEF237I 125  ALLOCATED TO DD1
IEF237I 121  ALLOCATED TO SYS01379
IEF237I 125  ALLOCATED TO SYSIN
IEF142I CSCJGJA STEP010 STEPA - STEP WAS EXECUTED - COND CODE 0004
IEF285I    JES2.JOB08268.SO0101                        SYSOUT
IEF285I    CSCJGJ.CSC.CNTL                              KEPT
IEF285I    VOL SER NOS= ACSCAC.
IEF285I    CATALOG.USER                                 KEPT
IEF285I    VOL SER NOS= ACSCAT.
IEF285I    CSCJGJ.CSC.CNTL                              KEPT
IEF285I    VOL SER NOS= ACSCAC.
IEF373I STEP /STEP010 / START 92179.1718
IEF374I STEP /STEP010 / STOP  92179.1718 CPU    0MIN 00.19SEC SRB    0MIN 00.01SEC

IEF375I JOB /CSCJGJA / START 92179.1718
IEF376I JOB /CSCJGJA / STOP  92179.1718 CPU    0MIN 00.19SEC SRB    0MIN 00.01SEC
```

Figure 18.4 MVS System Output from a Run of DUMPPROC (Instream)

(a) MVS reads in the proc and numbers all of it as one JCL statement. (b) MVS interprets the proc as JCL. (c) MVS shows the symbolic parameter substitutions.

```
EDIT ---- CSCJGJ.CSC.CNTL(L4SYMBOL) - 01.00 ----------------- COLUMNS 001 072
COMMAND ===> sub                                            SCROLL ===> PAGE
****** **************************** TOP OF DATA ********************************
000100 //CSCJGJA   JOB 1,'BIN 7 JANOSSY',CLASS=A,MSGLEVEL=(1,1),MSGCLASS=X,
000200 //  NOTIFY=CSCJGJ
000300 //*
000400 //*   THIS JCL IS STORED AT CSCJGJ.CSC.CNTL(L4SYMBOL)
000500 //*
000600 //* - - - - - - - - - - - - - - - - - - - - - - - - - - - - - -
000700 //DUMPPROC  PROC  TO='*'                 DEFAULT VALUE FOR &TO
000800 //STEP010   EXEC  PGM=IDCAMS
000900 //SYSPRINT    DD  SYSOUT=&TO              USE OF SYMBOLIC PARAMETER &TO
001000 //DD1         DD  DSN=&INPUT,             USE OF SYMBOLIC PARAMETER &INPUT
001100 //  DISP=SHR
001200 //SYSIN       DD  DSN=CSCJGJ.CSC.CNTL(CCDUMP),
001300 //  DISP=SHR
001400 //* - - - - - - - - - - - - - - - - - - - - - - - - - - - - - -
001500 //           PEND
001600 //STEPA     EXEC  PROC=DUMPPROC,
001700 //  INPUT='CSCJGJ.CSC.CNTL(WORKERS)'


JOB CSCJGJA(JOB01154) SUBMITTED
15.25.29 JOB01154 $HASP165 CSCJGJA  ENDED AT N1 CN(INTERNAL)
***
```

(a)
(b)
(c)

Figure 18.5 DUMPPROC with Two Symbolic Parameters and a Default

(a) TO= '*' is a default for the symbolic parameter &TO at line 000900. If the execution JCL does not give TO a value, MVS will use the default '*' as shown in Figure 18.6. (b) I have defined &TO as a symbolic parameter for print class and (as in Figure 18.3) &INPUT as a symbolic parameter for the data set to be dumped. (c) My execution JCL EXEC statement carries a default value only for INPUT, so MVS uses the default for the other symbolic parameter, TO.

Figure 18.6 shows you the top part of the MVS output produced by submitting the instream proc in Figure 18.5 for execution. You can see the two symbolic parameter substitutions after the interpreted JCL. The TO value * comes from the default on the PROC statement, and the INPUT value comes from the EXEC statement. If I had coded an actual value for TO on the EXEC statement in the execution JCL, the default would not have applied, because execution JCL takes precedence:

```
//STEPA   EXEC   PROC=DUMPPROC,
//   INPUT='CSCJGJ.CSC.CNTL(WORKERS)',
//   TO='A'
```

```
                    J E S 2   J O B   L O G  -- S Y S T E M   I B M 1  -- N O D E   N 1

15.25.27 JOB01154   IRR010I  USERID CSCJGJ   IS ASSIGNED TO THIS JOB.
15.25.28 JOB01154   ICH70001I CSCJGJ   LAST ACCESS AT 15:23:17 ON SATURDAY, NOVEMBER 28, 1992
15.25.28 JOB01154   $HASP373 CSCJGJA   STARTED - INIT  1 - CLASS A - SYS IBM1
15.25.28 JOB01154   $HASP395 CSCJGJA   ENDED

------ JES2 JOB STATISTICS ------
   28 NOV 92 JOB EXECUTION DATE
        17 CARDS READ
       154 SYSOUT PRINT RECORDS
         0 SYSOUT PUNCH RECORDS
        11 SYSOUT SPOOL KBYTES
      0.01 MINUTES EXECUTION TIME
```

```
   1 //CSCJGJA    JOB 1,'BIN 7 JANOSSY',CLASS=A,MSGLEVEL=(1,1),MSGCLASS=X,        JOB01154
     //  NOTIFY=CSCJGJ                                                            00020000
     //*                                                                          00030000
     //*     THIS JCL IS STORED AT CSCJGJ.CSC.CNTL(L4SYMBOL)                       00040000
     //*                                                                          00050000
     //* - - - - - - - - - - - - - - - - - - - - - - - - - - - - - - - -          00060000
   2 //DUMPPROC  PROC   TO='*'                                                    00070000
     //STEP010   EXEC   PGM=IDCAMS      ┌─────────────────────────────┐           00080000
     //SYSPRINT  DD     SYSOUT=&TO      │ Code any symbolic parameter │           00090000
     //DD1       DD     DSN=&INPUT,     │ defaults on the PROC statement │        00100000
     //  DISP=SHR                       └─────────────────────────────┘           00110000
     //SYSIN     DD     DSN=CSCJGJ.CSC.CNTL(CCDUMP),                               00120000
     //  DISP=SHR                                                                 00130000
     //* - - - - - - - - - - - - - - - - - - - - - - - - - - - - - - -            00140000
     //         PEND                                                              00150000
   3 //STEPA     EXEC   PROC=DUMPPROC,   ┌──────────────────────────┐             00160000
     //  INPUT='CSCJGJ.CSC.CNTL(WORKERS)' │ MVS/XA and MVS/ESA       │            00170000
   4 ++DUMPPROC  PROC   TO='*'            │ show symbolic parameter  │            00070000
   5 ++STEP010   EXEC   PGM=IDCAMS        │ value substitutions after │           00080000
   6 ++SYSPRINT  DD     SYSOUT=&TO        │ each affected line        │           00090000
     IEFC653I SUBSTITUTION JCL - SYSOUT=* └──────────────────────────┘
   7 ++DD1       DD     DSN=&INPUT,                                               00100000
     ++  DISP=SHR                                                                 00110000
     IEFC653I SUBSTITUTION JCL - DSN=CSCJGJ.CSC.CNTL(WORKERS),DISP=SHR
   8 ++SYSIN     DD     DSN=CSCJGJ.CSC.CNTL(CCDUMP),                              00120000
     ++  DISP=SHR                                                                 00130000
     ++* - - - - - - - - - - - - - - - - - - - - - - - - - - - - -               00140000
```

```
STMT NO. MESSAGE          ┌─────────────────────────────────────────────┐
                          │ MVS/ESA tells you the origin of the proc      │
                          └─────────────────────────────────────────────┘

   3 IEFC001I PROCEDURE DUMPPROC WAS EXPANDED USING INSTREAM PROCEDURE DEFINITION

ICH70001I CSCJGJ   LAST ACCESS AT 15:23:17 ON SATURDAY, NOVEMBER 28, 1992
IEF236I ALLOC. FOR CSCJGJA STEP010 STEPA
IEF237I JES2 ALLOCATED TO SYSPRINT
IEF237I 111  ALLOCATED TO DD1
IEF237I 111  ALLOCATED TO SYSIN
IEF142I CSCJGJA STEP010 STEPA - STEP WAS EXECUTED - COND CODE 0004
```

Figure 18.6 MVS/ESA System Output from DUMPPROC with &INPUT and &TO

MVS/XA and MVS/ESA show symbolic parameter substitutions after the affected
lines; the default coded on the PROC statement for &TO is '*'. MVS uses the
default for &TO because I did not give it a value on the EXEC statement.

I could also have omitted the PROC= on the EXEC statement because it defaults to PROC= (rather than PGM=) if you don't code it:

```
//STEPA   EXEC  DUMPPROC,                          PROC = omitted
//   INPUT='CSCJGJ.CSC.CNTL(WORKERS)',
//   TO='A'
```

I use PROC= in the examples in this book to simplify things. You have enough to think about without remembering so many of the more trivial MVS defaults!

18.7 Installing a Proc (Cataloged Procedure)

As a programmer or end user, you can easily build raw JCL, test it, convert it to an instream proc, create and insert symbolic parameters and defaults in the proc, and test it. To install the proc, you rip out the lines from the PROC statement to just before PEND and put them into a procedure library (proc lib). As a part of this process it's a good idea to put a comment line at the bottom of the proc to denote its end.

Figure 18.7 shows you my finished DUMPPROC. It's now fully generalized JCL and only eight lines long. It has no JOB statement at its beginning and no // null statement at its end. If I had authority to copy it to SYS1.PROCLIB as member name DUMPPROC, I could install it. But if you are like most programmers and end users, you can't write to the installation proc lib yourself. Instead, as a measure of control over what "goes into production," you pass your completed proc to an installation librarian or systems programmer who copies it to the proc lib. Once the proc is installed in SYS1.PROCLIB (or other similar system libraries), it's called a *cataloged procedure.*

18.8 Executing a Cataloged Procedure

To execute an installed proc, you simply use the JCL that remains from your instream proc testing after the heart of the JCL (the proc) has been ripped out. My execution JCL for DUMPPROC is listed in Figure 18.8. If you compare the line numbers on the JCL in Figure 18.8 with those in Figure 18.5 (the instream proc) you will see that the execution JCL is what was outside of the lines of hyphens earlier.

When you execute an installed proc, you'll only see the proc-supplied JCL once in your system output, not twice. MVS does not need to read in and temporarily store an installed proc; it simply gets it from the proc lib, applies your symbolic parameter substitutions, and executes the resulting JCL.

```
EDIT --- SYS1.PROCLIB(DUMPPROC) ---------------------------- COLUMNS 001 072
COMMAND ===>                                                  SCROLL ===> PAGE
****** **************************** TOP OF DATA ******************************
000100 //DUMPPROC   PROC   TO='*'
000200 //STEP010    EXEC   PGM=IDCAMS
000300 //SYSPRINT   DD     SYSOUT=&TO
000400 //DD1        DD     DSN=&INPUT,
000500 // DISP=SHR
000600 //SYSIN      DD     DSN=CSCJGJ.CSC.CNTL(CCDUMP),
000700 // DISP=SHR
000800 //*END DUMPPROC***
```

> # An Installed (Cataloged) PROC
>
> When you install a proc as a member of SYS1.PROCLIB or a similar
> "system" library it becomes a *cataloged procedure*. You see here an
> actual cataloged procedure I installed named **DUMPPROC**. It has no
> JOB statement and no // null statement. I added a comment at the
> bottom to explicitly mark its end, but this is entirely optional. (For an
> installed, cataloged proc, even the PROC statement is optional if the
> proc has no symbolic parameter defaults!)

Figure 18.7 How DUMPPROC Looks as an Installed Proc

```
EDIT --- CSCJGJ.CSC.CNTL(DUMPEXEC) ------------------------- COLUMNS 001 072
COMMAND ===>                                                  SCROLL ===> PAGE
****** **************************** TOP OF DATA ******************************
000100 //CSCJGJA    JOB 1,'BIN 7 JANOSSY',CLASS=A,MSGLEVEL=(1,1),MSGCLASS=X,
000200 // NOTIFY=CSCJGJ
000300 //*
000400 //*   THIS JCL IS STORED AT CSCJGJ.CSC.CNTL(DUMPEXEC)
000500 //*
001600 //STEPA      EXEC   PROC=DUMPPROC,
001700 // INPUT='CSCJGJ.CSC.CNTL(WORKERS)',         DATA SET TO PRINT
001800 // TO='A'                                    PRINT WITHOUT VIEWING
001900 //
```

> # Execution JCL
>
> Once **DUMPPROC** is installed in a proc library and becomes a
> cataloged procedure, you can execute it using JCL like this. The
> actual JCL of the proc is hidden from view. Anyone using the
> proc has to supply only a JOB statement and the appropriate
> values for the symbolic parameters.

Figure 18.8 Execution JCL for Cataloged Proc DUMPPROC   317

18.9 Private Proc Libs

MVS executes a cataloged procedure by drawing it in from the system library where procs are stored by name. SYS1.PROCLIB is the standard IBM-supplied name for the procedure library. An installation can create other similar libraries and concatenate them to SYS1.PROCLIB. But (unlike the case with a load module library) MVS has traditionally made it awkward for individual programmers to create personal proc libs.

Figure 18.9 shows you three ways that different configurations of MVS let you maintain your own procedure library. A procedure library is just a partitioned data set containing members with fixed-length, 80-byte records. MVS/ESA Release 4 and beyond makes it easy to use a new type of statement, JCLLIB, right after your job statement to name a private proc lib. In that environment you can "install" your procs in your own library and complete proc testing without systems programmer help.

In the pre-MVS/ESA Release 4 world, you can specify a private proc lib only with some help from a systems programmer. As you can see in Figure 18.9, under JES2 you use a /*JOBPARM statement naming a DDname coded by a systems programmer for MVS to identify your proc lib's name. Under JES3, you use a //*MAIN statement to make a similar specification.

18.10 Proc Rules and Guidelines

You have to follow some rules in turning raw JCL into a proc:

1. Procs can't contain a JOB statement.
2. Procs can't contain a // null statement.
3. Procs can't contain instream data or the delimiter /*.
4. Procs can't contain //JOBLIB statements.
5. Procs can't contain JES2 or JES3 control statements.
6. Cataloged procs should not contain the PEND statement.
7. Under MVS releases before MVS/ESA Release 4, procs cannot be nested. MVS/ESA Release 4 introduces the ability to nest procs up to 15 deep (that is, you can now invoke a proc within a proc.)

Private proc library in MVS/ESA Release 4:

```
EDIT ---- A1092JJ.LIB.JCL(SORTEXEC) - 01.04 ----------------- COLUMNS 001 072
COMMAND ===>                                                 SCROLL ===> PAGE
****** **************************** TOP OF DATA ******************************
000100 //A1092JJA   JOB  (1092,COB2),'JANOSSY',CLASS=A,MSGCLASS=X,
000200 //  NOTIFY=A1092JJ
000300 //     JCLLIB  ORDER=(A1092JJ.LIB.JCL)    ⬅
000400 //*
000500 //*   THIS JCL IS STORED AT A1092JJ.LIB.JCL(SORTEXEC)
000600 //*
000700 //STEPA    EXEC  SORTLIST,
000800 //  INDATA='A1092JJ.LIB.JCL(WORKERS)'
000900 //
```

Private proc library before Release 4, under JES2:

```
EDIT ---- A1092JJ.LIB.JCL(SORTEXEC) - 01.04 ----------------- COLUMNS 001 072
COMMAND ===>                                                 SCROLL ===> PAGE
****** **************************** TOP OF DATA ******************************
000100 //A1092JJA   JOB  (1092,COB2),'JANOSSY',CLASS=A,MSGCLASS=X,
000200 //  NOTIFY=A1092JJ
000300 /*JOBPARM PROCLIB=PROC08    ⬅
000400 //*
000500 //*   THIS JCL IS STORED AT A1092JJ.LIB.JCL(SORTEXEC)
000600 //*
000700 //STEPA    EXEC  SORTLIST,
000800 //  INDATA='A1092JJ.LIB.JCL(WORKERS)'
000900 //
```

Private proc library before Release 4, under JES3:

```
EDIT ---- A1092JJ.LIB.JCL(SORTEXEC) - 01.04 ----------------- COLUMNS 001 072
COMMAND ===>                                                 SCROLL ===> PAGE
****** **************************** TOP OF DATA ******************************
000100 //A1092JJA   JOB  (1092,COB2),'JANOSSY',CLASS=A,MSGCLASS=X,
000200 //  NOTIFY=A1092JJ
000300 //*MAIN PROC=08    ⬅
000400 //*
000500 //*   THIS JCL IS STORED AT A1092JJ.LIB.JCL(SORTEXEC)
000600 //*
000700 //STEPA    EXEC  SORTLIST,
000800 //  INDATA='A1092JJ.LIB.JCL(WORKERS)'
000900 //
```

Figure 18.9 How to Specify Private Proc Libraries

MVS/ESA Release 4 and beyond gives you the greatest ease in using your own
private procedure library, using the JCLLIB statement. You can use JCLLIB on your
own. Under earlier releases of MVS you need to work with a systems programmer
to inform MVS about the name of a private procedure library, which is equated
with a value such as PROC08 or 08.

You should also think about a naming convention that distinguishes between step names within your procs and step names in your execution JCL.
In the examples in this book I use stepnames in the form //STEP010 for
the lowest level JCL, such as JCL in procs. For execution JCL I use stepnames
like //STEPA, //STEPB, and so forth. I find that this helps me interpret
the MVS system output when I am executing procs, as the annotations on
Figure 18.4 indicate.

When you create symbolic parameters, you should include a default
for each on the proc statement and include a same-line comment there.
Make your symbolic parameter names as meaningful as possible given their
seven-character limit. Although you can use actual JCL words such as DSN
and SPACE for symbolic parameters, this is often confusing; I'd suggest you
use variations of these words such as DATNAME (data set name) and SPAC-
PRI (primary space).

18.11 Multiple-Step Proc Execution Under MVS/XA and MVS/ESA

Figure 18.10 shows you the flow chart for a two-step job stream that sorts
data and then uses IEBGENER to produce a formatted listing. Figure 18.11
shows you the instream proc named SORTLIST that I wrote to implement
this processing. I needed to store two sets of instream data to create this
instream proc. //SYSIN for the sort utility (line 3100) is in member name
CCSORTL and looks like this:

```
SORT FIELDS=(7,11,CH,A)
```

whereas //SYSIN for IEBGENER (line 4600) is in member name
CCGENER1 and looks like this:

```
GENERATE    MAXFLDS=99,MAXLITS=80
RECORD      FIELD=(5,1,,1),
            FIELD=(2,' ',,6),
            FIELD=(11,7,,8),
            FIELD=(2,' ',,17),
            FIELD=(10,18,,21),
            FIELD=(2,' ',,31),
            FIELD=(2,28,,33),
            FIELD=(1,'.',,35),
            FIELD=(1,30,,36),
            FIELD=(2,' ',,37),
            FIELD=(20,31,,39)
```

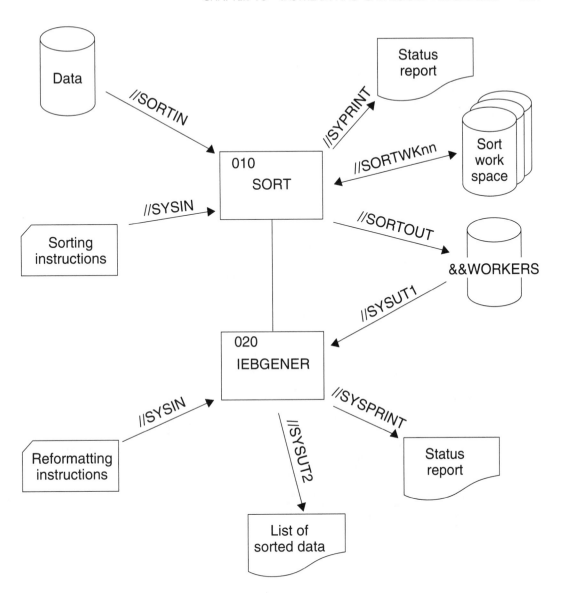

Figure 18.10   Flow Chart of Two-Step Sort and Report Job Stream

This job stream reads data into the sort utility, which outputs it to a temporary data set. Then the IEBGENER utility reads the sorted data and reformats it to produce a simple report. I implement this in a proc called SORTLIST in Figure 18.11.

```
  EDIT --- A1092JJ.LIB.JCL(SORTEXE) - 01.01 ----------------- COLUMNS 001 072
  COMMAND ===>                                                 SCROLL ===> PAGE
  ***** ************************** TOP OF DATA **********************************
  000100 //A1092JJA  JOB (1092,COB2),'JANOSSY',CLASS=A,MSGCLASS=X,
  000200 //  NOTIFY=A1092JJ
  000300 //*
  000400 //*    THIS JCL STORED AT A1092JJ.LIB.JCL(SORTEXE) AT GIS INFO SYSTEMS
  000500 //*
  000600 //* - - - - - - - - - - - - - - - - - - - - - - - - - - - - - - - - - -
  000700 //SORTLIST  PROC  INDATA='***',      NAME OF INPUT DATA SET
  000800 //   SYSPRT='*',                     PRINT CLASS FOR SYSTEM PRINT
  000900 //   DATPRT='*',        (a)          PRINT CLASS FOR DATA PRINT
  001000 //   DATSPAC='5,2'                   SORTED DATA SPACE 48 RECS/BLK
  001100 //*
  001200 //*    THIS PROCEDURE SORTS WORKER DATA ON POSITIONS 7-11 ASCENDING
  001300 //*    AND USES IEBGENER TO PRODUCE A FORMATTED LISTING
  001400 //*
  001500 //******************************************************************
  001600 //*                                                                *
  001700 //*    SORT WORKER DATA BY LAST NAME                               *
  001800 //*                                                                *
  001900 //******************************************************************
  002000 //STEP010   EXEC  PGM=SORT
  002100 //SYSOUT    DD    SYSOUT=&SYSPRT
  002200 //SORTWK01  DD    UNIT=SYSDA,SPACE=(CYL,1)   (b)
  002300 //SORTWK02  DD    UNIT=SYSDA,SPACE=(CYL,1)
  002400 //SORTIN    DD    DSN=&INDATA,                     <=== INPUT
  002500 //   DISP=SHR
  002600 //SORTOUT   DD    DSN=&&WORKERS,    (c)            <=== OUTPUT
  002700 //   UNIT=SYSDA,
  002800 //   DISP=(NEW,PASS,DELETE),
  002900 //   DCB=(RECFM=FB,LRECL=80,BLKSIZE=3840),  (d)
  003000 //   SPACE=(3840,(&DATSPAC),RLSE)
  003100 //SYSIN     DD    DSN=A1092JJ.LIB.JCL(CCSORTL),
  003200 //   DISP=SHR
  003300 //*
  003400 //******************************************************************
  003500 //*                                                                *
  003600 //*    LIST SORTED WORKER DATA                                     *
  003700 //*    FIELDS ARE SPACED FOR EASIER READING USING INSTRUCTIONS     *
  003800 //*    TO THE "IEBGENER" PROGRAM AT ITS //SYSIN DD STATEMENT       *
  003900 //*                                                                *
  004000 //******************************************************************
  004100 //STEP020   EXEC  PGM=IEBGENER
  004200 //SYSPRINT  DD    SYSOUT=&SYSPRT    (e)
  004300 //SYSUT1    DD    DSN=&&WORKERS,
  004400 //   DISP=(OLD,DELETE)                     (f)
  004500 //SYSUT2    DD    SYSOUT=&DATPRT
  004600 //SYSIN     DD    DSN=A1092JJ.LIB.JCL(CCGENER1),
  004700 //   DISP=SHR
  004800 //* - - - - - - - - - - - - - - - - - - - - - - - - - - - - - - - - - -
  004900 //        PEND
  005000 //STEPA     EXEC  SORTLIST,
  005100 //   INDATA='A1092JJ.LIB.JCL(WORKERS)',
  005200 //   DATPRT='A'
  005300 //
```

Figure 18.11 Instream Execution of SORTLIST Proc

(a) I coded four symbolic parameters in this proc, gave each a default value, and documented each with a same-line comment on the PROC statement.
(b) &SYSPRT is the print class for "system" output like the sort //SYSOUT.
(c) &INDATA is the name of the input data set. (d) &DATSPAC is the symbolic parameter for disk space for the temporary data set created by the sort program.
(e) I coded &SYSPRT at IEBGENER's //SYSPRINT; you can code the same symbolic parameter in at several points to substitute the same value in multiple places.
(f) &DATPRT is the print class for program output such as the list of sorted data.

Some installations require programmers to code comments in JCL to document the contents of control statements handled this way. If you do that, make sure you keep them up to date when you change the actual control card libraries!

Notice that I have defined four symbolic parameters in this proc, each with a default:

> &INDATA is the name of the data set to be processed
> &SYSPRT is the print class for //SYSOUT and //SYSPRINT outputs
> &DATPRT is the print class for "data" outputs such as reports
> &DATSPAC is the coding for the primary and secondary SPACE allocation values

In the execution JCL I have specified actual values for INDATA and DATPRT only. SYSPRT and DATSPAC will assume their default values in this run. I could change the handling of the system print and the amount of disk space allocated to data storage via the execution JCL.

Figure 18.12 shows you some of the output from a run of my instream SORTLIST proc. I ran this on a mainframe system operated by a service bureau, GIS Information Systems of Oak Brook, Illinois, under MVS/ESA. You'll notice several differences between earlier MVS output examples and this one in the area of the job log and usage information because this can be customized in an installation. But notice in particular how the symbolic parameter substitution values are now reported throughout the interpreted listing of the proc at lines 5, 8, 9, 12, and 14. In MVS/XA and later versions of MVS you will see symbolic parameter substitutions listed like this.

Figure 18.13a shows you how SORTLIST looks as an installed proc. Figure 18.13b shows you the execution JCL to run it as an installed proc.

18.12 Proc Overrides and Adds

Sometimes you have to execute a proc and change a value in it for which there is no symbolic parameter. In fact, in an extreme case someone may have developed a proc and not included any symbolic parameters! To run such a proc you code complete DD statements in your execution JCL after EXEC PROC= ... to override or add them to the proc. You code them in this form:

```
//procstepname.DDname  DD ...
```

where "procstepname" is the name of the step in the proc and "DDname" is the specific DD statement name. For example,

```
//STEP010.SYSOUT  DD  ...
```

(text continues on page 327)

J E S 2   J O B   L O G -- S Y S T E M   G I S A -- S Y S T E M   G I S A -- N O D E   G I S A N J E

```
00.43.43 JOB 1221  $HASP373 A1092JJA STARTED - INIT 2 - CLASS A - SYS GISA - DATE 92180
00.43.44 JOB 1221  IEF403I A1092JJA - STARTED - TIME=00.43.44
00.43.46 JOB 1221
00.43.46 JOB 1221
00.43.46 JOB 1221
00.43.46 JOB 1221
00.43.47 JOB 1221
00.43.47 JOB 1221
00.43.47 JOB 1221  IEF404I A1092JJA - ENDED - TIME=00.43.47
00.43.47 JOB 1221  -A1092JJA ENDED.  NAME-JANOSSY          TOTAL CPU TIME=   .14  TOTAL ELAPSED TIME=   .0
00.43.47 JOB 1221
00.43.47 JOB 1221  $HASP395 A1092JJA ENDED - DATE 92180
```

					--- TIMINGS ---				PG	-- PAGING COUNTS --			
-JOBNAME	STEPNAME	PROCSTEP	RC	EXCP	CPU	SRB	CLOCK	SERV		PAGE	SWAP	VIO	SWAPS
-A1092JJA	STEPA	STEP010	00	89	.09	.00	.0	2689	1	0	0	0	1
-A1092JJA	STEPA	STEP020	00	24	.05	.00	.0	826	1	0	0	0	0

```
----- JES2 JOB STATISTICS -----
  28 JUN 92 JOB EXECUTION DATE
      53 CARDS READ
     218 SYSOUT PRINT RECORDS
       0 SYSOUT PUNCH RECORDS
      17 SYSOUT SPOOL KBYTES
    0.06 MINUTES EXECUTION TIME
```

> I ran my SORTLIST proc on an MVS/ESA system operated by GIS Information Systems of Oak Brook, Illinois to show you how a service bureau tracks system usage. **RC** is the last digits of the return code (COND CODE) for each step. The other customized "timings" document machine usage for billing. **EXCP** means "execute channel programs;" each EXCP is a block of data read or written.

```
1 //A1092JJA JOB (1092,COB2),'JANOSSY',CLASS=A,MSGCLASS=X,                          JOB 1221
  //         NOTIFY=A1092JJ                                                         00002001
2 //STEPA    EXEC SORTLIST,                                                         00500000
  //         INDATA='A1092JJ.LIB.JCL(WORKERS)',                                     00510001
  //         DATPRT='A'                                                             00520000
    -
    -
    -
3 ++SORTLIST PROC  INDATA='****',         NAME OF INPUT DATA SET                    00070000
  ++       SYSPRT='*',                    PRINT CLASS FOR SYSTEM PRINT              00080000
  ++       DATPRT='*',                    PRINT CLASS FOR DATA PRINT                00090000
  ++       DATSPAC='5,2'                  SORTED DATA SPACE 48 RECS/BLK             00100000
  ***                                                                              00110000
  ***   THIS PROCEDURE SORTS WORKER DATA ON POSITIONS 7-11 ASCENDING               00120000
  ***   AND USES IEBGENER TO PRODUCE A FORMATTED LISTING                           00130000
  ***                                                                              00140000
  ***********************************************************                   *  00150000
  ***                                                                           *  00160000
  ***         SORT WORKER DATA BY LAST NAME                                      * 00170000
  ***                                                                           *  00180000
  ***********************************************************                      00190000
4 ++STEP010  EXEC PGM=SORT
5 ++SYSOUT   DD   SYSOUT=&SYSPRT
  IEF653I SUBSTITUTION JCL - SYSOUT=*
6 ++SORTWK01 DD   UNIT=SYSDA,SPACE=(CYL,1)                                          00240000
7 ++SORTWK02 DD   UNIT=SYSDA,SPACE=(CYL,1)
8 ++SORTIN   DD   DSN=&INDATA,
  IEF653I SUBSTITUTION JCL - DSN=A1092JJ.LIB.JCL(WORKERS),                          00250000
  ++       DISP=SHR                                                                 00260000
9 ++SORTOUT  DD   DSN=&&WORKERS,                                                    00270000
  ++       UNIT=SYSDA,
```

<=== INPUT
<=== OUTPUT

> MVS/XA and MVS/ESA list symbolic parameter substitutions immediately after the affected line

Many MVS installations customize their MVS system reporting by adding locally-designed messages like these. GIS Information Systems uses data recorded by MVS in the *job log* to show billing information such as the number of magnetic tapes mounted on drives and the number of disk or tape data blocks read or written. "Outsourcing" data processing makes it necessary to itemize more components of machine usage and cost than are often considered when a company owns or leases its own dedicated mainframe.

```
   ++    DISP=(NEW,PASS,DELETE),                                          00280000
   ++    DCB=(RECFM=FB,LRECL=80,BLKSIZE=3840),                            00290000
   ++    SPACE=(3840,(&DATSPAC),RLSE)                                     00300000
10 IEF653I SUBSTITUTION JCL - SPACE=(3840,(5,2),RLSE)
   ++ SYSIN    DD   DSN=A1092JJ.LIB.JCL(CCSORTL),                         00310001
   ++    DISP=SHR                                                         00320000
   ***                                                                    00330000
   *********************************************************              00340000
   ***                                                        *           00350000
   ***   LIST SORTED WORKER DATA                              *           00360000
   ***   FIELDS ARE SPACED FOR EASIER READING USING INSTRUCTIONS *        00370000
   ***   TO THE "IEBGENER" PROGRAM AT ITS //SYSIN DD STATEMENT  *         00380000
   ***                                                        *           00390000
   *********************************************************              00400000
11 ++STEP020  EXEC  PGM=IEBGENER                                          00410000
12 ++SYSPRINT  DD   SYSOUT=&SYSPRT                                        00420000
   IEF653I SUBSTITUTION JCL - SYSOUT=*
13 ++SYSUT1    DD   DSN=&&WORKERS,                                        00430000
   ++    DISP=(OLD,DELETE)                                                00440000
14 ++SYSUT2    DD   SYSOUT=&DATPRT                                        00450000
   IEF653I SUBSTITUTION JCL - SYSOUT=A
15 ++SYSIN     DD   DSN=A1092JJ.LIB.JCL(CCGENER1),                        00460001
   ++    DISP=SHR                                                         00470000
   ***                                                                    00480000

STMT NO. MESSAGE

IEF236I ALLOC. FOR A1092JJA STEP010 STEPA
IEF237I JES2 ALLOCATED TO SYSOUT
IEF237I 834  ALLOCATED TO SORTWK01
IEF237I 821  ALLOCATED TO SORTWK02
IEF237I 839  ALLOCATED TO SORTIN
IEF237I 70A  ALLOCATED TO SORTOUT
IEF237I 839  ALLOCATED TO SYSIN
IEF142I A1092JJA STEP010 STEPA -  STEP WAS EXECUTED - COND CODE 0000
        JES2.JOB01221.S000101                                SYSOUT
IEF285I SYS92180.T004343.RA000.A1092JJA.R0000001            DELETED
IEF285I VOL SER NOS= GISAW3.
IEF285I SYS92180.T004343.RA000.A1092JJA.R0000002            DELETED
IEF285I VOL SER NOS= GISAW2.
IEF285I A1092JJ.LIB.JCL
IEF285I VOL SER NOS= ERCCB3.                                KEPT
IEF285I SYS92180.T004343.RA000.A1092JJA.WORKERS             PASSED
IEF285I VOL SER NOS= GISAW1.
IEF285I A1092JJ.LIB.JCL                                     KEPT
IEF285I VOL SER NOS= ERCCB3.
GIS001I STEP /STEP010 / *--
GIS101I STEP /STEP010 / * STEP =    1   DASD EXCPS =    7   TAPE MNTS =   0   CPU SERV =   959 *
GIS102I STEP /STEP010 / * RC   =   00   TAPE EXCPS =    0   DD *(DATA) =  0   I/O SERV =   410 *
GIS103I STEP /STEP010 / * PGM  = SORT  OTHR EXCPS =   82                      OTH SERV =  1320 *
GIS001I STEP /STEP010 / *--
IEF373I STEP /STEP010 / START 92180.0043
IEF374I STEP /STEP010 / STOP 92180.0043 CPU 0MIN 00.09SEC SRB 0MIN 00.00SEC VIRT 1064K SYS 284K EXT
```

Figure 18.12 SORTLIST Proc Run under MVS/ESA at a Service Bureau

326   PRACTICAL MVS JCL EXAMPLES

```
EDIT --- SYS1.PROCLIB(SORTLIST) - 01.01 -------------------- COLUMNS 001 072
COMMAND ===>                                                 SCROLL ===> PAGE
****** *************************** TOP OF DATA *******************************
000100 //SORTLIST PROC  INDATA='***',      NAME OF INPUT DATA SET
000200 //   SYSPRT='*',                    PRINT CLASS FOR SYSTEM PRINT
000300 //   DATPRT='*',                    PRINT CLASS FOR DATA PRINT
000400 //   DATSPAC='5,2'                  SORTED DATA SPACE 48 RECS/BLK
000500 //*
000600 //*   THIS PROCEDURE SORTS WORKER DATA ON POSITIONS 7-11 ASCENDING
000700 //*   AND USES IEBGENER TO PRODUCE A FORMATTED LISTING
000800 //*
000900 //******************************************************************
001000 //*                                                                *
001100 //*    SORT WORKER DATA BY LAST NAME                               *
001200 //*                                                                *
001300 //******************************************************************
001400 //STEP010  EXEC  PGM=SORT
001500 //SYSOUT     DD  SYSOUT=&SYSPRT
001600 //SORTWK01   DD  UNIT=SYSDA,SPACE=(CYL,1)
001700 //SORTWK02   DD  UNIT=SYSDA,SPACE=(CYL,1)
001800 //SORTIN     DD  DSN=&INDATA,                <=== INPUT
001900 //  DISP=SHR
002000 //SORTOUT    DD  DSN=&&WORKERS,              <=== OUTPUT
002100 //   UNIT=SYSDA,
002200 //   DISP=(NEW,PASS,DELETE),
002300 //   DCB=(RECFM=FB,LRECL=80,BLKSIZE=3840),
002400 //   SPACE=(3840,(&DATSPAC),RLSE)
002500 //SYSIN      DD  DSN=A1092JJ.LIB.JCL(CCSORTL),
002600 //   DISP=SHR
002700 //*
002800 //******************************************************************
002900 //*                                                                *
003000 //*    LIST SORTED WORKER DATA                                     *
003100 //*    FIELDS ARE SPACED FOR EASIER READING USING INSTRUCTIONS     *
003200 //*    TO THE "IEBGENER" PROGRAM AT ITS //SYSIN DD STATEMENT       *
003300 //*                                                                *
003400 //******************************************************************
003500 //STEP020  EXEC  PGM=IEBGENER
003600 //SYSPRINT   DD  SYSOUT=&SYSPRT
003700 //SYSUT1     DD  DSN=&&WORKERS,
003800 //  DISP=(OLD,DELETE)
003900 //SYSUT2     DD  SYSOUT=&DATPRT
004000 //SYSIN      DD  DSN=A1092JJ.LIB.JCL(CCGENER1),
004100 //  DISP=SHR
004200 //*END OF PROC SORTLIST***
```

(a)

```
EDIT --- A1092JJ.LIB.JCL(SORTEXE) - 01.01 ------------------ COLUMNS 001 072
COMMAND ===>                                                 SCROLL ===> PAGE
****** *************************** TOP OF DATA *******************************
000100 //A1092JJA  JOB (1092,COB2),'JANOSSY',CLASS=A,MSGCLASS=X,
000200 //  NOTIFY=A1092JJ
000300 //*
000400 //*   THIS JCL STORED AT A1092JJ.LIB.JCL(SORTEXE) AT GIS INFO SYSTEMS
000500 //*
000600 //STEPA    EXEC  SORTLIST,
000700 //  INDATA='A1092JJ.LIB.JCL(WORKERS)',
000800 //  DATPRT='A'
000900 //
```

(b)

Figure 18.13 SORTLIST as a Cataloged Proc and Its Execution JCL

(a) My sortlist proc appears this way when it is installed as a cataloged procedure.
(b) This is the JCL that executes SORTLIST. This JCL looks no longer than the
execution JCL in Figure 18.8, but it invokes a much larger proc than DUMPPROC.
Since I did not specify values for SYSPRT and DATSPAC, they will assume defaults.

By definition, DD statements that you code after the EXEC PROC= ... with DDnames that are in the proc are "overrides" of those existing DD statements. DD statements that you code after EXEC PROC= ... with DDnames not in the proc are "adds" to the proc.

Versions of MVS before MVS/ESA were not very sophisticated in the way that they merged your overrides and adds with the proc. They passed through the proc and your overrides and adds only once, and your overrides and adds had to be in this strict sequence:

1. All overrides and adds in step sequence
2. Within a step, all overrides first, then any adds for the step
3. Within a step, all overrides in exactly the same sequence as the original DD statements in the proc

MVS/ESA provides more sophisticated handling of your overrides and adds, and these requirements no longer apply.

18.13 A Proc Override and Add Example

Figure 18.14 shows you my SORTLIST proc without any symbolic parameters. I left the //SORTIN DD statement for the sort step out of the proc. I would like to send the three print outputs of the proc to '*' instead of print class A, and I would like to change the space allocation at line 002500 when I execute the proc. You can see at the bottom of Figure 18.14 how I coded each add or override as a complete DD statement parameter (not as a character string substitution) to accomplish this. You can code only DCB subparameters individually in overrides, such as DCB=BLKSIZE=nnnn.

Figure 18.15 shows you the system output from my SORTX proc execution. MVS lists overridden JCL statements with +/ (instream execution) or X/ (installed proc execution). It puts the overriding statement above the statement being overridden.

18.14 Overriding EXEC Statements in Procs

You can override EXEC statements within a proc that you are invoking by using the format parameter.procstepname on the EXEC statement that invokes the proc. For example, this overrides the PARM parameter on the EXEC statement (//COB) for the compile step of the COBUCL proc:

```
//STEPA    EXEC  PROC=COBUCL,
//    PARM.COB='(SIZE=1024K,SXR,DMA,CLI,APOST',
//    'NOSEQ,NOADV,LIB,DYN')
```

(text continues on page 330)

```
EDIT ---- CSCJGJ.CSC.CNTL(SORTX) - 01.00 -------------------- COLUMNS 001 072
COMMAND ===>                                                 SCROLL ===> PAGE
****** *********************** TOP OF DATA ******************************
000100 //CSCJGJA    JOB 1,'BIN 7 JANOSSY',CLASS=A,MSGCLASS=X,MSGLEVEL=(1,1),
000200 // NOTIFY=CSCJGJ
000300 //*
000400 //*    THIS JCL IS STORED AT CSCJGJ.CSC.CNTL(SORTX)
000500 //*
000600 //* - - - - - - ( a ) - - - - - - - - - - - - - - - - - - - - -
000700 //SORTLIST  PROC
000800 //*
000900 //*    THIS PROCEDURE SORTS WORKER DATA ON POSITIONS 7-11 ASCENDING
001000 //*    AND USES IEBGENER TO PRODUCE A FORMATTED LISTING
001100 //*
001200 //*******************************************************************
001300 //*                                                                *
001400 //*    SORT WORKER DATA BY LAST NAME                               *
001500 //*                                                                *
001600 //*******************************************************************
001700 //STEP010   EXEC  PGM=SORT
001800 //SYSOUT     DD   SYSOUT=A
001900 //SORTWK01   DD   UNIT=SYSDA,SPACE=(CYL,1)
002000 //SORTWK02   DD   UNIT=SYSDA,SPACE=(CYL,1)
002100 //SORTOUT    DD   DSN=&&WORKERS,                   <=== OUTPUT
002200 //  UNIT=SYSDA,
002300 //  DISP=(NEW,PASS,DELETE),
002400 //  DCB=(RECFM=FB,LRECL=80,BLKSIZE=3840),
002500 //  SPACE=(3840,(5,1),RLSE)
002600 //SYSIN      DD   DSN=CSCJGJ.CSC.CNTL(CCSORTL),
002700 //  DISP=SHR
002800 //*
002900 //*******************************************************************
003000 //*                                                                *
003100 //*    LIST SORTED WORKER DATA                                     *
003200 //*    FIELDS ARE SPACED FOR EASIER READING USING INSTRUCTIONS     *
003300 //*    TO THE "IEBGENER" PROGRAM AT ITS //SYSIN DD STATEMENT       *
003400 //*                                                                *
003500 //*******************************************************************
003600 //STEP020   EXEC  PGM=IEBGENER
003700 //SYSPRINT   DD   SYSOUT=A
003800 //SYSUT1     DD   DSN=&&WORKERS,
003900 //  DISP=(OLD,DELETE)
004000 //SYSUT2     DD   SYSOUT=A
004100 //SYSIN      DD   DSN=CSCJGJ.CSC.CNTL(CCGENER1),
004200 //  DISP=SHR
004300 //* - - - - - - - - - - - - - - - - - - - - - - - - - ( b ) - -
004400 //          PEND
004500 //STEPA     EXEC  SORTLIST
004600 //STEP010.SYSOUT   DD  SYSOUT=*                      STEP010 OVERRIDE
004700 //STEP010.SORTOUT  DD  SPACE=(3840,(15,3),RLSE)      STEP010 OVERRIDE
004800 //STEP010.SORTIN   DD  DSN=CSCJGJ.CSC.WORKERS,DISP=SHR STEP010 ADD
004900 //STEP020.SYSPRINT DD  SYSOUT=*                      STEP020 OVERRIDE
005000 //STEP020.SYSUT2   DD  SYSOUT=*                      STEP020 OVERRIDE
005100 //
```

Figure 18.14 SORTLIST Proc with No Symbolic Parameters (SORTX)

This proc has no symbolic parameters for values I want to change in executing it.
But I want print class to be '*' for all SYSOUTs, I want 15 primary and 3 secondary
tracks of disk space for the //SORTOUT data set, and I want to input
CSCJGJ.CSC.WORKERS at the sort at DDname //SORTIN. I have to code overrides
to existing DD statements and code an added DD statement for //SORTIN. (a) No
symbolic parameter defaults are coded on PROC because this proc has no
symbolic parameters! (b) I put comments on each override or add to make it easier
to see them in the MVS system output. I'd suggest that you follow this practice.

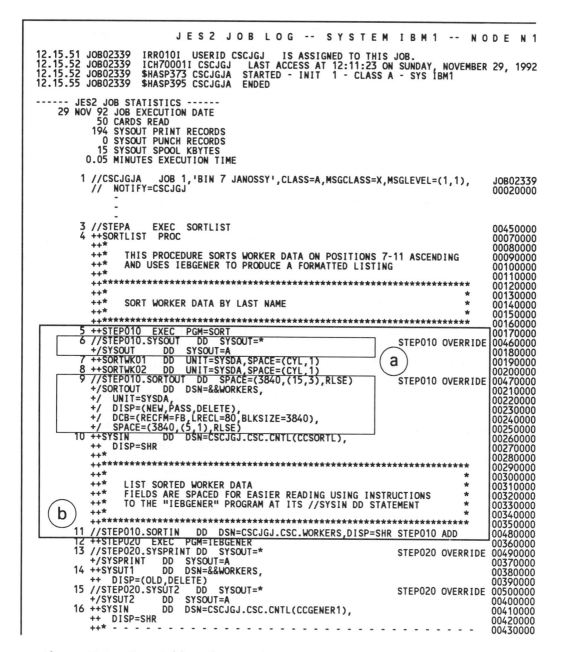

```
           J E S 2   J O B   L O G  --  S Y S T E M   I B M 1  --  N O D E   N 1
12.15.51 JOB02339  IRR010I  USERID CSCJGJ    IS ASSIGNED TO THIS JOB.
12.15.52 JOB02339  ICH70001I CSCJGJ   LAST ACCESS AT 12:11:23 ON SUNDAY, NOVEMBER 29, 1992
12.15.52 JOB02339  $HASP373 CSCJGJA  STARTED - INIT 1 - CLASS A - SYS IBM1
12.15.55 JOB02339  $HASP395 CSCJGJA  ENDED

------ JES2 JOB STATISTICS ------
   29 NOV 92 JOB EXECUTION DATE
         50 CARDS READ
        194 SYSOUT PRINT RECORDS
          0 SYSOUT PUNCH RECORDS
         15 SYSOUT SPOOL KBYTES
       0.05 MINUTES EXECUTION TIME

    1 //CSCJGJA    JOB 1,'BIN 7 JANOSSY',CLASS=A,MSGCLASS=X,MSGLEVEL=(1,1),   JOB02339
      // NOTIFY=CSCJGJ                                                        00020000
                          -
                          -
                          -
    3 //STEPA     EXEC  SORTLIST                                              00450000
    4 ++SORTLIST  PROC                                                        00070000
      ++*                                                                     00080000
      ++*     THIS PROCEDURE SORTS WORKER DATA ON POSITIONS 7-11 ASCENDING    00090000
      ++*     AND USES IEBGENER TO PRODUCE A FORMATTED LISTING                00100000
      ++*                                                                     00110000
      ++*************************************************************         00120000
      ++*                                                          *          00130000
      ++*     SORT WORKER DATA BY LAST NAME                        *          00140000
      ++*                                                          *          00150000
      ++*************************************************************         00160000
    5 ++STEP010   EXEC  PGM=SORT                                             00170000
    6 //STEP010.SYSOUT    DD  SYSOUT=*                    STEP010 OVERRIDE   00460000
      +/SYSOUT       DD  SYSOUT=A                                            00180000
    7 ++SORTWK01    DD  UNIT=SYSDA,SPACE=(CYL,1)                             00190000
    8 ++SORTWK02    DD  UNIT=SYSDA,SPACE=(CYL,1)                             00200000
    9 //STEP010.SORTOUT   DD  SPACE=(3840,(15,3),RLSE)    STEP010 OVERRIDE   00470000
      +/SORTOUT      DD  DSN=&&WORKERS,                                      00210000
      +/ UNIT=SYSDA,                                                         00220000
      +/ DISP=(NEW,PASS,DELETE),                                             00230000
      +/ DCB=(RECFM=FB,LRECL=80,BLKSIZE=3840),                              00240000
      +/ SPACE=(3840,(5,1),RLSE)                                             00250000
   10 ++SYSIN        DD  DSN=CSCJGJ.CSC.CNTL(CCSORTL),                        00260000
      ++ DISP=SHR                                                            00270000
      ++*                                                                     00280000
      ++*************************************************************         00290000
      ++*                                                          *          00300000
      ++*     LIST SORTED WORKER DATA                              *          00310000
      ++*     FIELDS ARE SPACED FOR EASIER READING USING INSTRUCTIONS *       00320000
      ++*     TO THE "IEBGENER" PROGRAM AT ITS //SYSIN DD STATEMENT  *        00330000
      ++*                                                          *          00340000
      ++*************************************************************         00350000
   11 //STEP010.SORTIN    DD  DSN=CSCJGJ.CSC.WORKERS,DISP=SHR STEP010 ADD     00480000
   12 ++STEP020   EXEC  PGM=IEBGENER                                          00360000
   13 //STEP020.SYSPRINT DD  SYSOUT=*                      STEP020 OVERRIDE   00490000
      +/SYSPRINT     DD  SYSOUT=A                                            00370000
   14 ++SYSUT1       DD  DSN=&&WORKERS,                                       00380000
      ++ DISP=(OLD,DELETE)                                                   00390000
   15 //STEP020.SYSUT2    DD  SYSOUT=*                     STEP020 OVERRIDE   00500000
      +/SYSUT2       DD  SYSOUT=A                                            00400000
   16 ++SYSIN        DD  DSN=CSCJGJ.CSC.CNTL(CCGENER1),                       00410000
      ++ DISP=SHR                                                            00420000
      ++*  -  -  -  -  -  -  -  -  -  -  -  -  -  -  -  -  -  -  -  -  -  -     00430000
```

Figure 18.15 Proc Adds and Overrides (SORTX)

(a) You see the override I coded for //STEP010's SYSOUT applied by MVS to line 6. MVS lists the override before the overridden statement, and the overridden statement's // is changed to +/ (X/ for an installed proc). //SORTOUT's SPACE parameter has also been overridden at line 9. (b) The DD statement added for //SORTIN is listed just before the EXEC statement for the next step.

You have to override EXEC statement parameters like PARM in their entirety; you are replacing them, not modifying them. If you have to override parameters in more than one step in a proc, you code the overrides in *step* sequence on the exec that invokes the proc:

```
//STEPA    EXEC  PROC=COBUCL,
//   PARM.COB='(SIZE=1024K,SXR,DMA,CLI,APOST',
//   'NOSEQ,NOADV,LIB,DYN'),
//   TIME.LKED=(,30)
```

18.15 Robust Proc Coding: The PDSREORG Proc

I have listed in Figure 18.16 a practical proc that uses several features of MVS JCL and proc coding. This proc is named PDSREORG. In addition to serving as a good example of proc coding, PDSREORG is useful in its own right for reorganizing partitioned data sets. It uses the IEBCOPY utility to do this. Unlike many PDS reorganization procs, PDSREORG doesn't require any control statements in a library. I built PDSREORG using a very conservative philosophy. I wanted it to be as bulletproof as possible and to provide backup of the PDS being reorganized if anything went wrong. (We use PDSREORG a lot at DePaul University, and I don't ever want it blamed for losing a student program library!)

At //STEP010, PDSREORG locates the partitioned data set that you want to reorganize. It does this with DISP=(OLD,KEEP) because the proc really does need exclusive access to the data set; it eventually deletes it! The newly reorganized PDS will always be placed on the same disk; it will never "migrate" to another disk as a result of using this proc. Due to the COND coding on them, //STEP020 and beyond execute only if the preceding steps return COND CODE 0000.

At //STEP020, the proc copies your input partitioned data set to another on the same disk, using a VOL referback to //STEP010, with a data set name made up of the original name and .NEWCOPY appended to it. That is, CSCJGJ.CSC.COBOL is copied to CSCJGJ.CSC.COBOL.NEWCOPY. This shows you how to code symbolic parameters for a part of the data set name. Here &PDS is the symbolic parameter holding the value CSCJGJ.CSC.COBOL:

```
//SYSUT1  DD  DSN=&PDS..NEWCOPY,
```

The two periods between &PDS and the literals .NEWCOPY are not a mistake. You need to code them to achieve the intended result.

The IEBCOPY copy process uses the default or supplied symbolic parameter values for DCB characteristics and space allocation, including quantity of directory blocks. That's why you can change any of these using

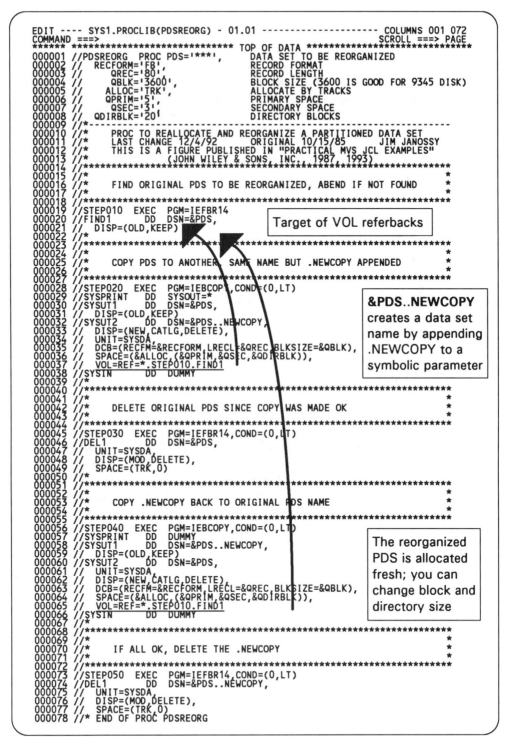

```
EDIT ---- SYS1.PROCLIB(PDSREORG) - 01.01 ------------------- COLUMNS 001 072
COMMAND ===>                                                 SCROLL ===> PAGE
****** *********************************** TOP OF DATA ***********************
000001 //PDSREORG  PROC PDS='***',      DATA SET TO BE REORGANIZED
000002 //     RECFORM='FB',             RECORD FORMAT
000003 //        QREC='80',             RECORD LENGTH
000004 //        QBLK='3600',           BLOCK SIZE (3600 IS GOOD FOR 9345 DISK)
000005 //       ALLOC='TRK',            ALLOCATE BY TRACKS
000006 //       QPRIM='5',              PRIMARY SPACE
000007 //        QSEC='3',              SECONDARY SPACE
000008 //     QDIRBLK='20'              DIRECTORY BLOCKS
000009 //*-------------------------------------------------------------
000010 //*     PROC TO REALLOCATE AND REORGANIZE A PARTITIONED DATA SET
000011 //*     LAST CHANGE 12/4/92      ORIGINAL 10/15/85      JIM JANOSSY
000012 //*     THIS IS A FIGURE PUBLISHED IN "PRACTICAL MVS JCL EXAMPLES"
000013 //*          (JOHN WILEY & SONS, INC.  1987, 1993)
000014 //****************************************************************
000015 //*                                                              *
000016 //*     FIND ORIGINAL PDS TO BE REORGANIZED, ABEND IF NOT FOUND  *
000017 //*                                                              *
000018 //****************************************************************
000019 //STEP010  EXEC  PGM=IEFBR14
000020 //FIND1     DD  DSN=&PDS,
000021 //  DISP=(OLD,KEEP)
000022 //*
000023 //****************************************************************
000024 //*                                                              *
000025 //*     COPY PDS TO ANOTHER, SAME NAME BUT .NEWCOPY APPENDED      *
000026 //*                                                              *
000027 //****************************************************************
000028 //STEP020  EXEC  PGM=IEBCOPY,COND=(0,LT)
000029 //SYSPRINT  DD  SYSOUT=*
000030 //SYSUT1    DD  DSN=&PDS,
000031 //  DISP=(OLD,KEEP)
000032 //SYSUT2    DD  DSN=&PDS..NEWCOPY,
000033 //  DISP=(NEW,CATLG,DELETE),
000034 //  UNIT=SYSDA,
000035 //  DCB=(RECFM=&RECFORM,LRECL=&QREC,BLKSIZE=&QBLK),
000036 //  SPACE=(&ALLOC,(&QPRIM,&QSEC,&QDIRBLK)),
000037 //  VOL=REF=*.STEP010.FIND1
000038 //SYSIN     DD  DUMMY
000039 //*
000040 //****************************************************************
000041 //*                                                              *
000042 //*     DELETE ORIGINAL PDS SINCE COPY WAS MADE OK               *
000043 //*                                                              *
000044 //****************************************************************
000045 //STEP030  EXEC  PGM=IEFBR14,COND=(0,LT)
000046 //DEL1      DD  DSN=&PDS,
000047 //  UNIT=SYSDA,
000048 //  DISP=(MOD,DELETE),
000049 //  SPACE=(TRK,0)
000050 //*
000051 //****************************************************************
000052 //*                                                              *
000053 //*     COPY .NEWCOPY BACK TO ORIGINAL PDS NAME                  *
000054 //*                                                              *
000055 //****************************************************************
000056 //STEP040  EXEC  PGM=IEBCOPY,COND=(0,LT)
000057 //SYSPRINT  DD  DUMMY
000058 //SYSUT1    DD  DSN=&PDS..NEWCOPY,
000059 //  DISP=(OLD,KEEP)
000060 //SYSUT2    DD  DSN=&PDS,
000061 //  UNIT=SYSDA,
000062 //  DISP=(NEW,CATLG,DELETE),
000063 //  DCB=(RECFM=&RECFORM,LRECL=&QREC,BLKSIZE=&QBLK),
000064 //  SPACE=(&ALLOC,(&QPRIM,&QSEC,&QDIRBLK)),
000065 //  VOL=REF=*.STEP010.FIND1
000066 //SYSIN     DD  DUMMY
000067 //*
000068 //****************************************************************
000069 //*                                                              *
000070 //*     IF ALL OK, DELETE THE .NEWCOPY                           *
000071 //*                                                              *
000072 //****************************************************************
000073 //STEP050  EXEC  PGM=IEFBR14,COND=(0,LT)
000074 //DEL1      DD  DSN=&PDS..NEWCOPY,
000075 //  UNIT=SYSDA,
000076 //  DISP=(MOD,DELETE),
000077 //  SPACE=(TRK,0)
000078 //* END OF PROC PDSREORG
```

Target of VOL referbacks

&PDS..NEWCOPY creates a data set name by appending .NEWCOPY to a symbolic parameter

The reorganized PDS is allocated fresh; you can change block and directory size

Figure 18.16 The PDSREORG Proc for Partitioned Data Set Reorganization

331

the proc. This copy process automatically produces a reorganized partitioned data set because only the most recent copy of each member is copied.

At //STEP030, the proc deletes the original partitioned data set if a copy of it has successfully been made. At //STEP040, the proc copies the new data set back to a data set of the original name. This process could be made more efficient by simply renaming the copy of the data set, but one of my goals for PDSREORG was to not use any control statements. Finally, at //STEP050, PDSREORG deletes the copy of the data set named .NEWCOPY if the run was successful.

Execute the installed PDSREORG proc in its simplest form and you'll get the default space allocation:

```
//STEPA    EXEC   PROC=PDSREORG,PDS='CSCJGJ.CSC.COBOL'
```

To change the quantity of directory blocks or space allocation, execute PDSREORG this way:

```
//STEPA    EXEC   PROC=PDSREORG,
//         PDS='CSCJGJ.CSC.COBOL',
//      ALLOC='TRK',
//      QPRIM='20',
//       QSEC='4',
//    QDIRBLK='15'
//
```

18.16 Using Symbolic Parameters for Data Set Names

You gain a vital flexibility if you code symbolic parameters for the first two parts of data set names. System security is usually based on data set name. When you test your procs and programs, you will have to use "test" data set names. When you install procs for production use ("for real") they have to refer to "live" production data sets with different names.

Figure 18.17a shows you how to code symbolic parameters in a proc for the first two parts of data set names. I called the leftmost part of the name &HILEV and the second part &GROUP. (You see here just the first part of a complete production job stream from another of my books, *Advanced MVS/ESA JCL Examples*, published by John Wiley & Sons in 1993). I used the &HILEV and &GROUP symbolic parameters in several places in this proc. The execution JCL shown in Figure 18.17b lets me supply the tape volume serial number of a transaction input tape and the front two parts of data set name when I run the proc. Using these symbolic parameters, I can easily change from using test data set names (like CSCJGJ.CSC.TRANS in our installation) to production data set names (like BT3700.MKT.TRANS) without changing any proc coding.

```
EDIT --- CSCJGJ.CSC.CNTL(PROC1801) ------------------------ COLUMNS 001 072
COMMAND ===>                                                SCROLL ===> PAGE
****** *************************** TOP OF DATA ********************************
000100 //PROC1801 PROC  TAPEVOL='XXXXXX',      VOL=SER OF INPUT TAPE
000200 //  HILEV='XXXXXXXX',                   DATA SET NAME 1ST PART
000300 //  GROUP='YYYYYYYY',                   DATA SET NAME 2ND PART
000400 //  TRSPC='(6,2)',                      TRANS SPACE 77 RECS/BLOCK
000500 //  MFSPC='(20,4)',                     MFILE SPACE 77 RECS/BLK
000600 //  PRSPC='(30,5)'                      PRINTLINE SPACE 30 RECS/BLK
000700 //*
000800 //*    JOB STREAM TO UPDATE CSCJGJ.CSC.MASTFILE SAVING REPORT
000900 //*
001000 //*********************************************************************
001100 //*                                                                  *
001200 //*    SORT THE TRANSACTIONS ON KEY AND TRAN TYPE CODE               *
001300 //*                                                                  *
001400 //*********************************************************************
001500 //STEP010   EXEC  PGM=SORT
001600 //SYSOUT    DD   SYSOUT=*
001700 //SORTIN    DD   DSN=&HILEV..&GROUP..TRANTEST,
001800 //   DISP=OLD,
001900 //   UNIT=(TAPE,,DEFER),
002000 //   DCB=(RECFM=FB,LRECL=80,BLKSIZE=1280,DEN=3,OPTCD=Q),
002100 //   VOL=SER=&TAPEVOL,
002200 //   LABEL=(1,NL)
002300 //SORTOUT    DD   DSN=&&TRANSORT,
002400 //   DISP=(NEW,PASS,DELETE),
002500 //   UNIT=SYSDA,
002600 //   DCB=(RECFM=FB,LRECL=80,BLKSIZE=6160),
002700 //   SPACE=(6160,&TRSPC,RLSE)
002800 //SORTWK01   DD   UNIT=SYSDA,SPACE=(CYL,1)
002900 //SORTWK02   DD   UNIT=SYSDA,SPACE=(CYL,1)
003000 //SYSIN     DD   DSN=&HILEV..&GROUP..CNTL(CC1801A),
003100 //   DISP=SHR
            .
            .
            .
```

(a)

DSN formed with
symbolic parameters
gives flexibility changing
data set names

```
EDIT --- CSCJGJ.CSC.CNTL(EXEC1801) ------------------------ COLUMNS 001 072
COMMAND ===>                                                SCROLL ===> PAGE
****** *************************** TOP OF DATA ********************************
000100 //CSCJGJA   JOB 1,'BIN 7--JANOSSY',CLASS=A,MSGCLASS=X,MSGLEVEL=(1,1),
000200 //   NOTIFY=CSCJGJ
000300 //*
000400 //*    THIS JCL IS STORED AT CSCJGJ.CSC.CNTL(EXEC1801)
000500 //*
000600 //STEPA     EXEC  PROC=PROC1801,TAPEVOL='ABC123',   <===INPUT VOL=SER
000700 //   HILEV='CSCJGJ',
000800 //   GROUP='CSC'
000900 //
```

(b)

Figure 18.17   Start of a Full-fledged "Production" Proc

(a) The symbolic parameters coded and documented in PROC1801 (from my book, *Advanced MVS/ESA JCL Examples*, John Wiley & Sons, Inc., 1993) include those for input tape volume serial number and the first two parts of all data set names. This lets me easily specify that test data sets be used in some runs (for testing purposes) and production-named data sets for other runs. //SORTIN reads a non-labeled 1600 bpi foreign tape that conveys transactions "keypunched" on a minicomputer and coded in ASCII. (b) With this execution JCL I am processing an input tape having volume serial number ABC123, and all data sets in the run will be named CSCJGJ.CSC.... . In my installation, names like this identify a programmer's own "test" data sets.

Appendix A

STORAGE MANAGEMENT SUBSYSTEM (SMS)

Storage Management Subsystem is one of the newest major features offered by MVS/ESA. SMS is available only with MVS/ESA; if your installation does not use this version of MVS, SMS is irrelevant to you. Even using MVS/ESA, the use of SMS is optional.

Storage Management Subsystem was designed to help an installation manage its disk space more efficiently. SMS has the potential to make your "writing" DD statements a lot easier to code, but that is not its primary purpose. To use SMS your installation has to make many decisions about categories of data sets and disk storage requirements and define names for each. Your JCL is simplified if a new data set can be created with the characteristics of an already-defined and documented category.

A.1 New JCL Parameters

SMS adds ten new JCL parameters, all of which deal with new cataloged disk data sets. (SMS does not deal with uncataloged data sets, ISAM, in-stream data, the SYSOUT print spool, or tape data sets.) You can use these new JCL parameters with data sets that are not managed by SMS as well as with SMS-managed data sets, as long as SMS is installed and active:

```
AVGREC
LIKE
REFDD
RECORG
KEYOFF
DSNTYPE=PDS
DATACLAS
SECMODEL
```

You can code these new parameters only for data sets that are managed by SMS:

```
STORCLAS (makes the data set SMS-managed)
MGMTCLAS
DSNTYPE=LIBRARY
```

You need a perspective on Storage Management Subsystem to know what your installation management is talking about when the decision is made to use it. I'll give you an overview of the new JCL parameters so you can see where some of them may already be relevant to your work.

A.2 AVGREC, LIKE, and REFDD

You can use AVGREC, LIKE, and REFDD with any data sets; the data sets do not have to be SMS-managed. (But SMS must be active or these parameters will be ignored.)

AVGREC lets you change the way the SPACE parameter works. If you code it like this:

```
//   RECFM=FB,
//   LRECL=80,
//   AVGREC=U,
//   SPACE=(80,(5000,2000),RLSE)
```

you are making "80" be a record length (not block size) and the primary and secondary allocations be unit record counts. If you code AVGREC=K, the primary and secondary allocations are scaled in thousands of records. Coding AVGREC=M makes the allocations in millions of records. Using AVGREC goes hand in hand with omitting the block size (BLKSIZE) from your JCL to let MVS compute it. Since coding BLKSIZE was a major reason for coding a DCB, MVS/ESA "promotes" the LRECL and RECFM DCB subparameters to be parameters of their own so you can eliminate coding DCB=(...). I showed you other examples of AVGREC, LRECL, and RECFM in Chapter 14.

LIKE lets you copy the characteristics of an existing data set to create a new disk or tape data set. It provides the same capability as referring to a cataloged data set with the DCB parameter to "copy in" its characteristics. Unlike naming a data set at the DCB, however, LIKE also copies SPACE parameter information, so it operates more broadly:

```
//   LIKE=CSCJGJ.CSC.CNTL
```

is roughly similar to

```
//  DCB=(CSCJGJ.CSC.CNTL)
```

REFDD works the same as LIKE except that instead of referring to a data set by name, you refer to a previous DD statement by stepname and DDname. REFDD works for new disk or tape data sets and copies information only from the DD statement, not from a cataloged access to the data set or its label. It makes sense to use REFDD to refer back to a DD statement where a data set is created:

```
//  REFDD=*.STEP020.SYSUT2
```

A.3 Partitioned Data Set Extended (PDSE): DSNTYPE

DSNTYPE lets you create a Partitioned Data Set Extended (PDSE) if your installation has made SMS active. A PDSE is faster to access than a regular PDS and you never need to reorganize (compress) it. You can use it for source code and JCL storage but *not* to house load modules.

Code the allocation of a partitioned data set extended exactly the same as for a regular PDS but include the extra parameter DSNTYPE=LIBRARY. Your mention of a nonzero quantity of directory blocks tells MVS that the data set is to be of partitioned organization. But you don't have to worry about the quantity of directory blocks that you specify for a PDSE because every PDSE can hold more than half a million members.

A.4 RECORG and KEYOFF: VSAM Data Set Support

Storage Management Subsystem makes it possible to create and delete VSAM data sets through JCL without explicitly executing the IDCAMS utility. To do this, you have to code DATACLAS (which carries the specifications normally made to IDCAMS), and you can also code the RECORG and KEYOFF parameters.

RECORG stands for "record organization" and can be RECORG=ES for entry sequenced data set, RECORG=RR for relative record data set, RECORG=KS for key sequenced data set (indexed file), or RECORG=LS for a "linear" data set.

KEYOFF stands for "key offset" and is coded KEYOFF=nnn. You code this if you are creating a key sequenced data set. It tells the displacement within the record where the key of the record starts.

Using RECORG and KEYOFF makes sense when your installation has already defined storage classes that supply the other VSAM data set characteristics you previously had to code as IDCAMS DEFINE specifications.

A.5 SECMODEL (RACF Only)

SECMODEL stands for "security model" and deals with the security associated with a data set when an installation uses IBM's security product RACF. You use it according to locally established documentation if your installation uses RACF.

A.6 Storage Management Subsystem Class Parameters

Three new parameters provided by the Storage Management Subsystem end in CLAS. These parameters are the ones that provide access to the heart of SMS functionality.

DATACLAS stands for a "data class" and specifies data set type, record length, space allocation, and VSAM data set options. Think of it as a copy library member containing DSORG, RECFM, LRECL, and SPACE parameters. Data classes are defined by the installation and are locally publicized as established standards. If a data class named XYZ123 describes the data set attributes you need for a data set that you are creating, you can code DATACLAS=XYZ123 and omit coding DCB and SPACE information. If you code DATACLAS *and* DCB or SPACE, your JCL overrides the data class specifications. You can use DATACLAS with tape data sets.

STORCLAS replaces the UNIT and VOL parameters if your installation has defined and named "storage classes." *If you code STORCLAS=name for a data set you are creating, the data set becomes system managed.* If you code UNIT and VOL with STORCLAS, they may be ignored. STORCLAS is similar in capabilities to symbolic device group names. If SMS is not active, STORCLAS is ignored. STORCLAS is also ignored for existing data sets.

MGMTCLAS "Management class" associates the data set with a locally defined name that can be used by the installation as a part of disk space management activities. It's an organizational tool that lets an installation create categories of backup schedules and migration-to-tape schedules and name each such category. An installation can gather data set performance information using the MGMTCLAS name and can process groups of data sets associated with each MGMTCLAS name. MGMTCLAS doesn't supplant any existing JCL parameters. You can code MGMTCLAS with DATACLAS or STORCLAS for new data sets but you do not have to unless your installation requires it. You code management class as MGMTCLAS=*name*, where *name* is up to eight characters in length.

Listed below is an example of a traditional DD statement that creates a disk data set. I've coded several additional versions of this to show you how it evolves into progressively more dependence on SMS:

Traditional JCL to create a disk data set for about 7,700 records:
```
//SYSUT2    DD  DSN=CSCJGJ.CSC.NEWSTUFF,
//   DISP=(NEW,CATLG,DELETE),
//   UNIT=SYSDA,
//   DCB=(RECFM=FB,LRECL=80,BLKSIZE=6160),
//   SPACE=(6160,(100,30),RLSE)
```

Simplified MVS/ESA JCL for 7,700 records, without SMS management:
```
//SYSUT2    DD  DSN=CSCJGJ.CSC.NEWSTUFF,
//   DISP=(NEW,CATLG,DELETE),
//   UNIT=SYSDA,
//   RECFM=FB,
//   LRECL=80,
//   AVGREC=U,
//   SPACE=(80,(7700,2310),RLSE)
```

Even simpler MVS/ESA JCL without SMS management (but a DATACLAS defines attributes and space):
```
//SYSUT2    DD  DSN=CSCJGJ.CSC.NEWSTUFF,
//   DISP=(NEW,CATLG,DELETE),
//   UNIT=SYSDA,
//   DATACLAS=USERTRAN
```

Full MVS/ESA JCL with SMS management (STORCLAS assumes the role of assigning the appropriate disk resource and so the new data becomes SMS managed):
```
//SYSUT2    DD  DSN=CSCJGJ.CSC.NEWSTUFF,
//   DISP=(NEW,CATLG,DELETE),
//   STORCLAS=TESTDATA,
//   DATACLAS=USERTRAN
```

Full MVS/ESA with SMS management including MGMTCLAS:
```
//SYSUT2    DD  DSN=CSCJGJ.CSC.NEWSTUFF,
//   DISP=(NEW,CATLG,DELETE),
//   STORCLAS=TESTDATA,
//   DATACLAS=USERTRAN,
//   MGMTCLAS=USER1
```

To code the later versions of this DD statement you would, of course, have to know what specifications your installation had established for the locally defined storage class TESTDATA and locally defined data class USERTRAN. Establishing and publicizing the nature of these classes is the job of your installation data administrator.

Storage Management Subsystem will ultimately make a tremendous impact on your JCL. But since it comes along almost 30 years after JCL was invented, it will take several years for most installations to fully adopt it. IBM's approach to the gradual implementation of SMS by most shops allows coexistence of older JCL with the newer forms of coding. Installations need to modify the "writing" DD statements of older job streams to include the new SMS parameters only when the data sets the job streams deal with become system managed.

Appendix B

DISK CAPACITIES CHART

Blocks per track	3380		3390		9345	
	Block size	Track capacity	Block size	Track capacity	Block size	Track capacity
1	47,476	47,476	56,664	56,664	46,456	46,456
2	23,476	46,952	27,998	55,996	22,928	45,856
3	15,476	46,428	18,452	55,356	15,074	45,222
4	11,476	45,904	13,682	54,728	11,158	44,632
5	9,076	45,380	10,796	53,980	8,818	44,090
6	7,476	44,856	8,906	53,436	7,214	43,284
7	6,356	44,492	7,548	52,836	6,088	42,616
8	5,492	43,936	6,518	52,144	5,262	42,096
9	4,820	43,380	5,726	51,534	4,600	41,400
10	4,276	42,760	5,064	50,640	4,102	41,020
11	3,860	42,460	4,566	50,226	3,672	40,392
12	3,476	41,712	4,136	49,632	3,304	39,648
13	3,188	41,444	3,768	48,984	3,010	39,130
14	2,932	41,048	3,440	48,160	2,744	38,416
15	2,676	40,140	3,174	47,610	2,512	37,680
16	2,484	39,744	2,942	47,072	2,314	37,024
17	2,324	39,508	2,710	46,070	2,144	36,448
18	2,164	38,952	2,546	45,828	1,980	35,640
19	2,004	38,076	2,376	45,144	1,850	35,150
20	1,876	37,520	2,212	44,240	1,748	34,960
21	1,780	37,380	2,082	43,722	1,618	33,978
22	1,684	37,048	1,946	42,812	1,516	33,352
23	1,588	36,524	1,850	42,550	1,414	32,522
24	1,492	35,808	1,748	41,952	1,352	32,448
25	1,396	34,900	1,646	41,150	1,250	31,250
26	1,332	34,632	1,550	40,300	1,182	30,732
27	1,268	34,236	1,482	40,014	1,128	30,456
28	1,204	33,712	1,386	38,808	1,052	29,456
29	1,140	33,060	1,318	38,222	984	28,536
30	1,076	32,280	1,250	37,500	950	28,500
31	1,044	32,364	1,182	36,642	888	27,528
32	980	31,360	1,154	36,928	854	27,328
33	948	31,284	1,086	35,838	820	27,060
34	916	31,144	1,018	34,612	752	25,568
35	852	29,820	984	34,440	718	25,130
36	820	29,520	950	34,200	690	24,840
37	788	29,156	888	32,856	656	24,272
38	756	28,728	854	32,452	622	23,636
39	724	28,236	820	31,980	588	22,932
40	692	27,680	786	31,440	554	22,160

Practical MVS JCL Examples (Janossy, John Wiley & Sons, Inc., 1993)

B.1 Raw Disk Track Capacity for 3380, 3390, and 9350 Disks

EBCDIC/ASCII COLLATION CHART

DECIMAL	BINARY	ASCII	CTL	HEX	NIBBLES		EBCDIC	OCTAL	CRUMBLES		
0	00000000	NUL	sp	00	0000	0000	NUL	000	00	000	000
1	00000001	SOH	A	01	0000	0001	SOH	001	00	000	001
2	00000010	STX	B	02	0000	0010	STX	002	00	000	010
3	00000011	ETX	C	03	0000	0011	ETX	003	00	000	011
4	00000100	EOT	D	04	0000	0100	PF	004	00	000	100
5	00000101	ENQ	E	05	0000	0101	HT	005	00	000	101
6	00000110	ACK	F	06	0000	0110	LC	006	00	000	110
7	00000111	BEL	G	07	0000	0111	DEL	007	00	000	111
8	00001000	BS	H	08	0000	1000	GE	010	00	001	000
9	00001001	HT	I	09	0000	1001	RLF	011	00	001	001
10	00001010	LF	J	0A	0000	1010	SMM	012	00	001	010
11	00001011	VT	K	0B	0000	1011	VT	013	00	001	011
12	00001100	FF	L	0C	0000	1100	FF	014	00	001	100
13	00001101	CR	M	0D	0000	1101	CR	015	00	001	101
14	00001110	SO	N	0E	0000	1110	SO	016	00	001	110
15	00001111	SI	O	0F	0000	1111	SI	017	00	001	111
16	00010000	DLE	P	10	0001	0000	DLE	020	00	010	000
17	00010001	DC1	Q	11	0001	0001	DC1	021	00	010	001
18	00010010	DC2	R	12	0001	0010	DC2	022	00	010	010
19	00010011	DC3	S	13	0001	0011	TM	023	00	010	011
20	00010100	DC4	T	14	0001	0100	RES	024	00	010	100
21	00010101	NAK	U	15	0001	0101	NL	025	00	010	101
22	00010110	SYN	V	16	0001	0110	BS	026	00	010	110
23	00010111	ETB	W	17	0001	0111	IL	027	00	010	111
24	00011000	CAN	X	18	0001	1000	CAN	030	00	011	000
25	00011001	EM	Y	19	0001	1001	EM	031	00	011	001
26	00011010	SUB	Z	1A	0001	1010	CC	032	00	011	010
27	00011011	ESC	[	1B	0001	1011	CU1	033	00	011	011
28	00011100	FS	\	1C	0001	1100	IFS	034	00	011	100
29	00011101	GS	]	1D	0001	1101	IGS	035	00	011	101
30	00011110	RS	~	1E	0001	1110	IRS	036	00	011	110
31	00011111	US	?	1F	0001	1111	IUS	037	00	011	111
32	00100000	sp		20	0010	0000	DS	040	00	100	000
33	00100001	!		21	0010	0001	SOS	041	00	100	001
34	00100010	"		22	0010	0010	FS	042	00	100	010
35	00100011	#		23	0010	0011		043	00	100	011

DECIMAL	BINARY	ASCII CTL	HEX	NIBBLES	EBCDIC	OCTAL	CRUMBLES
36	00100100	$	24	0010 0100	BYP	044	00 100 100
37	00100101	%	25	0010 0101	LF	045	00 100 101
38	00100110	&	26	0010 0110	ETB	046	00 100 110
39	00100111	'	27	0010 0111	ESC	047	00 100 111
40	00101000	(	28	0010 1000		050	00 101 000
41	00101001	)	29	0010 1001		051	00 101 001
42	00101010	*	2A	0010 1010	SM	052	00 101 010
43	00101011	+	2B	0010 1011	CU2	053	00 101 011
44	00101100	,	2C	0010 1100		054	00 101 100
45	00101101	-	2D	0010 1101	ENQ	055	00 101 101
46	00101110	.	2E	0010 1110	ACK	056	00 101 110
47	00101111	/	2F	0010 1111	BEL	057	00 101 111
48	00110000	0	30	0011 0000		060	00 110 000
49	00110001	1	31	0011 0001		061	00 110 001
50	00110010	2	32	0011 0010	SYN	062	00 110 010
51	00110011	3	33	0011 0011		063	00 110 011
52	00110100	4	34	0011 0100	PN	064	00 110 100
53	00110101	5	35	0011 0101	RS	065	00 110 101
54	00110110	6	36	0011 0110	UC	066	00 110 110
55	00110111	7	37	0011 0111	EOT	067	00 110 111
56	00111000	8	38	0011 1000		070	00 111 000
57	00111001	9	39	0011 1001		071	00 111 001
58	00111010	:	3A	0011 1010		072	00 111 010
59	00111011	;	3B	0011 1011	CU3	073	00 111 011
60	00111100	<	3C	0011 1100	DC4	074	00 111 100
61	00111101	=	3D	0011 1101	NAK	075	00 111 101
62	00111110	>	3E	0011 1110		076	00 111 110
63	00111111	?	3F	0011 1111	SUB	077	00 111 111
64	01000000	@	40	0100 0000	sp	100	01 000 000
65	01000001	A	41	0100 0001		101	01 000 001
66	01000010	B	42	0100 0010		102	01 000 010
67	01000011	C	43	0100 0011		103	01 000 011
68	01000100	D	44	0100 0100		104	01 000 100
69	01000101	E	45	0100 0101		105	01 000 101
70	01000110	F	46	0100 0110		106	01 000 110
71	01000111	G	47	0100 0111		107	01 000 111
72	01001000	H	48	0100 1000		110	01 001 000
73	01001001	I	49	0100 1001		111	01 001 001
74	01001010	J	4A	0100 1010		112	01 001 010
75	01001011	K	4B	0100 1011	.	113	01 001 011
76	01001100	L	4C	0100 1100	<	114	01 001 100
77	01001101	M	4D	0100 1101	(	115	01 001 101
78	01001110	N	4E	0100 1110	+	116	01 001 110
79	01001111	O	4F	0100 1111		117	01 001 111
80	01010000	P	50	0101 0000	&	120	01 010 000
81	01010001	Q	51	0101 0001		121	01 010 001
82	01010010	R	52	0101 0010		122	01 010 010
83	01010011	S	53	0101 0011		123	01 010 011

DECIMAL	BINARY	ASCII CTL	HEX	NIBBLES	EBCDIC	OCTAL	CRUMBLES
84	01010100	T	54	0101 0100		124	01 010 100
85	01010101	U	55	0101 0101		125	01 010 101
86	01010110	V	56	0101 0110		126	01 010 110
87	01010111	W	57	0101 0111		127	01 010 111
88	01011000	X	58	0101 1000		130	01 011 000
89	01011001	Y	59	0101 1001		131	01 011 001
90	01011010	Z	5A	0101 1010	!	132	01 011 010
91	01011011	[	5B	0101 1011	$	133	01 011 011
92	01011100	\	5C	0101 1100	*	134	01 011 100
93	01011101	]	5D	0101 1101	)	135	01 011 101
94	01011110	^	5E	0101 1110	;	136	01 011 110
95	01011111	_	5F	0101 1111		137	01 011 111
96	01100000	`	60	0110 0000	-	140	01 100 000
97	01100001	a	61	0110 0001	/	141	01 100 001
98	01100010	b	62	0110 0010		142	01 100 010
99	01100011	c	63	0110 0011		143	01 100 011
100	01100100	d	64	0110 0100		144	01 100 100
101	01100101	e	65	0110 0101		145	01 100 101
102	01100110	f	66	0110 0110		146	01 100 110
103	01100111	g	67	0110 0111		147	01 100 111
104	01101000	h	68	0110 1000		150	01 101 000
105	01101001	i	69	0110 1001		151	01 101 001
106	01101010	j	6A	0110 1010	¦	152	01 101 010
107	01101011	k	6B	0110 1011	,	153	01 101 011
108	01101100	l	6C	0110 1100	%	154	01 101 100
109	01101101	m	6D	0110 1101		155	01 101 101
110	01101110	n	6E	0110 1110	$>$	156	01 101 110
111	01101111	o	6F	0110 1111	?	157	01 101 111
112	01110000	p	70	0111 0000		160	01 110 000
113	01110001	q	71	0111 0001		161	01 110 001
114	01110010	r	72	0111 0010		162	01 110 010
115	01110011	s	73	0111 0011		163	01 110 011
116	01110100	t	74	0111 0100		164	01 110 100
117	01110101	u	75	0111 0101		165	01 110 101
118	01110110	v	76	0111 0110		166	01 110 110
119	01110111	w	77	0111 0111		167	01 110 111
120	01111000	x	78	0111 1000		170	01 111 000
121	01111001	y	79	0111 1001	`	171	01 111 001
122	01111010	z	7A	0111 1010	:	172	01 111 010
123	01111011	{	7B	0111 1011	#	173	01 111 011
124	01111100	¦	7C	0111 1100	@	174	01 111 100
125	01111101	}	7D	0111 1101	'	175	01 111 101
126	01111110	~	7E	0111 1110	=	176	01 111 110
127	01111111	DEL	7F	0111 1111	"	177	01 111 111
128	10000000		80	1000 0000		200	10 000 000
129	10000001		81	1000 0001	a	201	10 000 001
130	10000010		82	1000 0010	b	202	10 000 010
131	10000011		83	1000 0011	c	203	10 000 011

DECIMAL	BINARY	ASCII CTL	HEX	NIBBLES	EBCDIC	OCTAL	CRUMBLES
132	10000100		84	1000 0100	d	204	10 000 100
133	10000101		85	1000 0101	e	205	10 000 101
134	10000110		86	1000 0110	f	206	10 000 110
135	10000111		87	1000 0111	g	207	10 000 111
136	10001000		88	1000 1000	h	210	10 001 000
137	10001001		89	1000 1001	i	211	10 001 001
138	10001010		8A	1000 1010		212	10 001 010
139	10001011		8B	1000 1011		213	10 001 011
140	10001100		8C	1000 1100		214	10 001 100
141	10001101		8D	1000 1101		215	10 001 101
142	10001110		8E	1000 1110		216	10 001 110
143	10001111		8F	1000 1111		217	10 001 111
144	10010000		90	1001 0000		220	10 010 000
145	10010001		91	1001 0001	j	221	10 010 001
146	10010010		92	1001 0010	k	222	10 010 010
147	10010011		93	1001 0011	l	223	10 010 011
148	10010100		94	1001 0100	m	224	10 010 100
149	10010101		95	1001 0101	n	225	10 010 101
150	10010110		96	1001 0110	o	226	10 010 110
151	10010111		97	1001 0111	p	227	10 010 111
152	10011000		98	1001 1000	q	230	10 011 000
153	10011001		99	1001 1001	r	231	10 011 001
154	10011010		9A	1001 1010		232	10 011 010
155	10011011		9B	1001 1011		233	10 011 011
156	10011100		9C	1001 1100		234	10 011 100
157	10011101		9D	1001 1101		235	10 011 101
158	10011110		9E	1001 1110		236	10 011 110
159	10011111		9F	1001 1111		237	10 011 111
160	10100000		A0	1010 0000		240	10 100 000
161	10100001		A1	1010 0001	~	241	10 100 001
162	10100010		A2	1010 0010	s	242	10 100 010
163	10100011		A3	1010 0011	t	243	10 100 011
164	10100100		A4	1010 0100	u	244	10 100 100
165	10100101		A5	1010 0101	v	245	10 100 101
166	10100110		A6	1010 0110	w	246	10 100 110
167	10100111		A7	1010 0111	x	247	10 100 111
168	10101000		A8	1010 1000	y	250	10 101 000
169	10101001		A9	1010 1001	z	251	10 101 001
170	10101010		AA	1010 1010		252	10 101 010
171	10101011		AB	1010 1011		253	10 101 011
172	10101100		AC	1010 1100		254	10 101 100
173	10101101		AD	1010 1101		255	10 101 101
174	10101110		AE	1010 1110		256	10 101 110
175	10101111		AF	1010 1111		257	10 101 111
176	10110000		B0	1011 0000		260	10 110 000
177	10110001		B1	1011 0001		261	10 110 001
178	10110010		B2	1011 0010		262	10 110 010
179	10110011		B3	1011 0011		263	10 110 011

DECIMAL	BINARY	ASCII CTL	HEX	NIBBLES	EBCDIC	OCTAL	CRUMBLES
180	10110100		B4	1011 0100		264	10 110 100
181	10110101		B5	1011 0101		265	10 110 101
182	10110110		B6	1011 0110		266	10 110 110
183	10110111		B7	1011 0111		267	10 110 111
184	10111000		B8	1011 1000		270	10 111 000
185	10111001		B9	1011 1001		271	10 111 001
186	10111010		BA	1011 1010		272	10 111 010
187	10111011		BB	1011 1011		273	10 111 011
188	10111100		BC	1011 1100		274	10 111 100
189	10111101		BD	1011 1101		275	10 111 101
190	10111110		BE	1011 1110		276	10 111 110
191	10111111		BF	1011 1111		277	10 111 111
192	11000000		C0	1100 0000	{	300	11 000 000
193	11000001		C1	1100 0001	A	301	11 000 001
194	11000010		C2	1100 0010	B	302	11 000 010
195	11000011		C3	1100 0011	C	303	11 000 011
196	11000100		C4	1100 0100	D	304	11 000 100
197	11000101		C5	1100 0101	E	305	11 000 101
198	11000110		C6	1100 0110	F	306	11 000 110
199	11000111		C7	1100 0111	G	307	11 000 111
200	11001000		C8	1100 1000	H	310	11 001 000
201	11001001		C9	1100 1001	I	311	11 001 001
202	11001010		CA	1100 1010		312	11 001 010
203	11001011		CB	1100 1011		313	11 001 011
204	11001100		CC	1100 1100		314	11 001 100
205	11001101		CD	1100 1101		315	11 001 101
206	11001110		CE	1100 1110		316	11 001 110
207	11001111		CF	1100 1111		317	11 001 111
208	11010000		D0	1101 0000	}	320	11 010 000
209	11010001		D1	1101 0001	J	321	11 010 001
210	11010010		D2	1101 0010	K	322	11 010 010
211	11010011		D3	1101 0011	L	323	11 010 011
212	11010100		D4	1101 0100	M	324	11 010 100
213	11010101		D5	1101 0101	N	325	11 010 101
214	11010110		D6	1101 0110	O	326	11 010 110
215	11010111		D7	1101 0111	P	327	11 010 111
216	11011000		D8	1101 1000	Q	330	11 011 000
217	11011001		D9	1101 1001	R	331	11 011 001
218	11011010		DA	1101 1010		332	11 011 010
219	11011011		DB	1101 1011		333	11 011 011
220	11011100		DC	1101 1100		334	11 011 100
221	11011101		DD	1101 1101		335	11 011 101
222	11011110		DE	1101 1110		336	11 011 110
223	11011111		DF	1101 1111		337	11 011 111
224	11100000		E0	1110 0000	\	340	11 100 000
225	11100001		E1	1110 0001		341	11 100 001
226	11100010		E2	1110 0010	S	342	11 100 010
227	11100011		E3	1110 0011	T	343	11 100 011

DECIMAL	BINARY	ASCII CTL	HEX	NIBBLES	EBCDIC	OCTAL	CRUMBLES
228	11100100		E4	1110 0100	U	344	11 100 100
229	11100101		E5	1110 0101	V	345	11 100 101
230	11100110		E6	1110 0110	W	346	11 100 110
231	11100111		E7	1110 0111	X	347	11 100 111
232	11101000		E8	1110 1000	Y	350	11 101 000
233	11101001		E9	1110 1001	Z	351	11 101 001
234	11101010		EA	1110 1010		352	11 101 010
235	11101011		EB	1110 1011		353	11 101 011
236	11101100		EC	1110 1100		354	11 101 100
237	11101101		ED	1110 1101		355	11 101 101
238	11101110		EE	1110 1110		356	11 101 110
239	11101111		EF	1110 1111		357	11 101 111
240	11110000		F0	1111 0000	0	360	11 110 000
241	11110001		F1	1111 0001	1	361	11 110 001
242	11110010		F2	1111 0010	2	362	11 110 010
243	11110011		F3	1111 0011	3	363	11 110 011
244	11110100		F4	1111 0100	4	364	11 110 100
245	11110101		F5	1111 0101	5	365	11 110 101
246	11110110		F6	1111 0110	6	366	11 110 110
247	11110111		F7	1111 0111	7	367	11 110 111
248	11111000		F8	1111 1000	8	370	11 111 000
249	11111001		F9	1111 1001	9	371	11 111 001
250	11111010		FA	1111 1010		372	11 111 010
251	11111011		FB	1111 1011		373	11 111 011
252	11111100		FC	1111 1100		374	11 111 100
253	11111101		FD	1111 1101		375	11 111 101
254	11111110		FE	1111 1110		376	11 111 110
255	11111111		FF	1111 1111		377	11 111 111

I'd like to thank Ron Stevens, a true gentleman and scholar, for his help in preparing this table. Ron wrote a program that generated the 256 bit patterns and formatted the binary representations of each in the groupings that made most sense for numeric, hex, and octal demonstration. The artwork for this appendix is the original from the first (1987) edition of this book.   -JGJ-

Appendix D

IBM UTILITY PROGRAM RETURN CODE REFERENCE

IBM utilities are programs supplied either as part of the MVS operating system or licensed separately by IBM. They are written in Assembler language by IBM systems programmers. You execute utility programs the same way as any other programs, that is, by using the EXEC statement. Documentation supplied by IBM in manuals tells you what DDnames each utility program expects in JCL.

Each utility program reads instructions that you code to tell it what you want it to do. Your instructions take the form of 80-byte records called control statements. Each utility reads its control statements at its DDname //SYSIN. Because many of these utilities were written by different people almost 30 years ago, inconsistencies exist between them in the way different utilities expect their control statements to be coded. For example, field positions within records are coded differently for DFSORT, IDCAMS, IEBGENER, and IEBPTPCH.

All of the utilities communicate processing results to you via the return code, the four-digit number that you can test in subsequent job steps with the COND parameter. All utilities indicate successful processing with the return code 0000. *Almost all utilities assign a different meaning to other return code values.* I have listed the COND CODEs used by each IBM utility here for your convenience.

DFSORT
General purpose sort/merge utility. Competing products such as CA-SORT and Syncsort issue similar condition codes.

    0000 Successful execution
    0004 (Not used)
    0008 (Not used)
    0012 (Not used)
    0016 I/O error or out of sequence error; step terminated
    0020 //SYSOUT DDname or message DDname missing

IDCAMS

Multipurpose Access Method Services utility. IDCAMS can copy, print, dump, catalog, uncatalog, rename data sets, delete unexpired data sets and PDS members, define, alter and delete VSAM data sets, and list catalog entries. It can also create, alter, and delete generation data groups bases.

0000   Successful execution
0004   Problem in a noncritical function; not usually fatal
0008   Error in requested function; some aspect bypassed
0012   Serious logical error; function abandoned
0016   Severe error; IDCAMS command processing terminated

IEBCOMPR

Compares data sets or whole partitioned data sets. One data set is read at //SYSUT1, and the other is read at //SYSUT2. The report produced at //SYS-PRINT identifies records that differ but shows them only in hexadecimal.

0000   Successful completion
0004   (Not used)
0008   Unequal comparison; processing continue
0012   Unrecoverable error; step terminated
0016   User routine passed 0016 (rarely used)

IEBCOPY

Copies or merges partitioned data sets; copies selected members. This utility is used for "compressing" (reorganizing) partitioned data sets. State the input PDS at //SYSUT1 and the output at //SYSUT2 and you can code DUMMY at //SYSIN.

0000   Successful completion
0004   Recoverable error; investigate
0008   Unrecoverable error; step terminated

IEBDG

Creates test data in patterns. The control statements read at //SYSIN are tedious to code, but you may consider using this utility to create test data that contains packed decimal (COMP-3) values.

0000   Successful completion
0004   User routine passed 0016 (rarely used)
0008   Error in control statements; processing continues
0012   Error during I/O; step terminated
0016   Unrecoverable error; step terminated

IEBEDIT

Manipulates JCL statements in batch mode.

0000   Successful completion

0004   Error; output may not be usable
0008   Unrecoverable I/O or control statement error
0012   (Not used)
0016   (Not used)

IEBGENER
Copies and optionally reformats records or inserts literal characters in fields.

0000   Successful completion
0004   Warning error; probable successful completion
0008   User requested processing of data set labels only
0012   Unrecoverable error; step terminates
0016   User routine passed 0016 (rarely used)

IEBIMAGE
Creates and maintains forms control buffer (FCB) modules in SYS1.IMAGELIB control data set, electronically replacing physical carriage control tapes for printers; also creates or modifies printer character tables for certain laser printers, also housed in SYS1.IMAGELIB.

0000   Successful completion
0004   Operations performed; exceptions encountered
0008   Some operation not performed; investigate messages
0012   Severe exceptions encountered; possible termination
0016   Catastrophic exception; execution terminated
0020   //SYSPRINT data set could not be opened; terminated
0024   Control statements/parameters invalid; terminated

IEBISAM
Copies ISAM data set to sequential data set (obsolete).

0000   Successful completion
0004   User routine passed 0004 or 0012
0008   Error terminated the operation
0012   User routine passed value not 00, 04, 08, or 12
0016   Error terminated the operation

IEBPTPCH
Produces formatted print from records; the control statements you code at //SYSIN can indicate two lines of titles up to 120 bytes each, and fields can be positioned in printlines in a sequence different from their positions within input.

0000   Successful completion
0004   Data set empty or PDS specified has no members
0008   PDS member specified does not exist
0012   Unrecoverable error or incorrect user routine return code
0016   User routine passed 0016 (rarely used)

IEBUPDTE

Modifies lines in sequential or partitioned data set in batch mode. Programmers more commonly use TSO/ISPF for many of these functions now.

0000	Successful completion
0004	Incorrect syntax or use of control statement
0008	(Not used)
0012	Unrecoverable error; step terminated
0016	User routine passed 0016 (rarely used)

IEHATLAS

Recovers data from damaged disk volumes; attempts to write on the defective track and reads back the data written. If a track is judged defective, this utility assigns an alternate track to replace it. Can produce a list of data on the defective track and can be used to place reconstructed data on the alternate track. The disk address of defective tracks is obtained from a dump or backup data. A more common recovery procedure is to entirely recreate a corrupted data set from a tape backup.

0000	Successful completion; alternate track assigned
0004	Device does not have software-assignable tracks
0008	All alternate tracks are in use
0012	Requested main memory not available
0016	I/O error in alternate track assignment
0020	Error other than data check or missing address marker
0024	Error in VTOC Format 4 DSCB record
0028	Alternate track information not reliable
0032	Error in count field of last record on track
0036	Errors in Home Address or in Record Zero
0040	Errors even after alternate track assignment
0044	(Not used)
0048	No error found and no alternate assigned
0052	I/O error; cannot reexecute the EXCP for it
0056	System does not support track overflow
0060	Track address indicated does not belong to data set

IEHDASDR

Initializes disk volumes, assigns alternate tracks for defective ones, and dumps or restores disk contents (used by operations personnel).

0000	Successful completion
0004	Unusual condition but result satisfactory
0008	Operation did not complete successfully
0012	(Not used)
0016	Error invoking utility or opening input or //SYSPRINT

IEHINITT

Applies volume label and tape mark to a tape (used by operations personnel).

0000	Successful completion; //SYSPRINT present
0004	Successful completion; //SYSPRINT DDname not present
0008	Errors encountered and reported at //SYSPRINT
0012	Errors encountered and //SYSPRINT DDname not present
0016	Error in reading control statement or data set

IEHLIST

Lists partitioned data set members or disk VTOC (volume table of contents). Programmers routinely use TSO/ISPF to accomplish these tasks now.

0000	Successful completion
0004	(Not used)
0008	Error encountered; request ignored; processing continues
0012	Permanent I/O error encountered; step terminated
0016	Unrecoverable error reading data set; step terminated

IEHMOVE

Move or copy data sets including OS catalogs (obsolete) but not ISAM or VSAM data sets. Can also rename or replace specified members of a partitioned data set. Most of these functions are now performed by IDCAMS.

0000	Successful completion
0004	Specified function not completed; processing continues
0008	Abnormal condition but recovery has been completed
0012	Unrecoverable error; step terminated
0016	Impossible to open //SYSIN or //SYSPRINT

IEHPROGM

Creates, modifies, and deletes OS passwords. Other functions formerly accomplished with IEHPROGM, such as creating generation data group indexes (bases), are now handled by IDCAMS.

0000	Successful completion
0004	Error in control statement name field or in PARM field of your EXEC statement
0008	Incorrect control statement or invalid request
0012	I/O error on disk VTOC, //SYSIN, or //SYSPRINT
0016	Unrecoverable error; step terminated

IEWL (Also HEWL)

The standard MVS linkage editor. IEWL combines object files produced by language compilers with service routines to create an executable load module. It accepts control statements at //SYSIN that identify DDnames pointing to libraries containing input object module or load module members. The resulting load module is written at //SYSLMOD as a member of a partitioned data set.

0000	Successful completion; processable load module created
0004	Warning messages listed; execution was successful
0008	Error message listed; load module execution may fail
0012	Severe errors in load module; execution impossible
0016	Operation terminated; incomplete load module produced

IGYCRCTL

The VS COBOL II compiler; this system software processes your COBOL source code statements to create a source code listing and an object file for linkage editing. VS COBOL II supports 1985 ANSI COBOL standards. Note: The return codes listed here may be posted by the compiler as it processes your source code. As you execute your program, it may post a return code in the range of 1000–1999 to indicate a runtime error ("user abend"). Return codes in this range are built into your program load module automatically by the compiler. Runtime return codes are documented in IBM manuals for the VS COBOL II compiler and in error messages printed in your system output.

0000	(I) Successful completion; informational messages only
0004	(W) Warning errors only; object module is not flawed
0008	(E) Error; object module flawed
0012	(S) Severe error in source code; object module flawed
0016	(U) Unrecoverable errors caused compiler to terminate

IKFCBL00

The VS COBOL compiler; this system software processes your COBOL source code statements to create a source code listing and an object file suitable for linkage editing. VS COBOL follows the 1974 ANSI COBOL standards. Note: The return codes listed here may be posted by the compiler as it processes your source code. As you execute your program, it may post a return code such as 0519 or 3505 to indicate a runtime error. Return codes such as 0519 and 3505 are built into your program automatically by this compiler. VS COBOL runtime return codes are documented for your convenience at the end of Appendix E in this book.

0000	Successful completion
0004	(W) Warning errors only; object module is not flawed
0008	(C) Caution; object module flawed
0012	(E) Serious error in source code; object module flawed
0016	(D) Disastrous problem in source code; object module flawed
0505	Compiler has failed and prematurely terminated due to gross source code syntax error and is unable to issue appropriate error messages

Additional utility programs exist for CICS, DB2, and SMS and are documented in the IBM manuals associated with those products. All newer IBM utilities follow the general return code interpretation conventions exhibited by the IDCAMS utility.

Appendix E

SYSTEM COMPLETION CODE REFERENCE

MVS tells you why a job failed using a three-position hexadecimal value known as the *system completion code.* When a program abends (ABnormally ENDs), the system completion code is printed in the job log. You can usually find the system completion code most quickly by using the TSO/ISPF "find" command within SDSF for the word "abend" as in Figure E.1.

When you find the word "abend" in the job log and the system completion code following it, you sometimes have to look above in the system print to find the same code followed by a suffix, usually called a *reason code.* The location of the system completion code and the suffix varies for different kinds of problems. This is admittedly not very user-friendly in either location or content.

IBM documents system completion codes in *MVS/370 Message Library: System Codes,* IBM publication GC38-1008. I have listed the most commonly occurring system completion codes here for your convenience and provided explanations of each in plain language.

001   Record Length/Block Size Discrepancy

Your problem is in conflicting record or block size specifications in the program or JCL, damaged tape or disk media, a hardware error on a tape or disk drive, or incorrect logic attempting to read after end of data set has been reached.

001-0	A discrepancy exists between the record length and block size specified in the program or JCL and these values in the data set label. Examine and correct your JCL or program.
001-2	An error was detected in closing the data set.
001-3	QSAM error could not be resolved by MVS.
001-4	You probably forgot to code BLOCK CONTAINS 0 RECORDS in the FD for a file in a COBOL program. The blocking defaults to one record per block if the phrase is omitted, which almost always conflicts with the actual blocking of the data set if it is blocked.
001-5	You attempted I/O after the end of a file was reached.

```
EDIT ---- CSCJGJ.CSC.CNTL(APPE1) - 01.00 -------------------- COLUMNS 001 072
COMMAND ===> sub                                         SCROLL ===> PAGE
***** **************************** TOP OF DATA ****************************
000100 //CSCJGJA   JOB 1,              ACCOUNTING INFORMATION
000200 //   'BIN 7--JANOSSY',          PROGRAMMER NAME AND DELIVERY BIN
000300 //   CLASS=A,                   INPUT QUEUE CLASS
000400 //   MSGLEVEL=(1,1),            HOW MUCH MVS SYSTEM PRINT DESIRED
000500 //   MSGCLASS=X,                PRINT DESTINATION X A L N OR O
000600 //   NOTIFY=CSCJGJ              WHO TO TELL WHEN JOB IS DONE
000700 //*
000800 //*******************************************************************
000900 //* COMPILE AND LINK USING VS COBOL II                             *
001000 //*******************************************************************
001100 //STEP010  EXEC COB2CLJ,
001200 //      PDS='CSCJGJ.CSC.COBOL',
001300 //    MEMBER='XXXXXXXX',
001400 //    LOADLIB='CSCJGJ.CSC.LOADLIB'
001500 //        `
```

> You get this message when a job ABENDs (abnormally ends). You then have to examine the top part of your output, called the "job log," to see why the job failed.

```
JOB CSCJGJA(JOB00328) SUBMITTED
10.21.18 JOB00328 $HASP165 CSCJGJA  ENDED AT N1 - ABENDED CN(INTERNAL)
***
```

```
  SDSF OUTPUT DISPLAY CSCJGJA  JOB00328  DSID    2 LINE 0        COLUMNS 02- 81
  COMMAND INPUT ===>                                         SCROLL ===> PAGE
  ****************************** TOP OF DATA ******************************
                      J E S 2  J O B  L O G  --  S Y S T E M  I B M 1  --  N

  10.21.15 JOB00328  IRR010I  USERID CSCJGJ   IS ASSIGNED TO THIS JOB.
  10.21.16 JOB00328  ICH70001I CSCJGJ   LAST ACCESS AT 10:19:19 ON SATURDAY, NOVEM
  10.21.16 JOB00328  $HASP373 CSCJGJA   STARTED - INIT  1 - CLASS A - SYS IBM1
  10.21.17 JOB00328  IEC141I 013-18,IGG0191B,CSCJGJA,COB2,SYSIN,111,USER00,CSCJGJ.
  10.21.17 JOB00328  IEA995I SYMPTOM DUMP OUTPUT
                     SYSTEM COMPLETION CODE=013
                      TIME=10.21.17  SEQ=34315  CPU=0000  ASID=0101
                      PSW AT TIME OF ERROR  075C1000   E8799C  ILC 2  INTC 0D
                        NO ACTIVE MODULE FOUND
                        DATA AT PSW  00E87996 - 4100395E  A0D4DE0  39025820
                        GPR  0-3  00E87B58  A0013000  00005B8  00E871FA
                        GPR  4-7  008DBD68  008DB34C  008DB FC  008DB34C
                        GPR  8-11 008DB31C  00FD6918  58FC86 8  008DB094
                        GPR 12-15 00000008  00000000  00E873 0  00000018
                     END OF SYMPTOM DUMP
  10.21.17 JOB00328  IEF450I CSCJGJA COB2 STEP010 - ABEND=S013 U0000 REASON=000000
  10.21.18 JOB00328  $HASP395 CSCJGJA ENDED
  ------ JES2 JOB STATISTICS ------
     28 NOV 92 JOB EXECUTION DATE
```

> The system completion code such as S013 following the word ABEND often requires a suffix to be meaningful. You have to look farther up in the job log to see the same code with its suffix. The line carrying the suffix also contains the DDname (such as SYSIN here) to help you find the problem.

E.1 TSO/ISPF Job Abend Message and Job Log Placement of the System Completion Code

013   Conflicting DCB Parameters at Open

The actions you need to take to resolve a completion code of 013 depend on the specific reason code value received. Check the OPEN, FD, and SELECT/ASSIGN statements in the program and your job control language spelling of data set names.

013-10   Dummy data set needs buffer space; specify BLKSIZE.
013-14   The DD statement must specify a partitioned data set but currently does not.
013-18   The member you specified was not found in the partitioned data set.
013-1C   I/O error searching partitioned data set directory.
013-20   Block size is not a multiple of record length or is incorrect for variable length records.
013-34   Record length versus block size is inconsistent, or a dummy data set needs buffer space.
013-50   You tried to open a printer for other than output.
013-60   Block size is not equal to record length for unblocked data set.
013-64   DUMMY can only be used for sequential data sets.
013-68   Block size cannot be greater than 32,760.
013-A4   SYSIN or SYSOUT data sets must be sequential.
013-A8   Invalid record format for SYSIN or SYSOUT data set.
013-D0   Partitioned data set (PDS) cannot carry record format of FBS or FS.
013-E4   The number of concatenated partitioned data sets (PDS) exceeds the limit of 16.

04E, 04F   DB2 Database Error

A connected user task or a task internal to the DB2 database has been terminated because the operating system has detected an internal DB2 error. Refer to *IBM DATABASE 2 Messages and Codes*, IBM publication SC26-4113, for problem resolution suggestions.

0C1   Operation Exception

The computer is being directed to perform a machine language instruction that is not valid or that has not been implemented on the particular model of computer. Several things can cause an OC1:

- //SYSOUT DD statement is missing from your JCL. Check to see if this DDname is present in your JCL for the step. DISPLAY, TRACE, and EXHIBIT in a COBOL program direct output to this DDname.
- The value after the AFTER ADVANCING phrase in a COBOL WRITE statement is outside the range of 0 to 99.

- A subscript value exceeds the bounds of the table with which it is associated, causing inappropriate access to a memory location.
- A data set was not open when an I/O was directed to it.
- Files have not been closed before a STOP RUN is executed.

0C2   Privileged Operation Exception

The program has attempted to invoke an operation available only to specially authorized programs. Several things can cause an 0C2:
- A DD statement is missing or incorrect.
- A data set was not open at the time I/O was directed to it.
- A subscript is uninitialized or carrying a value out of bounds for the table that it is associated with.

0C3   Execute Exception

An OC3 results from seriously incorrect program logic. You may get this error in circumstances similar to those for 0C1 or 0C2.

0C4   Protection Exception

The program is attempting to access a memory address that is not within the memory area it is authorized to use. This can occur for several reasons:
- A SELECT/ASSIGN statement is missing.
- Your ASSIGN clause indicates an incorrect system name.
- You omitted the USING phrase after the procedure division heading in a CALLed program.
- A DD statement is incorrect or missing.
- A subscript or index is not initialized or has taken on a value outside the bounds of the table with which it is associated.
- You tried to access a field in the FD of a file that is not open.

0C5   Addressing Exception

The program is attempting to access a memory location that is outside the bounds of available real storage on the machine. Several things can cause this:
- A subscript or index is out of bounds for the table it is associated with.

- You left a subscript or index uninitialized (no VALUE clause or SET).
- You tried to close a data set a second time.
- You made an improper exit from a performed paragraph, which might occur when logic within the paragraph does a GO TO exit but the paragraph had not been performed THRU the exit.
- You supplied incorrect DD statement DCB values or forgot to code DCB parameters.
- You tried to read or write a data set before opening it.
- You tried to access a field in the FD of a COBOL program before an output file is opened, before reading the first record from an input file, or after execution of the AT END option for an input file.
- You coded a CALL using incorrect parameters.

0C6   Specification Exception

This exception indicates a problem with the alignment of a data field on a memory word boundary. Several things can cause a 0C6:

- You let a subscript take on a value outside the bounds of the table it is associated with.
- You coded an improper exit from a performed paragraph; this can occur when logic within the paragraph does a GO TO exit but the paragraph had not been performed THRU the exit.
- You used COMP fields for record storage, as opposed to use for internal program values only, and you positioned them without regard to forcing alignment on word boundaries with the SYNC option.
- You made inconsistent usage of COMP linkage area fields between a calling program and a called program.
- You used a multiplier or divisor larger than 15 digits and a sign in a decimal arithmetic operation.
- You omitted a DD statement or coded it incorrectly.

0C7   Data Exception

This is the single most common cause for job failure on IBM mainframes. A 0C7 indicates an attempt to perform an arithmetic operation on nonnumeric data. You can get 0C7s for many reasons:

- Forgetting to validate the contents of numeric fields (read from outside files) before trying to use them in arithmetic operations.
- Using a subscript or index value out of bounds.
- Forgetting to initialize a working storage field.
- Moving nonnumeric data to a COBOL output picture such as $ZZ,ZZZ.99.

0C8   Overflow Exception, Fixed Point

A computed value is too large to be accommodated by the indicated receiving field. You can get this by dividing one value by another value that is too small (forcing a very large result), repeated computation involving the same fields within a loop, or multiplication of numbers that are too large.

0C9, 0CA, 0CB, 0CC   Divide or Overflow Exception

A value that results from a division that is too large to be accommodated by the indicated receiving field. This is usually caused by division by zero but can also be triggered by division by a value that is too small or repeated computation involving the same fields within a loop.

0CD   Underflow Exception, Exponent

The result of a floating point (COMP-1 or COMP-2) computation is so small that it cannot be represented. This may occur in multiplication by too small a number, division by too large a number, or a program loop involving repeated computation with the same quantities.

0CE   Significance Exception

A computation involving floating point COMP-1 or COMP-2 data resulted in an absolute zero quantity, one possessing an all-zero fraction.

0CF   Divide Exception, Floating Point

You tried to divide by a floating point COMP-1 or COMP-2 number that has a zero fraction.

106   Cannot Load and Run Program

A problem prevents MVS from running the program named on an EXEC statement. Try coding a larger REGION on the EXEC statement for the program. For reason code -0F, investigate to see if the load module library (partitioned data set) has been damaged.

122   Job Cancelled with Dump

Check your program logic and its use of files. The program may have appeared to be in a loop, not outputting, or producing a large amount of I/O. It may have demanded a data set that was not available.

137   I/O Error on Tape Data Set Labels

This usually results from flawed media or a malfunctioning device or an error in trailer label writing. Before recreating a data set that cannot be processed, try different devices to access it. Cleaning a tape may restore it to readability.

213   Open of a Disk Data Set Failed

A 213 is usually caused by an illogical DD statement where MVS cannot process a data set it has been asked to access. Check your JCL for incorrect DSN and VOL= SER and check to see if the data set exists.

214   Tape I/O Error

A hardware or tape media error exists, or a tape mark is missing after the data. Have the tape cleaned and/or retry the operation on a different tape drive. If these actions fail, you must recreate the data set.

222   Job Cancelled Without a Dump

Check your program logic and its use of files. The program may have appeared to be in a loop, not outputting anything, or generating a large amount of I/O. It may have demanded a data set that was not available. The operator who cancelled the job may have been required to provide a comment or reason with his/her dump action; ask the operator for that reason.

237   Invalid Block Count or Data Set Name

Failure in data set label verification processing. If the data set is not cataloged, you may have coded an incorrect VOL=SER. If the VOL=SER is correct, have the tape cleaned and attempt to process it. If these steps do not resolve the problem, you must recreate the data set.

2FB   JES3 Address Space Error

Contact the operations group to report this problem with Job Entry Subsystem 3 (JES3). You cannot correct this type of system problem on your own.

2F3   System Failure Occurred During the Run

The computer system or MVS "crashed" while your job was running. Check to see if some of the data sets created by the job are on the system; if so, delete them and resubmit the job. Alternatively, modify the JCL to avoid trying to recreate the files already created and resubmit the job.

313, 314, 317, 414, 417   I/O Error on Disk VTOC

This is a hardware problem. The data set being accessed very likely must be recreated because a defective volume or device is involved. Notify the operations group, because a VTOC error affects large numbers of jobs.

322   Job Cancelled: Exceeded Time Limit

The TIME parameter on the job card or on an EXEC was too low. Check your program logic for loops. If your logic is correct, increase the TIME parameter.

413   Open Failed for a Tape Data Set

A system completion code of 413 usually means that you coded an illogical DD statement or that MVS cannot locate a specified tape data set. A hardware I/O error may also be the problem.

513   Open Failed for a Multiple Tape Data Set

This problem occurs if you try to open more than one data set on the same tape at the same time.

522   Job Timed Out

The job had no activity for 30 minutes or more and was cancelled by MVS. This type of cancellation is unusual and is often caused by program error or unavailable data sets. You can also receive a 522 cancellation during a TSO session if you don't press the <*Enter*> key or a <*PF*> key every few minutes.

613   Tape Data Set Open Failed

The tape or drive may need cleaning. Tape cleaning may eliminate the error, but also try using a different drive, because this is usually a hardware problem.

614   Close Error on a Data Set

A defective disk, tape, or device. Notify the operations group so that media can be replaced or hardware maintenance initiated.

637   Tape I/O Error or Improper Concatenation

The system is having a problem reading a tape. Defective tape or disk media or hardware is probably at fault. Have the tape and drive cleaned. You may have to recreate the data set on a different volume if several devices have trouble reading it. 637 has several very detailed reason codes, but they all deal with tape errors.

706   Program Module Is Not Executable

The linkage editor marked the module "not executable," which means that it was recognized as incomplete or flawed. Check the diagnostic messages from the linkage editor when the program was compiled and linked. Also check your JCL or the proc used for linkage editing; it should test the return code of the linkage edit step and raise visible attention when a nonexecutable load module is created.

713   Open Failed: Data Set Is Not Expired

You tried to overwrite or "MOD onto" and extend an existing data set. This can happen if you code DISP=OLD to overwrite an existing data set or DISP=MOD to extend (append to) a data set. MVS seeks permission from the operator to do this when the data set label specifies an expiration date that is still in the future.

FORTRAN programs may require use of the VOL "IN" subparameter because this language sometimes opens data sets for both input and output processing, depending on the way in which the data set is first accessed (see Chapter 15).

714, 717, 737   I/O Error Writing Trailer Label or Tape Mark

You have probably encountered defective hardware or tape, or the tape and/or tape drive need cleaning. Notify the operations group and rerun the job.

722   Outlim or JOBPARM Print Limit Exceeded

Your job tried to send more lines to SYSOUT than your OUTLIM or JES3 MAIN statement allows. If the job really should produce more print output, increase the limits and rerun it.

804, 80A, 878   Program Needs More Memory

Check the REGION value on your JOB or EXEC statement. You may need to increase it because your program demands more memory than MVS is being allowed to let it use.

806   Program Load Module Cannot Be Found

Your JCL requested a program that could not be found. This may be a program named on an EXEC statement and housed in other than the default load library, but you left out a //STEPLIB DD or //JOBLIB statement that names the library. You can also get this problem when one program CALLs another and MVS can't locate the CALLed program. Check your EXEC statement or source code CALL for a misspelled program name. It is also possible that the load module was deleted or never created or that an I/O error occurred while MVS searched the directory of the load module library.

813   Open Failed; DSN in Label Does Not Match JCL

The DSN parameter and volume serial number are not consistent with what is contained in the tape data set label. Check the spelling of the data set name in your JCL and the volume serial number you coded.

837 Error Occurred at the End of Volume

Check your logic to make sure your program is operating correctly. It may be outputting too much data as a result of a logic loop. You need to specify more volume serial numbers explicitly or code the VOL parameter to indicate a larger volume count.

913 Security Problem

Several reason code values pinpoint the problem detected by the security system. To correct this problem you have to resolve your authorization to use the data set with your security coordinator.

922 Job Cancelled Due to Machine or MVS Failure

Actual processing of the job had begun but an MVS abend was experienced, the console restart key was pressed, or some other machine problem occurred that forced this job (and most likely all others) to be cancelled. There is almost certainly no error in the program; resubmit it.

A14 Error Releasing Disk Space at Data Set Closing

A defective disk or tape volume or device probably exists. Contact the operations group.

A22 Operator Forced Cancellation of the Job

No program logic may be in error. Check with the operator and find out why he/she cancelled the job.

B14 Close Failed Trying to Write a PDS Member

Except for a reason code of -18, the partitioned data set probably requires reorganization before you can rerun the job. You may have to allocate more directory blocks for the PDS by copying it to a new PDS using IEBCOPY with an appropriate SPACE parameter on the DD statement for the new data set. For reason code -0C, the deletion of existing members of the PDS and its reorganization may also resolve the immediate problem.

B14-04   Duplicate member name exists
B14-0C   PDS directory is full
B14-10   I/O error while writing the PDS directory
B14-14   DCB inconsistency in the program, JCL, PDS or directory
B14-18   Insufficient memory for closing actions (increase REGION size)

B37   Disk Volume Is Out of Space

You received all the primary space that you requested and as much of the secondary space as MVS could provide, but this was still not enough for the data set being written. A B37 usually means that you coded your SPACE parameter incorrectly or you have a logic loop involving a WRITE statement in your program. Check your program logic and SPACE coding for the data set.

C13   Error on Concatenated PDS

Correct your JCL; you are violating one of the rules that apply to concatenated data sets, such as trying to write to a concatenated PDS.

C37   DOS/VSE Data Set Cannot Be Read by MVS

The next volume of the data set contained more than 16 extents or has a nonallowable form of split cylinder space allocation. Some DOS data sets are not compatible with MVS and must be recreated to be read by MVS.

CFB   JES3 Initialization Problem

Contact the operations group; you cannot correct this problem on your own.

D37   Primary Space Exceeded, No Secondary

In writing a data set to a disk device, your JCL specified only a primary disk SPACE allocation, and this was exceeded. Change your DD statement associated with the data set to specify more primary space or provide a secondary allocation of space. *Caution:* Make sure you delete the partially created data set resulting from this job before rerunning the job!

DFB   JES3 System Support Module Problem

Contact the operations group; you cannot correct this problem on your own.

E37   Primary and Secondary Space Filled

An E37 indicates a lack of appropriate disk resources to receive output. Check your program logic for a loop involving a write statement. You may have to change your JCL to specify larger primary or secondary allocations. Delete the partially created data set resulting from this job before rerunning it. You can get an E37 under TSO when a TSO library needs to be reorganized. An E37-04 can also indicate that the disk volume table of contents (VTOC) is full. If no other explanation for the problem seems to apply, contact your operations group, because a filled VTOC is a serious problem that will affect many other jobs.

VS COBOL User (Runtime) Return Codes

In certain circumstances, VS COBOL programs will post an unusual user return code. This happens because VS COBOL builds in the return codes as an indication of specialized execution-time errors. The following VS COBOL return codes are *user return codes,* not system completion codes. They appear as four-digit decimal numbers, as if they had been moved by VS COBOL program logic to the RETURN-CODE register. These code values are documented in Appendix K of the *IBM OS/ VS COBOL Compiler and Library Programmer's Guide,* IBM publication SC28–6483. I have listed here only the most common ones.

0400, 0505   VSCOBOL Compiler Failure

You broke the VS COBOL compiler! Certain syntax errors can cause the VS COBOL compiler to fail. When this occurs, it posts a return code of 0400 or 0505 and quits. Because no abend occurs, you may think that your program actually ran and returned this code, but it was actually the compiler "giving up." Coding the word INDEX instead of INDEXED in defining a table to be searched can cause an 0505 user return code. You may also encounter it if you use the reserved word KEY as a data name. Resolving an 0400 or 0505 error involves carefully inspecting your source code, because the compiler can't provide much help in locating your syntax violation.

0519   Error in Logic Flow

The next instruction to be executed is not identifiable. You probably branched out of a PERFORM and fell through the bottom of your program or forgot to code a STOP RUN statement. Also check to make sure that called modules appropriately contain EXIT PROGRAM or GOBACK statements and that your use of the VS COBOL compiler PARM option DYN, needed for dynamically callable modules, is consistent in all compiles.

3505   Flow of Control Error

This error can occur if you use a GO TO out of one SECTION of code into another and eventually "drop out the bottom" of the program. This error can also occur when an Assembler or PL/I program CALLs a COBOL program. The Assembler program needs to issue a call to library routine ILBOSTP0 before calling a COBOL program, but this has not been done. The Assembler program must be corrected. This call initializes the COBOL environment so that the called program does not think it is the main program.

VS COBOL II   User (Runtime) Return Codes

Programs compiled with VS COBOL II generate return codes in the range of 1000 through 1999 for conditions similar to those that caused VS COBOL to issue 0400, 0505, 0519, and 3505 return codes. For example, 1037 is the return code from VS COBOL II corresponding to the 0519 return code of VS COBOL. You don't need a printed reference to the meaning of these codes. VS COBOL II puts a plain-text description of each of its automatic return codes into your MVS system output.

Appendix F

JCL ON DISKETTE AND A STUDENT WORKBOOK

JCL can be frustrating to manually enter and experiment with because it's so easy to make minor errors. The JCL in this book is error-free. All of the examples I've presented have actually been run on modern IBM mainframe computers; I downloaded the JCL and produced the illustrations directly. You can obtain all of the JCL for the figures in this book, error-free and complete on diskette (specify 5¼" or 3½" diskette) for uploading to your computer system, by sending $15 (US) in check or money order form to:

Practical Distribution Diskettes
P.O. Box 46078
Chicago, Illinois 60646

The diskette includes the program source code and data for the FSBT37xx programs executed in the JCL and procs in Chapter 18, in both VS COBOL and VS COBOL II versions. That source code is not listed in the book due to program size. With these programs you can actually run all load module and proc examples yourself and see full-size MVS system output. I've also included the COB2J, COB2CLJ, and PDSREORG procs.

Special Note to College and University Instructors

The JCL diskette is free to instructors as an aid in using this book in courses. Just send me a brief note via the above address using your institution's letterhead and mention the course for which you are considering using the book. Or contact me at DePaul University, (312) 362–8840.

An economically priced student workbook that parallels *Practical MVS JCL Examples* is available from Stipes Publishing Company, 10–12 Chester Street, Champaign, Illinois 61824, telephone (217) 356–8391. The workbook contains lecture and learning aids. In addition, the workbook contains a series of "copy, run, and answer the questions" exercises designed to be torn out and turned in by students for grading. JCL for those exercises is also on the diskette mentioned above.

A Note to Corporate Trainers

I conduct on-site corporate training on MVS JCL, TSO/ISPF for programmers and end users, VS COBOL and VS COBOL II, structured testing, action diagramming, and other mainframe subjects for some of the largest companies in the world. Consider bringing in the author of the book if you want something truly special and productive in on-site professional development!

INDEX